To Be a Teacher

Marilyn M. Cohn • Robert B. Kottkamp • Eugene F. Provenzo, Jr.

To Be a Teacher
Cases, Concepts, Observation Guides

Random House   New York

This book was developed for Random House by Lane Akers, Inc.

First Edition

9 8 7 6 5 4 3 2 1

Library of Congress Cataloging-in-Publication Data

Cohn, Marilyn.
 To be a teacher.

 Bibliography: p.
 Includes index.
 1. Teaching—Addresses, essays, lectures.
2. Teaching—United States—Addresses, essays,
lectures. I. Kottkamp, Robert. II. Provenzo, Eugene F.
III. Title.
LB1025.2.C623 1986   371.1′02   85–28156
ISBN 0–394–33606–2

Designed and composed by The Bookmakers, Incorporated, Wilkes-Barre, Pa.

Manufactured in the United States of America

For our parents: Gertrude and Marvin Moldafsky, Pearl and Ralph Kottkamp, and Therese and Eugene Provenzo, who helped us grow as persons and were our first teachers

For our wives and husband: Ginny Kottkamp, Asterie Provenzo, and Jay Cohn—our best friends and most important collaborators

And finally for the results of some of our collaborations: Derek and Cheryl Cohn, Nathan and Jeremy Kottkamp

CONTENTS

FOREWORD

This book, *To Be a Teacher*, is a powerful statement. It focuses on the right issues at precisely the right time. This remarkable work by Marilyn M. Cohn, Robert B. Kottkamp, and Eugene F. Provenzo, Jr., brings to light in a dramatic and helpful way both the complexities and the rewards of teaching. It challenges teachers already in the classroom to improve their work and introduces new teachers to this ennobling yet difficult profession.

Strengthening teaching in America is our most urgent obligation. Teachers are leaving the profession and retiring in large numbers. As many as one half of those who teach in our elementary and secondary schools will leave within the next five years. It is estimated that within a decade we will need more than a million and a half new teachers for the public schools.

At the same time, the nation's minority school enrollment will reach one-third by the mid-1990s. Of the total public school enrollment, the schools have been least successful in the education of students from differing ethnic and racial backgrounds. They also have been less successful with poor children who constitute a rapidly growing percentage of school enrollees. Today, thirteen million of the sixty-two million children under age eighteen live in poverty, compared with ten million of the sixty-nine million children in 1970.

One of America's top priorities must be a commitment to a core of teachers who are the brightest and the best. *To Be a Teacher* is the kind of book that will help us meet this urgent obligation. What makes this introductory text so valuable is the special blending of theory and practice—the moving from thought to action. As the authors state, "Teacher educators and those learning to become teachers have always had to face the problem of integrating two realities—the broader and more theoretical orientation of university-based preservice education and the concrete experiences of life in the school."

To help link ideas to action, the authors introduce us to five gifted teachers who teach in urban, suburban, and rural settings. These vivid portraits are believable, real people come to life. And through these case studies, each with a different model, we discover how excellence can be achieved in a variety of ways. We learn that there is no single, all-purpose model for teaching excellence, and we are reminded that character, integrity, mastery of subject matter material, along with dedication and understanding of the learning process are conditions common to all. Above all, we compellingly confront the fact that an excellent teacher is an authentic human being.

I also find it fascinating that in this remarkable book case studies are used not as ends in themselves but to take us back to teaching theory: the environment for learning, the structure of schools, the nature of the profession, and the process of teacher education. In these sections of the book the authors discuss rich vignettes and anecdotes. Finally, to illustrate fundamental points, we are presented with five vivid portraits of young people who are either in teacher education or in their first year of teaching. In meeting this "new generation of teachers" as well as veterans Ruth, Luberta, Sandy, Larry, and Jacquie, we come to appreciate anew that we are not going to have excellence in our schools until we give respect and dignity to the people who meet with young people every day.

To Be a Teacher should be of value to everyone who cares about the future of public education in the nation. And for anyone who plans to teach, I am not aware of a more important book to read.

Ernest L. Boyer
President, Carnegie
Foundation for the
Advancement of
Teaching

ACKNOWLEDGMENTS

This book is a collaboration. Like any collaboration it is often difficult to determine where one author's contribution begins and another's ends. Beginning with the original conceptualization of a book and continuing through successive writings and revisions, co-authors play different roles in the creation of a work—roles that often involve different skills and perspectives. Collaboration is often a difficult and painful process. It is also an enlightening one. Whatever the faults or limitations of this work, it is better because the three of us joined together to do it.

The three authors, Marilyn M. Cohn, Robert B. Kottkamp, and Eugene F. Provenzo, Jr., are a research team that first began to work with one another over a decade ago when they were students at the Graduate Institute of Education, Washington University. Together as students they shared many of the same professors and, despite their different disciplinary orientations, learned the importance of each other's perspectives and the value of establishing a creative and on-going dialogue with one another. Education is one of the few truly interdisciplinary fields found within the American university system. While this at times creates problems in terms of focus and definition, it also provides the opportunity for a creative synergism that can transcend disciplinary boundaries and isolation.

This particular work is the first book in a series of on-going collaborations that have as their primary purpose expanding our knowledge of the role of the teacher in American society. Marilyn Cohn took the lead in the conceptualization and writing of this particular book. While individual chapters and responsibilities were divided among the authors, it was her point of view that most often prevailed and set the tone for the overall work. Throughout the various revisions her perspective was used to draw together the inevitably diverse strands to make a whole piece of cloth. Despite this, as is the case with other research projects that we have under-way, this work is ultimately the collaborative effort of our research team and should be recognized as such.

Together we wish to thank those individuals at Washington University who were most responsible for helping us formulate our own ideas and perspectives on the nature and meaning of the teaching profession: Barry Anderson, Joan Beaning, Harold Berlak, William Connor, David Colton, Vivian Gellman, Barry Kaufman, Raymond Callahan, Richard de Charms, Bryce Hudgins, Richard Nault, Louis Smith, Alan Tom, and Arthur Wirth. In the case of Harold Berlak, Arthur Wirth, and in particular Louis Smith, the influence of their thought is immediately evident in the text.

Ernest L. Boyer, president of the Carnegie Foundation for the Advancement of Teaching, and Jim Steffenson of the Office of Educational Research and Improvement have provided important support and encouragement for our work. They deserve very special thanks.

Our spouses, Jay Cohn, Virginia Kottkamp, and in particular Asterie Provenzo, not only put up with us but nurtured us through the process of creating this book. In a sense, they represent a second layer in the collaborative process that enabled this book to move beyond the initial scratches on our yellow pads.

Special thanks go to Gordon Ames, John Pingree, Cynthia Shephard, Vivian Vieta, and Leslie Will for their technical assistance. Pat Frost, principal of West Laboratory School, William Renuart of David Fairchild Elementary School, and the teachers in their schools are thanked for their special help. Beverlee and Harold Kaminetzky are thanked for their sanctuary by the sea.

We are grateful to principals who invited us to observe in the five case study schools. The instructional leadership of William Benning of Jefferson School in St. Louis, Missouri, Robert Bredin at Conway School in Ladue, Missouri, Charles Martin at Hillsboro High School in Hillsboro, Missouri, William Jones of Robert E. Lee Junior High School in Miami, Florida, and Sanford Pridy of Lindbergh High School in St. Louis County, Missouri, was evident to us as we walked through the halls of their schools. We thank them for helping to create environments where both teachers and students can flourish. We have used photographs of these environments as an important source of documentation in this work. All the photographs were taken by Eugene F. Provenzo, Jr.

Burt Lummus, Jack Nelson, and especially Lane and Jean Akers of Random House are to be thanked for their editorial guidance.

Reverend Gary McCloskey helped in ways that only he and the saints can understand. Edward Mikel of the St. Louis Public Schools introduced us to Luberta Clay; for this we give him our special thanks. Tom Cooper of Florida International University and Carol Weinstein of Rutgers University are thanked for their special help on Chapter 5.

We are especially grateful to Karen Fairbank, Jim Ladwig, Audrey Oka, Meg Richardson, and Amy Spiegel for sharing their experiences and insights about the process of becoming teachers.

Finally, and most importantly, we wish to thank Ruth Christopherson, Luberta Clay, Sandy Snodgrass, Larry Wells, and Jacquie Yourist—dedicated and creative professionals. In the end, this book is a celebration of their excellence and of the commitment they and others like them have to the teaching profession.

Marilyn M. Cohn, Washington University
Robert B. Kottkamp, Hofstra University
Eugene F. Provenzo, Jr., University of Miami

INTRODUCTION

PURPOSES

This book is an introduction to schooling and to the profession of teaching in contemporary America. Its primary audiences are those considering a career in education and those in the process of becoming teachers. Its overarching aims are twofold: (1) to present a vivid description of what it means to be a teacher; and (2) to provide a set of lenses through which one can see and analyze the complexities of teaching, the challenges as well as the joys. Toward these ends, we, as authors, have made a number of assumptions that inevitably give a particular shape to the picture of teaching we portray. We wish to make these assumptions explicit at the outset.

ASSUMPTIONS

The first assumption is that an introductory text about teaching must be a blend of the theoretical and the practical. Teacher educators and those learning to become teachers have always had to face the problem of integrating two realities—the broader and more theoretical orientation of university-based preservice teacher education and the concrete experiences of life in classrooms and schools. *To Be a Teacher* attempts to address this dualism. The approach is to synthesize in a single book both the concrete images of what it is like to be a teacher in the field and the more abstract theoretical conceptions of teacher education. The vehicle is five case studies of highly successful elementary and secondary teachers in very different settings. These teachers are currently working in schools, and their names and the names of their schools are real.

Chapter 1 presents brief life histories of these individuals, including their reasons for becoming teachers. Chapters 2 and 4 present these teachers in the context of the schools and the communities in which they work. These introductory chapters are intended to provide a practical backdrop for understanding the theoretical underpinnings of the later chapters. In addition, included throughout the theoretical chapters are examples and references related to the experiences of each of the five teachers. Thus, through the use of case studies of real teachers, this book attempts to forge links between theoretical conceptions of teacher education and the practical realities of classroom life.

A second assumption is that teaching is a complex and demanding profession that requires one to *know*, to *think*, and to *act* simultaneously. Teachers are expected to know thoroughly both the content of what they teach and the generic theories and concepts of how to teach (pedagogy). At the same time, they are expected to have the capacity to think analytically and creatively about how to teach a particular course, class, or lesson and then to have the skills to put their thoughts into action. Finally, they are expected to be able to reflect critically upon their action and, where necessary, revise their initial thinking.

In Part I the reader will see five different instances of teachers' knowledge and thought put into action and will hear teachers' reflections upon their action. Part II will address the knowledge of subject matter and pedagogy teachers must have in order to create a physical, social, intellectual, and personal environment for learning.

The third assumption is that teaching has inescapable and interactive individual, contextual, and moral dimensions. How teachers think and act about what they know is inevitably influenced by who teachers are as individuals and the type of school and district in which they work. Moreover, the fact that teachers have the power to decide what is desirable for students in terms of what students should learn and how they should behave gives teaching a value-laden, or moral, dimension.

A case in point is the issue of discipline and classroom management. Every teacher enters the classroom armed with theories from teacher education courses as to how to establish and maintain control. The approach that a particular teacher chooses to take, however, may be highly influenced by the teacher's own individual needs, philosophical view of power and authority, and former experience as a student. All of these specifics, in turn, arise from each teacher's personal life history. At the same time, there are larger social or contextual circumstances that might also significantly affect teacher behavior in regard to discipline. These social factors that influence a teacher might include the norms, assumptions, and values of the broader society; the specific mandates of a local community, the rules and regulation transmitted through a superior (e.g., principal or superintendent); and the norms and beliefs of colleagues. Whatever ultimate form teacher behavior takes as a result of individual and social influences, it invariably represents a value decision as to how teachers should relate to students and how students should behave in school.

By presenting in Part I the personalities, philosophies, and life histories of five individual teachers, as well as the specific details of their differing school and community settings and examples of their classroom behavior, this book attempts to illustrate concretely how the individual and contextual dimensions of the teaching experience interact to produce particular teacher thought and action. Chapter 10 and Chapter 12 look more theoretically at the individual and contextual dimensions of teaching. The moral dimension is implied throughout but does not receive as much explicit attention.

A fourth assumption that gives shape to our picture is that teaching is a dynamic profession that changes over time. As teachers grow and develop in their careers, various issues assume greater and lesser importance. The early years of almost any teaching career are focused primarily on surviving and learning a new professional role. Typically, this includes struggling to maintain discipline, defining oneself as a person and as a member of a larger professional group, mastering subject matter, and coping with an almost overwhelming number of new responsibilities. Such efforts may well consume most of the new teacher's time and energy. Issues that are important in the early years of teaching become less consuming with the passage of time and are replaced by long-range career and advancement issues. For example, problems such as the need to fight apathy and to maintain enthusiasm emerge for many teachers, as does the need to learn new skills and to change along with rapidly shifting fields of knowledge. To focus exclusively on first-year survival issues tends to frighten away potentially excellent teachers. To focus exclusively on longer-range issues does not provide the support and orientation needed by beginners in the profession. *To Be a Teacher* attempts to capture the kaleidoscope of changing issues through the reflections and comments of five experienced teachers and through the comments of five novices introduced in Chapter 14.

A fifth assumption is that there are multiple definitions and exemplars of teaching excellence as well as common denominators that span individual and contextual differences. The use of the five case study teachers throughout the book is intended to give concreteness and meaning to this assumption. These particular teachers were selected deliberately because they were excellent in different ways and in different settings. Hopefully they communicate that there can be excellence in teaching anywhere but that it may take different forms and shapes.

It is important to define what this book means by *excellence* in teaching. The fact is, however, that no formal definition or established set of criteria guided the selection of the five teachers. We knew only that we were not looking for a small, exclusive club of superstars. Rather, our aim was to identify teachers who could represent the countless numbers of teachers in public schools who make a significant difference in the lives of their students by helping them to learn and grow. The final choices were clearly subjective, based upon years of experience and an implicit sense that excellent teachers are knowledgeable, skilled, reflective, and caring. Four of the five were known to us from our previous work either as teachers, supervisors, or researchers, and the fifth was recommended by a trusted colleague who worked as a school and teacher evaluator. Still, our intuitive judgments were consistently confirmed by administrators and peers who worked with these teachers.

This validation convinced us that there is a shared sense of excellence but one that is not easily articulated. The challenge for this text became the task of trying to add some clarity and preciseness to the concept of excellence through the analysis of these five teachers. As we observed and listened to these teachers we searched for ways in which they are alike and ways in which they are different. We struggled with the question of whether there was, in fact, a broad enough definition of excellence to encompass their differences. As you read this book we ask you to struggle along with us, but in Chapter 11 we will focus upon what we ultimately saw as common elements of excellence. We invite your agreement or disagreement.

The sixth and final assumption is that to learn about teaching and teachers, one must spend time in classrooms—observing, working, and analyzing what transpires. Classrooms are exceedingly complex environments and it is not always easy for novices or experienced teachers to see all that is actually happening. *To Be a Teacher* attempts to provide you with the necessary observational tools and lenses to become a skilled participant observer. Chapter 3 presents observational methods and techniques and some initial questions to focus one's observation. Each of the chapters in Part II then presents additional frameworks and questions to focus observations in different areas. Hopefully, through the experience of becoming a participant observer you will develop both a descriptive and an analytical sense of what classroom life is like and, more importantly, what it means to be a teacher.

ORGANIZATION

This book is organized in three parts, each of which has a separate purpose as well as a link to one another. The purpose of Part I is to provide a descriptive overview of elementary and secondary teaching in America, including systematic ways of looking at classrooms. Chapter 1 asks Who teaches in America? and draws upon brief personal life histories of the five case study teachers as well as upon research and national statistics for an answer. Chapter 2 focuses upon the two elementary case study teachers, Ruth Christopherson and Luberta Clay, describing in considerable detail what and how they teach in their differing suburban and urban environments. Chapter 3 presents some general methods and techniques for conducting classroom observations and introduces a specific set of questions with which you can begin to observe, describe, and analyze the influence of personal background and social context upon what teachers do in their classrooms.

These questions are then given to you as guidelines for examining the elementary classrooms of Ruth and Luberta and the secondary school classrooms of Jacquie Yourist, Larry Wells, and Sandy Snodgrass that are described at some length in Chapter 4. After using these questions with the case study material, you are encouraged to use them in your own fieldwork. Taken as a whole, Part I serves as a practical base for considering the more theoretical chapters that follow and as a methodological base for becoming a classroom observer. At the same time, it introduces you to the individual and social dimensions of teaching.

In Part II the aim is to move beyond the descriptive and look more closely and analytically at what is involved in classroom teaching. The thesis of Part II is that to be a teacher is to be responsible for creating a *physical, social, intellectual,* and *personal* environment for learning. Chapter 5 begins with the notion that teachers can manipulate the physical environment of a classroom to achieve certain learning outcomes. Next we consider the role of a teacher in creating the social environment of the classroom. The social environment, which involves the way in which teachers and students interact with each other in the classroom, is examined in two related chapters. Chapter 6 focuses on the establishment of a classroom social system, and Chapter 7 looks at issues of classroom authority and control. The challenge of creating a stimulating intellectual environment through curricular and instructional choices is the focus of the following two chapters. Chapter 8 examines what the schools teach, why they teach it, and what role a teacher has in that decision making. Chapter 9 considers the instructional role of a teacher, which involves decisions about how to teach the selected curriculum. Chapter 10 argues that although teaching is making decisions related to the physical, social, and intellectual environment of the classroom, it is also something more. In our view, to be a teacher is to relate to students as people and to establish a dialogue with them. Chapter 10 focuses on the role of a teacher in creating a personal and human environment for learning that has implications for both student and teacher growth. Finally, Chapter 11 returns to the problem of defining excellence in teaching and moves toward a definition based upon how the five case study teachers think and act in creating physical, social, intellectual, and personal learning environments for their students.

Taken separately, each chapter offers you a different set of conceptual lenses with which to gain increasing understanding of what it means to be a teacher. These lenses can be used to analyze both the five case study teachers and teachers in the field. Taken as a whole, Part II tells you that beyond the individual and contextual dimensions there is a core of knowledge that all prospective teachers need to acquire before becoming full-fledged professionals.

A word about sequence. The chapters in Part II build from the simple to the complex, from the concrete to the abstract. More importantly, they build substantively upon one another and convey an implicit progression of tasks that we believe underlies the process of becoming a teacher. Probably the first and simplest task of a teacher is to create a viable and conducive physical classroom arrangement. Next, a teacher has to consider the social environment and the establishment of rules and norms for working together in an orderly fashion. Only when there is physical and social order can a teacher then attend to the intellectual tasks of deciding what to teach, why, how. Finally, with the curricular and instructional tasks in hand, a teacher is in a position to attend to the more subtle but no less primary issues of how to respond to students as people and how to establish a quality of excellence in his or her own work. We recognize, of course, that teaching does not necessarily follow such a linear progression. Nonetheless, Part II follows this sequence because it is a logical one that can help the reader gradually gain an increasing awareness of the complexities of classroom teaching.

Part III moves outside the classroom and introduces some of the larger issues that should be considered by those who are contemplating a teaching career or who are in the process of becoming a teacher. Chapter 12 argues that to be a teacher involves membership in a complex organization that is affected by local communities, state and federal governments, and broad societal issues. Chapter 13 maintains that to be a teacher involves belonging to a profession that is characterized by certain career and work rewards and lifestyles. Chapter 14 examines the process involved in deciding to become a teacher and the training and first-year experiences that follow such a decision. The overall message of Part III is that there are numerous external forces, programs, and institutions that affect the career decision and daily life of the teacher.

In sum, *To Be a Teacher* is an effort to present a vivid and accurate picture of teaching by looking at the profession from different angles and points of view. In Part I our "cameras" span different communities, schools, classrooms, and teachers to give a sweeping panoramic view of teaching. In Part II our cameras zoom in to focus upon the classroom, different aspects of the teaching role, and the nature of excellence in teaching. In Part III we back away from the classroom to bring into view some of the external influences and considerations that impinge upon the classroom and one's decision to be a teacher.

PART ONE

CLASSROOMS AND TEACHERS

A Look at Contemporary America

Part I presents a general introduction to the teaching profession, five case studies of highly successful elementary and secondary teachers, and a systematic approach to becoming a skilled classroom observer. Chapter 1 addresses the question of who teaches in America through a look at the personal life histories of the case study teachers and a consideration of long-standing stereotypes and recent statistics. Case studies, in Chapters 2 and 4, of different types of teachers in a variety of settings provide a descriptive overview of the individual and social dimensions of teaching and a practical base for examining the theoretical issues raised in Parts II and III. Chapter 3 offers a methodological framework for identifying the complexities of classroom life in the case studies and in the field.

1

WHO TEACHES
IN AMERICA?

INTRODUCTION

At the heart of the educational process in America stands the classroom teacher. Observational studies in education suggest that the backgrounds, orientations, and personalities of individual teachers dramatically shape what transpires within classrooms and within the profession. Sociological research indicates that the sex, social class, and ethnic and geographical origins of the membership of a profession can significantly influence its definition and development. Teachers, inevitably, teach who they are as well as what they know.

This book about teaching and the teaching profession, therefore, begins by asking, Who teaches in America and why? Chapter 1 attempts to answer this question, first, by presenting brief life histories of the five different teachers who are featured throughout the text. By meeting these individuals and by learning something of their personal backgrounds and reasons for choosing to be teachers, it is possible to get a more general picture of who enters and stays in the profession. Next, against this backdrop of real, living teachers, this chapter considers some of the popular stereotypes or idealized versions of teachers, past and present. It concludes with what educational statistics and research reveal about who teaches in America today.

As you read this chapter look for:

1. The similarities and differences among the five teachers in terms of family and educational background and reasons for entering teaching.

2. The ways in which the stereotypes do or do not capture the actual characteristics of the five teachers.
3. The degree of fit between what educational research and statistics say about teachers in general and these five teachers in particular.

FIVE LIFE HISTORIES

Ruth Christopherson: Elementary School Teacher

Ruth Christopherson is 56 years old, white, and married to a researcher at Washington University's medical school. Ruth grew up in the conservative southern section of St. Louis, Missouri. Her mother was a housewife and her father was a bookbinder; neither finished grade school. The family belonged to the United Church of Christ, and religion played a major role in the household.

By the time she was in high school Ruth knew she wanted to be a teacher because she "loved working with children" and "enjoyed watching them learn." A seventh-grade teacher who exhibited great enthusiasm for teaching and put a lot of herself into the job influenced Ruth's choice of teaching as a career. A high school counselor, however, did not encourage that choice. She urged Ruth to select a field

Ruth Christopherson

that would be more rewarding financially. Nonetheless, Ruth eventually followed her own instincts and interests and completed a teacher education program at Washington University.

Her first job was in Edwardsville, a small town in Illinois across the Mississippi River from St. Louis. That experience convinced Ruth that teaching was going to be a snap.

> I could do the things my education courses had taught me because the children were from a community in which the teacher was highly respected and there were no discipline problems. I didn't have to learn how to handle discipline problems. There just weren't any.

This idyllic picture changed abruptly and dramatically when Ruth decided to leave Edwardsville to take a job in the St. Louis Public Schools. She had become engaged, and her fiancé lived in St. Louis. As Ruth smilingly recalls: "I wanted to be near the object of my affection."

Ruth entered a second-grade class midyear that prior to her arrival had seen a string of 13 substitute teachers. How did this class greet Ruth? Not exactly as she had hoped.

> They bit, they kicked, they ate the crayons and the paste; they used foul language. It was an interesting little group. After three days I lost my voice. I stayed home for two days and then went back. I decided there had to be a way. With help from a master teacher, I was able to bring about many changes. It was there that I learned to teach.

What Ruth learned was that she needed to find techniques that would motivate and help control students. She observed the techniques of others, and she created some of her own. As soon as she could control the students, the situation turned around for her.

> As you learn to control and motivate the children, your effort is directed in a different place. It's very tiring to work on discipline all day long, and it's much more satisfying to work on learning activities. And once you learn this and master this—but I shouldn't say master because you never master it—but once you learn good techniques for doing this, then it becomes easier.

Ruth is extraordinarily modest. She has indeed mastered the techniques of discipline and motivation and, therefore, has been free to devote almost all her energies to developing creative and stimulating classroom activities. Curricular ideas and instructional skills have won her the highest rating in her district's merit pay program and opportunities to develop programs for gifted students and for fellow teachers. By anyone's measure, Ruth is today a "master" teacher. All who know her are truly grateful that she ignored her high school counselor's advice and that she refused to let a bunch of out-of-control second graders conquer her. The independent spirit that got her through her early years is the very same spirit she has successfully developed in her students over the past quarter of a century.

At the end of this school year, Ruth intends to take early retirement. She looks forward to traveling with her husband, but she also looks backward with deep satisfaction on her decision to be a teacher.

Luberta Clay: Elementary School Teacher

Luberta Clay has been a classroom teacher for 31 years, but if you met her you would never believe it. She is a tall, slender, attractive black woman who looks almost 20 years younger than she is. Her posture and carriage have an elegance, a gentleness, and a dignity that suggest a highly privileged background, yet almost the opposite is true. She was born in the small town of Hannibal, Missouri, the eleventh child in a family where her father was a custodian for a large department store and her mother was a homemaker. The family was, however, not what Luberta would call poor.

> We were not poor because Dad worked, and Dad was a very planning-type person. He allotted his funds, as little as they were, very wisely. My brothers and sisters took jobs as soon as they were able; I did myself.

What kind of work did Luberta do? Since there were not a lot of opportunities in Hannibal she took what she could, which was working as a housekeeper. Interestingly enough, she recalls that kind of work as "an invaluable experience."

> It was like going to a finishing school. I worked for a banker, and you learned terrific ways to manage a home because you were the manager, with the guidance of the lady of the house. I wouldn't trade that experience for anything. That experience really, really helped shape my views on a lot of things. As I said, it taught me some little niceties of living that probably I wouldn't have gotten in my home. I think this was a very good thing to have happen.

There were also a few manufacturing plants in Hannibal. Luberta had one experience with factory work, but that only convinced her that she needed to find something quite different for her life's work.

According to Luberta, the fact that she ultimately picked teaching was really quite natural. She had two older sisters who were teachers, and she attended the school where one of her sisters taught. When Luberta went to school in the 1940s, all of the schools in Missouri were completely segregated. The all-black school she attended was a huge building that housed Grades 1 through 12. Because of her sister, Luberta became friends with many of the teachers in the school. Her friendship with these teachers clearly directed her toward entering the profession.

Luberta Clay

Growing up in Hannibal, which was the birthplace of Mark Twain, led her at first toward teaching high school English. When she received a scholarship to Lincoln University, an all-black state school in Jefferson City, Missouri, she chose literature as her major.

> The fact that I came from a town that had produced Mark Twain had a lot to do with my desire to go into literature. They had a lot of contests in Hannibal. You were encouraged to write and speak; it was competitive; and it was citywide. We were sort of reminded all the time about the value of writing. I think it was helpful.

When she graduated from Lincoln, her intention was to look for a job as a secondary teacher in English or in her minor, social studies. But once again her family ties influenced her. Her other sister, who was teaching at the elementary school in Palmyra, Missouri, 12 miles north of Hannibal, decided to get married and move. Her sister's position was offered to Luberta, and although she did not feel prepared to teach elementary school, she took it.

Luberta really got on-the-job training in Palmyra. Palmyra is a town of 2,000 people, and when Luberta moved there, the all-black elementary school, which consisted of Grades 1 through 8, had only two teachers. The other teacher was responsible for Grades 4 through 8, and Luberta was left to teach Grades 1 through 4. Luberta described the experience in Palmyra as a "real workout" for she had students as young as 5 years old and as old as 13 in the same classroom. Still, she smiles and laughs when she remembers.

> There were advantages though—the little guys would hear a year ahead what they were to learn the next year. . . . It worked both ways—both against and for the teacher. It was a challenging situation.

Luberta taught in Palmyra for five years before moving to St. Louis in 1958 and taking a job in the St. Louis Public Schools. She and her husband, who works for the United States Postal Service, have remained in St. Louis ever since. She has raised six children of her own while being an elementary school teacher who puts great time and effort into her work.

What is the secret that keeps Luberta so energized, so youthful? Basically, it is her passion and interest in children.

> I like people; I like children. They are so honest—they let you know where you stand with them. Children are so responsive. They will respond to you, especially if you reach out, and I really think I reach out to children—at least I try.

By reaching out to students, Luberta has touched and motivated countless numbers of inner-city children. Clearly, Mark Twain was not the only influential person to grow up in Hannibal, Missouri.

Sandy Snodgrass: High School Social Studies and Special Education Teacher

Sandy Snodgrass is a 35-year-old, white, divorced and recently remarried high school social studies teacher at Lindbergh High School in St. Louis County, Missouri. She has two boys, a 7 year old from her first marriage and a 1 year old from her second marriage.

Sandy grew up in a middle-class family in south St. Louis. Both her father and mother graduated from high school, but because of financial limitations neither went to college. Her father became a machine foreman for a large lead company and eventually moved up through the ranks. The very top positions in his company, however, were always awarded to those with a college degree. Sandy's mother stayed home while she was growing up but started to work part-time as a secretary when the youngest child in the family began high school.

Because neither parent had the opportunity to go to college, they were adamant about higher education for their children. In Sandy's words, "They pushed education down our throats." In fact, Sandy laughingly recalls her father's reaction when she told him that one of her single friends was pregnant: "He immediately asked: 'Will she finish college?' rather than, 'Will she get married?'"

The household Sandy grew up in clearly affected her choice of career and her approach to teaching. Because her mother was a Presbyterian, Sandy belonged to that church. Because her father was an agnostic who believed in exposure to different religions, she visited many churches and became familiar with a variety of religious perspectives. Her grandfather, who lived with the family, and her father were extremely liberal, and Sandy recalls serious discussions concerning the writings of Karl Marx and the rights of the working class and blacks. This background made her different from a lot of her friends in the conservative high school she attended, although she did her best to hide it. When Sandy talks about her high school experience, she describes herself as uncertain and out of the mainstream.

In high school I was very quiet, shy. I wouldn't say that I had a low self-image, but for instance, I graduated second in my class from high school but doubted that any college would want me. I doubted my academic ability. I didn't have a lot of faith. I thought I was lucky. I just thought — I did well in high school but get me in college and I'll be lucky to get through. I just doubted myself. . . . In high school most of the others were interested in being Suzie Cheerleader or being on prom court. I was never interested in that sort of stuff. I guess it was nice, but I would never see myself doing any of it. In high school I felt like an outsider.

Sandy Snodgrass

College, for Sandy, was a different story.

> When I got into college, I got around people who thought like I did, and I didn't feel so
> much like an outsider. I felt like I had a niche for myself. I was beginning to emerge as
> an outgoing person, which most teachers tend to be. You have to reach out to people.
> At the time I was thinking of becoming a teacher, I was still inward, but as I went
> through college I became more outgoing, reaching out to people. It was a confusing
> time for me when I was in college. I was just beginning to blossom. I was a late
> bloomer.

One aspect of Sandy's personality that really blossomed in college was her sense of
compassion and social service.

> In college I got involved in all these causes—working with poverty children, working
> with handicapped children, working with Vietnam disabled veterans at the veterans'
> hospital. My capacity for compassion developed. I still tend to pick out the kids who
> need large doses of that, and that quality started emerging in college. Before then I
> knew I had it, but I kept it to myself. A sort of a sensitivity for people's feelings came
> out in college. Probably there were people who knew me in high school that just
> thought I was stuck up. I was painfully shy, but they probably thought I was stuck up.
> Probably compassion, empathy, beginning to see other people's sides started to really
> come through in college.

Sandy did consider social work and nursing as alternative careers, but ultimately
her love for social studies and politics and her father's encouragement led her into
teaching: "To my father, teachers are exalted. He's got this old view that anyone
who educates is fantastic, and I wanted to please him." Although Sandy originally
may have leaned toward teaching because of her father's views, she now enjoys the
profession for the high degree of personal satisfaction it has brought to her.

Larry Wells: High School History Teacher

Larry Wells is white, in his mid-thirties, married, and has two children in grade
school. His wife works as a speech therapist in the same school district where Larry
teaches.

  Larry was raised in a small, rural town, Caruthersville, Missouri, where his father
was a grocery salesman and store owner. He describes the area in which he grew up
as "cotton country" and a place where there was strong antiblack and antiunion
bias. Larry's interest in education goes back to his childhood, and he was the first
person in his family to graduate from college.

> I think that perhaps I have been—I've always been—enamored with education. I think
> from my socioeconomic background, education was a way to get out of whatever it

Larry Wells

was I was in, which wasn't extremely poor or anything, but I come from a rural background where I think I was probably the first person to graduate from college. Education was, of course, very important to me throughout my whole life so I thought that in some ways, teaching was really neat. You know, I always respected teachers, but I never really thought I'd be a teacher. In fact, in the eighth grade, I distinctly remember saying, "I'll never be a teacher!"

The town of Caruthersville is less than 150 miles from Southeast Missouri State University, and when Larry decided to go to college "SEMO," by virtue of its proximity, was the logical choice. The fact that SEMO was formerly a teacher training institution (or normal school) that only offered a few majors beyond teaching probably contributed considerably to Larry's decision to become a teacher. Still, Larry recalls trying to decide between accounting and history: "I thought of accounting a lot, but I got bored with accounting. In history, I found I could study so many things, and it always fascinated me."

Once Larry settled on being a history major, his first thoughts were to teach at the university level. He soon realized, however, that the job market for history professors in the 1970s was bleak, and high school teaching seemed the natural alternative.

I just fell into teaching high school and remained there. There was nothing as far as a set plan or goal. Maybe subconsciously there was, but nothing really conscious.

Although these remarks suggest on the one hand that he simply drifted or fell into teaching, upon reflection Larry also talks about his own teachers who probably significantly affected his choice of career. First, he describes a fifth-grade teacher whom he "had a lot of respect for" and "really looked up to." He also describes a high school business teacher who:

> was an excellent teacher. He really got along well with the kids. He could tell you to be quiet in such a way that everybody said, "Gee, okay, we'll be quiet." He could tell you to really get on the ball and work in such a way that nobody really resented it.

Finally, Larry mentions the university history professor for whom he was a teaching assistant. In Larry's words this man was "a dynamic lecturer, a confrontive type of discussion leader who provoked students to discuss, who provoked their minds and tried to make them think." He then adds, "I believe in some respects that all three of the teachers who influenced me the most did that."

Although there were teachers all along the way who influenced Larry Wells's decision to become a teacher, it was the first principal he worked under who most influenced his approach to teaching.

> This school principal had an ability to motivate and to pat people on the back. He liked positive reinforcement. That's stuck with me. I like that. If you were wrong, he'd tell you. His criticisms at times hurt me. . . . He wanted us to experiment; he wanted us to be innovative; he wanted us to give positive feedback to the students; he wanted a school that had a good atmosphere. He didn't want the kids to feel like they were in prison. I like that idea. That affected me I think more than anything. I think that if I hadn't had that high school principal, I would not have been the same teacher. . . . I think in order to be confident, you've got to try things that are different and new. You must take those risks. If you succeed, you gain confidence. If you don't succeed, then you're still going to learn. Learning is going to make you even more confident. I think there's a lot to be said for that. You can't go out and jump off a cliff for the experience, but you've got to try things that are different. You have to be able to fail. There's nothing wrong with that whatsoever.

Larry Wells, however, rarely fails. He experiments, he innovates, and he succeeds.

Jacquie Blausey Yourist: Junior High French Teacher

Jacquie Blausey Yourist is white, in her mid-thirties, and from a middle-class farming family with French and German roots in northwestern Ohio. Her father graduated from high school but remained on the family farm even though he was offered a scholarship to attend a university. Her mother, who also graduated from high school and became a registered nurse, chose to be a housewife while Jacquie was growing up. Religion was a major force in Jacquie's home life. Her mother's strong commitment to Catholicism was pervasive.

Jacquie Yourist

In high school Jacquie was a leader both socially and academically. She was a class officer and the president of numerous clubs; at the same time, she ranked third in her class academically. Her favorite teacher, Thelma D'Almaine, who taught French and Latin, influenced Jacquie's decision to enter the teaching profession. Jacquie describes her in glowing terms: "She was fantastic. She instilled a love of learning in me as well a love of languages."

Another influential person in Jacquie's life was her aunt, Mary Blausey Roberts, who was principal of Jacquie's high school. She clearly served as an educational role model, and when she married the local superintendent, Jacquie's family really had an educational flavor. The family interest in education was further reinforced by the small community where Jacquie lived. As Jacquie puts it, "Teachers were put on a pedestal where I grew up. They were highly respected in the community."

In addition to the family and community forces at work, Jacquie personally found teaching highly appealing. It offered her "something to do" with her French, which she loved, and it gave her a chance to stay in school: "I enjoyed school. I liked being a student, and I thought that perhaps I could be a perpetual student all my life by being around a school."

During her college years at the University of Toledo, Jacquie was once again a leader. She was a member of various honor societies, president of the French Honor Society, resident advisor in her dorm, and a homecoming queen candidate.

By the time she had to declare her major, the decision was almost automatic—

she double-majored in French and history and enrolled in the teacher certification program. From the university, Jacquie got her first job in suburban Sylvania in the very school where she did her student teaching. It was there that she met Jay Yourist. When Jay decided to enter graduate school at the University of Miami, first he and then she moved south. They were married, established a home in Miami, and put their talents to work there. Today, both devote a lot of time and energy to highly successful careers. Jay, who has a Ph.D. in microbiology, became assistant professor of medicine and head of the Micro Computer Institute at the University of Miami. Jacquie teaches French, Spanish, and History in a junior high school where she also is director of student activities. It is a busy and sometimes all-encompassing job, but Jacquie appears to thrive on it. Both her move to become a teacher and her move to Miami have proved to be good ones for Jacquie Yourist.

TEACHERS IN AMERICAN SOCIETY: SOME STEREOTYPES

Five separate lives and five very different people—all of them are teachers. What is it that they hold in common with each other and their 2.1 million counterparts in America? Who teaches in America?

There are many stereotypes of the "typical" teacher. One that has been popular since the nineteenth century is that of the dedicated "schoolmarm." She is a woman, and she is single—perhaps on her way to being a spinster, perhaps one already. She is sincere but relatively humorless. She is sexless and socially unsophisticated, intelligent but not intellectual, maternal but firm and not too loving.

She is a type often described in literature. She is, for example, the character Miss Dove as created by the novelist Frances Gray Patton.

> All in all, in bearing and clothing and bony structure, Miss Dove suggested that classic portrait of the eternal teacher that small fry, generation after generation, draw upon fences and sidewalks with nubbins of purloined chalk. (Patton, 1954, p. 20)

Her very being commanded the attention of her students. She was not to be taken lightly. She wasn't someone whom you could question or manipulate.

> For Miss Dove had no moods. Miss Dove was a certainty. She would be today what she had been yesterday and would be tomorrow. And so, within limits, would they. Single file they would enter her room. Each child would pause on the threshold as its mother and father had paused, more than likely, and would say—just as the policeman had said—in distinct, formal accents: "Good morning, Miss Dove." And Miss Dove would look directly at each of them, fixing her eyes directly upon theirs, and reply: "Good morning, Jessamine," or "Margaret," or "Samuel" (never "Sam," never "Peggy," never "Jess." She eschewed familiarity as she wished others to eschew it). They would

go to their appointed desk. Miss Dove would ascend to hers. The lesson would begin. (Patton, 1954, p. 8)

Discipline was never an issue in Dove's classes. She was the mistress and the master.

Miss Dove's rules were as fixed as the signs of the zodiac. And they were known. Miss Dove rehearsed them at the beginning of each school year, stating as calmly and dispassionately as if she were describing the atmospheric effects of the Gulf Stream. The penalties for infractions of the rules were also known. If a child introduced a foreign object—a pencil, let us say, or a wad of paper, or a lock of hair—into his mouth, he was required to wash out his mouth with the yellow laundry soap that lay on the drainboard of the sink in the corner by the sand table. If his posture was incorrect, he had to go and sit for awhile upon a stool without a back-rest. If a page in his notebook was untidy, he had to copy it over. If he emitted an uncovered cough, he was expected to rise immediately and fling open a window, no matter how cold the weather, so that a blast of fresh air could protect his fellows from the contamination of his germs. And if he felt obliged to disturb the class routine by leaving the room for a drink of water (Miss Dove loftily ignored any other necessity) he did so to an accompaniment of dead silence. Miss

Portrait of a district schoolteacher. From *Harper's Weekly*, Vol. 17, p. 817

Ichabod Crane's schoolroom

Dove would look at him—that was all—following his departure and greeting his return
with her perfectly expressionless gaze and the whole class would sit idle and motionless
until he was back in the fold. It was easier—even if one had eaten salt fish for breakfast—to remain and suffer. (Patton, 1954, pp. 9–10)

The portrait of Miss Dove was created in a past now long gone, but her image
lingers on in the memory of the American culture.

Miss Dove is by no means the only stereotype of a teacher. There is a common
image of the slightly rumpled male teacher of indeterminate age. In its harshest
realization the image reveals itself in the likeness of Ichabod Crane, the principal
character of Nathaniel Hawthorne's *The Legend of Sleepy Hollow*, a petty tyrant—
and torturer of children—and even worse, a bore. In its most kindly embodiment
the stereotype is of the thoughtful, sensitive, caring, slightly eccentric, and dreamy
Mr. Chips, a teacher totally dedicated to his students, but somehow not completely

at ease in the adult world. As the British essayist Charles Lamb asked over one and one-half centuries ago:

> Why are we never quite at ease in the presence of a schoolmaster?—because we are conscious that he is not quite at ease in ours. He is awkward, and out of place, in the society of his equals. He comes like Gulliver from among his little people, and he cannot fit the stature of his understanding to yours. He cannot meet you on the square. . . . He is so used to teaching that he wants to be teaching *you*. (Lass & Tasman, 1980, p. 8)

In this stereotype the teacher is highly regarded for his knowledge of the subject he teaches and his erudition but is somehow considered inadequate to cope completely with the demands of the real world. He is the butt of Irish playwright George Bernard Shaw's dictum that "He who can does. He who cannot teaches."

Another stereotype of the teacher is the dynamic, hip and with-it young male or female teacher—the Gabe Kotter of the popular television program "Welcome Back Kotter." In that series, Gabe Kotter returns as a teacher to the high school where he was a student. He is someone who likes and understands the kids whom he teaches. He believes he can reach them because he knows "where they're coming from."

Kotter is a variation of the middle-class teacher who enters an inner-city school and decides to bring civilization to the natives. In a more comic vein this stereotype is described by Bel Kaufman in her extremely funny novel *Up the Down Staircase*. It is the beginning of the school year, and Miss Barrett meets with her homeroom class for the first time. The scene proceeds with a voice rising from the classroom:

> O, no! A *dame* for homeroom?
> You want I should slug him, teach?
> Is this homeroom period?
>
> *Yes. Sit down please.*
>
> I don't belong here.
> We gonna have you all term?
> Are you a regular or a sub?
> (Weis, 1967, p. 11)

The first moments of the class are clearly a testing of wills of both the teacher and the students. By the end of the class, the encounter reaches epic proportions in which the full powers and intellect of the teacher are pitted against the barbarisms, crudity, and native intelligence of the students. A student arrives at the end of class and rudely throws a late pass to her as he enters the room. She objects, saying:

That's no way to hand it to me. Throwing it like that on
my desk.

My aim is bad.

There's no need for insolence. Please take that toothpick
out of your mouth when you talk to me. And take your
hands out of your pockets.

Which first?

What's your name?

You gonna report me?

What's your name?

You gonna give me a zero?

I'm afraid I've just about——What's your name?

Joe.

Joe what?

Ferone. You gonna send a letter home? Take away my
lollipop?
Lecture me? Spank me?

All I asked——

Yeah, All you asked.

I don't allow anyone to talk to me like that.

So you're lucky—you're a teacher!

(Weis, 1967, p. 21)

There are many variations on this stereotype. Sidney Poitier finds himself teaching
in a London slum school in the movie *To Sir With Love*. In his case through sheer
force of personality he takes a group of disenchanted teenage dropouts and brings
meaning to their lives.

Although the Poitier characterization may romanticize teaching to the point
that it is no longer real, it does reflect what is a very real missionary motivation

underlying why many people become teachers. All of the five teachers introduced at the beginning of this chapter entered the profession because they somehow felt that they could reach students in a special way. Ruth Christopherson, for example, describes how she wants to

> motivate a child to function on his or her own. . . . To figure things out—and to give them that feeling of accomplishment—"I've done it myself"—and show them where to go with it from there.

In teaching French and Spanish, Jacquie Yourist hopes that she teaches her students

> a little about other people and other cultures, civilizations, so they can develop an idea of their own world in perspective to these other faraway places.

The ability to reach out and touch students, to make a difference in their lives, is a theme that comes up again and again in discussions with teachers about their work.

Yet another stereotype of the teacher is the "mover of men" (or one would hope in today's more enlightened era also a "mover of women"). This teacher is someone not quite mortal who can move and shape the students whom he or she teaches by the sheer force of will and the strength of ideas. This notion has much of its origins in the autobiographies of famous people who credit teachers with having had a profound impact on their development, as well as from personal experiences with a particularly effective or influential teacher.

The journalist and political analyst Theodore H. White, for example, describes a teacher whom he could never forget in *In Search of History*.

> How can I say what a ten-year old boy remembers of a schoolteacher lost in time? She was stout, grey-haired, dimpled, schoolmarmish, almost never angry. She was probably the first Protestant I ever met; she taught history vigorously; and she was special, the first person who made me think I might make something of myself. She was the kind of teacher who could set fire to the imagination of the ordinary children who sat in lumps before her, and to do so was probably the chief reward she sought. (Lass & Tasman, 1980, pp. 255–256)

The reality of teachers such as these—ones who could move and shape people's lives in important ways—recalls the often quoted comment of the American historian Henry Adams that a "politician may shape a moment, but a teacher affects eternity."

In doing so, however, there is also an important responsibility implied. If one sets out to shape and mold one's students, one must ask the question, toward what end? In a remarkable passage written when he was an adult, one of this century's most powerful and dynamic political leaders recalled the teacher who had most influenced him when he was young. Like Theodore White's teacher, the subject this teacher taught was history.

> It was perhaps decisive for my whole later life that good fortune gave me a history teacher who understood, as few others did, this principle . . . of retaining the essential and forgetting the non-essential. . . . In my teacher, Dr. Leopold Poetsch of the high school in Linz, this requirement was fulfilled in a truly ideal manner. An old gentleman, kind but at the same time firm, he was able not only to hold our attention by his dazzling eloquence but to carry us away with him. Even today I think back with genuine emotion upon this grey-haired man who, by the fire of his words, sometimes made us forget the present; who as if by magic, transported us into times past and out of the millennium mists of time, transformed dry historical facts into vivid reality. There we sat, often aflame with enthusiasm, sometimes even moved to tears. . . . He used our budding national fanaticism as a means of educating us, frequently appealing to our sense of honor. This teacher made history my favorite subject. And indeed, though he had no such intention, it was then that I became a young revolutionary. (Lass and Tasman, 1980, pp. 30–31)

The author of this passage, of course, was Adolf Hitler, and the book in which he wrote these words *Mein Kampf*.

Stereotypes, although misrepresenting and oversimplifying the world, often contain certain elements of truth. Many characteristics and traits in the preceding descriptions can be found in the five case study teachers. At the same time it is abundantly clear that stereotypes do not capture the totality of being a teacher. Each of the teachers introduced in this book is a unique individual. Yet despite their uniqueness they are members of a profession with certain identifiable characteristics and traits. The concluding part of this chapter looks at some of these characteristics and traits in detail.

THE "TYPICAL" AMERICAN TEACHER

Some Educational Statistics

There is an old joke to the effect that the average American couple has 2.4 children. No one, of course, has ever been able to describe what raising 40 percent of a child is like. Making generalizations from statistics obviously has its pitfalls. Nonetheless, statistics can provide useful insights into the teaching profession at large when used in conjunction with other types of data—and occasionally a bit of common sense.

The typical American teacher today does not look much like Miss Dove or the

Ruth at work

other stereotypes presented earlier in this chapter. Instead, she is a woman in her thirties who has taught for 12 years, most often just in a single school district. During these 12 years she has returned to her local college or university and has received a master's degree. She is white, married, and the mother of two children.

She teaches in a suburban elementary school, surrounded by other women faculty members similar to herself. Her school's principal, however, is in all likelihood a man. She typically has about 23 students in her class. Counting her after-school responsibilities, she puts in a longer work week than most blue-collar workers and brings home a slightly lower salary (Feistritzer, 1983, pp. 24–26). In fact, when school is in session, the average teacher works 46 hours a week. This is compared to an average work week of 35 hours for nonagricultural workers (Sykes, 1984, p. 74). The typical teacher is a member of the Democratic party but is not politically active.

Think quickly for a minute of a hypothetical third-grade teacher who has been working at a local suburban elementary school for the past 10 or 12 years. What image immediately comes to mind? It was probably of a woman. The facts support the image. According to figures put together in 1982–1983 there were 981,162 women and 195,449 male elementary school teachers in the United States.

Now think quickly for a moment about a high school science teacher. If you thought immediately of a man, you were at least partially justified. Men make up slightly more than half of the teaching population at the secondary level. Estimates for 1982–1983 show 487,713 male and 474,148 female teachers at the secondary level. What this means when elementary school figures are combined with second-

Luberta at work

ary school figures is that the ratio of women to men in the profession is over 2 to 1 in favor of women.

Teaching is clearly a feminized profession and, as such, is affected by many of the biases and prejudices that are held against women. In the American work force, wage discrimination is very much a reality. Men consistently make more money than women for the same work. Since women predominantly make up the population of teachers in the United States, it is not surprising that the profession as a whole suffers from relatively low salaries when compared to similar types of work. It can be argued that there is even discrimination within the profession between elementary and secondary school teachers. Women predominate at the elementary level, and the salaries of elementary school teachers are lower than those of their secondary school counterparts. Similarly, greater prestige is associated with teaching at the secondary rather than the elementary level. In point of fact, strong arguments could be made to the effect that an elementary school teacher's job is ultimately more taxing than a secondary school teacher's.

If men are underrepresented as teachers—particularly at the elementary level—then the same is true of minority groups in general. Only 1 in 10 teachers is black. And only about 2 out of every 100 teachers are Hispanic. These figures are particularly important to keep in mind when considering the ethnic composition of students attending school in the final decades of this century. At the present time, students from ethnic and racial minorities represent 26 percent of the total school-age population. By 1990 these figures are projected to increase to 30 percent of the total school enrollment. What this means is that many teachers currently working in the schools are instructing students who are probably of different ethnic and social backgrounds than themselves. This will increase as a trend unless more minority teachers are recruited into the profession.

Historically teaching has provided an important vehicle for social mobility. As the educational sociologist Dan Lortie (1975) has pointed out in his classic work, *Schoolteacher,* teaching is clearly "white collar work." It provides a important means for people to enter the middle class who are of blue-collar or lower-class origin. Precise figures concerning the social origins of teachers are not available, but even among the five case study teachers in this book the use of teaching as a vehicle for class and social advancement is clear. Sandy Snodgrass's father was a foreman in a lead company. Neither he nor Sandy's mother went to college. Sandy's father clearly felt it was important that his daughter graduate from college. Not only did Sandy's father see college education as providing his daughter with important advantages and opportunities that he had not had, but graduating as a teacher meant for him that his daughter was entering an "exalted" position.

Neither Ruth Christopherson's mother nor father finished elementary school. Ruth's father was a bookbinder and her mother was a housewife. Larry Wells's

Sandy at work

Larry at work

father was a grocery salesman and small-store owner. Luberta Clay's father was a custodian. Jacquie Yourist's father was a farmer. Her mother, a registered nurse, had the most formal education of any of these teachers' parents. When the five teachers for this book were selected, their social or economic backgrounds were not considered in any way. Yet they fit a general pattern of many other teachers in the United States.

Ironically, the very success of the educational system and, in particular, teachers has led to an undermining of the profession's status. As the high schools and colleges have graduated more and more students, as more parents of children in the schools have become educated, the status of teachers has declined. Historically, the teacher was the most—or one of the most—educated individuals in a community. This is no longer the case, and as a result, the special status of teachers has diminished considerably. In the past many parents were reluctant to challenge a teacher about what he or she was doing with their child because they did not feel competent to do so. Now far fewer parents feel in awe of the teachers who instruct their children.

Five Attractors to Teaching

Besides the sociological characteristics that unify the teaching population, there are to some extent personal and individual characteristics that set teachers apart from other types of professionals. Some of the most important of these can be seen by looking at what attracts teachers to the profession. Dan Lortie (1975), in *Schoolteacher*, cites the following five major attractions: (1) the service theme, (2) the interpersonal theme, (3) the continuation theme, (4) the time compatibility theme, and (5) the material benefits theme.

The Service Theme According to Lortie (1975), people who are attracted to teaching are usually *service*-oriented. They enter teaching primarily for the opportunity to help or inspire young people. The service theme in teaching receives support from almost all religious orientations stemming from the Judeo-Christian heritage. For many, teaching is secular missionary work, a place to enact a deep sense of responsibility to give of oneself. Lortie (1975) wrote that "teachers have been perceived as performing a special mission in our society," and from his interviews with teachers he found that they see the occupation as "a valuable service of special moral worth" (p. 28). Sandy exemplifies this theme when she refers to her sense of compassion and social service that developed in college. Recall her words:

> In college I got involved in all these causes—working with poverty children, working with handicapped children, working with Vietnam disabled veterans at the veterans' hospital. My capacity for compassion developed. I still tend to pick out the kids who need large doses of that, and that quality started emerging in college.

Jacquie at work

The other occupations that Sandy considered, social work and nursing, were service-oriented as well.

The Interpersonal Theme According to Lortie a second attractor to teaching is what he calls the *interpersonal* theme. Teaching is a people-oriented profession. Teachers spend most of their working hours interacting with other people—specifically children or young people. The essential behaviors of teaching—talking, counseling, managing, directing, and instructing—are all performed with children or adolescents. In fact when teachers have been asked to describe their reasons for entering the profession, the largest single category of responses has been summarized by the "desire to work with young people," or the more general orientation "to work with people" (Lortie, 1975). Ruth Christopherson fits this theme neatly for she says she entered teaching because "she loved working with children" and "enjoyed watching them grow."

The Continuation Theme Lortie labels another attractor to the profession the *continuation* theme. He means by this that teaching is appealing because it permits people to continue their positive experiences with school or learning. Sandy and Larry, for example, initially liked the idea of teaching because it would enable them to build upon their interest in history and politics. For Jacquie Yourist, teaching gave her "something to do with her French as well as an opportunity to stay in school." Recall her statement, "I liked being a student, and I thought that perhaps I could be a perpetual student all my life by being around a school."

The Time Compatibility Theme Another attraction is what Lortie labels the *time compatibility* theme. Unlike many other professions, teaching affords not only relatively large blocks of free time but also free time that is compatible with raising a family. This is a particularly important characteristic for women, one that allows them to be mothers and professionals. For Sandy Snodgrass, the mother of two small children, the opportunity to be at home at 4:00 P.M. each afternoon and to have summer vacations that she can share with her children is now extremely important.

The Material Benefit Theme Finally, Lortie found that teaching as a profession is attractive to people because of the *material benefits* it provides. Teaching, of course, has never been known for such benefits, and there are, in fact, norms that suggest that teachers should enter the profession only for altruistic reasons. Nonetheless, some do find teaching materially rewarding. Material benefits involve security and prestige as well as salary, and many teachers are pleased with the generally secure nature of the job. Also, many teachers do earn a reasonable living. Although the salaries provided to teachers are clearly lower than those received for similar work in other professions, teaching salaries are often second salaries in a family or are significantly better than the salaries of a teacher's parents, whose social and class origin is often lower than that of the typical teacher. This is by no means a justification for low teacher salaries but merely a partial explanation of why large numbers of teachers are willing to work for fewer material benefits than their professional counterparts in other fields (Lortie, 1975, pp. 27–31).

There are of course other reasons why individuals choose to enter teaching. Influential teachers and family members, for example, are also mentioned by our case study teachers. Nonetheless, the five attractors cited by Lortie stand out as the major factors that might be said to motivate the typical teacher.

CONCLUSION

This chapter has considered the question of who teaches in America by looking at brief life histories of five particular teachers, by presenting some sterotypes from literature and the media, and by examining some of the research data currently available on the general teaching force in America. In effect this book begins with a focus on the individual and the premise that family and community background as well as personal characteristics and experiences will deeply affect why and how a person teaches.

In *The Sociological Imagination* C. Wright Mills (1959) makes a more general case for the way in which an individual life history affects the society within which the person functions and works.

> We have come to know that every individual lives from one generation to the next, in some society; that he lives out a biography and that he lives it out within some historical sequence. By the fact of his living he contributes, however minutely, to the shaping of this society and to the course of its history, even as he is made by society and by its historical push and shove. . . . No social study that does not come back to the problem of biography or history and of their intersections within a society has completed its intellectual journey. (p. 6)

Individuals, in part, create their society; and teachers, in part, create their classrooms and their profession. To understand fully the nature of teaching in relation to the culture of the schools and to the larger society, we must begin with the personal backgrounds and qualities of those who chose to teach.

At the same time, however, C. Wright Mills also points out that society shapes an individual. Teachers are inevitably pushed and shoved by the traditions, values, and policies of the community and schools in which they work. Chapter 2 turns to the work settings of two of our five teachers so that you can begin to consider some of the contextual forces that appear to influence them and begin to see some of the day-to-day realities of their classroom lives.

DISCUSSION QUESTIONS

1. What are some of the major similarities and differences you find among the five teachers with regard to family background and motivation to become a teacher?
2. The five case study teachers in this book chose teaching as a profession a number of years ago. Do you think the motivations of those entering teaching today are similar or different? Explain.
3. Think about why you have become interested in education and teaching as a career. List some of the main attractions of teaching for you as an individual. Discuss with others in your class how your interests and motivations are similar to or different from theirs.
4. What do you think may be the source of some of the stereotypes about the teaching profession in the United States? What do these stereotypes suggest about the way in which the profession is perceived by the general public? Is there any element of truth in these stereotypes?

ACTIVITIES

1. Interview three education majors in either secondary or elementary education at your college or university and ask why they have decided to become teachers. Ask: What characteristics of the profession do they find appealing? What characteristics of the profession do they see as problematic or drawbacks? Have they been encouraged or discouraged by peers, parents, and advisors about going into the profession?
2. Interview three seniors at your school who have not chosen teaching as a career. Ask: Why have they selected the occupation they have? What characteristics of the selected occupation are most appealing and least appealing? Did status, money, or type of work figure most prominently in their decision?

REFERENCES AND SOURCES

Feistritzer, C. Emily. (1983). *The condition of teaching: A state by state analysis*. Princeton: Princeton University Press.

Greene, Maxine. (1973). *Teacher as stranger: Educational philosophy for the modern age*. Belmont, CA: Wadsworth.

Kozol, Jonathan. (1981). *On being a teacher*. New York: Continuum.

Lass, Abraham H., & Tasman, Norma L. (Eds.). (1980). *Going to school: An anthology of prose about teachers and students*. New York: Mentor.

Lortie, Dan C. (1975). *Schoolteacher: A sociological study.* Chicago: University of Chicago Press.

Mills, C. Wright. (1959). *The sociological imagination.* London: Oxford University Press.

Patton, F. G. (1954). *Good morning, Miss Dove.* New York: Dodd, Mead.

Weiss, Jerry (Ed.). (1967). *Tales out of school.* New York: Dell.

2

EXCELLENCE IN THE ELEMENTARY SCHOOL

INTRODUCTION

Teaching is at once an individual and a social endeavor. Who teachers are as individuals and as members of a profession deeply affects what they do in the classroom. Where teachers work and the nature of the student population they face each day also significantly affect their classroom behavior.

This chapter portrays two of the five case study teachers in their community, school, and classroom contexts. You will first visit Ruth Christopherson at work in her sixth-grade classroom in a wealthy section of St. Louis County and then travel downtown to inner-city St. Louis and Luberta Clay's fifth-grade classroom. Although these observation sites are relatively close geographically, they nonetheless are representative of differing models of teaching excellence in highly diverse settings. They suggest that what is seen as educational excellence in one situation or locale may not be seen as excellence elsewhere; what is excellent according to one set of values may not qualify as excellent in another's value system. Each educational setting has its own political and social history, its own student population, and its own resources and constraints that shape its particular definition of excellence. The act of teaching can never be fully understood in isolation. What Ruth, Luberta, or other teachers do or do not do in their classrooms is, in large part, determined by their school and community context.

Each case study presents a fairly detailed and therefore lengthy description of a single day. Ruth's case study attempts to capture the first day of school from beginning to end. The aim is three-fold: (1) to portray a slice of elementary school life as it occurs in suburban mid-America; (2) to project an image of how one school year begins and to suggest that many pupil behaviors that you observe in classrooms have been shaped systematically by the teacher from the first day of the school year; and (3) to present a vivid picture of the philosophy, pedagogy, and personality of Ruth Christopherson.

In Luberta's case the focus is on a single morning, and it conveys: (1) a slice of elementary school life as it occurs in urban mid-America; (2) one version of a "basics" curriculum; and (3) a vivid picture of Luberta Clay's philosophy, pedagogy, and personality.

As you visit these two classrooms look for: (1) the ways in which individual teacher characteristics and community or school context appear to influence what happens in the classroom; (2) the differences that set these particular teachers and contexts apart and the commonalities that hold them together; and (3) the reasons why each of these teachers might be considered excellent.

RUTH CHRISTOPHERSON: SETTING THE STAGE IN SUBURBIA

Community Context

It is August 31, 1983—the first day of a new school year for the children of the school district of Ladue, Missouri. It is also the first day of the last year of elementary school teaching for Ruth Christopherson. All but 4 of Ruth's 30 years as a teacher have been in Ladue, a suburb of St. Louis, Missouri.

As one drives down the streets of Ladue, one cannot mistake the economic success and elegant tastes of the majority of its residents. Clayton Road, which runs through the center of Ladue, is also the center of the community's commerce and civic activity. At the eastern edge of the suburb on Clayton Road are stately and immaculate red brick and white pillared colonial-style police and fire stations and city hall. On Clayton Road at the western edge of the suburb is a recently built cluster of exclusive shops and boutiques known simply as The Market Place. The Market Place is, however, anything but simple. Within the elegant country French shops with bay windows and shake roofs, one can purchase costly furs, custom-made jewelry, European and American designer clothes, luxurious lingerie, and one-of-a-kind gifts from every corner of the globe. At other points along Clayton Road are long-established specialty food, dress, jewelry, and needlepoint shops that cater to preppy and sophisticated consumers. Brass trim on the doors, striped awnings, and ceramic flowerpots filled with red geraniums beckon passersby and promise a pleasant social as well as shopping experience.

To the north and south of Clayton Road are the residences of the wealthy — large, gracious homes on rambling, tree-lined lots of several acres. Each house is in-

The Market Place, Clayton Road, Ladue, Missouri

dividual in design—an American Colonial here, a French Provincial there, an English Tudor across the street. Many homes are hidden from view down long winding roads or behind heavily wooded areas. Those that are clearly visible from the main streets have green, well-manicured lawns and profuse flower gardens despite the drought-like conditions of the summer. Underground sprinkler systems, well-paid gardeners, and housewives devoted to house and garden account for the surprisingly lush lawn conditions.

Amidst these extraordinarily affluent surroundings there do exist a few modest areas, one of which is almost a slum. These neighborhoods are few in number and do not detract from the overall ambiance of achievement and material well-being. There is, however, considerable diversity within the school population. The Ladue School District encompasses the adjoining suburb of Olivette, which has a far more heterogeneous citizenry. Within the various residential subdivisions live upper-middle-class whites, middle-class whites and blacks, and lower-class blacks. In addition, like all other school districts in the St. Louis metropolitan area, Ladue is participating in a voluntary desegregation plan that involves busing a small percentage of inner-city blacks into the community.

Conway School

Conway School, where Ruth Christopherson teaches, is one of the district's four elementary schools. Surrounded by trees and lovely homes, its stately red brick co-

A home in Ladue

lonial exterior almost fades into the residential and peaceful curves of Conway Road. It is 8:45 A.M. and already 80 degrees. As always, the first day of school in St. Louis is a hot and humid one that looks and feels very much like the middle of summer. The circular school driveway is lined with recent-model station wagons, Audis, BMWs, and Mercedes. Many of the Conway mothers, particularly those with kindergarteners or first graders, like to drive their children to school on the first day. Still there is ample room for the big yellow school buses that deposit the majority of the school's students at the front steps.

Out from the buses and cars jump smiling, well-scrubbed, healthy-looking boys and girls. Almost all of the boys are wearing Polo or Izod T-shirts, designer shorts or jeans, and Nike running shoes. The girls wear a similar "uniform," but their outfits have been selected with more forethought. One girl's turquoise shorts match her pink and turquoise T-shirt and turquoise Polo socks. Another girl's red shorts are teamed with a red and navy striped shirt and a red ribbon around her blond ponytail. Both boys and girls energetically climb the four steps that lead to the white double doors.

Inside the center hall are young, attractive, and tan mothers, in their tennis outfits or brightly colored skirts. They chat informally with each other and teachers, who generally look considerably older and more matronly. A few fathers are present, and they look crisp and businesslike in white shirts, khaki or pinstripe suits, and conservative club ties. Some parents have cameras ready to record the first day of school. In the background are carts filled with an array of audiovisual equipment. Television sets, movie and slide projectors, and tape recorders are ready for easy entry into the classroom of any teacher who requests them.

"Mrs. C's" Classroom

8:55 The 24 sixth graders who have been assigned to Mrs. Christopherson begin to head down the center and right hallways toward "Mrs. C's" room. Some dash through the doorway; others enter more slowly. Many of the girls come into the room in clusters and in animated conversation; a number of the boys are involved in good-natured shouting and shoving. Smilingly, Ruth greets each and every one by name, even those who are newcomers to Conway School. "Sit at the desk where you see your name tag for now," she repeats frequently; "we'll talk about how we want to reorganize the furniture and seating arrangements this afternoon."

As the students reach their designated desks, they find a folder with their name on it. Jeff, a tall, thin, dark-haired, fair-skinned boy who was in Mrs. Christopherson's first-grade class five years ago takes his seat at the back of the room. He opens his folder and finds—as all the other children do—the following mimeographed message on the first sheet:

> Today we start a new school year—a fresh beginning for you and for me. I hope it will be a year of great accomplishment and many happy times.
>
> Mrs. Christopherson

Conway School

Jeff,

   Shades of first grade! Here we go again. Do you remember any events from the good old days in 1-C? I hope this will be a super year for both of us. Let's do it!

                              Mrs. C

Mrs. C's note to Jeff on the first day of class

Jeff, as all the others do, also finds a personal, handwritten note.

Jeff smiles momentarily—perhaps recalling some funny event from his first-grade days. The flashback is over quickly, though, for he starts to examine the remaining contents of the folder—a list of school supplies and a schedule.

His schedule looks different from last year's because this year, for the first time, the sixth grade is departmentalized. Each of the three sixth-grade teachers will teach reading and language arts, but Ruth will be responsible for all math instruction; Mr. Moyle will handle science, and Mrs. Bialecki will teach social studies.

9:05 Ruth is in the process of taking attendance and lunch count. Her manner is crisp and businesslike. She pauses only briefly when an overweight, blond girl in unflattering shorts awkwardly enters the classroom. Several students sigh loudly and rudely, and one yells out, "Here comes trouble!" Ignoring the inappropriate student behavior, Ruth greets the latecomer by name and smilingly says, "Come in—there's your seat over there." When attendance and lunch count is over, Ruth introduces four newcomers to Conway—Chris from Chicago, Amy from South America, Jeff from neighboring Parkway School District, and Mike from California. As their names are called, each jumps up from his or her desk with an embarrassed look and then quickly sits down. Ruth reminds everyone:

> We need to help the new students with moving, and we *will* be moving. At 9:40 we are going to the gym to hear an explanation of the new schedule from Dr. Bredin. If it gets

near 9:40 and I don't seem to notice, please tell me. (*She writes 9:40 on the board*) Now let's go over the folders. Any questions?

She begins with the list of supplies, reading aloud a few key items she thinks might need explanation. When she finishes she adds, "For this week, I'll have supplies, in case you don't get a chance to go to the store. But I'd appreciate it if you could have most of them by next week."

The next order of business is the schedule, and Ruth explains:

> This room will be your homeroom, and we will have spelling, reading, and writing in here every morning. Your first move will be at 10:00. Some have math, some have science, some have social studies. Math is in here. Let's see where the new people go. (*She walks around to look at schedules of newcomers and to give a few words of direction*)
>
> 11:00 to 12:00 is a real ringer. Look at it. You could be going to vocal music, library— any of the new people have library? Watch out—this is a big building—first time I came here I got lost. Some will go to art, some to computers. (*Again she checks folders of new people*) Anybody taking band or strings? Any questions about anything in the folder?

Ruth then shifts gears somewhat:

> Sixth grade was the very first class I taught and one of my happiest times, and now I am ending with sixth grade. I started to say, "*I am going to make it the happiest class,*" but what's wrong with that statement?

A student says, "You should say *we*."

> That is exactly right. It has to be all of us working together. You know, I once had a student named Charlie—Charlie had a lot of tricks. If I said go out, he went in; if I said go in, he went out; if I gave him crayons to draw with, he would eat them (*students laugh*). I think I know all of the tricks, but if you come up with any new ones, I'll tell you.

Ruth then passes out what she calls a *student survey* and gives directions for filling it out as they go along.

> RUTH: Just write in phrases—it's too hot for complete sentences. . . .Under *life at home* just give me some idea of what's going on there. Do you have any animals? If you are going to use your guinea pig as an excuse this year—like your guinea pig ate your homework—then you should write down you have a guinea pig, or dog, cats, chickens, fish. Write down if you have brothers and sisters and be nice to your siblings. Some kids write down "bratty brother." Say something nice. . . . I am asking you to fill out your activity schedule

CONWAY SCHOOL

STUDENT SURVEY   6-C   PAGE 1

Name: _____

Date: _____

Address: _____   Phone: _____

_____   Birthday: _____

Life at Home:

Activities Schedule:

M		Sixth	
T		Grade	
W		At	
T		Conway	
F		School	
S			
S			

Feelings About Sixth Grade Year:

Student survey

so I can take it into consideration when I assign homework. Anybody have early morning swimming or soccer practice? I know you're busy. I usually have a policy of no homework on weekends. Let's see if you like that? (*Big show of hands, smiles, and head nodding*) Okay, how many like homework on Monday night? (*No one raises a hand*) Boys and girls, I have to rephrase. We will have

Student Survey	6-C Page 2
Reading	
Writing	
Spelling	
Math	
Science	
Social Studies	
Action	

Suggested Method for Handling Academic or Behavioral Problems Should the Need Arise:

Student survey

homework—which night is best? Be sure to fill in your birthday. And on your birthday—beware! I play tricks. How many of you have summer birthdays? Oh, good—you could get it any time. I am a birthday pest. Who will be my first victim? Under *subjects* on page 2, just write how you feel about different subjects. If you think math is boring put it down, but it's only boring if you make it that way—we will unbore you. If you say "yuk," it's my challenge to change it. We'll fill this out at the end of the semester and the end of year and see if there are any changes. Be honest—if you hate reading, put it down—no one else will see it. I will be honest and respect your feelings, and I expect the same. At the bottom, put down your suggestions for handling problems, although I don't think we'll have to deal with any. I like to take care of problems as soon as they arise. What are some ways we can handle problems?

STUDENT: Talk to parents.

STUDENT: Talk to principal.

STUDENT: Talk to us.

RUTH: (*Draws a triangle on the board and labels it*)

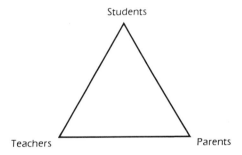

The three of us are in partnership for your education, and one of our goals is getting you ready for junior high. I call parents when something good happens as well as when there are problems.... Finally, on the back of the second sheet, please write down your experience with computers for Mrs. Bachman. Draw a smiling face if you like them or a frowning face if you don't. I will show her only this part of the survey. Everybody will get one half hour on computers each day, some will get more. Some kids last year wrote compositions—Laurie did one over the summer. Also last year some kids did graphs. Mrs. Bachman will tell you about different options.

9:35 Ruth collects the surveys and uses the few remaining minutes to answer questions and check students' understanding of their schedules.

You are pioneers in a new type of program—it's going to be great. Let me test you. David, where will you be going at 11:00? Laurie, where will you be? Andy, where are you at 11:00?

9:40 Ruth takes her class to the gym where they meet with the two other sixth-grade groups and the principal, Dr. Bredin. Dr. Bredin talks of responsibility, trust, confidence, and being role models for the younger students. He explains that under the new system they have 5 minutes to change rooms and be in the appropriate seat with their materials; he reminds them that when they change rooms they will be sitting in another student's desk, so they must be respectful, and he concludes:

> We think it will work because we know you and have confidence in you. It's more responsibility for you and for the teachers. Every teacher now has 69 students, but all of us will get to know each other better. Thank you for your cooperation.

9:50 Ruth uses the remaining 10 minutes before her first math class to give a spelling pretest. The test is preceded by a reminder that pretests do not count, they simply give her information. The word list includes *banish, senior, agreement, inquire, wealth, invitation, manufacturing, prisoner.*

10:05 Ruth takes the attendance for her first math class and expresses surprise that those who are supposed to be there are, in fact, there: "We worked all day yesterday on this schedule, but we still weren't sure if it would work!" She then introduces a lesson on the Cartesian coordinate system by saying that it is a highly useful system that can be used from kindergarten through college. The lesson begins with some preliminary questions and answers.

RUTH: Anybody know what the Cartesian coordinate system means? What is a *system?*

STUDENT: Something that works together.

RUTH: What are some examples of systems?

STUDENT: A school system.

STUDENT: A computer system.

RUTH: Good. Anyone have any ideas about *coordinate?*

STUDENT: All together.

RUTH: Good. Dr. Bredin has to coordinate all parts of the school. Cartesian comes from Descartes, a famous mathematician.

RUTH: (*Observes some unnecessary milling around*) One suggestion—it's much easier to learn math if you pay attention. I don't think I have to say any more. (*Passes out a chart with a grid and two number lines, and puts the same on the board*) Where do you think Descartes put 0? (*Hands go up*) Come to the board and do it. (*A student puts a zero in the correct place*) Where would 4 be? (*A student responds correctly*) What do you think Descartes did with the other line? (*A student answers correctly*) That's right. Did you know Descartes?

Cartesian Coordinates

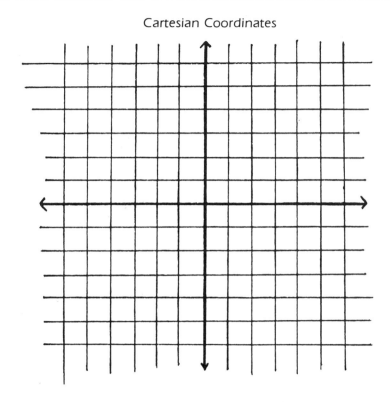

Cartesian coordinate grid

STUDENT: No (*grinning*).

RUTH: I'm going to call out pairs of numbers and I want you to plot them on your sheet. The rule is that the first number is on the horizontal and the second number is on the vertical line. (*Calls out pairs of numbers such as 2,1; − 3, − 1 and walks around to observe—some are doing it correctly, others are having some difficulty*) Never be afraid to say you don't understand—we need to clear that up quickly. Sometimes you feel embarrassed—I used to be that way. Tell me privately, if necessary, but please tell me. Also, I do not have patience with people who do not pay attention because that makes my job harder, so if that's going to be a problem, we'll have to do something. I hope it's not a problem. Okay, are we ready to play games? First rule, give others a chance—for some, this is brand new. It always happens that someone makes a mistake and other kids go, "Oh no!" Please give everyone a break. Here are the rules of the game. We will have two teams, X's and O's. You tell me where you want me to put the mark—*3,3*, or *4,4*—and I'll put it on the board. The first team with four in a row wins, but you have to recognize it—one group won but didn't know it.

STUDENT: What do we win?

RUTH: A kiss. We don't always have prizes. You can say you understand the Cartesian coordinate system—that's something to be proud of.

The students play a game until Team X wins. Next the focus is on using negative numbers. First they practice plotting pairs of negative numbers, and then they play a second game with them. The last math activity is a diagnostic test on the addition of large numbers. Ruth gives three addition problems (e.g., *6,050 + 982 + 12,004 = ?*), and then asks the students to write her a note on their feelings about math. As she collects the test, she asks, "What will I learn from this?" The class ends with this invitation and reminder:

Anybody who wants to practice the Cartesian coordinate system, please come in before school. We'll practice on a big board. Practice is the best way for understanding. Okay. It's time for your move—you have five minutes.

Ruth teaching mathematics

11:00–11:30 Ruth is free and goes to the teachers' lounge to grade papers. The lounge is air conditioned, but the rest of the building is extremely warm. The temperature outside is now over 90 degrees.

11:30–12:00 Ruth is responsible for monitoring the computer room and library, which are next to each other on the basement floor.

12:00–12:15 Ruth has cafeteria duty.

12:15–12:45 Ruth eats lunch with other teachers.

12:50 Ruth conducts her second math class. Except for her opening, good-humored line, "So you're all here for ballet?" this class is much like the first class on the Cartesian coordinate system.

1:30–2:10 Ruth has a break. She spends it getting ready for her homeroom students who will also be her third math class at 2:15 P.M.

Because the building inside and temperature outside are uncomfortably warm, and because she knows her last class will be coming from gym where they will have been running outside in the heat, Ruth prepares cold towels for their faces. She takes to her room a large plastic bowl filled with ice cubes from the kitchen and fills it with water. Then she tears off many sheets of paper towel, wads them up, and puts them into the water. As the students come through the doorway flushed and perspiring and out of breath, Ruth hands them a cold, wet towel to wipe off their faces. Needless to say, they are surprised and delighted. Some quickly come back for seconds.

2:15 Ruth begins her third and last math class with her homeroom group. The lesson is once again essentially the same, and her approach is to encourage them to learn through playing games and asking questions. At one point, when a number of students seem to be having difficulty, she announces:

> There was a person in the last class who went to a different school last year and who was having difficulty but didn't want anyone to know. I tried to convince him to ask questions, and at the end of class he came up to me and said he still didn't understand a particular part of the lesson and needed help. I thought that was great. You have to ask when you don't understand. And don't just say, "I don't get it," because I will just have to say, "What don't you get?" I need to know *what* you don't get.

A few minutes later two boys in the back ask Ruth for help and she responds: "Great, I'll position myself in back of the room. Some people can say it in front of others; some have to say it privately; but you have to say something."

Toward the end of the period, Ruth gives this group a set of problems to solve rather than a diagnostic test on addition. The problems are difficult and she tells them so: "These are not easy—you will have to work to figure them out. Try a lot of different things. You can work together."

Cut out these pieces.
Arrange them to form a triangle.

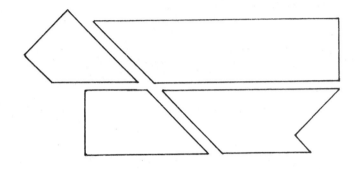

Arrange 6, 5, 3, 3 to
equal 4.

Arrange 9, 1, 8, 2 to
equal 7.

$$\frac{(9+5)+7}{3}$$ $$25 + {}^-6$$ $$\frac{6^2}{2}$$ $$\frac{(2 \times 13) - 0}{2}$$ $$(3 \times 6) + {}^-2$$

$$(4 \times 4) + 9$$ $$2^3 + 10$$ $$(\frac{10}{2} \times 6) + {}^-10$$

Seatwork for students

She then works through a problem that is similar to some of those on the sheet. The example is: *Arrange 6, 7, 8, 9 to equal 4 using any arithmetic operations you know.* After students have begun to work on their problems, some individually come up to ask questions or show Ruth the results. Ruth continually reinforces question asking and problem solving with these kinds of comments:

> John asked a good question. Robert asked another good question—he asked can you turn the pieces over. The answer is yes. All of you, Jeffrey found one way to put the pieces together, but there are other ways to get a triangle.

3:00 Ruth asks students to stop working on the math problems so that they can make some homeroom decisions: "I could have made a lot of decisions before, but I wanted you to be involved." After a discussion featuring pros and cons, they decide to have class officers, to change officers each semester, and to arrange their seats in islands of two desks. Ruth asks them to write down on a piece of paper the names of three or four people with whom they would like to be paired. The day ends with Ruth asking their reactions to the new departmentalized system and then, with humor, role playing their mothers by asking, "What did you learn today in school?"

3:30 Ruth leads the class to the gym where students are lined up for the buses. Other perspiring, flushed teachers lead students to the gym. As the numbers swell, the breeze from the big fan in the corner of the gym can no longer be felt. Still, students and teachers alike look like the first day of school was a good one. The bus boarding takes place without incident. Ruth, looking surprisingly energetic, quips with other teachers as she heads back to her room to gather up the work she will take home. How will she spend the evening? "With a tall glass of iced tea and my feet propped up," she responds smilingly as she walks towards her car. It was a long hot day for Mrs. C, but she had prepared well for it, and she clearly felt energized by the results.

Setting the Stage: A Closer Look

The focus has been on a single day of Ruth's long teaching career, but this description of the first day reveals much of what Ruth has stood for as a teacher for 30 years. The concern that she shows for her students on a hot day, her interest in individuals as shown through her personal notes to each student, and her respect for her students as whole persons who have something to contribute to the organization of their classroom are actually manifestations of a broader philosophical position on classroom management and control. In Ruth's words:

> The real control of behavior, of course, is intrinsic control—it's really building a concern for the environment and for what's happening in those individuals so that they care about their particular place. It's letting them know that I'm thinking of them and

their well-being as we plan, but at the same time they must realize that we're going to have a lot of work to do.

Ruth emphasizes, however, that a teacher has to work consciously to build such an environment. Her approach is to know each student really well, and that takes a lot of time and effort.

One thing I try to do is get acquainted enough by talking to them individually about their personal lives so that I can ask them about what's going on. This is very important to kids, and I'm finding it more important to sixth graders even than to first graders to know about their personal lives. You know one of your students wants a guitar for his birthday, and so you ask, "Did your parents shop yet?" Or you ask, "How's your hockey team?" or "How's your aunt's sick cat?" But the point is that you really know something about their personal lives to show them that you care about them as people outside of school. Every morning I try to have something to say when they come in or when I see them—and then they get to the point where they're writing little notes telling me things. . . . One of the boys had been watching this guitar in the store, and he got his parents right to the point where they were going to buy it, and his mother called the store to tell them to hold it, and it had been sold just half an hour ahead of time. This is the kind of thing you can talk to them about, commiserate with their feelings and bring other things in to talk about feelings and disappointments. The personal note that I wrote to one of my former students this year asked if he remembered falling off the bars in first grade. After class he came up to me and showed me his scar. For those who are brand new to the school, I put questions on their sheet and then they'd come up and tell me the answers to the questions—you know, things I didn't know about them. I think this personal attention makes them feel like human beings and that you care about them as people. I think that's important, but here again it takes work, and it takes preparation to do this.

In addition to revealing Ruth's desire to create an environment where students can feel the teacher's concern and interest in them as people, the first-day transcript shows a strong and deliberate attempt to make students comfortable about asking questions. By telling students over and over that they need to ask, by giving them the option to ask privately or publicly, and by praising publicly those who do ask questions, she is establishing a climate in which students feel free rather than afraid to say, I don't understand or I need help. At the same time that she is giving them the freedom to ask, however, she is giving them the responsibility for stopping the teacher when something is unclear or incomprehensible. This responsibility in turn implies an active role for the learner as well as the teacher.

Active student involvement is indeed one of the hallmarks of Ruth's teaching. Just as she teaches the Cartesian coordinate system by having students play games on the first day, she finds ways to teach almost every math concept during the year through student activities. When she taught the concept of prime numbers, for example, she first elicited from students the definition of *prime numbers*: numbers with only two divisors, the number *1* and the number itself. Then she distributed a chart with numbers from 1 to 100 and asked students to work in six teams to find all the prime numbers and to color all those that were not, all within a 20-minute time limit. The students started working immediately and became very involved in the task. Ruth circulated and made comments like:

> You're seeing patterns—that's a good observation.
> Your group really found a bonanza.
> A famous mathematician says there are 25 prime numbers. How many are you finding?
> He says there are five in the first row. What do you think?

Groups who have only four in their first row begin to reexamine. Groups who are not close to 25 begin to recheck. As the time is running out Ruth says, "Two more minutes," but no one wants to stop. When she finally calls time a number of students keep working. Some yell, "Mrs. C, we think we've got it; we're almost finished." Ruth asks students for a report as to how they went about the task. Some say they looked for patterns, others say they went one by one. When she observes that some students are still working, Ruth responds:

> I know it's hard to stop when you are close, but I want to tell you about this famous mathematician, Eratosthenes. He made a sieve, and we are going to check his sieve.

She reads row by row, and students check their findings against those of Eratosthenes.

Ruth helping a student

With this active approach Ruth has students wanting to do math beyond the assigned time. Students are actually enjoying the task for its own sake. Much of the joy seems to come from the fact that the activity has been carefully construed so that students can figure out patterns and discover answers on their own. According to Ruth, her major goal is to

> motivate children to function on their own—to figure things out—and to give them that feeling of accomplishment, that I've-done-it-myself feeling and to show them where to go with it from there. One thing that made me focus this way was a quotation that I read from Descartes some time ago. He said he had left many things unsaid to leave for others the joy of discovery, and I think basically this is one thing I try to build upon—whenever there's a chance the children could discover something, I let them do it.

What skills and knowledge does a teacher have to have to arrange such discovery? As Ruth sees it:

> To be able to do this you have to set the stage for it as the teacher. When you ask the big question, enough background is there on the answer. You really need to know the right questions to ask to set it up for them so that they can reach that I-did-it feeling. It's knowing your subject and actually thinking through yourself the steps that you're going to take to lead the child to this discovery.

The best days that Ruth has had as a teacher have been those when she has set the stage so well that she can just stand back and respond to the "production" of the children. She has been particularly pleased

> at the end of units on economics when we put everything together using all the skills—mathematics, science—when we produce things and market them and then give the money to somebody. This makes the kids feel good, lets them see how all this education has a meaning. More education needs to be meaningful in their lives rather than just isolated bits of knowledge.

When Ruth tells of the specific projects from the economics unit, her pride is unmistakable.

> One group, the very first one I did, decided to make table decorations for the holidays and planned to sell 150. They went out and took orders for 650 of them, so we worked before school, during lunch. We had parents coming in and we got everybody involved— that's a really, really good feeling. They've made magazines, they've made bookmarks and sold them around the school. Another group had a sort of country store where you could have your silhouette or handprint made, different things the kids thought of themselves.

Mrs. C. 9:15 Sentences 9:30 Cartoons 9:50 Workbook	Cindy Mrs. C. 9:30 GS-1 Lesson 8 Spelling 3 times Let's try for 100%	Meg Mrs. C. 9:30 GS-1 Family Pictures	Mike Mrs. C. 9:30 GS-1 Family Pictures	David Mrs. C. 9:30 GS-1 Family Pictures Outline R-L Brain Lesson	Sara Mrs. C. 9:30 GS-1 Family Pictures
Jessica B. GS-1 W Work on Final Copy	Jessica R. GS-1 W Work on Pencil Story	Lauren GS-1 Fraction Practice	Grant GS-1 W Pace yourself so you finish by 10:05	Chris F. GS-1 W	Steve GS-1 W Make Final Copy on Guitar Story
Chris D. GS-1 W Rework Mailbox Story	Brian GS-1 W Work on Social Studies Project	Jeff S. GS-1 W Speech Write Neatly	Cache Read Galaxies 27-32 Finish Unit 7 Spelling - Work on Unit 8	Jeff G. GS-1 W TV story was very nice!	Bill GS-1 W Personification Story Use your time well.
Scott GS-1 W Copy story in NEAT writing.	Chris F. Mrs. C. 9:50 Take math test you missed. Hope you feel better!	John Mrs. C 9:50 Unit 8 Spelling Write each word 3 times Story	Rachel Mrs. C 9:50 Personification Story	Amy Mrs. Grommet 9:05 Math - Long Division Mrs. C 9:50	Susie Mrs. C 9:50 Work on Halloween Bulletin Board

Individual student assignments (tickets)

Such projects are clearly learning experiences of a social nature, but Ruth also believes that learning must at times be highly individualized. During language arts each morning she issues individual assignments (she calls them *tickets*) to each student, with some receiving personal compliments or words of encouragement.

"Setting the stage" is how Ruth views her role as a teacher—setting the stage for discovery, for meaningful group activities, for individual progress, and for self-reliance. The task is an intellectually challenging and incredibly time consuming one that requires a high degree of knowledge, organization, creativity, drive, patience, good humor, and energy. Ruth has all of these qualities in abundance plus a genuine love for and interest in children. But now that the curtain is about to go down on Ruth's long-running, award-winning stage hit, the question is, How many other Ruths are there waiting in the wings?

LUBERTA CLAY: HELPING URBAN CHILDREN
REACH FOR THE GOOD LIFE

Community Context

Each day, Luberta Clay rides two buses to and from her teaching job at Jefferson School in St. Louis. She leaves her home in the fashionable Central West End of St. Louis, a recently renovated neighborhood of gourmet shops, boutiques, art galleries, singles bars, restaurants with sidewalk cafés, newly built, stylish condominiums, and old but still elegant apartments, duplexes, and large townhouses. The Central West End is where many young urban professionals (yuppies) and wealthy elderly women choose to live and where all segments of St. Louis city and county choose to come for street life. When Luberta arrives at Jefferson School on the north side of the city, however, she is in one of the most depressed and dangerous sections of the city.

Luberta feels safe walking in and out of Jefferson School during daylight hours, but she would hesitate to walk in the neighborhood alone at night. Directly across from the school are the Vaughn Tower Apartments, a high-rise housing project for low-income residents. Many of these apartments stand abandoned in a state of disrepair, including countless broken windows. A block away to the left is a lumberyard; to the right is a junkyard. In front of the junkyard is an almost vacant lot. At one end there are several dented, smashed, and rusted cars; at the other, a small group of elderly, disheveled black men hang out on tree stumps and broken chairs. On the next block is a liquor store that has customers as early as 8:00 A.M. On the block past the liquor store are abandoned slum buildings.

The Vaughn apartments opposite Jefferson School

The once proud city of 1904 World's Fair fame has seen both better and worse days. In its heyday during the early 1900s the city of St. Louis was a thriving and vital manufacturing center, with streetcar construction and shoe industries that were second to none. Downtown department stores, theaters, restaurants, and office buildings were bustling with people and activity. In its worst days, it was a city of decay. As businesses and factories moved westward into the suburban shopping malls and industrial parks, many downtown areas became dilapidated and deserted. City services diminished, crime flourished, and black ghettoes grew. During the last 10 to 15 years, however, there have been signs of recovery. The Gateway Arch on the riverfront has been an important tourist attraction and a symbol of rejuvenation. New hotels and office buildings have been and are still being built. The Central West End has been revitalized, and Laclede's Landing is a popular new development of shops, restaurants, and bars on the waterfront. Several major shopping malls and entertainment centers are under construction, convention business is up, and slick publicity is making an attempt to market "surprising St. Louis." Still there are sections of the city, such as the area where Luberta works, that are badly in need of rehabilitation.

The St. Louis Public Schools system has also had its ups and downs. Most of the problems have revolved around money or the lack thereof. A statute that requires a two-thirds vote (as opposed to a simple majority) to pass a school tax hike has consistently prevented the system from raising necessary revenues. The result is large classes, reduced services (physical education, art, and music have been either eliminated or severely cut back), limited materials and support resources, and some disgruntled and demoralized teachers.

There have been other serious problems as well. One of the major ones has been the issue of integration. In 1972 a group of north side parents (the area where Luberta teaches) filed suit against the school system, arguing that the all-black schools their children were attending could not provide a quality education. The suit started a chain of suits and countersuits that lasted for years. Ultimately, after complex legal negotiations, a "voluntary" desegregation plan was developed that encompassed both the city and county of St. Louis.

The voluntary desegregation plan is described by many as successful. Magnet schools, which are specialty schools designed to attract both black and white students from city and county, have done just that. Today there are formerly all-black city schools and formerly all-white county schools with partially or totally integrated student bodies. Because the school population in the city is predominantly black, however, there are still all-black schools in the city; these schools have recently been given enrichment centers for equity purposes, and Jefferson School is one of the schools that now has a science enrichment center, which all students attend several times a week.

Another problem with the St. Louis Public Schools, as with every large public system, is a centralized bureaucracy. There are 127 schools in the district, and the

Hanging out near Jefferson School

Mantia's liquor store

central office tries to monitor them all closely through paperwork. Each teacher, for example, is expected to fill out a weekly sheet that states how many minutes are being allocated to each subject. Recordkeeping such as this is often an unsatisfactory resolution for all concerned. For teachers it can be a time-consuming burden. For central office administrators it can convey little of what is actually happening in classrooms.

Jefferson School

Despite the press toward conformity, Jefferson School has a principal who encourages his teachers to be creative and innovative within the district's curricular guidelines. When you walk into the building you feel the resulting warmth and individuality. The outside of the building is nondescript. The two-story red brick building with windows that are opaque at the top looks rather cold and uninviting. Inside, however, one feels a commitment both to academic excellence and to a healthy learning environment. In the front hall is a big sign with three words: Believe, Work, Achieve.

Inside, the walls of the first floor halls are covered with children's art work and student posters that encourage adults to vote *yes* on an upcoming tax hike. One that catches the eye of the visitor is entitled Today's Children, Tomorrow's Leaders. On the walls of the second floor halls there are more displays of children's art, one of

ST. LOUIS PUBLIC SCHOOLS
TEACHER'S PROGRAM 19 84 /19 85

Original Program ☒
Program Change ☐
Date 10-19-84

NAME Clay, Luberta
ROOM all

SCHOOL Jefferson
LEVELS/GRADE/PROGRAM Grade 5

STUDENT'S INSTRUCTIONAL TIME

COMPLETE FOR YOUR CLASS
(or homeroom)
(Home) Room Number _____
Total minutes per week students are receiving instruction:
Language Arts 753
Mathematics 220
Social Studies 208
Science 135 Health - 86
Art and Music 150
Physical Well Being _____
# of P.E. Periods _____
P.Wk. _____ Tot. Min. _____
Total Min. P.Wk. _____
(P.E. + Recess)

	MONDAY			TUESDAY			WEDNESDAY			THURSDAY			FRIDAY		
	TIME	LGTH.	ACTIVITY	TIME	LGTH.	ACTIVITY	TIME	LGTH.	ACTIVITY	TIME	LGTH.	ACTIVITY	TIME	LGTH.	ACTIVITY
	8:15⁹:²⁰	5	Org.	8:15⁹:²⁰	5	Org.	8:15⁹:²⁰	5	Org.	8:15⁹:²⁰	5	Org.	8:15⁹:²⁰	5	Org.
	8:20⁹:⁰⁰	40	Math	8:20⁹:⁰⁰	40	Math	8:20⁹:⁰⁰	48	Math	8:20⁹:⁴³	23	Math	8:20⁹:⁰⁰	8	Math
	9:00⁹:²⁸	28	Lang.	9:00⁹:²⁸	28	Lang.	9:08⁹:²⁸	20	Reading	8:43⁹:²⁸	45	Science	8:30⁹:¹⁵	45	P.E.
	9:28¹⁰:²⁸	60	Art	9:28¹⁰:⁰⁰	30	Art	9:28¹⁰:³⁰	60	Music	9:28¹⁰:⁰⁰	28	Math	9:17⁹:⁵⁰	33	Math
	10:28¹¹:⁰⁰	28	Lang.	10:03¹¹:³⁰	41	Reading	10:30¹¹:³⁰	58	Lang.	10:00¹⁰:⁴³	43	Health	9:50¹⁰:³⁵	45	Science
	11:00¹¹:³⁰	30	Spell-Write	10:45¹¹:³⁰	45	P.E.	11:35¹²:⁰⁵	30	Lunch	10:43¹¹:²⁸	45	P.E.	10:35¹¹:³⁰	55	Spell-Write
	11:35¹²:⁰⁵	30	Lunch	11:35¹²:⁰⁵	30	Lunch	12:05¹²:¹⁵	5	Org.	11:35¹²:⁰⁵	30	Lunch	11:35¹²:⁰⁵	30	Lunch
	12:05¹²:¹⁵	5	Org.	12:05¹²:¹⁵	5	Org.	12:15¹:⁰⁰	45	Spell-Write	12:05¹²:¹⁵	5	Org.	12:05¹²:¹⁵	5	Org.
	12:15¹²:⁵⁵	43	Health	12:15¹²:⁵⁵	43	Oral Lang	1:00¹:⁵⁰	50	Soc. St.	12:15¹:¹⁰	55	Lang.	12:15¹:⁰⁰	45	Lang.
	1:00 1:45	45	Science	1:00¹:²⁸	28	Library	1:50²:¹⁵	25	Penmanship/Lang	1:10¹:²⁸	18	Soc. St.	1:00 1:50	50	Soc. St.
	1:45²:⁵⁰	63	Reading	1:30²:¹⁵	45	Soc. St.	2:15²:⁵⁰	35	Reading	1:30²:¹⁵	45	Soc. St.	1:50²:⁵⁰	60	Reading
	2:50²:⁵⁵	5	Org.	2:17²:⁵⁰	33	Reading	2:50²:⁵⁵	5	Org.	2:17²:⁵⁰	33	Reading	2:50²:⁵⁵	5	Org.
	2:55		Dismissal	2:50²:⁵⁵	5	Org.	2:55		Dismissal	2:50²:⁵⁵	5	Org.	2:55		Dismissal
				2:55		Dismissal				2:55		Dismissal			

DAILY TOTALS IN MINUTES

	MON.	+	TUES.	+	WED.	+	THURS.	+	FRI.	+	WEEKLY TOTALS	+
1. Instructional	292	+	230	+	281	+	290	+	296	+	1,389	+
2. Non-Instructional	78	+	140	+	89	+	80	+	74	+	461	+
3. SCHOOL DAY TOTAL	370	+	370	+	370	+	370	+	370	+	1,850	+
4. Lunch	30	+	30	+	30	+	30	+	30	+	150	+

SIGNATURE OF PRINCIPAL

Form IN-92 Rev. 8/84

Luberta's teacher program

The entrance to Jefferson School showing an urban renewal project

which is covered with student pictures of What I Like to Do. The floors and walls are clean, the halls are quiet and there is general sense of order and well-being.

Luberta Clay's Classroom

Luberta Clay's fifth-grade classroom is on the second floor. Inside, the atmosphere is cheerful and sunny. The room is relatively large, and with careful arrangement, it accommodates 30 students comfortably. Bulletin boards covered with bright yellow paper are colorfully decorated. Vivid posters cover almost every inch of wall space, and there are large chalkboards on three sides of the room. Most student chairs face the front chalkboard, but some face a side chalkboard.

The children are all black, neatly dressed, and well-groomed. The boys are in blue jeans, T-shirts, and tennis shoes, and most of the girls are in dresses. They appear to be very comfortable in the classroom setting with each other and with their teacher.

Luberta moves in the classroom with the confidence and relaxed manner of an experienced professional. She is well-organized, smooth, and almost maternal as she takes time to speak to individual students with obvious affection and interest. Her daily basics curriculum can be described in terms of minutes allotted to language, art, spelling, health, science, and reading, but life in Luberta's classroom is a great deal more. In her room one finds the basics embedded in a broad context and transmitted with understanding, high expectations, encouragement, and caring. A typical Monday morning captures the essence of the blend.

Morning Preparation—Language and Math

8:20 The morning begins with Luberta preparing students for some of the individual seatwork that will be expected of them during the day. The first assignment is language, and she directs Michelle to walk over to a stack of workbooks on a table and begin to read some of the topics on two particular pages. This workbook has practice exercises on topics the students have been studying in their regular language books, and Luberta is attempting to put some variety into the practice by giving them a different workbook. The student who reads is slow and stumbles a bit, and Luberta asks for patience from the rest: "Class, bear with us for a moment." As Michelle reads Luberta repeats, "Capital letters—everybody who recognizes that topic hold your hand up (*a lot of hands go up*), sentence punctuation (*a lot of hands go up*)." The process continues with subjects and predicates. When Michelle finishes, Luberta gives explicit directions.

LUBERTA: Thank you, Michelle. (*Speaks to the class*) I thought you might enjoy seeing the same topics in another book. When you get them, you are to read and write down the directions that you think are

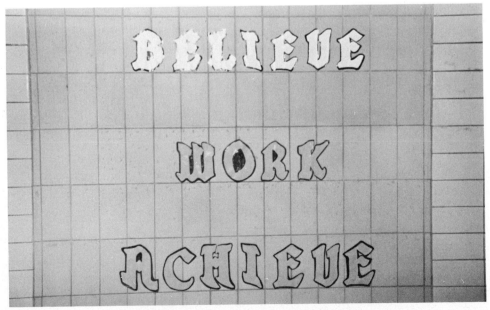

The sign in the front hall of Jefferson School

Luberta teaching language arts

necessary in order to let the reader know what you are doing— everybody understand that, that's what we usually do—then write the sentence but do not write in the book. Transfer to a sheet of paper—you will do the two pages indicated. (*Turns her attention to some math problems that are on the chalkboard*) Now for math, one of you please volunteer—oh good, Consuela. As usual, we have started right in this morning, and I'm watching the clock, but don't you do it—you relax, but I'm watching the clock. You are going to try the problems on the board. Now remember, these are just exercises. They are just problems, and when you work with them check each and every one to make sure you got the right answer. Anyone want to ask a question about checking? Everyone understand how we check addition? Subtraction? Multiplication? Division? Now, would you give me some stories that require or call for our using those numbers in a situation like that. Could you do that for me? Take A. Give me a problem story that would require us to put the numbers down in that fashion and add them. Try it, Consuela.

CONSUELA: (*Looks at problem A—6,958 + 5,834 + 3,506 + 531 = ?—and then begins to respond softly and slowly*) Some girls ate 6,958 pieces of candy, and the next day they ate 508—no 5,834—and the next day they ate 3,506, and the next day they ate 531. How many did they eat in all?

LUBERTA: All right—any disagreements? I don't know about you, but I'm satisfied with that story—all that was necessary to do was to put them together. Very good, Consuela. Okay, I think the second one's a little more difficult for some people, but not for you who are dynamite math people, and efficient—by the way, what do I mean by *efficient?*

STUDENT: Quick and correct.

LUBERTA: That's right and that's kind of what math is all about. Now who can give us a story for B. Okay, Vernon, do you want to try it?

VERNON: (*Looks at problem B—6,483 ÷ 8—and responds*) Jim has 6,483 bottles. He divided the 6,483 bottles in 8 parts. How many was left?

LUBERTA: That's interesting, your last remark—"How many was left?" I know I'm going to get some hands on that. How many *were* left? (*Pause*) Are we sure that there is going to be a leftover amount? What do you think about that, Rochelle?

ROCHELLE: He should have said, How many are in each group?

LUBERTA: Yes, that's what we are normally accustomed to, Vernon. We are accustomed to hearing division examples sound like that—how many were in each group or stack or pile or box or wherever you put them? Now you took your superset and you asked us to divide it into 8 parts. That was very good. I think your last question was a little confusing though. Do you want to give a question on your own which would sound a little more like division?

VERNON: How many did he put in each box?

LUBERTA: Yes, that is more nearly what I'd like to hear and the reader would like to hear. Now let's look at C. Who will give us a situation for doing this computation on the board. I know the numbers are large. I don't care if your problems sound ridiculous—the idea is just that you give us something that requires subtracting. Erica?

ERICA: (*Looks at problem C—87,548 - 42,559—*There were 87,548 people at the party. 42,559 people left. How many people were left?

LUBERTA: Okay, that's interesting; I would agree. Oh Sean, do you have something to say?

SEAN: 87,548 people were at the party. 42,559 people were left out.

LUBERTA: Did you say were *left* or *left out?*

SEAN: Were left out. (*Silence*)

LUBERTA: Well—we have all these people at the party. What's going to happen? (*Silence*) Well, let me give you a hint, if you have those people leave, then you would have your situation in hand.

SEAN: (*Persists*) 87,548 people were invited to the party, and 4,259 did not go. How many were at the party?

LUBERTA: Okay. They were invited and they didn't come. Now I know you didn't mean to read that last number as you did because you have been reading it correctly all along. Would you read that last numeral—the subset again?

SEAN: 42 thousand 500 and 59.

LUBERTA: (*Smiling and in a kind, motherly tone*) Now you know I'm going to scold you for that *and* in there. The only reason that I scold about that *and* in there is because when you write the number for some kind of test or skill you are not supposed to add the word *and*. That's the only problem. Okay, a lot of people do that, but when you are trying to be very correct, don't do it. Can we move on quickly to E. Who can handle that—who can put it in story situation? And then I'm going to let you talk together and get your voices going. Okay, Zina.

ZINA: (*Looks at E—1,637 × 82— and begins in a loud and clear voice*) 1,637 pieces of pie and 82 pieces of pie. 1,637 pieces of pie were eaten. How many——(*Silence*)

LUBERTA: We can see them—we can see all those pieces of pie. Now, what's going to happen? (*Long silence*)

LUBERTA: You in trouble?

ZINA: Can someone help me out?

LUBERTA: (*Smiling and with a little chuckle*) They sure will help you out. Taronda!

TARONDA: There were 1,637 pieces of pie. There were 82 people who ate the pie. How many were left?

LUBERTA: (*Smiling, chuckling with good humor*) Well, no. I am going to say it fast—that's not the situation there. C'mon, we need some more help here. Michelle?

MICHELLE: There were 1,637 pieces of pie. There were 82 pieces of pie. There was twice as much pie in another tray.

LUBERTA: Okay! Maybe before we get too bogged down with this we'd better get the picture. We are going to have one of those numbers over and over again. All right, if we are going to have 1,637 then that number is going to have to be repeated or worked with how many times? Erica.

ERICA: There were 1,637 pieces of pie on the plate and there were 82 different plates.

LUBERTA: Oh, I'm kind of getting the picture now. Now there is a larger plate that will hold 1,637 pieces of pie? Okay, that'll work, but you have to have how many of these plates?

ERICA: 82.

LUBERTA: And each of them will have to have how many pieces of pie?

ERICA: 1,637 pieces.

LUBERTA: Right—as long as we have that clear you are home free. Okay, let's move on 'cause as I said I'm watching that clock. Okay. *D*—There are our old friends fractions back. C'mon Tiffany, I haven't heard from you this morning—say something about that.

TIFFANY: (*Looks at* seven-eighths + one-eighth *but says nothing*)

LUBERTA: Give us a fast story situation. (*Silence*) Tiffany, maybe I was unfair. Are you ready? You didn't have your hand up, and I pounced on you. All right, you want me to pass on?

TIFFANY: Yes.

LUBERTA: Okay, Makesha? (*Silence*) You're thinking, "Well, I didn't have my hand up either." (*Luberta laughs and Makesha and a few others giggle*) Well, I have to call on someone. Someone has to give this story—it's the last one. Rochelle?

ROCHELLE: There was seven-eighths of a circle and a person added one-eighth of another circle to it. How much of the circle was there?

LUBERTA: Okay. You took care of that neat and fast. Okay. Sit up everybody. I'm going to let you talk—would you talk to me this morning about some big thoughts that I haven't heard for a while. Exercise your voices. Okay.

Luberta's students following a lesson

A group of students begin to recite in unison a pledge entitled The Power of Knowledge.

1. I now realize that the greatest power in the world is the power of knowledge.
2. I want to be smart. Dumb, misinformed people go through life missing so many rewards that could be theirs.
3. I will learn my basic skills and be expert in them.
4. I will read books on the subjects that interest me most. But I will also read books and articles on other subjects to broaden my awareness of what is happening in the world around me.
5. I will discuss at dinner time what I have learned or questioned at school today.
6. I will study the ideas and dreams of our history to see how they can help me today.
7. I will set aside some time each day to think about my future, to discuss it with people I respect, and to work on accumulating the knowledge that can guarantee that future.
8. I pledge this to those who love me and are trying to help me succeed. More important, I pledge it to myself.*

* This is a reprint of a pledge taken from a Missouri National Education Association publication.

Current Events

LUBERTA: Okay. Since you said that so convincingly I'm going to come right back and ask whether you talked to your parents about our discussion on the president? Did anyone go down and see the president? If you didn't get there, don't feel bad. I didn't either.

There is then 15 minutes of sharing experiences (some of the children had gone to see President Reagan at the Gateway Arch), and a review of earlier explained positions of President Reagan and Mr. Mondale on how to solve the deficit. After a student defines deficit as *a shortage of money* and Luberta adds *big debt*, Luberta probes until the students come up with the candidates' different ways to handle the deficit, and she ends with the importance of knowing what is happening in your government and knowing your presidents.

Vocabulary

Luberta quickly shifts into a vocabulary review with this simple statement: "Now I'm coming at you with something different. 'John dived in the pool,' and I am emphasizing *dived*." A lot of hands go up. A student answers *plunged*.

LUBERTA: Many people have given their names and addresses to vote. (*Lots of hands*)

STUDENT: *Register*.

LUBERTA: The skiers glided over the incline. (*A sea of hands*)

STUDENT: *Slopes*.

Students in Luberta's classroom participating in a discussion

This goes on with 10 more sentences and 10 more enthusiastic responses from the students. Throughout the review, comments like these from Luberta are interspersed: "If you can get this, you are really super." "Now I'm going to be able to trick you with this one." "It's marvelous how you can remember these words." After she reads the last one she asks, "Did I leave any out?"

STUDENT: *Prohibition.*
LUBERTA: What is prohibition? It is a noun, we know that. We learned *-tion,* didn't we? All right, Zina.
ZINA: Bootlegging.
LUBERTA: Bootlegging? (*Everybody laughs loudly, including Luberta*) Just a minute. You taught us that, I didn't. Okay. Now will you straighten up? What is prohibition?
STUDENT: It means being against something.
LUBERTA: Okay. That's a good review. Is there anything else I forgot?
VARON: *Physician.*
LUBERTA: Oh, that's a good one. You all have had so many words I don't know how you remember them all. What's a physician?
STUDENT: Doctor.
LUBERTA: Okay. That's very good. You did very well. I'm proud of you.

The Halloween Play

Next Luberta asks Zina, who played the witch in the school Halloween play, if she wants to do her part for the class. Zina smiles broadly and says yes. Luberta then asks the class if they would like Zina to perform a part from the play, and they shout in unison, "Yes!" To the class Luberta says, "Relax," and to Zina she says, "Go for it."

Zina stands in front of the class and delivers an expressive speech as a witch, with the body movements to match. The students listen attentively and then applaud her enthusiastically.

Math Seatwork

Michelle passes out paper; it is time for students to do their math problems. Luberta gives the students about 5 minutes to shuffle their pages and get settled, and then she asks, "Is it reasonable to expect to be able to hear a pin drop now?" A few answer yes. "Okay. I'll expect to hear the pencil sharpener but nothing else."

Luberta moves to the board to write the spelling words for the day and the students begin to work. The students look alert and conscientious; the room is indeed quiet enough to hear a pin drop. After about 15 minutes there are periodic interruptions. The principal walks in to talk to Luberta, and the class says in unison, "Good morning!" Students ask Luberta about certain math problems. Luberta says,

"Who else has finished Number 2 — Melissa. Go check with Melissa. If two or three of you get the same answer it's probably a good answer."

Luberta walks around and monitors the work. At one point she announces, "Everyone tighten up, you have 8 more minutes to go. We will be moving on to spelling. Sorry about that, we have to move, but don't rush and make mistakes! If you don't finish, you will be able to finish later. I want you to be correct. This is not a timed test, I just have to start spelling."

At another point, Luberta notices that a number of students are having difficulty with problem *D*, which involves adding seven-eighths and one-eighth.

> LUBERTA: Who will give me a name for 1? (*The responses are many—three-thirds, four-fourths, ten-tenths, five-fifths, seven-sevenths, three-thirds, eight-eighths, nine-ninths, thirteen-thirteenths, ninety-ninetieths*)
> Good—when you get to *D*, I know you will remember Mr. who?
> STUDENTS: (*In unison*) Mr. Whole Number.

Spelling and Art

Michelle passes out paper, and Luberta asks if anyone wants to stand up and stretch. Everyone gets up.

> LUBERTA: From here on in, you can wiggle your toes, where?
> STUDENTS: Inside your shoes.
> LUBERTA: Right, so stretch now.

Luberta asks them to look at the board at new spelling words which are homonyms. She elicits the definition of homonyms from one of the students: "words that sound alike but are not spelled alike and do not mean the same." The words on the board are:

fair	foul	rap	loan	main
fare	fowl	wrap	lone	mane
seem	flare	right	due	sent
seam	flair	write	dew	cent
				scent

Luberta begins to explain that these are important and tricky words when she is interrupted by "Judge Dailey" who says it's time for students to vote for class president, and the students file out quietly.

When the voting is over, it is 9:30 A.M. and time for art class in the art room. After art, the spelling lesson continues with a pretest. Luberta reads aloud sentences with homonyms, and students need to select the correct word. When a student gets confused, she says, "It's probably my fault—I probably was not as clear as I should be. Let me repeat it." After they are given the assignment of looking up

Students doing seatwork

each word in the dictionary and recording the definition in the vocabulary notebooks, the agenda shifts to math once again.

LUBERTA: (*Firmly*) Tighten up—this will be difficult. (*Smiling and relaxed*) I just said that to get your attention. I want to do something that I haven't done in a long while, but you need to be very quiet. This will be interesting, it's a listening exercise. I need sharp minds. I'm going to give you an arithmetic sentence, and I want you to snap to it. (*She asks one student to keep score*) 21 divided by 3 times 4.

STUDENT: 28.

LUBERTA: 5 times 5 plus 5 divided by 3 plus 6.

STUDENT: 10.

LUBERTA: You really have to concentrate. 18 minus 0 times 2 divided by 6.

STUDENT: 6.

Many more follow. When no one gets the answer after a few seconds, Luberta just goes on. Consuela is the winner with five correct answers, and she receives as a prize a small yellow notebook to keep a record of her assignments.

The rest of the morning is devoted to independent spelling and language seatwork. Students look up their spelling words in the dictionary and do the exercises that were assigned in the new workbook that morning. When students have difficulties Luberta helps or asks students to help each other. Finally she says, "I'll stop talking, and you stop talking, and let's try to get as much done as possible. It's a great opportunity to put your vocabulary words in your notebook so that you don't have homework. It's almost lunchtime. If you are really quiet, I might turn on the radio."

The students work very quietly on their spelling and language. One student, who has been given special permission to write a get-well note to a student who was in an accident, comes up to Luberta for approval and an envelope. Luberta responds: "Since it's your letter, I won't correct it, but did you edit it?"

Michelle is one of the first to finish, and she tells Luberta so. Luberta responds:

> Michelle, for the first time in your life, you have 3 whole minutes to yourself. Do you have anything to read in your desk? If not, come up to the reading table and get something.

To Zina who's already reading: "You do a lot of reading, I can tell. That's very good." At 11:30 A.M. Luberta ends the morning with these words:

> I think you'd better put your things away, and let's start thinking about going into the beautiful sunshine for a little while. Who remembers our autumn poem?

A lot of hands go up. They recite it in unison and then file out to Luberta's praise: "This was a very good morning."

A Very Good Morning: A Closer Look

The morning has been a good one and a full one. It has been fast paced, varied, and focused primarily on basic skills. Math, spelling, oral language, punctuation, and vocabulary had center stage, and art and current events provided a backdrop. Still there has been time for relaxation, sharing, and encouragement within the press to adhere to the district's curriculum guidelines and to keep students on task; there has been time devoted to developing group cohesiveness and to addressing individual needs. No time has been devoted to discipline problems—there simply weren't any. Clearly, over her years of experience, Luberta has developed a repertoire of ideas and strategies for creating a classroom environment that encourages students to work productively, cooperatively, and enjoyably.

The emphasis on variety in the classroom, Luberta believes, is one of her most effective practices. She varies the activities and she varies the material.

> Personally, I like to work with the flow from one activity to another. Not so fast that it's confusing to the kids; by that I mean that we give 25 minutes to math, and almost nonstop we flow right into a language activity; and I don't hesitate to come back to math either. It cuts down on problems; it really does because they don't have time to retrench.

I have found it helpful to use many textbooks. Textbooks have a different approach to the same thing, and the children sparkle a little when they get a different book. It keeps their interest. Books are my main instrument, but of course they are the first thing that children tire of, so you have to have other materials for variation. . . .

A second approach that she believes in is an emphasis on meaningful understanding and application of the basic skills.

We're in basic skills—they're stressed—however, in fifth grade I should hope that we're stressing them with the idea of having them strong enough so that the children can use them not so much to learn to read but to read to learn, as they say!

In math she maintains they must understand the principles involved, and that's why she spends so much time helping students develop number stories.

They do have a problem understanding if you don't let them sort of "deep think" the whole business of numbers. I guess maybe not being the best mathematician myself and having had to struggle to learn, I realize the difficulty of a young person understanding the principles that are involved. . . . Math takes a lot of repetition, and I think we do enough of that. But math is also supposed to be practical, and they are supposed to be able to use it. We're learning these numbers to use, so if you don't apply them to some kind of situation that they create, then they will never have a clear understanding of the concepts.

A third major strategy Luberta has developed is to use other students to help her.

The kids help a lot. I have 30 students, but I have 10 great helpers in here because my children believe they can do anything. And some of them can do much. . . . They need to feel real good about themselves and others too. . . . The children even do bookkeeping. They file papers for me; they can give me 5 minutes here and 5 minutes there.

I try to let them share. Why be secretive about an answer? Children can be terrific in teaching each other. They seem to know that magic word to say to each other while I might stand all day to try to make a point. They're so successful at getting each other to understand things they are trying to learn. It works with every subject. I let the kids get in there—they're harder on each other than the teacher would be. By the same token, they're more skillful teachers of each other. . . .

And the children aren't opposed to getting some help. They don't feel less than the next guy if they don't know it. We try to let them know that none of us knows all things. I certainly don't, and the important thing is to know where to find it. If your buddy has the information, then go there.

But perhaps it is Luberta's relaxed and encouraging management style that makes it all work. It is a style that starts with the perceptions of the students and that respects their feelings.

> They will have to be comfortable with whatever rules we have in here. They'll have to see the need for allowing each other to hear and to give each other a chance to talk. We just work at it. If someone gets a little pushy, we just say, "Hey, wait, it's not your turn," and we can be rather brisk if we have to. We can snap a whip [laughter]. But on the whole we don't have to do a great deal of it. They seem to want an atmosphere where they can hear.

> If you respond to what you're feeling, they're feeling practically the same thing. I know that they are. Sometimes they begin to squirm and get restless, and I understand because I am getting restless too. But I feel like I'm privileged because I can get up and move in and out. . . . If it's been a long day for me, it's been a long day for them too. I react to what happens to me, and I'm sure they are reacting to what's happening to them.

It is a style built upon the assumption that the classroom group is a family. When any problem arises, it affects all the members of the family and so students as well as the teacher need to be involved.

> I bring the whole classroom in on a problem with an individual. I feel that they are part of it. If someone behaves in a manner that obstructs, well, it happens to all of us. And we all bring pressure to bear on the individual. . . . This is our little world in here, and let's hope we're family; we're that close.

It's a style that is gentle in nature.

> If you try to coerce them into doing something or force the work, it doesn't work. With force, they usually sulk for a long time, and then where do you go from there—hit them harder or yell it louder? You have to think of something that's going to be lasting.

Luberta notes, however, that many of her students expect, at first, a tougher or a more forceful style or approach from adults—particularly parents:

> There's a misunderstanding sometimes, at first, when they come to a situation, and they do not know me. They see my approach as weakness, because they have had to be strong themselves. They have had to elbow themselves through a lot of situations, and if you don't show evidence of being strong they think, "Well, this is going to be a pushover." But if you persist, and they find out that you're for real, they accept it.

Luberta says regretfully that she has very little contact with most of the parents of her students, but on the occasions when she has been able to talk to some, they have recommended that she use physical punishment as needed.

People have pressured these children into doing a lot of things—they tell you what to do, and you are expected to automatically do it and not think about it too much, just do it. Sometimes they come from a home where the punishment is physical, and before it was outlawed, parents would say, "Spank them," and if you didn't do it, the children who had expected this to be done thought you weren't being strong enough. But they can adjust—it just takes a while.

Luberta is glad that her students can and do adjust because she is not sure that she could ever become tough:

My idea is to be a little low key with it. It wouldn't work for me to try to be tough. . . . I have to be what I am, and children can sense if you are going to be a rigid disciplinarian or whether you are going to be a little more relaxed, and I'm one of those people who is more relaxed myself in more relaxed situations. So it just occurs naturally. Now there are certain children who need a different kind of guidance or direction, but generally it's just a gut feeling you have about what's going to work with a particular group. The boys and girls this year have responded well to little discussions on right and wrong things to do in the classroom. The sense of what's right is an outgrowth of What do you want in here? You want to learn, and if you are going to learn then there will have to be a certain type of behavior that allows you to learn. You have to be a good listener; you have to be a good watcher; and you are going to have to be able to contribute, offer something—some answers or some questions. And if we are going to have that we have to have people working together. Then we talk about goals or outcomes.

Luberta does, in fact, have some very clear goals that she is trying to accomplish for each student.

I want him to have a good life for himself. I want the child to expand himself as much as he possibly can and get to know that what he will be is not necessarily what the kid sitting beside him is going to be . . . do the very best that he can, because I don't want to overwhelm him by expecting extraordinary things of a child who cannot do extraordinary things. But if he can, then I would say, Yes, you have to do that. I want the child to know that education is important. I feel it's important. I believe if there is any answer to a good life for a child, it is education— knowledge is coming at us so fast today. I certainly can't teach him all the new things, but hopefully with techniques for learning the child can keep up on his own.

Luberta Clay aims high. She wants every student to reach his or her full potential, to be an independent learner, and to have a good life. What is even more important, she has the pedagogical strategies and the human skills to turn those aims into realities.

TWO CONTRASTING MODELS: SOME QUESTIONS

The elementary classrooms of Luberta and Ruth are alike in some fundamental ways, yet they are different in many others. Focusing for the moment on the differences, several factors that might account for them immediately come to mind. First, of course, is the obvious fact that Ruth and Luberta are individuals with differing backgrounds, personalities, skills, and teaching styles. Their classrooms, in part, reflect their unique characteristics. A second and probably less significant source of variation may stem from differences at the fifth- and the sixth-grade levels. A third and powerful differentiating factor grows out of the dramatically contrasting settings in which these two teachers work. Although it is difficult to pinpoint with any certainty the multitude of ways in which community context impinges upon any individual teacher, it is apparent that it has major effects. It was, in fact, this conviction that led to the selection of teachers working in different types of communities. In the broadest of terms teaching is teaching no matter where it occurs. Day-to-day, however, teaching in an economically deprived urban setting is quite different from teaching in an affluent suburban or a middle-class environment.

In the particular cases of Ruth and Luberta, for example, differences in socioeconomic class and ethnic background of the students, the size and organization of the school districts, and the amount of financial and parental support available affect considerably what happens in their classrooms. In order to focus your thinking upon the nature of these differences and the impact they might have on a teacher's daily classroom behavior, try to answer in writing the following questions:

1. In what ways do the student and parent populations of the two teachers differ? Cite specifics wherever possible.
2. In what ways do the financial resources of the districts differ? What evidence do you see of this difference in the schools or classrooms?
3. Compare and contrast the physical surroundings of each school. How might these surroundings affect each teacher? their students?
4. What differences might there be between working in a large centralized system like the St. Louis Public Schools and in the small, more decentralized district of Ladue?
5. What differing goals and aspirations does each teacher appear to hold for her students?
6. In what ways are the skills and content taught in each class different?
7. In what ways do the teachers' instructional strategies differ?
8. What connections might there be between the differing goals, skills, content, and teaching strategies and the differing contexts?

In the course of looking for differences, some of the similarities between Ruth and Luberta will surface. With regard to similarities between the two teachers, write the answers to the following questions:

➜ 9. What is the most striking similarity between Ruth's thoughts and actions and Luberta's?
   10. Do you think this similarity is coincidental, or does it represent a generic characteristic of excellent teaching?

To answer these questions look back through the case studies if necessary. This will be a time-consuming task, but the process of grappling with these questions is important for several reasons. First, it can help you begin to see concretely how social context as well as personal life history and style of an individual teacher can significantly affect what happens in classrooms. Secondly, it can help you to begin to understand why there are multiple definitions of teaching excellence and how, at least in part, they are socially constructed. Finally, it will introduce you to a process of analysis that is an essential part of becoming a competent observer and teacher. In order to understand what is actually going on in classrooms, an observer or a teacher must be able to identify and collect relevant data and then analyze it.

A central aim of this book is to teach you how to engage in such analysis, step by step. This set of questions is the first step, for it asks you to try your hand at gathering and analyzing some of the case study data presented. To help you along at this early stage answers to the preceding questions are presented below. The answers are not comprehensive. Rather they attempt to hit some of the key points. The intent is to give you some guidelines and models for the kinds of conclusions you should be able to reach from careful consideration of the case studies. Hopefully, you will go beyond these answers and come up with other important points. After you have done your own thinking and writing consider the following material which gives some of our thoughts regarding commonalities and differences.

TWO CONTRASTING MODELS: SOME ANSWERS

Student and Parent Populations

Ruth works with mostly white, middle-, upper-middle-, and upper-class students and parents. As one might guess from the nature of the community, the vast majority of parents are highly educated professionals who expect their children to achieve and to attend prestigious colleges and universities. These parents consider education their first priority and demand that their children be taught a college preparatory curriculum that begins with a highly academic program in the elementary grades. The advanced math work that students are doing at the beginning of sixth grade suggests that students are meeting the high expectations of parents and teachers. In return it appears that Ladue parents are willing to support the district enthusiastically both at home and at school. On the first day Ruth explains to her students that there are three partners working together for their education—the teacher, the student, and the parents. If Ruth could not count on parental support, she probably would not mention it. Ruth also talks of parent participation when her class needed help with its table decoration project one Christmas. In point of fact, Conway School uses parents as volunteers throughout the entire school program.

Luberta's students and parents are quite a different matter. They are all black and most would be considered poor. The vast majority of parents have had little formal schooling and many are unemployed. Many survive on welfare checks and live in government-subsidized housing projects that are in a general state of disrepair. Luberta tells us that she rarely sees or talks to parents. She does, however, urge students to involve their parents in school work. The Power of Knowledge pledge reminds students to discuss at dinner what they have learned in school, and she follows up the pledge by asking if students talked with their parents about a class discussion on the president. The Power of Knowledge pledge and the sign in the front hall of Jefferson School that exhorts students to Believe, Work, and Achieve suggest that the administration, as well as Luberta, feels that students come to school without a sense of the importance of school from their parents. Luberta responds by devoting great effort toward helping students develop an appreciation of the values of education and the motivation and skills to get an education that leads to a good life. She tries to accomplish her aims in a low-key, warm, and family-like environment. Her students, however, are used to a tougher approach.

Financial Resources

Although no figures are presented in the two case studies, it is reasonable to assume that the Ladue School District has more money to spend on pupils and teacher salaries than the St. Louis Public Schools system. That is, in fact, the case. It was mentioned that Ruth is a teacher who receives the highest rating on Ladue's merit pay plan, and the very existence of such a plan suggests that Ladue is a district that is not only committed to excellence but willing and able to pay for it. In Ladue's merit pay system teachers are systematically evaluated throughout the school year by their building principals, and those with the highest rating are given considerably more money for the next year than those who received middle or low ratings. Teachers who have received the highest ratings for a long time earn salaries that are on a par with other comparable professions and considerably above national salary norms for teachers. Also one can see from the case study that Conway School is able to provide teachers and students with an extensive array of audiovisual equipment and computer hardware. A final indication of the financial advantages of Ladue is the fact that Ruth has a class size of 24.

Luberta on the other hand has 30 students, and 6 extra students usually means less teacher time available for individual attention. The large class size that Luberta has to contend with is directly related to the fact that the St. Louis Public Schools in recent years have been unable to muster the two-thirds vote necessary to pass tax levies. In addition to larger classes, city schools have experienced cutbacks in course offerings, materials, and equipment. Many of the buildings are badly in need of repair, and many teachers suffer from low morale resulting from less than ideal working conditions. Clearly, Luberta is not one of these. She feels that she has all she needs to be a good teacher and she views some of the additional funds and programs that have been available through the voluntary desegregation plan as real bonuses. These include the money that was given to Jefferson School for a science enrichment center and for the partnership program that allows her to do some joint activities with an all-white school in south St. Louis.

Physical Surroundings

The starkly different physical settings of these two teachers are portrayed in several photographs in this chapter. Conway School is situated in a beautiful and peaceful residential area near a charming and attractive shopping center whereas Jefferson School is in the middle of one of the most dilapidated and dangerous sections of the city. The high-rise projects with their broken windows and the unemployed males drinking in the junkyard early in the morning cast a shadow of despair and gloom on the school. The neighborhoods surrounding Conway project a sense of order and security, a feeling of educational and material success; the neighborhoods adjacent to Jefferson suggest a sense of disorder and insecurity, a feeling of educational and material failure and hopelessness.

One can only guess that Ruth finds her surroundings pleasant. From what Luberta says about education as the key to the good life, one can also only guess that, for Luberta, the good life is to be found miles from Jefferson School. For both Ruth and her students there appears to be a genuine continuity between school and community. In great contrast, the surroundings of Luberta and her students seem to be in direct conflict with the school. Jefferson School in general, and Luberta's sunny classroom in particular, strikes the observer as an oasis in an urban desert.

Size of School System

The two elementary case studies give very little information about the school districts. Ladue school district is a small system with only four elementary schools. These four schools feed into a single junior high and a single high school. Because there are so few schools, lines of communication proceed somewhat informally. In the city system, however, the task of communicating among 127 schools is exceedingly complex. With largeness generally comes an attempt to centralize, and the city schools are no exception. Central office personnel issue guidelines for the entire system and they seek to monitor what goes on at the individual building and classroom level through paperwork. The weekly teacher program that Luberta is expected to fill out is but one example of the paperwork designated to ensure that time is well spent according to district guidelines. It is reasonable to assume that as a result of working in a large system Luberta devotes more time to paperwork than Ruth and has less freedom in terms of what she teaches and how.

Goals and Aspirations

Both Ruth and Luberta hold independent learning as a goal for students. Ruth, for example, wants "to motivate students to function on their own to figure things out." Similarly Luberta says, "Knowledge is coming at us so fast today — I certainly can't teach them all the new things, but hopefully with techniques for learning, a child can learn on his own."

Although learning how to learn is a shared priority, there are also some differences between the two teachers' stated goals. Ruth's major aspiration is for students to experience and learn from "the joy of discovery." Her ongoing goal for herself is to set the stage so that students can reach that "I did it" feeling, and she works deliberately to structure lessons so that such discovery can occur. Luberta, on the other hand, continually strives to help each student understand the importance of education for his or her future.

> I want the child to know that education is important. I believe if there is any answer to
> a good life for a child, it is education.

The periodic recital of the Power of Knowledge pledge attests to this valuing of education as a priority. In a sense Luberta must work hard to instill in her students the belief in the importance of education that Ruth's students already assume when they come to her.

Content and Skills

The transcripts of classroom activity show both Ruth and Luberta teaching mathematics. The content and skills that Ruth is working on with students are clearly at a higher level than what Luberta is presenting to her students. Although there is less than one grade-level difference, Ruth's students' skills seem considerably more advanced. The Cartesian coordinate system and the problems that Ruth assigned for diagnosis on the first day assume a knowledge and understanding of fundamental operations. In contrast, Luberta is working on the basic operations of addition, subtraction, multiplication, and division. As can be seen in the way she has students put math problems into stories, she is intent upon their grasping the meaning and practical relevance of these skills.

Some insights as to what each teacher works on in language skills can also be gleaned from the transcripts. In Luberta's classroom students are working on capital letters, sentence punctuation, subjects and predicates, and vocabulary. On the first day Ruth gives a spelling pretest, and from the individual tickets we can also see that during the year her students work on spelling and sentences. In addition the tickets in Ruth's classroom reveal that students are writing and revising stories. Although there is insufficient data here to make any inferences, it appears that Luberta focuses more on helping students to learn specific language skills whereas Ruth emphasizes the use of these skills in creative writing assignments.

One final note regarding content and skills. Ruth tells her students that each of them will spend at least a half hour a day at the computer and suggests by her references to students "who wrote compositions" and "did graphs" that students will be using the computer for creative activities as opposed to drills. Luberta's weekly teacher's program shows that computer skills are not part of the curriculum.

Instructional Strategies

It is in this area that one can see the most striking differences. In Ruth's classroom the accent is on discovery and active problem solving. Ruth consistently plans lessons in which students can play strategy games, search for patterns, and take on projects that involve creating some product. While her students work on their projects Ruth integrates the various content and skill areas whenever possible. One of the highlights of every year is her economics units where math, science, and language skills come together.

A second characteristic of Ruth's instruction is its individual nature. Her tickets show that wherever possible she attempts to address individual needs through different assignments. In considerable contrast Luberta emphasizes comprehension and practice of basic skills using large-group instruction. Luberta believes that all of her students need the basics and that those who are more skilled are wonderful teachers for the less skilled. All students, therefore, do the same math problems and language activities. She has students talk out the math stories together and recite the Power of Knowledge pledge in unison in the morning; in the afternoon they read aloud to one another. Luberta, however, worries that the necessary repetition could become boring, and so she strives for variety in activities and materials.

Effect of Context on Classroom

After examining some of these contextual and classroom differences, we conclude that the varying school settings play a considerable role in shaping the thought and action of each teacher. Luberta stresses the values of education and basic skills because they are, in her view, the key to getting her students out of their present environment. Her students obviously entered fifth grade without basic computational and learning skills, and she works daily to see that they get those skills, but in a meaningful way. By having students make up stories that represent the operations she is teaching them to understand what they are doing and why. With such understanding she is hopeful that relevant transfer will occur later when they need to use such skills. Large-group instruction is probably her choice for many different reasons, some of which are individual and some of which are contextual. One likely contextual reason is the difficulty of organizing small groups or individual assignments with a class of 30. Another contextual reason may be that most of her students can benefit from additional practice or review of basic skills, even those who are more advanced. Also when everyone is working on the same problems, the faster students can help the slower students, which could in turn lighten Luberta's load. Teaching the large group is also a way to build the family feeling she desires. Whereas the importance of establishing a family atmosphere in her room is probably partly a reflection of her individual style and background, it may also stem from a belief that her particular students can benefit from a warm, cooperative family environment.

Ruth, on the other hand, has students who already come to her classroom with a strong commitment to school and a strong desire to succeed. She does not have to sell them on the value of an education. Their parents function as partners in the educational process, and their support is a given. Also, Ruth has students who are already skilled in many of the basics, and she pushes them to use the basics to solve problems creatively and, in turn, to learn how to think and to discover patterns on their own. Ruth's philosophy and personality would probably lead her to teach any group in a creative, active, and integrated way, but with the Conway sixth graders she knows they have the fundamentals and feels free to concentrate on higher-order intellectual tasks. With only 24 students she has more time available for monitoring individual assignments.

Similarities

The most obvious similarity between the two teachers is the way in which they respond to students. Both exhibit caring, respect for, and belief in their students.

Both encourage students to ask questions and to find answers without fear of embarrassment or failure. Both work toward making their students independent learners with confidence in themselves as competent, initiating human beings. A more extended discussion of Ruth's and Luberta's responses to students, as well as other similarities between them, will appear in Part II of this book.

Coincidence or Characteristic

With only two cases to consider it is difficult to assess whether the fact that Luberta and Ruth respond to students similarly is a coincidence or a generic characteristic of excellent teaching. After meeting the three secondary teachers you will have more data to consider. Still, you can make some hunches, and one data source to back up a hunch is your own experience with teachers whom you might consider excellent. Would you say that they responded to you as Luberta and Ruth do to their students or somewhat differently? As part of an ongoing interest in clarifying the meaning of excellence in teaching, this matter of teacher response will be pursued in several other places in the book.

CONCLUSION

The case studies of Ruth and Luberta offer you some concrete images of what elementary teaching in general is like and of how it may differ depending on an individual teacher and a particular context. Both teachers are excellent at what they do, but for the most part, what they do is different. This notion of the various images of excellence has some boundaries, however. That anything goes is *not* the message. Rather, the message is that excellence can have what Sarah Lawrence Lightfoot (1983) has called a "staged quality." Lightfoot, writing about *The Good High School*, analyzes case studies of six good but different schools. She argues that a school that sets and achieves its goal of basic skills for everyone can be as good a school as one in a position to set loftier goals. Excellence occurs in stages. Schools have to achieve basic skills for students before they can move to a higher stage of accomplishment. Consequently, Luberta is excellent because she teaches what she sees as necessary—the basics—with expertise and effectiveness, whereas Ruth is excellent because she expertly pushes students who have the basics to use them creatively. Perhaps another characteristic of excellence in teaching is the ability to carefully diagnose student needs and then set appropriate goals for one's particular class. To better understand the concept of excellence in teaching, this book will pursue these notions as well as more examples of the individual and contextual dimensions of teaching using the three secondary case studies in Chapter 4. Chapter 3, however, will first consider some ways of studying classrooms more systematically through the methods and techniques of participant observation.

DISCUSSION QUESTIONS

The text of Chapter 2 posed a series of comparative questions that focus on the social context of Ruth's and Luberta's classrooms. The following discussion questions focus on the individual and personal dimensions of teaching.

1. How do Ruth's and Luberta's family backgrounds and motivations to teach differ from one another?
2. Knowing something of Ruth's and Luberta's personal backgrounds, discuss the extent to which their social and economic status have been advanced as a result of their having chosen teaching as a profession.
3. What if any evidence do you see that Ruth's and Luberta's personal backgrounds affect their particular teaching style or behavior in the classroom?
4. If Ruth and Luberta were to trade jobs, to what degree would they have the same approach to teaching students? To what extent are their teaching characteristics individual? Contextual?

Consider the following questions related to the nature of instruction at the elementary level.

1. Using the the two case studies, what does the day-to-day life of an elementary school look like? What are the principal activities? What are the pleasures? What are the problems?
2. What are the implications for teachers like Ruth or Luberta in terms of their working on an almost continuous basis with the same students? Do you think that it is significant that as adults they spend most of their working day with children rather than other adults? How is this different from other professions you have considered? What are the advantages or disadvantages of this situation?
3. Think back to your own elementary school experience. What would you have liked and disliked about having either Ruth or Luberta as your teacher?
4. What do you think is unique, if anything, in Ruth's and Luberta's teaching that is a result of their working in an elementary versus a secondary setting?
5. To what extent do you think your own views of education and the teaching profession have been shaped by your elementary school experience?

REFERENCE AND SOURCE

Lightfoot, Sarah Lawrence. (1983). *The good high school: Portraits of character and culture.* New York: Basic Books.

3

LOOKING AT SCHOOLS, CLASSROOMS, AND TEACHERS

INTRODUCTION

The preceding chapter described in some detail the classrooms of Ruth Christopherson and Luberta Clay with a focus on teacher thought and action in two different settings. In addition it posed a number of questions and offered some analysis of that descriptive account. The data for these case studies were collected through a qualitative research method known as *participant observation*. Participant observation has been defined as "conscious and systematic sharing insofar as circumstances permit in the life activities and on occasion in the interests and effects of a group of persons" (Kluckhohn, 1940). In simpler terms this means spending time in a particular environment observing and participating in order to understand better how the individuals who live there think and act. Most cultures have their own particular meanings that are known only to those who live within the culture. The underlying assumption of participant observation is that by immersing oneself in the culture and systematically observing and recording firsthand experiences, one can gain insights into and understanding of that culture.

Schools and classrooms can be thought of as cultures, and to understand fully what is involved in teaching one must have some insight into the nature of these cultures. Classrooms, in particular, are dynamic and complex physical, social, intellectual, and personal environments characterized by innumerable interactions and multiple layers of meaning. Participant observation can be a powerful tool for learning to comprehend the complexities of the teaching-learning process and what it means to be a teacher.

This chapter focuses on the rationale, methods, and techniques of participant observation and how prospective and experienced teachers can use this approach to gain a greater understanding of the multifaceted processes of schooling and teaching.

PARTICIPANT OBSERVATION IN THE CLASSROOM: THREE EXAMPLES FROM RESEARCH

Numerous studies have been done by educational researchers employing the method of participant observation. This section briefly explores some of the different types of insights gained by three well-known classroom observers: George Spindler, Ray C. Rist, and Louis M. Smith.

George Spindler

George Spindler is frequently credited with founding the field of educational anthropology. During the early 1950s he began to observe classrooms systematically in West Coast elementary schools.

It is worth noting that when he began his work as a classroom observer Spindler (1982) came very close to quitting his research.

> I sat in classes for days wondering what there was to "observe." Teachers taught, reprimanded, rewarded, while pupils sat at desks, squirming, whispering, reading, writing, staring into space, as they had in my own grade school experience, in my practice teaching in a teacher training program, and in the two years of public school teaching I had done before World War II. (p. 24)

After weeks of observation Spindler had taken hardly any notes. Everything that he observed seemed obvious; nothing was noteworthy.

Spindler's problem was one that faces almost everyone the first time he or she goes into the field to observe a class. Initially everything seems obvious. This is particularly the case when observing in a highly familiar setting. Things appear so commonplace that their significance is overlooked. As Margaret Mead has suggested, "If a fish were to become an anthropologist, the last thing that it would discover would be the water" (Spindler, 1982, p. 24).

It was not until Spindler began to look beyond the obvious and superficial aspects of the classroom he was observing that he began to understand the various interactions and rituals present. In time specific patterns began to emerge encompassing cultural values, reinforcement, social class structure, and communication. A world very different from the one that he had assumed to exist came into focus.

Spindler's early work involved observing a young male elementary school teacher. Over a six-month period he regularly observed this teacher at work in the classroom. His collection of data included:

1. Personal autobiographical and psychological data from the teacher.
2. Evaluative ratings by the teacher's superiors.
3. Self-perceptions provided by the teacher.
4. Observations of the teacher in his classroom interaction with students.
5. Interviews with students.
6. The teacher's evaluations and analyses of his students.
7. Sociometric data obtained from the students regarding their perceptions of one another.
8. Interviews with the teacher's superiors.

While acting as an observer Spindler also participated in the life of the classroom and the school. He followed the teachers around wherever he could and became a friend to many of the children.

The teacher Spindler observed was perceived by his superiors to be extremely competent. He seemed knowledgeable, fair, and just to all of his students, and sensitive to their needs. He perceived himself in the same light, as having no favorites in his class and as making fair decisions. The teacher's class included students from a broad spectrum of ethnic and economic backgrounds: Mexican Americans, Anglo-Americans, and Japanese Americans from lower-, middle-, and upper-middle-class groups.

Spindler eventually discovered that the teacher ranked those students who were most like himself (i.e., Anglo, middle-, and upper-middle-class) as having the highest academic and personal ability. He assumed that these children were most popular with their peers and that they were the leaders of classroom social groups. In reality Spindler found through his observations and interviews with the children that they had a very different perception of who was most popular. He found that many of the children felt the teacher had favorites—a fact not in agreement with the teacher's self-perception.

Closely observing the teacher, Spindler concluded that the children's perceptions were accurate. Overall, the teacher encouraged and most often praised those children who were from backgrounds similar to his own. Children who were from different backgrounds he unconsciously treated as less capable and acceptable. Spindler's (1982) observations carry with them important implications: the realities perceived by the teacher and the children were clearly different. Neither the teacher nor his administrators realized he discriminated against many of the children with whom he worked (pp. 25–26).

Spindler's early research is noteworthy for prospective and experienced teachers because it suggests that teachers' self-perceptions may not conform to the reality perceived by a majority of students. What is significant is that Spindler's teacher would probably have had a very different understanding of himself and his class if he had been taught to observe his relationship with them more accurately. As a participant observer who critically noted his own interaction with his students and their interaction with one another, he might have come to understand a different reality. Without such an understanding it is doubtful that he could be either just or fair with many of his students or, ultimately, helpful in terms of meeting their needs as learners.

Ray C. Rist

A second example of how classroom observations can provide us with a greater understanding of children, teachers, and classroom events can be seen in the work of Ray C. Rist. Rist (1973) was interested in studying children as they progressed through the school system and he became involved in following a class of mostly poor, black, inner-city children from their entry into school as kindergarteners through their third-grade year. Through his own observations and interviews as well as the examination of relevant school records Rist discovered that the single most important variable that teachers responded to with students was their social and class background.

For example, Mrs. Caplow, the kindergarten teacher whom Rist observed during his first year of longitudinal studies, segregated the children in her class into three separate groups by the eighth day of school. This division of the children was accomplished by assigning them to one of three work groups. Rist concluded that the teacher, without having administered any type of intelligence or achievement test, had determined within a few days who were the bright and the slow learners.

The children at the first table were described by Mrs. Caplow as being the fast learners. The children at the other two tables "had no idea of what was going on in the classroom" (Rist, 1973, p. 89). Rist (1973) concluded that Mrs. Caplow's normative reference group for her students was

> mixed black-white, well educated middle class, and the attributes considered most desirable in such a group became the basis for her evaluation of the students. Those who possessed these particular characteristics were expected to succeed, while those who did not could be expected not to succeed. A child could attain highly prized middle-class status in the classroom by getting along with adults; by demonstrating facility in standard American English, leadership ability, and a neat and clean appearance; by coming from a family that was educated, employed, living together, and interested in the child; and by the ability to participate well as a member of a group. (p. 89)

Significantly, the values and characteristics outlined above conformed to those of Mrs. Caplow's own middle-class background. Her normative group conformed closely to her own background and belief system.

Collecting data on variables related to the social and economic background of the children in Mrs. Caplow's class, Rist (1973) discovered the following:

1. Children at the first table (the "fast learners") did not include any families who were on welfare. In the case of Table 2, two of the families of the children were on wel- and at Table 3, four of their families were on welfare.
2. Children assigned to Table 1 had parents who were consistently better educated than those children at Tables 2 and 3.
3. Of the nine children at Table 1, six had parents who lived together. The eleven children at Table 2 had three [sets of parents] who still lived together and the children at Table 3 had only two parents who still lived with one another. (p. 88)

Unconsciously, within the first few days of her students' experience in school, Mrs. Caplow had established a pattern defining who would be successful and who would fail. Rist's research over the next three years clearly demonstrated that the pattern established and the roles defined by Mrs. Caplow continued to follow her students through their education.

Such findings have important implications at a number of different levels. Rist's interviews with Mrs. Caplow clearly indicated that, like Spindler's teacher, she thought that she was fair and doing a good job with the children. When asked by Rist (1973) at the end of the year why she believed a number of the children in the class had done poorly on the standardized intelligence tests that had been administered by the school, she explained:

> Very few of the children in my class are exceptional. I guess you were able to notice this from the way the children were seated this last year. Those children at Table 1 gave consistently the most responses throughout the year and seemed the most interested in what was going on in the classroom. The children at Table 2 and most all of them at Table 3, at times seemed to have no idea of what was going on in the class and were often in another world often by themselves. It just appears that some can do it and some cannot. (p. 176)

Mrs. Caplow obviously had no idea that she had to a large degree assigned the students at the beginning of the year to either succeed or fail—that her response to the children in her classroom was in large part shaped and molded by her own prejudices and belief system. The children whom she taught were from the same city and probably even the neighborhood in which Luberta Clay works. It is clear that the differences in expectations for students between these two teachers is enormous. To a large extent each teacher's attitude determines the performance and success of his or her students. It is perhaps an obvious fact, but if you expect very little from students you will probably get very little. If you expect a great deal, as Luberta Clay demonstrates, you will probably receive it from students.

Without question, Mrs. Caplow's educational practices are discriminatory and unfair. They tend to perpetuate existing class and social structures and to discourage children from lower social and economic backgrounds from taking advantage of the potential opportunities afforded them by the education system.

Rather than being a liberating process schooling becomes a restrictive and inhibiting experience that saps the strength and ultimately destroys the confidence of many children.

Significantly, such insights could only have been obtained through observation and interview. Reviewing standarized test scores and developing a psychological profile of each of the children, while helpful, could not have provided the insight that resulted from the process of observation.

Louis M. Smith

A third example of how classroom observations can illuminate the schooling process comes from the early work of Louis M. Smith. During the late 1960s he wrote, in collaboration with William Geoffrey, *The Complexities of an Urban Classroom* — perhaps the most intensive observational study that has ever been made of a single classroom. Geoffrey was an elementary classroom teacher in an urban setting as well as a student in one of Smith's graduate courses. During class one evening Geoffrey invited Smith downtown to see "how a middle class teacher copes with a group of lower class youngsters." Smith accepted Geoffrey's invitation and challenge by arranging to become an observer in his class.

Sitting in the back of Geoffrey's classroom all day, every day, for a full semester, Smith took copious field notes. At the same time, Geoffrey kept daily notes and discussed in detail with Smith his perceptions of what was going on in both the class and the school in general. What emerged from Smith's analysis of countless concrete events and classroom interactions were conceptualizations and models of various aspects of the instructional process and teacher and student behavior that comprise the classroom social system.

For example, Smith carefully observed Geoffrey establishing control at the beginning of the school year. From his analysis of those initial observations he eventually concluded that a four-step process was at work. The first step, labeled by Smith "grooving the children," involved giving students innumerable tasks and directions during the first few days of school, as well as stressing the notion that they needed permission to do things. It was repeated again and again. In Smith's notes he recorded that Geoffrey "utilized the word 'permission' over and over again. In the field notes, recorded before 9:00 A.M. on the first morning, 'permission phrase appears and reappears'" (Smith & Geoffrey, 1968, p. 68).

With clarity and consistency, Geoffrey introduced those aspects of behavior that he wanted students to internalize eventually. Smith's observations further revealed that Geoffrey's behavior had an underlying serious tone that was communicated to the students. Beyond being clear, the rules that Geoffrey presented held specific consequences for the students if they were not followed. The second step, which involved what Smith described as Geoffrey's "I mean it!" quality, can be found in the following field notes:

"Who's been eating sunflower seeds?" Susan says she has. "Don't dine on them in the school room. I'll confiscate them. Who knows what confiscates means?" (Keep them.) "Any time that I collect food you will be lucky to see it again." Geoffrey moves about checking papers. (Smith & Geoffrey, 1968, p. 70)

Incidents like this one where Geoffrey explicitly stated that food will be confiscated according to Smith gave an I-mean-it quality to Geoffrey's rules.

A third step in establishing beliefs about classroom behavior Smith identified and labeled "following through." Smith's field notes revealed that Geoffrey consistently followed up on rules and procedures that he had previously established.

Geoffrey's fourth and final step was "softening of the tone" of classroom management. According to Smith, once rules and regulations were clearly set in place and operational, Geoffrey "usually softened the criticism and maintained the task oriented quality of the group through drama, humor and incidental learning" (Smith & Geoffrey, 1968, p. 71). Throughout this final phase Geoffrey was working toward shifting individual student beliefs about following the teacher's rules to a more commonly held group perspective on acceptable classroom behavior. In other words, Geoffrey worked first to establish rules and procedures, then to get students to take them seriously and to follow them. Once that was accomplished, however, Geoffrey moved on to the more difficult task of getting the class as a whole to believe sincerely that the teacher's rules were really good for everyone involved. Teacher rules become norms when students internalize them and accept them as the way "we" behave in this classroom. Smith put it this way:

As Geoffrey made the class rules clear, he was dealing with belief systems: as he tried to build an emotional commitment on the part of the children to these beliefs he was engaged in a more complex task of shaping normative structure. (Smith & Geoffrey, 1968, p. 71)

As a result of these observations Smith conceptualized classroom control as visualized in Fig. 3.1. Smith and Geoffrey's work provides many teachers and teacher educators with a new means of looking at the age-old problem of establishing control. This model, together with the many others introduced elsewhere by Smith and Geoffrey, clearly demonstrates how classroom observations can extend understanding of not only what it means to be a teacher but also the nature of the instructional process. Without the ability to conceptualize what goes on in the classroom at a more abstract level teachers are forced to rediscover each day—as though they were beginners teaching their first classes—what teaching is all about. The use of observational methods to generate models and theories provides one means by which both the classroom teacher and the educational researcher can make sense out of the day-to-day routines and teaching experiences.

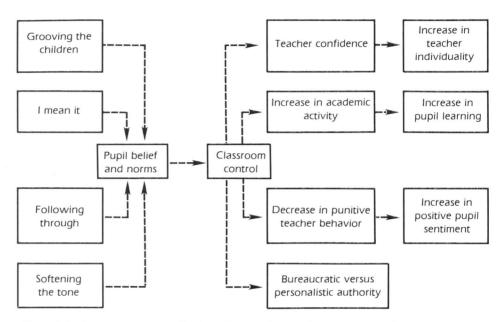

Figure 3.1   Summary conceptualization of antecedents and consequences of classroom control

The examples provided by Spindler, Rist, and Smith and Geoffrey suggest three qualitatively different outcomes resulting from the observation of classroom instruction. Spindler's work reveals that observational methods can help teachers become aware of what it is they actually do in the classroom. Clearly, Spindler's work suggests that a teacher's personal perceptions do not necessarily conform with student perceptions and realities. Although Rist's work also documents essentially the same phenomenon, its social and political implications are of a much greater significance. Social status and class assignment in American society, as Rist demonstrates, may in fact be much more rooted in the day-to-day activities of the classroom teacher than has been previously noted. Finally, Smith and Geoffrey's research suggests the power that observational research has in providing an understanding of the dynamics of instruction, including classroom control.

These are just a few examples of the types of insights that have evolved as a result of the work of educational researchers using observational methods and techniques. The chapters that follow will continue to explore in detail other findings from observational research. At this point, however, we consider how an educational researcher's observational methods and techniques can contribute to the insight of both the beginning and the experienced teacher.

ON BECOMING A PARTICIPANT OBSERVER

The use of participant observation for classroom research is rooted in the methods of anthropologists. Margaret Mead, the famous anthropologist, is a case in point. Her classic work, *Coming of Age in Samoa*, describes how she traveled to a Samoan village, got herself accepted as a visitor and observer, and collected data on her experiences. She then analyzed her data, and through her written description and analysis, the meaning and significance of the culture emerged.

Louis M. Smith and William Geoffrey were also interested in studying a culture by means of participant observation, but their culture was much closer to home. Instead of observing a distant, nonwestern culture, they selected the culture of Geoffrey's classroom. Smith and Geoffrey, in the introduction to their book, describe their study as a "microethnography of the classroom." This phrase describes well the idea of using a classroom as a site for ongoing observational research. *Micro*, of course, means small, and *ethnography* refers to the study of people in groups through or by means of observation. The term *microethnography* highlights an important difference in scope between a participant observation study of an entire Samoan village and one of the more tightly defined and limited culture of the classroom. There are obvious advantages in dealing with such a limited microcosm. A classroom is a manageable social unit. The findings derived from research can be used on a personal level, as well as generalized to the larger culture in which the observations take place. Furthermore, it is relatively easy to enter such a setting as an observer and to be readily accepted. Students and teachers alike are used to having outsiders moving in and out of classrooms. In addition, the organization of the school day and year allows an observer to begin and end research in well-defined time periods.

This book uses the term *participant observer*, rather than microethnographer, to refer to those who study classrooms and schools through observation because it means exactly what it says. One gathers data by participating in and observing in the classroom or school. The term participant observer, however, is broadly used to encompass different levels of activity either at the participation or the observation end of the continuum. When a full-time teacher is a participant observer, the accent is clearly on participation. This means that she or he would be observing while actively participating (teaching). Any written notes would have to be recorded after class. This, in fact, was the role of William Geoffrey when he collaborated with Louis Smith in writing *The Complexities of an Urban Classroom*. Geoffrey wrote summary notes of his observations after he finished his classroom teaching. When a prospective teacher is a participant observer, the accent is usually on observation. Opportunities to assist the teacher or students or to teach a lesson may occur only occasionally, if at all. More often than not the prospective teacher in the role of participant observer will be seated in the back of the room, observing and recording — much like Louis Smith.

The significance of the participant observation model for experienced teachers is that it provides them with a means by which to observe and interpret what it is that they actually do as instructors and as social and cultural agents. Classrooms are action-oriented places where it is very easy for teachers to be unaware of the effect of some of the literally thousands of interactions they have with students on a daily basis. Participant observation provides an immediate and powerful means of gaining insights about what teachers do. They have the opportunity to look at and to analyze the factors that are shaping and influencing their actions.

For prospective teachers, participant observation is significant in a number of different ways. It provides a means for going beyond the past experiences of the students' own schooling. Many people falsely assume that they understand what classroom life is like because they have been students for a large portion of their own lives. Being a student in a classroom, however, is not preparation for being a teacher. A simple analogy comes to mind: Just because one has ridden in cars all of one's life does not mean that one necessarily understands what is involved in the process of driving. Being a passenger and being a driver are very different, as are being a student and being a teacher.

The latter point has been made with considerable insight by the educational sociologist, Dan Lortie, in *Schoolteacher.* According to Lortie (1975), although most prospective teachers have already spent an average of 13,000 hours in classrooms as students, they still cannot be expected to understand the perspective of a teacher for two major reasons:

> First, the student sees the teacher from a specific vantage point; second the student's participation is imaginary rather than real. The student is the "target" of teacher efforts and sees the teacher front stage and center like an audience viewing a play. Students do not receive invitations to watch the teacher's performance from the wings; they are not privy to the teacher's private intentions and personal reflections on classroom events. (p. 62)

Given the limited nature of a student's perspective, this kind of observation ultimately is of limited value and may, in fact, be detrimental in that it provides a false, or at least a superficial, understanding of what it means to be a teacher.

According to Lortie what students learn about teaching from being students is "intuitive and imitative rather than explicit and analytical." Instead of being based upon an understanding of pedagogical and social principles that can be generalized, their knowledge is based on limited personal experiences. Lacking a sense of the problematic nature of teaching as well as pedagogical skills, students cannot perceive the teacher as being involved in complex decision making. The result is a distorted impression of the teaching profession.

Participant observation for the prospective teacher is particularly important in that it permits a former student to make the transition from being an observer of teaching to being an active inquirer into the teaching process. Teaching involves not just preparation and presentation of curricular materials but engagement in the social and cultural dynamics of the classroom and the larger educational setting.

The prospective teacher—or for that matter any teacher—who does not take advantage of the observational perspective provided by the methods of participant observation is at best a "stranger in a strange land." The development of observational and, in turn, reflective skills can help prospective teachers begin to define themselves professionally.

In addition, the insights gained through participant observation can help a prospective teacher make an informed and critical decision regarding whether or not to become a teacher. Few professions provide individuals with opportunities to explore and to understand the nature of the profession—its rewards and limitations, its daily realities, and its long-range satisfactions—before they actually make a commitment to the profession. Participant observation by a potential teacher in actual classroom settings makes this exploration a very real possibility.

METHODS AND TECHNIQUES OF PARTICIPANT OBSERVATION

According to McCall and Simmons (1966) participant observation is not really a single method. It is instead a characteristic blend or combination of methods and techniques employed to study certain types of behavior. These methods and techniques may include direct observation, in-depth interviewing, document analysis, and direct participation. You may use one, or all, or some combination of these methods in your own fieldwork.

One of our undergraduate students, Audrey Oka, began a midterm participant observation report with the following comment:

> Preparing to be a "classroom microethnographer" is similar to learning to drive a car. One can try to get a feel for it by reading and doing simulations, but the skill is learned and developed only through experience. One must take powers of observation and perception into the classroom and attempt to record interactions as quickly and accurately as possible. Over the course of five weeks this (aspiring) microethnographer has progressed in her ability to collect data in the classroom to the point where she feels some sense of control over the situation. (See Appendix A for her full report.)

The purpose of the following section is to provide "a feel" for how to become a participant observer in the field. Although guidelines and general suggestions are provided it is necessary to emphasize the importance of direct experience and the development of your own style in conducting observations.

Entering the Classroom

Successfully entering into an observational setting requires attention to both details and feelings. In effect it calls for good manners and diplomacy. First and foremost you need to gain entry through permission of the appropriate school personnel. Your instructor should be able to guide you toward the proper procedures to follow. Once you have permission to enter a classroom your next task is to be as unobtrusive as possible. Clothing should be subdued and blend in with the setting. In almost every instance your initial entry will be for the purpose of observation, not teaching. It is important to be at once pleasant and friendly but sufficiently distant to permit the "usual" to occur. It is not appropriate to comment or interject your feelings or opinions unless asked to do so by the teacher. To do so without permission would be to alter and redefine the observational setting and to redefine your role. If you do not get in people's way it is likely that you will be welcomed and absorbed quietly into the classroom. A fly on the wall—with spiral notebook and pen in hand—is the ideal model for most classroom observers.

Learning to Collect Data

The primary purpose of any field observation is to collect data, which can be used as the basis for analyzing the setting you are observing. *Data* refers to the information an observer collects from the setting in which he or she is working. As noted above, in participant observation of schools and classrooms data can come from multiple sources including: direct observation (notes on classroom activities); interviews with key participants (e.g., teachers, students), document analysis (e.g., a statement of school goals, teacher lesson plans, student work samples), and direct participation (helping a teacher or a student or teaching a lesson). An observer should look for as many different sources of information as possible in order to gain insight into the nature of the setting and the phenomenon being observed. An interpretation or analysis can only be as good as the data upon which it is based.

Collecting classroom data requires careful organization. Most important for a beginning field observer is the purchase of a spiral notebook for record keeping. At first this may seem trivial, but loose sheets of paper even in a notebook get lost and misplaced. In addition, the fact that one cannot move the pages of a spiral notebook around forces a chronological and sequential organization. This is extremely important as you accumulate large amounts of data. As you record each new set of observations make a point of noting the time, the date, and the place.

The information kept in field notes should remain absolutely confidential. It is important to use code names for the people you are observing, as well as the setting you are in. It is important to be discreet about freely discussing what it is that you are observing with other people. Several years ago, a student conducted a series of classroom observations in Miami, Florida. She returned home to New Jersey for

Thanksgiving vacation and went out to a restaurant with some relatives. While at the restaurant she described in very negative terms a teacher she had been observing in Miami. Unknown to her, the principal of the Miami school in which she was conducting the observation was sitting at the table next to her. The principal was extremely angry at the student's lack of discretion and professionalism as an observer and had the student removed from his school.

Shakespeare said that "discretion is the better part of valour." This is certainly the case when conducting field observations. It is difficult to get into trouble if you keep your observational data confidential. Obviously, in a proper context (a university class, for example, or with a fellow student participant observer) discussing such materials is not only appropriate but necessary. A good habit to establish is always to refer in any notes, discussions, or analyses to the subjects under observation using code names.

Tape recorders, film, and videotape equipment are often used by professional researchers during observational research. This equipment is not only very costly but also cumbersome and obtrusive. For a beginning observer it is usually best not to use such equipment. Even a tape recorder can greatly complicate the process of data collection. Batteries fail, tapes break, microphones capture only the loudest speakers, and recording levels are not turned up high enough. All too often important and irretrievable data are lost.

Questions to Guide the Observation and Interview Process

When entering a classroom for the first time, the natural tendency is to look everywhere to get an overall sense of the nature of the setting. After the initial overview, however, observers often find it useful to have some guiding questions to give a focus to the observation. There are so many things happening simultaneously in a classroom that it is often difficult to know what to watch first. For example, should the observer focus on the teacher, the students, the verbal interactions between students and the teacher, the verbal interactions among the students, the content of the lesson, the teacher's pedagogical strategies, the room arrangement?

There are countless numbers of categories and questions on which to focus observations. As a student, you may be given a focus for your observations or expected to decide on a focus yourself. In either case, it is generally helpful to have some questions ready to guide your observations. This book will present in different chapters different sets of questions and categories for giving a focus to your observations. In effect, it will provide you with different lenses through which you can look at classrooms. With each set of questions or lenses, you will be able to see another facet of the role of the classroom teacher. By the end of the text you should have enough categories and questions to enable you to see the complexities of the teaching-learning process and what it means to be a teacher.

Following are two sets of questions that reflect the dual emphases of Part I—the individual and contextual dimensions of teaching. The first set of questions can be asked in formal or informal interviews with teachers. The second set of questions can be used to guide observations or to conduct interviews with school personnel.

THE TEACHER AS AN INDIVIDUAL

1. Why did you choose a career in education? Did you consider other career choices? If so, what?
2. What are the occupations of your mother and father? How did family and friends react to your decision to teach?
3. How long have you been in the classroom? How long do you plan to teach?
4. What is your educational background? What kinds of elementary and secondary schools did you attend? What kind of a college or university did you attend?
5. Were there any teachers who influenced your decision to teach or your teaching style?
6. What are you trying most to achieve with students? What goals do you hold for students? What methods and strategies do you use to achieve these goals?
7. What is your greatest satisfaction in teaching?
8. What is your greatest frustration in teaching?
9. To what degree do you think the context of the school affects what you do in the classroom?
10. If you had to do it all over again, would teaching still be your career choice?

SCHOOL AND COMMUNITY: THE CONTEXT

1. What is the nature of the community in which the school is located? What is the ethnic, religious, and socioeconomic composition of the community? of the school?
2. Where in the community is the school situated? What are the immediate physical surroundings of the school?
3. Is the school system large or small? centralized or decentralized?
4. What is the physical condition of the school?
5. What level of financial support does the community give the school?
6. What are the material resources of the school (books, laboratories, audiovisual equipment, computers)?
7. What evidence is there of parental support of the school? Are there parent volunteers present in the school?

8. What is the nature of the relationship among ethnic groups in the school? Have there been racial problems? busing problems? Are classes racially balanced or do minority students tend to wind up in the same class?

9. How do students dress? Is there a predominant "uniform" or do different groups dress differently? What does the dress reveal about the school population?

10. What evidence is there in the classroom that goals, content, skills, or teaching strategies are influenced by the context?

Interview Techniques

Included in the previous section are not only observational questions but also interview questions. Together they provide a powerful means of collecting important information on the classroom and school under study.

Observations when carefully conducted are unobtrusive. They do not necessarily require the researcher to confront the subject being observed. Questions are formulated in order to provide a means by which to focus the observation. Thus, asking the question, How do the students dress? allows the researcher to organize the information that he or she is collecting. The question projects the researcher into a series of internal subquestions with each subject they are observing: Are the clothes new or old? Do the clothes reflect the influence of the student peer group or families they come from? Do differences in dress reflect differences in student status?

In contrast, interview questions by their very nature necessitate direct involvement with the subject. For example, to ask a teacher, What was your parent's occupation? is to confront the subject at a direct level about personal information. As a result, researchers need to be very careful regarding the interview process.

To begin with, researchers must assure a subject being interviewed that they will be responsible in the use of the information being given. Thus, if a teacher tells you that his or her greatest frustration is dealing with the school's administration, then you have an obligation to make sure that you do not repeat this fact in an inappropriate context (to another teacher in the school, in front of students, and so forth). If you can build trust and confidence you probably will be able to collect useful data much more easily.

Asking good questions and getting useful answers is a fine art. It is often necessary to elicit more detailed answers than are frequently volunteered by the subject being interviewed. For example, a question you might ask is, If you had it to do all over again would you still be a teacher? A simple answer "yes" is obviously not enough. It is necessary to draw the subject out. Why did you say yes? What satisfactions have there been for you? would be appropriate follow-ups.

Careful note taking, particularly when one is not using a tape recorder, is critical. A researcher must succeed not only in the difficult task of carefully listening and recording a response but also in anticipating the questions that will follow. Often you will find that the process of note taking will inhibit your subject's response necessitating that you simply talk with him or her and record what was said afterwards.

Of course, taking notes about a conversation after the fact poses a whole series of problems itself, the most important of which is forgetting exactly what the subject said or unconsciously distorting what was said to fit what you wanted to hear. In our own research we have found frequently that our memory of what was significant in a recorded interview was different from what we actually heard in a replay of the tape.

It is recommended that you do your note taking during the interview process whenever possible. Probably the most efficient and accurate way to do this is to try to record what appear to be key phrases or ideas instead of complete sentences. For example, when an interviewee says:

> I think the reason I became interested in teaching—let me think, that was when I was a junior in college—was because I had this interest, you know, I suppose it was perfectly normal—in becoming an historian, and teaching social studies at the high school level allowed me to study history

the notes could simply read, "became interested in junior year in college in studying history—teaching let him pursue interest."

At the same time that you are asking questions and listening for responses you will probably be forming some impressions or interpretations of what is being said or how it is being said. It is important to record these impressions, but they should be separated from what the interviewee has actually said. One way to make a distinction between the words of the interviewee and your own thoughts is to enclose your impressions in parentheses. The following section on recording field notes develops the idea of separating what actually is said or done from the observer's interpretations of what is said or done.

Recording Field Notes

Recording observational data can take several forms. How data are recorded often depends on the nature of the setting and the observer's level of participation. The following section outlines in detail three of the most basic strategies used in recording field notes: *formal field notes, informal field notes,* and *summary observations.*

Formal Field Notes At the heart of the data collection process are formal field notes. These are notes taken when an observer focuses on a lesson or activity and wishes to capture it in its entirety. The important characteristic of formal field notes is that they are primarily *descriptive* in nature. Descriptive note taking involves recording only that which actually occurs in the classroom setting. It consists of statements such as:

> There are 11 boys and 12 girls in this fifth-grade classroom.
> Mrs. Jones answers a student's question with another question.
> Two boys are shoving one another in the back of the room.

Although it may seem obvious to advise observers to record only what is actually happening, the reality is that there is a human tendency to record interpretively rather than descriptively unless specifically trained to do otherwise.

Interpretive note taking involves recording personal interpretations and reactions to events as they occur. The following field notes are at the interpretive level:

> The girls are expected to be much quieter than the boys.
> Ms. Jones's way of responding to students' questions is confusing.
> The two boys seem to be seeking attention from the teacher by fighting in
>   the back of the room.

Some observers even move beyond the interpretive level and record their notes partially or entirely in an *evaluative* mode. Evaluative note taking involves recording your value judgments (good or bad) as they occur and might read as follows:

> It is good that the number of boys and girls in the class is about equal.
> I don't like the way Ms. Jones answers student questions.
> Ms. Smith is a poor teacher because she permits fights in the back of the
>   classroom.

It is important to note that although the importance of descriptive note taking is emphasized it is not an argument against interpretation and evaluation per se. On the contrary, the very purpose of observation is to enable observers to make interpretations and judgments regarding classroom activities. The argument is one of sequence. Description should precede interpretation, and interpretation should precede evaluation. The idea behind this sequence is both logical and simple. Before observers can undertake interpretation and evaluation they must have an accurate and full picture of what actually has taken place. In other words, observers need a descriptive data base upon which to build later interpretation and evaluation.

It is likely that observers and teachers often reach erroneous conclusions precisely because they have not followed this sequence. The problem is usually one of premature interpretation that stems from the bias of the observer. Each of us brings to our observations a framework of experiences and prejudices that tend to color our perceptions. For example, an observer who as a student hated being called on in class might automatically describe as unfair a teacher who calls on nonvolunteers as well as volunteers. A teacher who dislikes a certain student may falsely conclude when a disturbance occurs in the vicinity of that student that the student is in fact responsible. The only way to guard against such tendencies is to become highly conscious of your inclination to interpret situations from your own perspective and to work explicitly and deliberately to record *first* that which you actually see. As you record what is happening at a descriptive level, you will of course have some hunches, questions, or preliminary judgments as to why something is happening—these too should be recorded, but separately from the descriptive notes!

To show how the multilevel note-taking process is often done the following section presents some of the notes recorded by one of the authors on the first visit to Conway School and Ruth's classroom. Look back at Ruth's case study to see how these notes were eventually used.

EXCERPTS FROM RUTH CHRISTOPHERSON'S FIRST DAY

AUGUST 31

8:45 Cars line the circular driveway—new Country Squire station wagons, Audis, BMWs, Mercedes. It is already very warm— temperature is, according to my car radio, 80 degrees. Yellow school buses on the driveway in front of entrance.

Inside center entry hall is crowded with kids, parents with cameras, teachers. Also equipment on carts to either side of the center hall—globes, film and slide projectors, tape recorders, TV sets.

Mothers and a few fathers chatting in clusters with each other and several teachers. Mothers are mostly tall, slim, young, tan, and blond. Several have hair pulled back in ponytails like their daughters. They wear tennis outfits, brightly colored, and flowered skirts. Fathers are dressed for business—freshly pressed white or blue shirts, khaki or blue cord pants or suits, club ties—young, tan, and slim, too.

(The affluence of these parents is obvious—they also clearly take good care of themselves with outdoor exercise. They look like they have spent the summer at the country club or in the Bahamas—they also look like the kind of parents who send their children to private school. How does Conway compete with the more private options in Ladue? Check to see how many go on to private schools—also check to see what percentage of parents are this affluent.) **Int.**

Several teachers are smiling and talking with parents. The teachers look middle-aged—some are grey—and others dress in matronly fashion. (The contrast between parents and teachers is striking. An obviously middle-class faculty teaching mostly upper-middle- and upper-class kids—does this cause any problems?) **Int.**

Ruth's Classroom: 6th Graders—Homeroom

9:05 Everyone is seated at desks and Ruth reads the roll and takes the lunch count. (Her tone is businesslike and her pace is crisp.) **Int.** One girl walks in late and several students voice displeasure with loud sighs, oh's, and ah's. One student says aloud, "Here comes trouble." The girl is blond, overweight, and wearing ill-fitting shorts. Ruth greets her by name with a smile and says, "Come on in—there's a seat over there." (Ruth ignored the negative and rude comments of the students—is she trying to extinguish it by ignoring it and by treating the girl as all the others?) **Int.** She introduces four new students to Conway School.

9:10 Ruth: "We need to help the new students with moving, and we *will* be moving. At 9:40 we are going to the gym to hear an explanation of the new schedule from Dr. Bredin. If it gets near 9:40 and I don't seem to notice, please tell me." She writes *9:40* on the board.

"Now let's go over the folders. Any questions?" Ruth talks about each item on the supply list. She concludes: "For this week, I'll have supplies—in case you don't get a chance to go to the store. But I'd appreciate it if you could have most of them by next week." (She comes through as considerate and reasonable.) **Int.**

9:20 Ruth explains the schedule: "This room will be your homeroom, and we will have spelling, reading, and writing in here every morning. Your first move will be at 10:00. Some have math, some have science, some have social studies. Math is in here. Let's see where the new people go."

She walks around to look at schedules of newcomers and to give a few words of direction. Continues with schedule: "11:00 to 12:00 is a real ringer. Look at it. You could be going to vocal music, library—any of the new people have library? Watch out—this is a big building—first time I came here I got lost." (She is preparing newcomers for mistakes and that it is okay to make mistakes—but she does it so naturally!) **Int.** "Some will go to art, some to computers." Again she checks folders of new people. "Anybody taking band or strings? Any questions about anything in the folder?"

Individual students ask questions and she answers everyone by name. (I can't believe that on the first day and in the first half hour she is calling everyone by name—she couldn't know all of these kids. Did she systematically learn names before school began?) **Int.**

"Mr. Moyle and Mrs. Bialecki and I have never done this moving around before. We had so many meetings, but we are still not sure how it will work." (The message here is that we teachers are not great authorities—just human beings trying hard and hoping to make this new schedule work.) **Int.**

"Sixth grade was the very first class I taught and one of my happiest times, and now I am ending with sixth grade. I started to say, 'I am going to make it the happiest class,' but what's wrong with that statement?"

Student: "You should say *we*."

"That is exactly right. It has to be all of us working together. You know, I once had a student named Charlie—Charlie had a lot of tricks. If I said go out, he went in; if I said go in, he went out; if I gave him crayons to draw with, he would eat them." Students laugh.

"I think I know all of the tricks, but if you come up with any new ones, I'll tell you." (Here, she exhibits a sense of humor and her notions of working together. It all flows so naturally, it's hard to believe how carefully she is laying out what she expects.) **Int.**

9:25 Ruth then passes out what she calls a *student survey*. "Just write in phrases—it's too hot for complete sentences. . . . Under *life at home* just give me some idea of what's going on there. Do you have any animals? If you are going to use your guinea pig as an excuse this year—like your guinea pig ate your homework—then you should write down you have a guinea pig or dog, cats, chickens, fish. Write down if you have brothers and sisters and be nice to your siblings. Some kids write down 'bratty brother.' Say something nice."

Student: "I can't think of anything nice to say about my brother."

"I am asking you to fill out your activity schedule so I can take it into consideration when I assign homework. Anybody have early morning swimming or soccer practice? I know you're busy. I usually have a policy of no homework on weekends. Let's see if you like that." Big show of hands, smiles, and head nodding. "Okay, how many like homework on Monday night?" No one raises a hand. "Boys and girls, I have to rephrase. We will have homework— which night is best? Be sure to fill in your birthday. And on your birthday—beware! I play tricks. How many of you have summer birthdays? Oh, good—you could get it any time. I am a birthday pest. Who will be my first victim?"

(Ruth is amazing—in the first 30 minutes she has accomplished a great deal: roll, lunch count, supplies, schedule, and now student survey and still has managed to convey herself as a person—fun-loving, interested, caring, considerate, *but* serious about work.) **Int. & Eval.**

Although the majority of the notes from Ruth's classroom are clearly at a descriptive level, note that there are comments *in parentheses* that are interpretive and evaluative. For the purposes of illustration they have been marked **Int.** or **Int. & Eval.** All but the last of these parenthetical comments were labeled **Int.**, or interpretive, because they indicate some initial interpretations or questions that need to be checked out through further data. The material within the last parentheses, in addition to making some initial interpretations, makes some judgments; e.g., *Ruth is amazing*. This statement has therefore been labeled **Int. & Eval.** for interpretive and evaluative.

It is important to note that sometimes interpretation and evaluation occur simultaneously and cannot be easily separated or distinguished. Although the fine distinctions between interpretation and evaluation can be significant, it is the separation of description from the other two categories that is most important. Description represents what took place in the classroom; interpretation and evaluation represent what an observer initially feels is important or thinks about what took place.

Many observers use the technique of inserting within parentheses ongoing personal questions and comments, both interpretive and evaluative, into their descriptive field notes. This practice serves two important functions. First, it reinforces the idea of separating description from interpretation and evaluation. Second, and perhaps more importantly, it permits the observer to keep track of important insights and ideas gained while in the field. These ideas can be extremely valuable when the data are analyzed for a final report. For example, an observer might record an impression that the way a teacher selected students for a science fair project seemed sexist. If there are recurring instances of what appears to be sexist treatment of children scattered throughout a set of field notes, the idea of sexism in the classroom may turn out to be a major theme or pattern explaining classroom dynamics and behavior. In order to see how the recorded interpretations and evaluations eventually helped to analyze Ruth, look once again at the notes and the case study.

The practice of separating an observer's thought processes from descriptive notes has been employed extensively by Louis M. Smith. Smith (1979) calls these parenthetical comments involving interpretation and evaluation "interpretive asides" and explains how they have operated in his own and his students' work.

> Along the way, a variety of ideas, insights, and interesting associations of ideas, events and people arise. We tend to jot these down into the notes as "(Obs— ...)." They seem to "pop out" in the normal give and take of observing and talking with people in the setting. Often they have a free-associational quality ("reminds me of ... ") and sometimes they are simple perceptual comparisons or contrasts. . . . It seems sensible to make at least a quick note of the insights or "bright ideas" that seem to be arising effortlessly along the way. My hunch is that many get lost if not jotted down at the time. . . . Students whose notebooks are full of these seem to move the analysis along much easier than those whose notes are more limited. (p. 333)

In summary, a good set of formal field notes starts with descriptive note taking, almost a transcript of the class. At the same time these descriptive notes are interspersed with interpretive and evaluative comments set aside within parentheses.

Informal Field Notes There are many opportunities to collect data informally outside the context of direct classroom observation. For example, while walking through the halls of the school an observer might look carefully at how other teachers in the school are dressed or carry themselves in comparison with the teacher under observation. An observer also might note whether or not there are groups or cliques of students or teachers congregating with one another. It is important to record all thoughts triggered by these kinds of experiences in the general context of the school setting. These notes may be either descriptive, interpretive, or evaluative. If they are interpretive or evaluative, however, they should be identified as such. This can be done using parentheses in much the same way as with the formal classroom observation discussed previously. For an example of these informal field notes see the first part of the notes on Ruth's first day. They were jotted down by the observer in the driveway and front hall before class started.

Summary Observations The third type of note taking is summary observation (Smith, 1968). Essentially this involves writing down in a summary form memories of the key events and incidents that took place during observations. Summary observations are used most frequently in situations where it is difficult or impossible to take notes on the spot. For example, if an observer is talking informally with a group of students outside of class it is likely that they will "clam up" if the observer starts taking notes. On such occasions it is best to forget about note taking and instead to summarize the observations at a later time.

In addition, if an observer assumes some teaching duties within a classroom observational setting (e.g., leading a reading group at the elementary level) recording any observations will obviously have to wait until the teaching is over. Because summary notes are recorded from memory, they will necessarily have a more sketchy quality. To guard against losing important information and insights, it is crucial to record summary notes as soon as possible following the observation.

Summary observations are also useful for those who are functioning strictly as observers. Often at the end of the day after reading a set of field notes or recalling some of the major events of the day, important insights, patterns, and connections will surface that can contribute to a final understanding and interpretation of a classroom setting. An example of this kind of summary observation recorded after the event is as follows:

Summary Observation
December 20th
Larry Wells's American History Class

The students seemed more hyperactive than I have ever observed them to be. Could it have been because of the holiday that starts the day after tomorrow? Does this mean that teachers can expect little in the way of serious work tomorrow and, more generally, on the several days preceding holidays? Should different kinds of activities be arranged in order to take this into consideration? How many of the teachers do in fact prepare different types of classes for different times of the year? Ask Larry if this is a conscious part of his planning. It might be interesting to talk to other teachers about this as well.

Rich data and *rich field notes* are phrases used by experienced observers to refer to field notes that are filled with complete descriptions, accurately recorded dialogues, and powerful images that give a clear picture of the social setting and its meaning for the participants. Rich data are also filled with perceptions, preliminary interpretations, and insights that will serve as important clues in eventually making analytical sense of what has been observed.

Interpreting the Data during Observation

The interpretation of data is a process that takes place both during the observational period and following it. The following material considers several different steps toward interpretation that take place as part of the observational process.

Narrowing the Observation Field One of your first tasks as an observer during the early stages of a classroom observation is the need to find a focal point around which to organize and develop your observations. During the first few times in a setting it is best to attempt to record everything possible. Selective observation can only come after you have developed a general sense of the setting you are observing. Through general observation, more specific aspects of the classroom environment and social interaction become evident. It is then important for you to select those key elements that appear to be either the most significant or the most interesting.

In undertaking a recent ethnographic study of an entire school, for example, one of the authors spent the first two visits assessing the overall operation of the school. The required courses of the curriculum; behavior in the halls, cafeteria, and smoking areas; teacher-pupil interaction in the classroom; and relationships between administrators and teachers were among the areas initially examined. Recognizing, however, that in a 20-day period of observation it would only be possible to examine in depth one particular aspect of the school, the observer decided to focus primarily on teacher-pupil interactions related to instruction in the classroom.

The selection of this topic was by no means a random one. The observer sensed that the students in the school were not engaged in or excited by intellectual activity. The overall impression was of a warm, pleasant social environment in which relatively little thinking and learning took place. The question was, Why? Based upon the initial observations in the setting, it appeared that understanding teacher-pupil interaction around instruction would be central to understanding the school in general. Although the other areas could not be ignored, of necessity they assumed secondary importance. (Cohn & DiStefano, 1985.)

Searching for Patterns Once you have narrowed your field of observation, it is important to begin to search for patterns. In the ethnographic study of an entire school mentioned above the observer first narrowed the focus to teacher-pupil interaction in the classroom and then began to look for patterns related to pedagogy. The observer looked to see whether teachers were lecturing, conducting discussions, showing films and videotapes, using simulation games, arranging experiments, or reading from a text. At the same time the observer watched students to see whether they were listening, talking, writing, conducting experiments, doing research, or giving reports. Next the observer began to look for patterns related to subject matter. Were the teacher-pupil interactions in the English department different from those in math, science, and history? This in turn led to a search for patterns related to the three-level tracking system in the school. Were interactions in regular classes different from those in remedial or advanced classes? Finally, there was a look at individual class periods. Were interactions different at the beginning, middle, and end of each class session?

Ultimately, the observer found a model of teacher-pupil interaction that ran almost through the entire school. The model consisted of 20 minutes for lecture (usually from an outline shown with an overhead projector) and 30 minutes of supervised independent seatwork including worksheets, textbook questions, and reading assignments.

With only a few exceptions faculty members firmly adhered to the notion that "teaching is telling" and that "knowledge is given"—something to be presented and digested rather than something to be examined, questioned, applied, or discovered. In the advanced classes as well as those aimed at the average or below average student teachers were invariably doing almost all of the talking. They presented the information, posed the questions, and in most instances answered their own questions.

The chemistry teacher, for example, who had some of the best students in the school, conducted questioning as follows:

TEACHER: *(Working from an overhead projector)* Anyone have an idea of how to go on from moles to molecules?

STUDENT: Multiply.

TEACHER: Okay, multiply. *(The teacher then writes out a formula on the overhead projector)* Now how would you change from grams to molecules? *(write on overhead* G Molecules)

STUDENT: We haven't done this.

TEACHER: If you look at Step 1 *(a previously given formula)* it will tell you how to go from grams to moles. Then if you put moles to molecules, you can get the answer or if you want, you can do the reverse.

This lack of opportunity for students to figure out for themselves (i.e., what to multiply or what formulas might be combined to go from grams to molecules) or to participate actively in any way in class was typical throughout the academic curriculum. The passive role of students in class after class could, in part, account for the lack of intellectual excitement that the observer initially sensed.

Checking Out Ideas and Themes   A third type of interpretation during observation involves checking out ideas and themes. As an observer forms impressions, ideas, and possible explanations, it is helpful while still in the field to check out some of these ideas. One way to accomplish this is to discuss impressions with some of the people in the setting—teachers or students. If, for example, an observer is getting the impression that athletics is the most important part of the students' school life, he or she might say to a teacher something such as: "I've noticed a lot of school activities seem to center around athletic events. What role do you think athletics play in this school?"

A second means of checking out ideas involves looking for *counter instances*. If, for example, an observer starts to notice that the classroom teacher frequently gives unclear directions and begins to suspect that such a lack of clarity might contribute to problems in the learning environment, it is probably a good idea to search for occasions when the directions are very clear. If none can be found the observation is probably quite accurate. If, however, the observer discovers a significant number of counter instances, the initial impression could be wrong.

Interpreting Data after Observation

Once you have collected all of your data, you are faced with the problem of identifying the themes and patterns that will allow you to develop a final intepretation or analysis. Essentially the task is to figure out what it all means. There is, however, little understanding of exactly how skilled observers successfully draw significant interpretations from their data. Despite this fact, certain generalizations about the final interpretive and writing processes can be made.

Louis M. Smith has explained that for him the process involves a number of different steps. After an initial skimming of the total set of field notes he slowly reads the data from beginning to end searching for comparisons and contrasts, antecedents, and consequences. As important items and issues are communicated through the various images, dialogues, and descriptions Smith (1979) asks a simple two-part question: How are they alike and how are they different?

> The similar things are grouped and given a label that highlights their similarity. The different things are grouped, insofar as possible, and given labels. There always is a large "miscellaneous" category of items which seem important, but which do not fit anywhere. The *seem* is critical. There is always a hunch lurking behind the *seem* and, given more data, more time, and more thought, the pieces find a place in relation to one another. Earlier we called this the "jigsaw puzzle analogy." (p. 338)

Smith also describes a related but different process that he uses during interpretation. Drawing on the work of sociologist Robert Merton, Smith (1979) suggests that an observer look for the unexpected and the unanticipated.

> At a practical level, while in the field, the thinking, searching, and note recording reflected not only a consciousness of similarities and differences, but also an attempt to look for unexpected relationships, antecedents, and consequences within the flow of items (p. 338).

An example of the unexpected comes from one of the author's research experiences in a central city magnet school that had both a college preparatory and a vocational curriculum. When looking for the similarities and differences between these curricula, the observer's initial assumption was that there would be more active problem solving and intellectual stimulation in the college preparatory courses. In fact, the vocational education program was, in the observer's final opinion, much more intellectually challenging. This could be explained in part by the fact that there were vocational teachers who made courses such as auto mechanics into a problem-solving experience. Students were asked, How does this engine work and why? They were expected to develop hypotheses about how the engine worked and then to test out these hypotheses through experimentation with a real engine. In contrast, many of the students in the college preparatory classes were memorizing formulas, filling out study guides, and taking tests that involved feeding information back to the teacher. Needless to say, the vocational education students appeared happier and more challenged. This unanticipated finding led the observer in subsequent research projects to always look out for the unexpected.

Other observers who have discussed the processes of interpreting observational data suggest that beginners start by developing coding categories. They argue that as one reads the data, certain words, patterns, phrases, and events will naturally stand out. Developing a coding system involves searching for regularities and patterns as well as topics the data cover and developing labels that represent these topics and patterns. These labels are the coding categories.

Content analysis is yet another interpretive process that can be used to score classroom observation data such as transcripts of teacher-pupil interactions or conversations of students with one another. A scoring system could easily be developed, for example, to indicate whenever a teacher made a sexist or a discriminatory remark. The observer could make a transcript of the teacher's comments and conversations, which could then be scored. Content analysis provides a particularly effective means of isolating and quantifying the thematic content of certain types of written and spoken information.

Finally, whenever you are involved in the interpretation of field data, you will find it helpful to try to ground your interpretations in existing literature. In the case of beginning observers in the field for the first time in order to learn something about the instructional process, referring to an introductory text such as this one is extremely helpful. As you gain more background and insight you can turn to the more specialized studies of teaching that are available in the literature.

Writing an Ethnographic Report

The final product of a series of classroom observations typically takes the form of an ethnographic report or case study. The quality of the report depends on two key factors: (1) the existence of a rich data base from which to work and (2) the thoughtful and creative interpretation of the data.

An ethnographic report can take many forms. A particularly effective format for a beginning observer involves a two-part organization. The first section of the report provides a summary description or a narrative of the behaviors and events that were observed. It often tells a story that includes *what* occurred *when* and *who* was involved. The second part of the report involves the interpretations, findings, and conclusions. It generally seeks to explain *how* and *why*. The case studies of Ruth and Luberta can serve as examples. In Ruth's case study, pages 32 to 46 are essentially descriptive in nature. They are followed by pages of interpretations and analysis. Similarly, in Luberta's case study pages 51 to 61 are descriptive, and the following pages interpret and analyze the descriptive data.

There is no single correct way to write an ethnographic report. However, the most effective reports always include a large number of concrete examples, vivid images, extended dialogue, lively illustrations, and anecdotes to support the interpretations, evaluations, and conclusions of the observer.

In order to give a more concrete idea of what an ethnographic report done by a beginner might look like, we have included one in Appendix I written by Audrey Oka, an undergraduate math and secondary education major at Washington University in St. Louis. While enrolled in a field-based educational psychology course she wrote this report after five weeks of observation that focused on the physical and social climate of her observational setting.

CONCLUSION

This chapter interrupted the portrayal of the five case study teachers in their professional settings in order to provide some methods and techniques for conducting observations and writing case studies or other kinds of ethnographic reports. Chapter 4 will give you the opportunity to use some of the insights provided in this chapter to analyze the three secondary school teachers.

Participant observation has been and will continue to be a highly productive mode of educational research capable of shedding light on the dynamic and multifaceted aspects of school and classroom life. Further, as this chapter indicated, participant observation can be an equally productive methodology for prospective, beginning, and experienced teachers. With the prospective teacher the accent will probably be on observation, whereas with beginning and experienced teachers the accent will invariably be on participation. In either case, however, the process of looking, recording, and reflecting upon what takes place in classrooms can illuminate underlying patterns of behavior that are difficult to see in the day-to-day press of classroom interaction. Moreover, for a prospective teacher, participant observation can provide anticipatory socialization to the teaching profession. By carefully observing and analyzing what teachers do, you can begin to understand what it means to be a teacher and to decide if it is a wise career choice. This chapter, therefore, has introduced some of the methods and techniques of participant observation so that you can begin to do your own fieldwork and case studies as well as to analyze the case studies in this book.

There are some who argue that the task of making prospective teachers into skilled participant observers is overly ambitious. The argument is that participant observation is an abstract and difficult endeavor that should be reserved for educational scholars who plan to pursue a career in research. We agree with the first part of the argument — participant observation is abstract and difficult — but strongly disagree with the second part. Our stance is that participant observation is both useful and necessary for practitioners and would-be practitioners who want to reach a deep understanding of classroom life. Teachers must be skilled in their action and thought. Participant observation can help teachers engage in more thoughtful reflection of their daily action.

Given both the difficulty and necessity of participant observation, this book will proceed slowly and systematically and give you many opportunities to develop and practice your skills. This chapter presented some terminology and mechanics and cited two categories—the individual and social or contextual dimensions of teaching—that you can begin to look for in your own fieldwork and in the case studies in this text.

Later chapters will offer other categories and questions. Part II is designed to present a variety of lenses through which to view classrooms during fieldwork. Chapter 5 focuses on the physical environment; Chapters 6 and 7 focus on the social environment; Chapters 8 and 9 focus on the intellectual environment; Chapter 10 focuses on the personal environment; and Chapter 11 focuses on the overall concept of excellence in teaching. After each of these chapters, you will find questions to guide your observations and to guide your formal and informal interviews with teachers. These questions, as well as the end-of-chapter activities and discussions, should enable you to become a careful and thoughtful observer.

After each of the chapters in Part III there will be additional activities and discussion questions to further enhance your ability to see what is happening in schools and in the profession. By the end of the text, you should begin to possess some skills as a participant observer as well as an appreciation of the methodology. It will be a difficult and abstract enterprise but one well worth the effort.

DISCUSSION QUESTIONS

1. Participant observation is a research method that includes many different ways of collecting data. What are the advantages and disadvantages of using direct observation, in-depth interviewing, document analysis, and direct participation as separate means of data collection? What are the advantages of combining these different ways of collecting data?
2. As demonstrated in this chapter both teachers and field researchers have to contend with preconceptions and sometimes prejudices they bring to a particular setting. How can these be minimized or avoided for both teachers and field researchers? How important is it to be aware of one's point of view?

ACTIVITIES

1. Following is a list of statements about students in a classroom setting. To practice your ability to distinguish between *descriptive* statements (those that are directly observable) and *interpretive* statements (those that the observer infers), check the appropriate category next to each statement.

Statement	Descriptive	Interpretive
Johnny is an aggressive boy.		
Mary hit Steven in the stomach.		
Susie is hyperactive.		
Roberto is quite intelligent.		
Charlie underlined all the verbs in the sentence.		
Steven cried after recess.		
Cheryl is a troublemaker.		
Rita got out of her seat and walked to the pencil sharpener.		
Fred added the two columns of numbers.		
Ann is very talented.		

2. Watch a videotape of a classroom with the rest of the students in your class, and take descriptive notes putting your interpretations and evaluations in parentheses. Exchange your notes with others and let them, as well as your instructor, give you feedback on (1) the amount of data you were able to record and (2) your ability to separate descriptive notes from your interpretive and evaluative statements. Afterward, discuss the difficulties of an accurate and full set of field notes.

REFERENCES AND SOURCES

Cohn, M. & DiStefano, A. (1985). *Ridgefield High School*. In V. Perrone and Associates, *Portraits of high schools*. The Carnegie Foundation for the Advancement of Teaching. New Jersey: Princeton University Press.

Kluckhorn, C. (1940). The participant-observer technique in small communities. *American Journal of Sociology, 46,* 343.

Lortie, D. C. (1975). *Schoolteacher*. Chicago: University of Chicago Press.

McCall, G. J., & Simmons, J. L. (Eds.). (1969). *Issues in participant observation: A text and reader*. Reading, MA: Addison-Wesley.

Rist, Ray. (1973). *The urban school: A factory for failure*. Cambridge, MA: Massachusetts Institute of Technology Press.

Smith, L., & Geoffrey, W. (1968). *The complexities of an urban classroom: An analysis toward a general theory of teaching*. New York: Holt, Rinehart & Winston.

Smith, L. (1979). *An evolving logic of participant observation, educational ethnography, and other case studies*. In L. Shulman (Ed.), *Review of research in education*. Itasca, IL: Peacock.

Spindler, G. (1982). *Doing the ethnography of schooling: Educational anthropology in action*. New York: Holt, Rinehart & Winston.

4

EXCELLENCE IN THE
SECONDARY SCHOOL

INTRODUCTION

Chapter 2 presented case studies of two elementary teachers in their school and community context. Chapter 3 paused to consider the rationale, methods, and techniques of participant observation to help you get started with your own fieldwork and case studies. This chapter continues the presentation of case studies, with the spotlight on three secondary school teachers.

First there will be a visit to Sandy Snodgrass's high school classroom in Lindbergh, Missouri—a middle-class suburb in the southern section of St. Louis County where Sandy will teach a psychology class and interact with special education social studies students. The second stop will be in the countryside to observe Larry Wells's high school social studies classroom in Hillsboro, Missouri. The final destination will be in downtown Miami, Florida, in the "rough" neighborhood where Jacquie Yourist teaches French and history to junior high students.

This chapter conveys a general overview of teaching at the secondary level; specific instances of secondary teaching in suburban, rural, and urban schools; and the personality, philosophy, and pedagogy of three secondary teachers. The emphasis is the same as in Chapter 2—the individual and contextual dimensions of teaching. Therefore, look once again for:

1. The ways in which individual teacher characteristics and community or school context appear to influence what happens in the classroom.
2. The differences that set these particular teachers and contexts apart and the commonalities that hold them together.

3. The reason why each of these teachers might be considered excellent.

In addition, note any ways in which teaching at the secondary level appears different from teaching at the elementary level.

SANDY SNODGRASS: STRIVING FOR A PERSONAL RELATIONSHIP WITH STUDENTS

Community Context

The locale is Lindbergh School District in south St. Louis County. The district encompasses 23 square miles of land that in the 1940s and early 1950s was mostly rural. In the late 1950s and throughout the 1960s tremendous change, development, and population growth took place in this area. Today there are still some farms, but much of the land is now covered with tract developments of different vintages and styles—colonial, Cape Cod, ranch, and split level. In addition, there are businesses along major roads, a large shopping mall, and large new tracts of garden apartments. The school district covers several incorporated municipalities as well as a large area that remains unincorporated and is served by St. Louis County police and other services.

Those who moved to Lindbergh School District during the growth spurt were largely blue- and white-collar workers and other representatives of the middle class, many of them of German and Italian extraction who moved the 6 to 10 miles from south St. Louis to the suburbs. They were part of a national trend in those years, moving away from the central cities of the nation. The political persuasion of the residents is predominantly conservative. The majority of parents want for their children an emphasis on the basics, strong discipline, and preparation for further education. They want their children to be financially successful adults. As with Sandy's family, a large number of the parents are not college educated themselves but have a great desire for their children to receive some form of higher education. Roughly 75 percent of the high school graduating classes go on to participate in some sort of continuing or higher education.

The Lindbergh School District was consolidated from a number of independent elementary districts early in the growth period. The district enrollment peaked in 1970 when 12,343 students attended schools in the system, 4,000 of them in the high school where Sandy Snodgrass teaches. In the last decade there has been a precipitous decline in students forcing the riffing (reduction in force) of many teachers and the closing of several elementary and one of two middle schools. Today the high school has a population of about 2,500, including roughly 150 St. Louis city students transported to Lindbergh as part of a voluntary city-county desegregation plan. Most of the students who attend the high school from within the district are also bused to and from school each day.

Lindbergh High School

Lindbergh High School, named for Charles Lindbergh, is a collection of nondescript tan and red brick one-, two-, and three-story buildings, originally built to separate junior and senior high schools. The newer buildings are air conditioned, but many of the rooms lack windows. The school fronts on Lindbergh Boulevard, originally built as the U.S. Highway 61–66 bypass for St. Louis, but today a major and busy thoroughfare with commercial and business stretches along it. The high school property extends for a considerable distance in back of the school and includes a track and football field as well as numerous other playing fields.

The Classroom

The class is psychology, and the students are juniors and seniors. A quick glance around the room, which features desks arranged in two large semicircles, reveals a superficial sameness in terms of student appearance. The girls for the most part wear slacks and jeans with clingy knit tops and have long, teased hair. The care with which their make-up has been applied and their hair has been arranged suggests that a major interest is to be attractive to the boys. The boys, many of whom respond enthusiastically to the overtures of the girls, also have longish hair and wear either T-shirts or oxford-cloth shirts with their jeans and tennis shoes. The

Sandy talking to her students

look is middle-class white. The absence of ethnic minorities or suburban preps and sophisticates is striking. Beneath the surface, however, there is considerable variation—particularly in terms of intellectual ability. In this class some of the highest achieving students in the school sit alongside some of the least able, including those in special education. Psychology at Lindbergh High School is a popular elective with students all along the academic continuum.

The teacher is Sandy Snodgrass. Although she is a 16-year teaching veteran her youthful appearance and manner belie her age. Her dark hair is permed; her figure is trim; her dark brown eyes twinkle with spirit; her dress is casual—tailored jeans and a plaid blouse. Her approach with students is clear but, at the same time, relaxed, personal, and playful. The class begins this way.

> Okay. Today we're going to start Chapter 11. We'll be looking at how groups operate and we will begin by doing some group experiements. One experiment will be with what is called *circle communication* and the other will be with *wheel communication*.

She draws on the board.

Circle Communication

0

0   0

0   0

Wheel Communication

O   O

O

O   O

It's easier to do these experiments than to explain them. The first one we will do is circle communication and the first thing you need to do is to divide yourselves into six groups.

The students move easily and smoothly into six groups.

Step 1, and my favorite part, is that you can't talk—you can only communicate on paper. You can communicate on paper to anyone who is in your group.

Sandy then passes out a worksheet and asks a student to read the explanation at the top of the worksheet:

A group of 15 experts considered miracle workers by those who have used their services have agreed to provide these services for members of this class. Their extraordinary skills are guaranteed to be 100 percent effective. It is up to you to decide which of these people can best provide you with what you want.

Sandy then gives the class instructions: "Your group must select 5 of the 15 experts in 15 minutes. Your group must agree on all five, but you must communicate only on paper."

The groups look interested and begin by reading the list of experts from whom they have to choose. The choices are difficult, for the list includes such "experts" as:

1. **Dr. Dorian Grey** A noted plastic surgeon, he can make you look exactly as you want to look by means of a new painless technique. (He also uses hormones to alter body structures and size!) Your ideal physical appearance can be a reality.
2. **Baron VonBarrons** A college placement and job placement expert. The college or job of your choice in the location of your choice will be yours! (He also provides immunity from the draft if you wish.)
3. **Drs. Masters Johnson and Fanny Hill** Experts in the area of sexual relations, they guarantee that you will be the perfect male or female, will enjoy sex, and will bring pleasure to others.
4. **Dr. Yin Yang** An organismic expert, he will provide you with perfect health and protection from physical injury throughout your life.
5. **Dr. Knot Not Ginott** An expert in dealing with parents, he guarantees that you will never have any problems with your parents again. They will accept your values and your behavior. You will be free from control and badgering.

6. **"Pop" Larity** He guarantees that you will have the friends you want now and in the future. You will find it easy to approach those you like, and they will find you easily approachable.
7. **Rocky Fellah** Wealth will be yours, with guaranteed schemes for earning millions within weeks.

After reading with smiles on their faces the students in each group start passing notes to one another. They are obviously engrossed in the task. In some groups the note passing just goes around the circle. In others one person starts to assume leadership and begins to pass notes back. In one group, a student writes his choices on a large piece of paper and holds it up so everyone in the group can see it. Most students immediately pick Experts 1 and 10 but have difficulty making choices among the rest. No one, however, breaks the imposed silence, even when Sandy walks around and teases: "Oh, I love the quiet; I wish we could do this every day."

When 15 minutes are up she stops the exercise and collects the worksheets and the group choices. Some complain that they are not finished, but she responds:

> Never mind, we'll discuss the problems you had tomorrow, but now we have to get into the second communication game. We are going to play something called the Moon Game. In this game you can't talk either, but you can pick a certain person to receive all of your messages, and you will have more time.

She refers to the board and indicates that this time they will be using a wheel communication pattern with someone in the middle to handle all of the written communication. When one group seems to be having trouble getting anyone to volunteer to be in the center, Sandy quips, "Force is a nice way to decide who goes in." Then Sandy passes out the Moon Game and goes over the situation:

> Imagine yourself as an astronaut who has crash landed on the moon and must decide how to reach your mothership 200 miles away. The only supplies that have not been ruined by the crash are the 15 items listed below. Rank in order of usefulness.

The 15 items range from oxygen to matches, and the task for each group is to come up with a ranked list. The conditions are that each person can only communicate with the person in the center of their wheel by written communication.

As the students get to work one girl laughs out loud. Sandy quickly responds, "Carrie, you're not supposed to be having so much fun." This comment brings more laughter.

Sandy circulates to observe varying approaches. All but two girls seem involved — they're using the opportunity for passing notes to discuss plans for Friday night.

About five minutes before the bell is to ring Sandy calls time, collects the sheets, and reads the answers. She jokes with those who say their group got a low score and says she would not want to crash in space with them.

RANK IN ORDER

Imagine yourself as an astronaut who has crash-landed on the moon and must decide how to reach your mother ship 200 miles away. The only supplies not ruined by the crash are the fifteen items listed below. Rank in order of usefulness.

Items

_____ box of matches

_____ food concentrate

_____ fifty feet of nylon rope

_____ parachute silk

_____ solar-powered portable heating unit

_____ two .45 caliber pistols

_____ one case of dehydrated Pet milk

_____ two 100-pound tanks of oxygen

_____ stellar map (of the moon's constellation)

_____ self-inflating life raft

_____ magnetic compass

_____ five gallons of water

_____ signal flares

_____ first-aid kit containing injection needles

_____ solar-powered FM receiver-transmitter

1. Your group must come up with a list.

2. You may communicate only with the person you are "linked" to and only in writing.

The Moon Game

She concludes by saying the purpose of the game is not to figure out the right answers for the astronauts.

The purpose is to begin to understand group communication. Tonight I'd like you to think about our group work today in the wheel and in the circle and then answer the questions on this sheet. She passes out sheets with the following questions:

1. Describe how your group was organized and how you got your job done (both times).
2. Was there a leader (in the circle)? Who? How did he or she emerge?

Sandy working with her students

3. Which time was a solution reached the quickest?
4. Which way did you enjoy it the most?
5. Discuss any problems you encountered in either group.

When the bell rings students are still talking about their scores in the Moon Game and the choices they made among the 15 experts. Student interest has been high throughout the class, and it remains so even afterward. Sandy goes into the hall to wait for her next class, which is a history class for special education students—slow learners because of emotional or behavioral problems, learning disabilities, or retardation. In Missouri there is an eighth-grade competency test that every student must pass in order to graduate from high school. One of the major goals of this course is to help those who have failed the social studies portion of the test.

As Sandy stands in the hallway she jokes with many of the students. A girl from another psychology class comes to the classroom to take a make-up test and Sandy banters with her:

SANDY: (*Laughingly*) It's on my desk in the social studies office—you'll recognize my desk immediately—it's the messiest one.
STUDENT: I don't know why I'm even bothering—I'm going to get an A on this test, remember.

SANDY: Oh, that's right! Because you gave me two chocolate chip cookies yesterday, I promised you an A— well, let's just go through the motions anyway.

Soon the special education students begin to enter. As they walk in the door Sandy greets each one by name. To one retarded boy Sandy puts her arm across the door and says, "You can't come in here until you whisper sweet nothings in my ear." He leans over and whispers, "I love you, Mrs. Snodgrass."

Reflections on Changes in a Teaching Career

Actually a lot of students love Sandy Snodgrass, and she loves them. Watching her in action it is apparent that she teaches because she enjoys her students. It was not, however, always that way. Originally she became interested in teaching because of her love for social studies in general and politics in particular. The situation is different now.

Now that I have taught, it isn't the love of politics that keeps me in teaching. That changed. The change now is that I enjoy the kids. They are not interested in the subject matter. They hate politics. And I enjoy the kids. I especially enjoy the slow kids. So it's not so much the subject matter as working with the kids. Whatever they give me to teach them, it would essentially be the same. You can give me a different subject, but my method, my style, those things are basically the same.

Change, in fact, has been a constant throughout Sandy's teaching career. She talks, for example, of how change in her personal life has changed the way she responds to students.

I have changed a lot. I continually change it seems. I think the past few years I have gone through personal problems in my own life that have really helped me with the kids—having gone through a divorce—when a kid mentions something about a stepfather or stepmother, I really tune into that. And once they find that I am divorced they open up. I am more keenly aware of the personal problems, I guess, of kids. Because it was hard for me to go to work and teach with problems at home, now I am more aware that if these kids have problems it is hard for them to come to school. I sort of hone in on it. I sort of have a sixth sense with kids. I can tell which kids are going through unhappy times at home. I have become more sensitive. At one time I would have just thought, "You're from a divorced home, well, that's too bad, isn't it? It's a shame your parents are failures." Whereas now I'm not as condescending in my attitude toward children of divorce. At one time I would see on a kid's record a different name from the parents and say, "Oh my, a child from a broken home." But now that I am in that situation and have a son, I don't want him to be categorized or all of his problems blamed on the fact that he comes from a broken home. So I think I have liberalized my thoughts on that because of my own problems.

Another change that has surprised her is a renewed interest in working with what she calls the "slow kids."

When I first started teaching I would just look down on them. And I looked at the people who taught them and thought, "Well you just can't do anything else. That's why you are working with them." And I thought to myself, "I would never have a room that was so loud and where kids were squirming around." And now when I think of teaching some of the slow kids—some of the things they did to me or I let them do—years ago I would never have believed that I would have changed that much in regard to them. And now I really enjoy teaching them. . . . I used to think, "Why don't you just quit school? You don't belong here." My attitude toward them has changed. Rather than babysitting with them now I feel that I am finally teaching them something, but it took me years to get to that point and know what to teach them.

One of the insights Sandy eventually learned was never to assume what students should be able to do.

When I first worked with the special education students, I took too much for granted. I assumed that they knew things they didn't know. Therefore, I would be teaching from a base they hadn't even touched on yet. Now I don't assume anything. It's an individual approach which has been helped by the fact that the classes are smaller.

In addition Sandy now feels that she gets a great deal of assistance from Special School District that wasn't available in the past.

Years ago we knew they were slow, but we didn't know anything else about them. Today Special School District can effectively diagnose and pinpoint certain problems. If I know that a kid's problem is auditory, and he can't understand information he hears, doesn't process right, then I'll do visual things with him. Years ago we didn't know what their problems were, and I would have essentially babysat those kids, giving worksheets or things to keep them busy. Now I feel that they are making progress.

Much of her ability to work effectively with these and regular students Sandy attributes to still another change—a change in philosophy.

I think that I am more patient than I used to be. At first, I wanted to change the world. I was going to save all these children from themselves. Now, it's more or less just a day at a time. Instead of thinking of their whole future or the whole school year with them, it's just each day, and if we don't get as far that day as I had intended—fine, no problem. We'll just do it tomorrow. Whereas before I almost felt under a time schedule—Okay, now let's get this done because we have to get on to the next thing. Patience is something that for me has been very difficult, but I am a lot more patient than I used to be. And I expect more from them. My goals for them are higher than they used to be—not academically as much, but I just expect certain things from them, and I won't take anything less. Whereas in the past I would say, "Oh well, he can't help it. He's slow," now I find that if you require them to do certain things, like bringing a pencil to class, most of them can do it, whereas before I was supplying them with pencils every day.

Given these changes Sandy now finds herself working to achieve a positive personal relationship with individuals and a positive social climate in the classroom.

I really strive for a personal sort of relationship — they will not work for you if they do not have a personal relationship or feeling toward you. The regular student will work for a grade. But with the slower kids you first have to sort of establish a personal relationship before you can get down to any basic teaching. And with the regular kids I still do that; I think that's part of me. Not that I want all of my classes to like me. But I want to feel comfortable with them and they with me. I am more concerned that when they leave the class they will have a good attitude toward the subject than that they will remember anything specific. And that way if they are interested in it they will pursue it further. And I think that with adolescents if they enjoy a class and the teacher they are more apt to pursue it than if they think the teacher doesn't care. I think that can sour them on the subject. So basically I suppose I strive for good feelings between me and the students — not a popularity contest. There are kids who hate my guts, and I don't care, but I like a relaxed atmosphere where a kid can speak up, challenge me if he likes, add something to our discussion or whatever. I really strive for that relaxed atmosphere where each kid feels that he is part of the class, not just sitting there but that he has contributed.

Because Sandy is so successful at establishing personal relationships many students come to her with personal problems, and she thrives on these one-to-one interactions.

I had this last year — a kid comes up and says: "I'm pregnant, and I don't know what to do." After talking to her, finally she talked to her mother. I talked to her, I talked to her mother; it was very rewarding. Ten years from now she won't remember my government course, but she might remember that at a time of need a teacher was sympathetic and helped her out. The one-on-one problems, I really thrive on them. It would be very hard for me to be impersonal. I like to get involved if the student wants me to get involved. . . . I guess now the kids seek me out more because as the school gets smaller your reputation gets around more.

These one-to-one encounters afford Sandy a feeling of satisfaction because she feels she has made a positive and important impact on an individual's life. Being able to have an impact on students academically as well as personally is also important to her. Sometimes the simplest gestures on the part of the students make her feel that what she does both inside and outside the classroom makes a difference. For example, Sandy describes a good day as follows.

Students in one of Sandy's classes

A good day is when you have been going on and on about the presidency for days—and a kid who is very slow comes in with an article he has cut out of the newspaper, and you think that he probably never looks at the newspaper. He comes in saying, "Look, we talked about this in class yesterday." And you are surprised that he remembered. It's little things like that. Or a kid running in saying, "Last night on the news they said exactly what you said." Like you didn't make it up after all—something that you said in class, and they follow up on it. You mention something and they go home and talk to their parents about it, and then they will come back and comment about it—the fact that the things you said or talked about do have some importance for them. I think that at times we do worry that the things that we teach them are important, and that they aren't really paying any attention at all. Or they will come in and say, "thank you; I got the scholarship that you wrote the recommendation for." Or a kid coming up to tell you that he talked to his parents about something like you suggested and now everything is fine. Those are the things that really make my day. Or just a kid in the hall saying, "Oh, hi! I haven't seen you in a while." Or a kid coming into the room saying, "I really enjoy your class; what are we going to do today?" Sometimes that's all it takes to make my day.

Extracurricular activities are also a source of satisfaction for Sandy, particularly since she's found a level of participation that fits her family life. Instead of being a club sponsor with heavy, ongoing responsibilities as she did when she was single,

Sandy now enjoys being a "help-out." "I can just help out when I want and when I'm needed, and I can go home when I need to."

There are, of course, difficult days as well as good ones. These are days during which things start to go downhill because of some kind of confrontation with a student or the entire class.

> You'll be doing something that you think is important, and in the middle of it some kid will belch and the whole class starts laughing. Usually I can handle that by making some comment and then move on. There are times when maybe I am just tired of it. They don't know when I'm tired of it, and they will look at you really astonished and think well that really upset her today, and usually they respect that and sort of straighten up. Or a kid comes to class and maybe he's just been in trouble in the office. And he'll walk in saying that the principal is no good and start cussing him out, getting the class sort of stirred up, and he won't settle down. And the whole class will start out, "Yeah, that principal, he's no good, and bla, bla, bla," and it will continue for a while and you can't get them back. I'll go with it for a while, and then I'll want to get back to task. Sometimes they don't want to. This happens more with the slower kids. And finally you'll say, "Okay, let's get it out of your system and get back to work." And they don't want to, and they just keep going on and on and on. Or a belligerent kid who comes to class and maybe he's had a problem with another teacher or maybe he's just—there are some kids—who knows why they do the things they do—who will try to pull out matches or something and try to set his neighbor's paper on fire. Things like that I'm not real tolerant towards. Usually it doesn't really bother me, but when you've had it two classes in a row, one thing after another, it's usually things that just pile up one on top of another, and then when you walk into the next class you're in a foul mood. They'll say, "Boy, you're in a nasty mood today," and sometimes that's all it takes. "You're right, and I want to have a good day now so you all help me along. I'm in a bad mood. Help me to get out of it."

More often than not, however, Sandy helps herself out of it through her delightful sense of humor. For Sandy, humor is an icebreaker and a way to get through a bad day. She usually starts by trying to amuse herself, and the results are contagious—the students are amused as well. She has found that it is hard for students to behave hostilely while they are laughing. How does Sandy amuse herself? Sometimes it is with in-class bantering.

> They'll come to class, and I'll say things like, "My feelings are really hurt today." And they'll say, "Oh, what did we do, what did we do?" And I'll say, "I don't know if I can teach today because John was absent yesterday, and he knows that I can't go on when he's not here." Just stupid stuff like that, and they just love it. And I just do it mainly to keep myself amused. I can't understand it completely, but in doing it, it amuses them, and they'll laugh, "Oh, John, tell her that you are sorry for being absent yesterday." These are the slow kids. If I did this with the regular kids they would think I was crazy. With them I entertain myself too. With the higher kids it's a higher form of humor, sarcasm and wit. And they'll say, "Oh, that Mrs. S. she's crazy," or something. I guess

when I started teaching I was too insecure to do that. I would have thought that they would think that I am stupid. Whereas now I don't care. I have a good time and if they want to join in the fun that's okay. You have to do it to entertain yourself.

Sometimes it is by planning fun classroom activities like the communication games. At other times it is by joking with kids in the hall and playing practical jokes.

They'll come to class, and I'll tell them something outrageous, and they'll believe it. Just continually amusing myself, joking with other teachers, sending a kid down to another teacher's room. The two of us have concocted a little trick to play on that teacher; that's fun.

Clearly, Sandy has learned over her 16 years how to cope with the bad days and, better yet, how to ensure that there will be many good ones. Sandy not only teaches psychological theories; she makes them work for her. She knows "how people tick" and that, she maintains, is really what it takes to succeed as a teacher.

I used to think that it was only important that you knew your subject matter in order to teach, but I don't feel that way any more. I think you could give me anything to teach as long as it wasn't some advanced science or math, and I could go in there and do a good job—an English class, a basic science class. So I don't think knowledge of a subject is as important as I once did. I mean you need to know your subject but . . . I think you need to know how to handle people basically, because so many of the problems in your class are not with kids asking questions that you can't answer but with kids doing things that you need to respond to immediately. . . . Every day is different, and you can't prepare yourself for what is going to happen. You walk into your room one day and a kid ODs right in front of you. There is no way you can prepare for that. A girl walks up to you and says she is going to have an abortion tomorrow, and what do you think about that? Just constant newness—which makes it exciting, but at times makes it hectic. You just have to develop a feel for people and what makes them tick and how to respond to any given situation. I think it's more of a human nature sort of knowledge than a subject matter knowledge.

Sandy surely has human nature knowledge, whatever it is, and she uses it well. She uses it to develop personal relationships with students and to build a positive, social climate for classroom learning. Most of all, however, she uses it to reach the slower kids whom others so often try to avoid. She acknowledges that the challenges they present are great at times, but so are the rewards.

Most of my rewards do come from the slower kids. . . . I suppose that they are the ones that you have your worst days with too. The highs are higher and the lows are lower than with the other classes. When you have a low you're ready to resign. Maybe that's why you enjoy them more because when you have a high it's really a high.

Sandy is really high on teaching. And that is why when a retarded boy whispers, "I love you, Mrs. Snodgrass" in her ear, he is probably speaking not just for himself but for a lot of his classmates.

LARRY WELLS: TAKING STUDENTS BEYOND THEIR RURAL ENVIRONMENT

Community Context

Located approximately 45 miles southwest of St. Louis, Missouri, Hillsboro is a rural community "in transition." Until the late 1950s Hillsboro was a small, stable, homogeneous community. Most of its residents were farmers and staunch supporters of community and school. In 1953, for example, there were a total of 147 students in the high school and 18 in the graduating class. A long-time resident and teacher recalls the "good ole days":

> We couldn't have had a more supportive community. We never had a bond issue that was voted down. Anything the school wanted we would get. [But] they were a little shortsighted in terms of inviting business in. They wanted to keep it the little ole Hillsboro. Anything new was taboo—including supermarkets. Discipline problems were nil. All you had to do was talk to a parent and everything was taken care of. The few who drove back and forth from the city were old Jefferson Countians. If we did get newcomers from the city, they would fall in line with our students.

The 1960s and 1970s, however, brought dramatic population changes to Hillsboro. As the cost and complexities of urban living increased, many middle- and lower-class white St. Louis families found a move to Hillsboro appealing. The cost of land was cheaper, the pace was slower, the air was cleaner, and the pressures for integration were nonexistent. Gradually, acres and acres of farmland were prepared for homesites instead of crops, and the new landowners were mostly blue-collar workers with jobs in the automotive plants and factories of St. Louis. Hillsboro, in effect, became a bedroom community or what Larry Wells calls a "ruburb."

With the shift in population came a change in family and school-community relations. A serious increase in divorce, teen-age pregnancy, child and drug abuse meant many broken families with children being shuttled from one parent to another and from one community to another. As the school population became more scattered and students had to be transported long distances by bus, the one-time cohesive quality of the Hillsboro School District disappeared. Despite, or perhaps because of, these upheavals in family and school life, the new population established strong ties with their Baptist, Mormon, and Pentecostal churches.

The visitor to Hillsboro today finds that the blue-collar worker predominates but that there are also a significant number of welfare recipients and a small local farming elite. Religion still exists as a powerful force in the community. School meetings are scheduled so as not to conflict with church activities; at football games, the superintendent of schools gives an invocation in which he thanks God for the "good men on the field" and prays that "all will be safe." Moreover, fundamentalist groups and individuals exert a new conservative presence in the schools by pressing for the removal of "unsuitable" books, magazines, and films.

Perhaps the only surprise that the visitor to Hillsboro today encounters is the absence of growth in terms of small businesses or industry. The increase and shift in population has not been accompanied by any economic development. Although Hillsboro is the largest district in Jefferson County in terms of square miles, it takes only a few minutes by car to tour the center of Hillsboro and to observe the courthouse and adjoining offices, the three eating establishments, a bank, a drugstore, and several small two-story buildings that house the local physicians and lawyers. There is still no main street, no newspaper. With so small a commercial tax base, Hillsboro is heavily dependent on state funding (about 50 percent) for the financing of its schools. It is little wonder that the high school principal talks first and foremost about state budget cuts and their devastating effects on his school.

Hillsboro High School

Hillsboro High School, where Larry Wells has been a social studies teacher for his entire career of 11 years, is located just off the main highway and behind the complex of elementary, middle, and junior high school buildings that serve the district. As one drives toward the high school parking lot a relatively new and undistinguished single story brick building comes into view. Emblazoned upon the side wall next to the entrance is a ferocious-looking white hawk and the words in large white lettering Hillsboro High School—Home of the Hawks.

Once inside, however, the feeling is anything but ferocious. The foyer leads in three directions: to the right (at an angle) is a large cafeteria where the predominant color is a bold and bright blue; straight ahead is a long hallway lined with

Downtown Hillsboro

Hillsboro High School

Going to one's locker

Getting in shape

brightly colored lockers; to the left is a wider main corridor that leads to the rest of the building. The main office is to the immediate left of the main corridor and across from it is a weekly activities board that announces everything from athletic events to student birthdays. The main corridor opens into a wider area dominated by filled trophy cases. To the right is the gym, to the left are the counseling offices. An armed services recruitment stand is located directly across from the gym. In the main corridor senior class composite portraits dating back to 1975 adorn the walls. Throughout the rest of the windowless building the dry-wall interior partitions are mostly bare except for an occasional poster or handwritten announcement regarding a Teenage Christian Fellowship meeting.

While students are in classes, the building looks relatively clean, free of vandalism and well maintained. Before, between, and after classes all one can see and hear are boisterous, friendly adolescents talking, laughing, shouting, and kissing. Sexual intimacies, sarcastic barbs, and caring greetings are exchanged. A few students walk slowly and self-consciously along. One senses that for most of the students this is where the real action of school takes place and where the social winners and losers can most clearly be seen.

The boys are dressed in jeans, T-shirts (especially football and rock group shirts), and running shoes. The girls wear more feminine versions of this uniform, but few

An encounter between classes

Students on their way to class

boys or girls sport designer labels or famous brand names. Other girls are in dresses, either conservative and plain or clinging and dressy. The two looks are supplemented by either straight, long hair, and no make-up or spike heels, plentiful make-up, and feathered hair. Individual students not deeply involved in conversation give a friendly smile, nod, or a hello to visitors. The halls are crowded but manageable.

The main office has a pleasant atmosphere with popular music on the radio, students and teachers wandering in and out looking for a specific form or a ladder, and lunch tickets being sold. The two secretaries joke with the principal, Chuck Martin, as well as with students and teachers who stop by to strike up a conversation.

A former P.E. instructor and coach, Chuck Martin is in his second year as principal. The visitor is struck by his youthful appearance (he is in his early thirties), but his short neatly styled red hair, casual but careful dress, direct manner, and big smile suggest that he is quite comfortable in his new position.

He appears at once energetic and calm, firm and accessible. Students and teachers who ask to see him usually do. Although Larry Wells describes Martin's leadership style thus far as laissez faire, both he and the rest of the faculty praise him as an administrator who gives his teachers autonomy and freedom, particularly in the areas of curriculum and instruction. From Martin's perspective the teachers are in a better position to make such decisions.

> Sometimes I find myself in a position where I am working with someone who almost has a doctor's degree in English, and I am trying to tell him how to teach and what to teach—so that's where I feel inadequate—in curriculum—I don't feel confident enough to walk into an art class and say what they should be doing. I see myself as organizing and facilitating so they can do what they want. They're okay. I really think that they know what to do, and they feel that they are in a better position to know what should be done.

Despite Martin's feelings of inadequacy regarding the specifics of various disciplines he is quite confident of his ability to recognize good teaching. When asked to name his outstanding teachers the name of Larry Wells came to his mind immediately.

Larry Wells's Classroom

To get to Larry Wells's classroom it is necessary to walk past the main office into the wider hallway and down the central corridor. The room itself is a rather typical 20′ × 20′ classroom. The students' desks are arranged in two semicircles in front of the chalkboard. Larry teaches at the front of the classroom where he has a lectern and an overhead projector. His own desk is crowded into a corner in the back of the classroom. Behind his desk there are photographs of Larry and eight different class trips to Washington, D.C. They include pictures of Larry and his students in front of the Capitol building and in the office of Missouri senator Thomas Eagleton. Reproductions of paintings by the nineteenth-century American artist Frederick Remington are taped to the wall over the blackboard. Color reproductions of paintings of famous Americans, including Robert E. Lee, Daniel Webster, and Daniel Boone, are scattered on the walls of the class. A globe of the world stands at the front of the room and a map of the United States is prominently displayed on one of the walls. Adjacent to the lectern is a tall chair from which Larry directs his classes.

On any given day during any given topic Larry can be seen actively moving about — gesturing, joking, asking pointed questions, telling stories — to involve and interest his students. Larry entered the teaching profession with a strong commitment toward his subject area of history and a desire to model the methods of the three teachers who had stimulated his own thinking. He assumed that the subject matter itself would provoke interest and attention from his students. The task of motivating students, however, was much more difficult than he had anticipated.

> I naively thought I would come into classes and have students read the material, and we would discuss it in an intellectual manner, and I would ask Socratic questions, which I still attempt to do. But the biggest shock I had in the early seventies was that the students couldn't read. There were maybe five in the class, six, who could read well, who understood. There were probably 20, 18 maybe, who could read, but they didn't always understand what they read. Then you've got the other 6 or whatever is left over from 30, who literally couldn't read at all. My little fourth-grade daughter can read better than many high school kids as far as reading aloud. That's not even all there is to reading, but as far as reading and knowing what you read, perceiving it, that was the biggest shock to me. I just didn't expect the kids to be that illiterate in high school.

Part of becoming an effective teacher, for Larry, was adjusting to the realities of the classroom in which he was teaching. Larry had to find a means by which he could help students with limited interest and reading ability to see the relevance of distant places, people, and events from the past. The challenge for Larry as a teacher was to make history relevant to a group of rural students, many of whom had never gone beyond the limited boundaries of their homes in Hillsboro and Jefferson County, Missouri.

Larry eventually developed a style of presentation that involved common-sense language, concrete examples, and friendly, humorous undercurrents that made him and the ideas he was attempting to introduce accessible. In a certain sense Larry represents a translator and a re-creator of times and situations long past. In a discussion about mercantile theory in eighteenth-century France, for example, he describes how the manufacture of cloth was very strictly regulated by the government: "In France, for example, there were laws on the books that told how many

Larry in his classroom

stitches could be included in the cloth that they manufactured." After stressing the point several times that mercantilism involves the strict regulation of the economy by the government, he attempts to connect the ideas with the present and the experience of the students by asking: "What would Ronald Reagan think of mercantilism in that respect?" Larry's ability to link the historical concepts he presents to the students and their own experience is a hallmark of his teaching.

At another point during the same class he introduces the idea of the importance of establishing a favorable balance of trade between different nations. Going beyond a historical example he points to one of the girls in the class and announces: "Vicki here is a big shirt manufacturer. She has a big factory in Massachusetts." Stepping from his lectern he walks up to Vicki and asks her directly, "Do you like the idea of our putting a tax or tariff on all the shirts manufactured in Taiwan, Korea, and China?" Vicki replies, "Oh, yeah, that will make their shirts more expensive than mine." Larry turns to a boy across the room and asks him, "Is that right, Steve?" Steve replies, "Yeah." And Larry continues, "Darn right!" and then asks the question, "Is it relevant to talk about tariffs today or is it just an old issue? We don't have those types of problems of imports versus exports today, do we? None of your parents work for automobile manufacturers, do they?" Many students nod their heads yes and five or six hands immediately go up. "Oh, they do?" Larry says in feigned surprise. "Do you think that if we said to your fathers that we ought to put a $2,000 tax on these Hondas and Toyotas that they would like it or not?" The students, who now are caught up in the issue and finally understand it, respond that such a tax would be okay. Larry then goes on to develop the point that imposing such a tax is by no means a simple or clear-cut matter. He asks, for example, what would be the response of the countries who were having their import items taxed?

What Larry is doing is forcing his students, who find concepts like balance of trade and mercantilism irrelevant, to become actively involved through their own experience in these topics. Through clever presentation and manipulation of the subject he makes it relevant and comprehensible. Equally significant is the fact that he shows the students that there are not necessarily clear-cut and obvious answers to complex problems.

> I want the kids to see that the world is not all black and white, that the world is various shades of grey, and that because other people don't agree with us does not necessarily mean that they have the wrong idea. You must appreciate other people's values and other people's cultures and sort of understand why they do things the way they do. If we don't have that kind of idea, we are more and more polarized. This is supposed to be a country of various ideas. That's what makes it great. I really believe that.

Making his students realize that there are many different points of view in the world is one of the most important things Larry tries to convey through his teaching. Equally important to him is the idea of teaching students how to think.

> I like to ask questions that make their heads sort of click and maybe see why people do what they do. Education, I think, is useless if all you do is simply memorize things and stick them in a compartment and regurgitate it when you need it. With most compartments, the material never comes out again. It's lost, but if you can use the material you learn, then it will be with you. But that's hard to do.

Larry feels that a very real tension exists between what he likes to do with the students and what he can do in light of the value system of the community, the practices of his faculty peers, his own lack of training, and the content he has to cover.

Larry sees the community as an obstacle because in his view many of the parents are

> very conservative, straight-laced, white folk who generally say to their kids, "Obey, obey; keep your mouth shut." Then the kids come to class expecting to do that, and somebody says, "Hey, talk about this, talk about that, give me your ideas," and they haven't any.

Larry also sees some of his fellow teachers as working against him. He talks of teachers who underestimate, falsely label, and write off the majority of students who are not academically motivated or college-bound: "I get so tired of hearing 'They can't do this; they can't do that.'" He speaks of those who take the easy way out and say, "Open your heads and I'll pour stuff in."

At the same time, Larry recognizes that neither he nor his fellow teachers were really trained to develop the students' thinking skills.

> I never had a class in how to teach kids to think. I don't ever remember anybody say-ing, even in methods of teaching, here's how to make the kids think; here's how you provoke them; here's how you make those little minds click. It's simply an individual thing that you might have somebody who's interested in that and does it and somebody else who presents simply facts, facts, facts.

Further, he acknowledges that it is easy for any teacher to become preoccupied with covering the material rather than helping students actually learn it. Within the current shortened semester schedule, he finds himself falling into the trap in World History by eliminating provocative projects and simulation games in order "to get to Vietnam."

Without question these obstacles lead to periods of frustration. There are other kinds of occupational dissatisfaction as well. For example, Larry dislikes having to function as a policeman patrolling the halls, the bathrooms, and the cafeteria. Equally annoying is the paper work—reading long essay tests, recording grades. And every now and then Larry, like most other teachers, becomes angry about the relatively low salaries of the teaching profession. Why, he wonders, do people who enter teaching with the idea of doing something good and important have to sacrifice themselves to a lifetime of less than standard professional wages? In his particular case he has felt compelled to work almost every summer as a meat cutter in order to keep his head above water. It irritates him also that meat cutters earn more money than most teachers.

Despite these drawbacks Larry finds the satisfactions of teaching far outweigh the dissatisfactions. First and foremost he talks of the intellectual satisfaction of making students aware of what they need to know to be a good citizen in this democracy. Sometimes this includes what he calls storytelling.

> I don't believe in lectures, but I do believe in storytelling. If you can tell history as a story and see the looks in the kids' eyes, you can see that they are there with you, that's neat, I like that. I like to have the kids on the edge of their seats.

Almost equally as satisfying, however, are the personal relationships. Larry, for example, speaks movingly of a young girl with family and boyfriend problems whom he counseled last year.

I understood when she was down and why. I talked to her about it and explained to her that everybody has these problems periodically. She's been a lot better this year. She came by today to say thank you for understanding and everything. That was sort of neat. You have situations like that which make it satisfying. If I were a meat cutter someplace or an accountant someplace, I wouldn't have that. That's different.

Perhaps the most unanticipated area of satisfaction has been his participation in extracurricular activities. Larry has served as department chair, sponsor of the student council for 9 out of his 11 years, and cosponsor of the Washington, D.C., trip for the past eight years. In addition, Larry has been extremely active in his teacher association, which is a state and local chapter of the National Education Association. He has been president, vice president, chief negotiator, chair of the welfare committee, and editor of the newsletter. Larry says he never really thought about this aspect of teaching before he entered the profession.

When I was getting a master's in history, I never thought about being a student council advisor. I never in my wildest dreams thought I would take people to a big city far away on a bus. That's a lot different. I never thought about being involved in teacher

A student council meeting

organizations where we would try to advance teacher conditions, teachers' salaries, and education. I never dreamed about those kinds of things.

Yet it has been these extracurricular activities that have led to Larry's sense of personal growth in leadership and communication skills and have provided some of his most rewarding experiences. He speaks, for example, enthusiastically of the leadership workshop he and his cosponsor arrange every fall for the new student council.

We go off to a nice little resort for the weekend. We spend the night, and we have workshops and activities and a nice little campfire sensitivity session in the evening. And I'm always real proud of that. I think we do a real good job. The kids get a lot out of it.

He becomes even more animated when he describes the Washington trips he has led for the last eight years.

Larry and his students with Congressman Gephardt

That is teaching on a school bus, which is fantastic for me, because I'm a tour guide. Before we see Mr. Eagleton or Congressman Gephardt we talk about what they do, and we're going to meet them tomorrow, so we have to talk about what kind of questions we're going to ask them and, boy, the kids all of a sudden get really interested because we have to talk to them. When we go to Gettysburg we can see the spots that I teach about in school. That's really neat to me. I really like that. Of course, the organization and management of taking 30 kids 1,000 miles and back, and have them really come back with a good feeling, having learned a lot, that's something really special to me.

The truth of the matter is, however, that whether on a school bus to Washington or within a self-contained classroom in Hillsboro, Larry has an image of teaching that involves widening his students' horizons through active experience. For example, in trying to convey what he is for and against in terms of teaching style, he uses the extended metaphor of a river trip.

I have a colleague who teaches as though he's on the Delta Queen [a paddle-wheel riverboat] and we're all sitting here on the Delta Queen. He's got the microphone in his hand, and he's talking about over here is this and over there is that, and everybody's just sitting there looking back and forth. When I think of myself, and I hope—you know I don't always do this—my kids are in the canoe, and they're coming down the stream, and we go along the routes where it's somewhat wavy, and we go along the rapids, and they turn over sometimes. You've got to let them turn over and get wet and paddle back upstream sometimes, go back through a little obstacle here, but along the way, they're going to experience that river much more than somebody who's on the Delta Queen, who's just listening.

Those experiences seem to have an impact on his students, and Larry gets the feeling that "something has clicked," that "what I want to get across gets across. That's a good day!" Of course, arranging those kinds of experiences requires ongoing effort.

I'm always thinking. I take a shower in the morning, and I'm thinking. There will be times when I'll be sitting at my desk, I've got to walk from my desk up to the podium, and I'm still thinking how am I going to introduce it? I've found that those usually work better. The improvisations seem to go better than when I write it on a sheet of paper. That's fine, and that's good, but I think it's more natural if you improvise somewhat and go with it. That might sound very unprofessional, but . . . that's the way I teach too. I don't teach in a straight line. I think that is sometimes bad for the students. I teach in crooked lines; I bounce here and there. I'm trying to weave it all together somehow. I think if you teach in a straight line—next time you take a trip on a highway, the interstates are very boring usually. If you go off the highway and go along the little curves here and there and go down the hills and back up the hills it's more interesting; it keeps you awake more. . . . I think teaching is like that.

Students in Larry's class

And as Larry works to make school interesting for his students, he clearly makes it interesting and fun for himself as well.

> I have fun just talking to students. I have fun in the classroom; I really do. There are things we can teach, even things that aren't really the topic; we'll have discussions and jokes. I'll joke with the kids. That's fun. Relating with the other teachers is fun. Participating in various things the school does is fun. It's much more fun than, say, working as a meat cutter. I don't get a big thrill out of telling dirty jokes to the other guys with a saw. I don't get a thrill out of making comments about the people out there shopping. I do have fun here. I've had other jobs. I used to work for the highway department. I've worked for the agriculture department for a little while. This is much more interesting, much more fun.

Teacher burnout? Not for Larry Wells; at least not now. He's too busy taking his students off the boring highways and exploring the hills and curves; he's too busy leading canoe trips down the river, battling the rapids, and paddling upstream; he's too busy having fun.

JACQUIE YOURIST: AN ACTRESS IN AN INNER-CITY DRAMA

Community Context

It is 6:45 A.M. As Jacquie Yourist and her rider, Grace, drive from the suburbs toward the city of Miami and Robert E. Lee Junior High School, they listen intently to the news on the radio. The big story today as it has been for weeks is the Luis Alvarez trial. The announcer reviews the latest testimony from the trial and then summarizes the precautions being taken by the Miami Police Department to minimize the effects of riots expected if the verdict is not guilty.

Luis Alvarez is a Miami police officer accused of gross negligence in the December 28, 1982, shooting of Nevell Johnson, Jr., in the Overtown Video Arcade. Johnson had stolen a .22 caliber revolver and was carrying it in his waistband when a conflict between the two men started. Alvarez claims self-defense, arguing that Johnson was reaching for his revolver and that he shot first to protect himself. The shooting sparked three days of civil disturbance in downtown Miami.

Jacquie and Grace are extremely interested in the trial developments because they teach in the part of Miami where renewed rioting is predicted. The principal of their school has already called a faculty meeting to discuss procedures if rioting should begin and to establish a code phrase that will be read over the PA system to alert teachers to implement those procedures.

Jacquie's rider is agitated by the possibility of trouble. Jacquie appears to share her concern but is at the same time much calmer. She talks of her previous experiences with violence stemming from gang fighting, and she expresses some confidence in the students themselves. Soon an editorial comes over the radio that captures their attention once again. The speaker is denouncing the media for exacerbating the public hysteria surrounding the trial. He argues that the constant talk of riots makes them almost inevitable. Whether Jacquie and Grace are victims of media hype or harsh realities is not exactly clear. What is clear, however, is that they both head toward school this morning with the threat of violence hanging over their heads.

Did Jacquie's teacher education program prepare her for teaching in an inner-city school in what is considered to be a tough neighborhood? Had she much previous experience with the Cuban refugees, Haitians, and Black Americans who live in this neighborhood and work, when they can, in the nearby, low-paying, garment factories? The answer in each case is a resounding "No."

Jacquie moved to Miami directly from a teaching position in an upper-middle-class suburban district outside of Toledo, Ohio. She had done her student teaching in a junior high school in that district — Sylvania City Schools — and she was hired

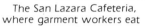

The San Lazara Cafeteria,
where garment workers eat

Houses in the Robert E. Lee
Junior High School neighborhood

as a first-year teacher there to take over the job of her cooperating teacher who moved to the high school.

High expectations reigned in Sylvania City Schools. The students were college-bound and the parents took an active interest in the quality of preparation their children were receiving. A brand-new language lab and tape system were installed in her building while she was there, so her facilities were excellent.

Robert E. Lee Junior High School

When Jacquie first arrived in Miami she found employment as a substitute teacher in the city schools. One year later, however, she was hired at Robert E. Lee Junior High School to teach French and Spanish. Robert E. Lee Junior High School is a very old, rundown but architecturally beautiful Spanish-style structure built in 1924. The three-story white stucco building, which forms a square around a big courtyard, has a red ceramic tile roof and large archways. The white stucco walls are yellowed and cracked, and the roof has many broken and missing tiles. Each side of the square opens onto the brick patio of the courtyard that is lined with palm trees and bushes. Some of the grounds seem in need of more care. The hallways and walkways are all open air, and when standing in the courtyard during the early morning hours, the feeling is that of a past-its-prime, deteriorated but charming resort hotel.

Around 8:45 A.M. as the hallways and courtyard begin to fill with students, the resort ambience begins to fade. A walk through the building a few minutes later completely destroys the earlier image. All along the hallways are traditional-looking classrooms. The rooms have been recently painted a medium blue and the darker blue desks lined in rows suggest some current effort to brighten the school atmosphere. Like Jacquie, a number of teachers come early to do paper work, and they can be seen working at their desks or talking to a few students who are hang-

Robert E. Lee Junior High School

ing out nearby. At one end of the first floor is a cafeteria where students on welfare are eating a free breakfast.

The students are neatly dressed but not stylishly so. Brightly colored T-shirts or blouses with slacks or jeans are the norm but not the designer variety. Almost all of the students are dark-skinned, but since there is a mix of Hispanics, black Americans, and Haitians, there are considerable differences in skin tone. Forty-four percent of the students are black, 53 percent are Hispanic, and 3 percent are white, non-Hispanic (see Figure 4.1).

Students who are here today, however, may be gone tomorrow, for Robert E. Lee Junior High School has one of the poorest attendance rates in the area. Average daily attendance for Grades 7 through 9 for the 1982–1983 school year was 86.6 percent. Nearly 60 percent of the students are enrolled in the free/reduced price lunch program. Over 16 percent of the students have limited proficiency in English.

For Jacquie, Robert E. Lee was at first almost shockingly different from her school in suburban Toledo. She remembers well the difficult transition.

I'll never forget the first day that I taught at my school. We were on the same pathway as the Miami International Airport, and the planes flew right overhead, and I thought they were going to crash into the school. You just had to stop class, what you were saying, and let the planes go over. Oh, there were so many things that were different. . . . The black and Hispanic cultures were virtually unknown to me. . . . The school was very old. . . . At one time it was very stylish. . . . It's a beautiful school; it's just that they haven't kept it up

ROBERT E. LEE JUNIOR

LOCATION NUMBER: 6371

ADDRESS: 3100 NW 5 Ave., Miami   PRINCIPAL: WILLIAM R. JONES   GRADE ORGANIZATION: 7–9
PHONE: 576-2424   AREA: NORTH CENTRAL   CONGRESSIONAL DISTRICT: 18

SCHOOL CHARACTERISTICS, 1983-84

EXCEPTIONAL STUDENT CENTER: NO	ADULT SCHOOL: NO	TRADITIONAL BASIC SKILLS: NO
COMMUNITY SCHOOL: NO	COMPREHENSIVE HIGH SCHOOL: NO	CHAPTER I: YES
		AFTER SCHOOL CARE: NO
DATE SCHOOL ESTABLISHED: 1924	PERCENT OF UTILIZATION PERMANENT FACILITY: 86	SCHOOL/PARK SITE: YES
NUMBER OF ACRES: 8.26	ASSIGNED PROGRAM CAPACITY: 939	NO. OF STUDENTS TRANSPORTED: 27
		NUMBER OF INSTRUCTIONAL
LIBRARY MEDIA ITEMS PER PUPIL: 16 (1982-83)	BOOKS CIRCULATED PER PUPIL: 2 (1982-83)	MICROCOMPUTERS: 0

STAFF CHARACTERISTICS, 1983-84

	WHITE NON-HISPANIC		BLACK NON-HISPANIC		HISPANIC		ASIAN/AMERICAN INDIAN		TOTAL	MALE	FEMALE
	NO.	%	NO.	%	NO.	%	NO.	%	NO.	NO.	NO.
PRINCIPAL			1	100					1	1	
ASSISTANT PRINCIPAL			1	50	1	50			2	1	1
COMMUNITY SCHOOL COORDINATOR											
CLASSROOM TEACHERS	15	41	11	30	10	27	1	3	37	14	23
EXCEPTIONAL STUDENT TEACHERS	4	50	3	38	1	13			8	2	6
GUIDANCE COUNSELORS			3	100					3	1	2
LIBRARIANS	1	100							1		1
TEACHER AIDES			3	100					3		3
CLERICAL/SECRETARIES			3	60	2	40			5		5
CUSTODIANS/SERVICE WORKERS			4	67	2	33			6	6	
OTHER											
TOTAL FULL-TIME STAFF	20	30	29	44	16	24	1	2	66	25	41
TOTAL PART-TIME STAFF	5	16	12	38	15	47			32	3	29

NUMBER OF BEGINNING TEACHERS: 0   PERCENTAGE OF INSTRUCTIONAL STAFF WITH MASTERS DEGREE: 39   AVERAGE SALARY FOR INSTRUCTIONAL STAFF: $20146.85

REGULAR PROGRAM
PUPIL/TEACHER RATIO: 22:1   PERCENTAGE OF INSTRUCTIONAL STAFF WITH SPECIALISTS DEGREE: 0

EXCEPTIONAL STUDENT PROGRAM
PUPIL/TEACHER RATIO: 9:

AVERAGE YEARS TEACHING IN FLORIDA: 7   PERCENTAGE OF INSTRUCTIONAL STAFF WITH DOCTORS DEGREE: 0

TEACHER SALARY RANGE	NUMBER
$14–18,999	19
$19–23,999	21
$24–28,999	5
$29,000 +	

STUDENT CHARACTERISTICS

STUDENT MEMBERSHIP, 1983-84

GRADE	WHITE NON-HISPANIC NO.	%	BLACK NON-HISPANIC NO.	%	HISPANIC NO.	%	ASIAN/AMERICAN INDIAN NO.	%	TOTAL NO.	% NOT PROMOTED 1982–83	DROP-OUT RATE 1982–83
7	14	3	201	47	213	50			428	37.1	
8	9	4	112	44	132	52			253	20.1	
9	3	1	95	39	147	60			245	12.6	
OTHER											
TOTAL	25	3	409	44	492	53			926		

SUBJECT AREA INFORMATION

SUBJECT AREA	AVG. CLASS SIZE	# OF PUPILS IN A.P. COURSES	# OF PUPILS IN ADV. COURSES
MATH	22.1		
SCIENCE	32.6		18
LANGUAGE ARTS	23.0		
SOCIAL STUDIES	35.1		
FOREIGN LANG.	25.0		
ART	26.8		
MUSIC	36.0		
PHYSICAL ED.	53.5		

TOTAL FULL-TIME EQUIVALENT STUDENTS & AVERAGE COST 1982–83

	NO.	%	AVG. COST PER FTE
BASIC EDUCATION	664.09	71	$1819.71
EXCEPTIONAL STUDENT	43.59	5	4552.19
EDUCATIONAL ALTERNATIVE	90.39	10	
VOCATIONAL EDUCATION	137.79	15	1993.73

PERCENT OF STUDENTS WITH LIMITED ENGLISH PROFICIENCY: 16.2

NUMBER OF GRADUATES, 1982–83

STANDARD DIPLOMA
CERTIFICATE OF COMPLETION
EXCEPTIONAL STUDENT DIPLOMA
TOTAL

PERCENT FREE/REDUCED LUNCH: 59.3

% OF ATTENDANCE: 7–9   86.6 (1982-83)

NO. OF STUDENTS WITH OUT-OF-SCHOOL SUSPENSIONS, 1982–83: 61

NO. OF STUDENTS REFERRED TO ALTERNATIVE EDUCATION, 1982–83: 14

NO. OF STUDENTS RECEIVING CORPORAL PUNISHMENT, 1982–83: 172

STUDENT ACHIEVEMENT

STANFORD ACHIEVEMENT TEST SEVENTH EDITION APRIL 1983 ADMINISTRATION

GRADE	NUMBER TESTED	MEDIAN PERCENTILE READING COMPREHENSION	MATHEMATICS COMPUTATION	MATHEMATICS CONCEPTS	MATHEMATICS APPLICATIONS
7	231	16	19	24	16
8	190	22	26	21	15
9	145	26	40	26	17
ALL GRADES	553	22	25	21	16

STATEWIDE STUDENT ASSESSMENT TEST OCTOBER 1983 BASIC SKILLS – PART I AVERAGE PERCENT MASTERY

GRADE	READING	WRITING	MATHEMATICS
8	89	87	75

APRIL 1983
GRADE 10 – PART II
PERCENT PASSING

COMMUNICATION	MATHEMATICS
65	

6371

NOTE: FOR EXPLANATORY NOTES PLEASE SEE PAGE i.

M.I.S. 23084 (10-83)

Figure 4.1   Robert E. Lee Junior High School profile

too well. At least when I arrived it was badly in need of paint. Since then they've fixed it up a bit, but still there are very few supplies. There was one set of books to be used for all classes. Students were not allowed to take them home, and that was one thing that I was really shocked about because before it was just understood that the student would have a book to take home for homework. In the beginning I was really, really fearful because the school had a very bad reputation—I think it developed that reputation back in the time of integration where there were all sorts of riots and protests. It still has a bad reputation today.

Over the years, however, Jacquie has grown to prefer her position at Robert E. Lee to her former one. One reason that she gives is that she genuinely enjoys her students. An early morning visit to her classroom immediately validates that fact. Just before first-hour class each morning Jacquie stands out in the open-air hallway in front of her room and welcomes students with enthusiasm and warmth. Tall, slender, blond, and elegantly but simply dressed, Jacquie looks very much like a high-fashion model, but her special word or two to each student who enters is clearly the manner of a caring teacher.

First Hour: Act I

When the bell rings Jacquie moves quickly inside and greets the class as a whole in French. The students stand politely until she tells them in French to sit down. In fact, from beginning to end, Jacquie conducts almost the entire class in French, even though these are first-year students. And from the beginning to end the pace is lively, fast, and often pure fun.

For example, on one unusually chilly Miami morning (the temperature was about 60 degrees and many of the youngsters came to school in fur-lined parkas) Jacquie begins class with banter about the weather. Then, noticing that one girl has a stuffed animal she stops, picks up the animal, and starts asking questions about its name and dress. The students are clearly amused. Then she shifts from the dress of the animal to the color of their clothing. Calling on individuals she asks them to name the color of their shoes, shirts, and sweaters. When students make a mistake she feigns great disbelief. When they are correct she feigns great ecstasy. No matter what the student response, Jacquie replies with exaggerated facial expressions and good humor. Quickly she moves to the board and writes various colors in English words and asks them to respond in chorus with the appropriate French word. Jacquie then shifts the questioning to sports. She asks: "Do you like football?" "Do you like baseball?" "Are you a good tennis player?" Next she moves the students to the text and the unit on sports. After reviewing the vocabulary she asks more questions, like "Which is your favorite professional football team?" As she calls on students she moves around, playfully pushing the jacket hood off of one student, showing the proper page to another who is not paying attention. When students respond incorrectly she probes to help them find the right answer. When they try to respond by

Jacquie teaching French

simply nodding their heads or giving a yes or no answer (in French), she refuses to accept it. Instead she insists, "You have to give me some information."

Her movement, her facial expressions, her good humor, her high expectations, and her "withitness" almost seem to mesmerize her audience. They follow her; they laugh with her; they respond to her. The sheer variety of activities are also involving for the students. They do a conversation followed by a verb conjugation contest at the chalkboard, followed by an exercise in which students first supply verb endings on the board and then practice them individually at their seats.

One of the sentences that Jacquie has created for the board is "*Charles aim__* [loves] *Marie.*" Everyone laughs because Charles and Marie are students in the class. Marie blushes. Charles is absent, and Jacquie jokes about how she never could have gotten away with it if he had been there.

During the last portion of the period she reviews the parts of the body and then leads them in singing the French song Alouette. In the middle of the song the bell rings, but Jacquie doesn't stop. She keeps singing but waves goodbye. The students gather their books and file out singing and waving back. Obviously a good time was had by all. Jacquie not only taught, she performed. The students not only learned, they were entertained.

Offstage Activities

Directly after first period each day Jacquie walks downstairs to the main office where she supervises student announcement of activities. In addition to teaching French, Spanish, and history Jacquie is coordinator of student activities at Robert E. Lee. According to Jacquie this position has now become the principal reason for her job satisfaction. The responsibilities of the activities coordinator are many and varied, and the supervision of student announcements is perhaps the smallest part. Jacquie explains the substance and status of this extracurricular position in these terms.

> I assist the principal, direct the activities program. I coordinate and schedule club activities. My student council is responsible for most of the major activities — fund raising for schoolwide events; social activities, like dances and the prom for ninth graders; charitable ones, like the United Way; helping initiate new clubs; promoting school spirit and pride. . . . This year I'm in charge of the newspaper, which I use as a means of unifying the school and boostering morale of students and teachers. . . . In my school you have the administrative staff, and the guidance staff, and then you have me. I'm kind of in between a classroom teacher and an administrator.

The activities that Jacquie directs seem to get as much of her creative energy as her classes do. During Spirit Week, for example, students could participate in twin

Jacquie supervising morning announcements

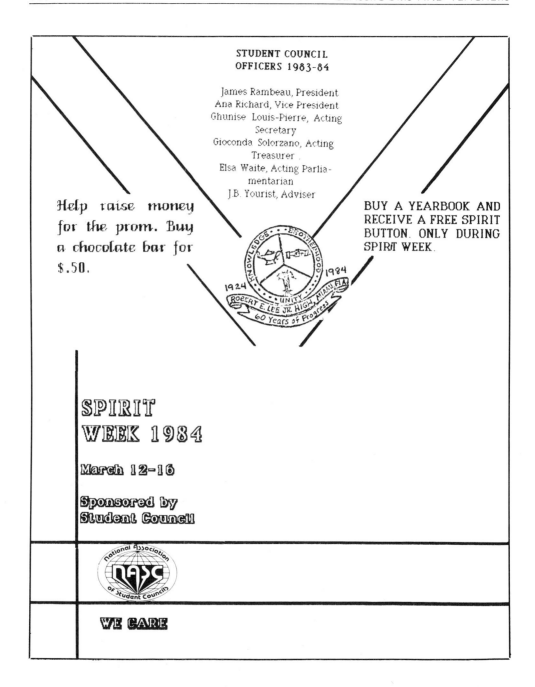

STUDENT COUNCIL
OFFICERS 1983-84

James Rambeau, President
Ana Richard, Vice President
Ghunise Louis-Pierre, Acting
Secretary
Gioconda Solorzano, Acting
Treasurer
Elsa Waite, Acting Parlia-
mentarian
J.B. Yourist, Adviser

Help raise money
for the prom. Buy
a chocolate bar for
$.50.

BUY A YEARBOOK AND
RECEIVE A FREE SPIRIT
BUTTON. ONLY DURING
SPIRIT WEEK.

SPIRIT
WEEK 1984

March 12-16

Sponsored by
Student Council

WE CARE

MONDAY, MARCH 12
TWIN DAY

Dress up with your friends as identical twins, triplets, etc. The most original group will be featured in the next issue of the **TRAVELLER**.

Marriage licenses will be on sale in the patio during lunch for $.50. (A license must be purchased in order to be married on Wednesday.)

TUESDAY, MARCH 13
HAT/ T-SHIRT DAY

Special permission has been granted to wear hats today. Combine your favorite hat with the T-shirt of your favorite team and be a winner on this day.

Marriage licenses will be on sale period 4. $.50 includes the rings and certificate. (The license will serve as a pass to leave class or the cafeteria to be married on Wednesday.)

WEDNESDAY, MARCH 14
DRESS UP DAY
WEDDING DAY

Students and staff are invited to dress up in their best clothes today.

Marriages will be performed during fourth period in the patio for those who have purchased a license. (No licenses sold today.) The license will serve as a pass to come to the patio at the appointed time to be married. (So don't lose the license.) Bigamy and polygamy are allowed.

THURSDAY, MARCH 15
60's DAY

Go back in time and dress as in the 1960's. For example:

GIRLS: straight skirts and white tennis shoes, sheath dress (like the wedge), mini-skirts, ethnic outfits (Indian, peasant skirts and blouses, African), beads, headbands, faded jeans, patches, T-shirts, peace symbols, "Preppie" look.
BOYS: ethnic looks, faded jeans, T-shirts, necklaces, headbands, also "Preppie" look.

FRIDAY, MARCH 16
PUNK ROCK DAY

Jump from the 60's to the present. Wear your leather and metal and prepare to enjoy the grand finale of Spirit Week '84 with a musical review of music from the 40's to the present. Presented by Miami Dade Community College at a time to be announced.

Schedule for Spirit Week at Robert E. Lee Junior High School

Traveller
SPECIAL EDITION

VOL. 30 NO. 5   JUNE, 1984

RAMBEAU, DIAZ, THOMPSON TAKE TOP HONORS

The 1984 awards assembly was held in the school auditorium on Tuesday, June 5 at 10:00. The following students received awards:

American Legion: Maria Diaz, James Rambeau, (runners-up: G. Louis-Pierre, R. Valencia)
Band: Denise Fulton, Deborah Stewart, Francis Bustos
Chorus: Jacqueline Miller
Drama: Vanessa Garnett
Debate: James Rambeau
Exceptional Education: Martin Anzola, Lenny Navarro, Marisol Rodriguez
Fine Arts: Alex Castro
Foreign Language: Fritz Octavien
Journalism: Maria Diaz
Language Arts: Henrietta Larkin, Itria Cruz, Robert Valencia, Keina Mcintyre (Ch.I), Marvin Lopez (E.S.O.L.)
Mathematics: Henrietta Larkin, Elsa Waite, Ghunise Louis-Pierre, Wilson Tinoco (Ch.I)

Maria Diaz and James Rambeau, winners of the American Legion Award

Physical Education: Rosanna Hernandez, Candelario Exposito
Science: Hector Cortez, Elsa Waite, Maria Diaz
Social Studies: Elsa Waite, Ghunise Louis-Pierre
Vocational: Marcella Broomfield, Ronald Kendrick, Pamela Hall, Martin Anzola, Ivan Espana
Playwriting awards: James Rambeau, Francis Bustos
Spelling Bee: Elsa Waite
Turnabout awards: Marcos Hoyos, Mr. Litt
United Way award: Ms.Link
Outstanding Athletes: Henrietta Larkin, Clifton Brown
Perfect Attendance: 2 years- Clifton Brown, Sonza Brown, Bernard Forges, 3 years-James Rambeau
Outstanding Service: Ana Richard, James Rambeau
Outstanding Citizenship: Elsa Waite, James Rambeau
Principal's Scholastic Awards: 7- Henrietta Larkin, 8- Itria Cruz, 9-Sherrell Thompson
Teacher of the Year: Mr. George

Itria Cruz, Sherrell Thompson, and Henrietta Larkin received the Principal's Scholastic Awards for highest grade point average.

The front page of the school newspaper edited by Jacquie and her students

day, hat-shirt day, dress-up–wedding day, 1960s day, and punk rock day. Students who brought marriage licenses on Monday or Tuesday could have a marriage ceremony performed in the courtyard on Wednesday. The newspaper she sponsors is equally interesting and highly impressive for a junior high school staff — 14 pages of features, activities, editorials, entertainment, sports, and student council news as well as two pages of photographs.

In addition to enjoying the creative and administrative aspects of the position, Jacquie strongly believes that it accords her special respect from the students.

> It really became my main reason for teaching. I give credit to my principal, Mr. William Jones, for suggesting that I take over student activities in 1981. Otherwise, it would never have occurred to me to undertake the position and the responsibilities. He has always supported and encouraged all my crazy ideas. I now think that this is why I have survived so happily at this school—the support from the principal along with the respect I receive from the students. . . . They often treat me differently from a regular. . . . I'm the one who organizes the major activities. . . . Of course, they don't want to get me angry or upset because I might say no. . . . I like the extra duties and the respect I get from the students because of that particular position, and I don't know that I would want to give it up.

Teaching as Acting

Jacquie's commitment to enjoying her students and making teaching fun has been with her from the very beginning when she observed her cooperating teacher in action.

> She was such an interesting teacher, she taught me everything I know, and she was just so helpful in the way she taught it to me—and such a good example. She made the students interested, and they loved her. She was almost like an actress in front of the classroom. She'd stub her toe and then swear in French. The kids learned a vocabulary word and were likely to remember it, too. It wasn't always by the book and that was probably what made it so interesting. Oh, she would have French dinners, and she would do all kinds of interesting things with the French Club. We both took students to France one time and it was just lots of fun. I realized then that you could make teaching fun, and now when I can't have fun in the classroom while teaching, I don't enjoy myself at all. It's especially important at junior high level where the students have such a short attention span. She taught me to enjoy teaching. I feel that the students are so perceptive, that on the days that I don't feel like being an actress they can sense that. But, in general, if they think you're having fun in the classroom then they know that you're not just there for the money.

Just as Jacquie initially admired her cooperating teacher because she was almost like an actress, she now has come to think of herself in the same terms.

> I've learned that I'm probably a frustrated actress because I enjoy being in front of a group and having an audience, which I never, never would have considered, ever. I was always very, very shy and deathly afraid of getting in front of a classroom, and in the last five years or so, I've just loved getting in front of a classroom to talk and teach.

Friday 21, 82
May.

To: Mrs. Youriot,

I just wanted to thank you for all you have done for us at Robert E. Lee. If it weren't for you where would we be now. (home maybe?)

Mrs. Youriot like you say proms are something to remember, well I'll tell you one thing, we won't only remember the memories of our prom, but also the memories of you "Mrs. J. Youriot" and all you have done for us.

Thank you!
Love always
Lelis Del'Castillo
Henry Roberts
Darren Fulton
Jim Perz
Rodrick C. Campbell
R.C. Anderson
Melisa Pinder
Laura Jackson

We
Love
you!

Letter to Jacquie from her students

In fact, Jacquie feels like a different person when she's at school or in the company of teachers.

I'm a totally different person at school than any place else. For the most part, most of my husband's friends have always been in the scientific field, and I have no one to talk to usually, and so I'm usually very, very quiet. But I'm totally different when I get together with other teachers. We have one friend who's a teacher at a school even worse than mine. He really had problems with discipline and the guns and rapes and everything, and occasionally he's come over to our house, and we'll have 25 people all of whom are in research or are doctors, and then this one teacher and I will get off in a corner and talk. You know, we'll talk and talk and talk and talk, and they have to come and pull us away.

Without question, through a career of teaching Jacquie has found a meaningful way to express herself as a full human being. At the same time she has found a forum for influencing and broadening the perspectives of young adolescents.

The junior high age group is very, very vulnerable, very impressionable. The kids that I deal with really have little concept of anything except themselves and their families day to day, the foods they like, the movie stars, the magazines. In teaching French and Spanish I hope that I teach them a little about other people and other cultures and civilizations, so they can develop an idea of their own world in perspective to these other faraway places. Also, especially in Miami, I want to develop an appreciation of people with different cultures and different backgrounds. This is what some of them really need because there are so many different nationalities down here. So I like to think that I teach them a little about other people and a little about the world and how other people may have different customs.

I often think about—every year—how many people I really touch. And if, let's say I have 60 French students, I'm lucky if there are 5 who have really excelled and who are going to go on with French in high school, and maybe pick up a third or a fourth language.

The rest of them I think just get a general background. They leave, and I don't think they usually go on beyond their first or second year, but many times they'll come back to visit me years later and they'll say, "Oh, I didn't take any more French, but I found myself in a French restaurant, and I remembered how to say this and that." I had one boy who came back to tell me that in the army they had asked him what country he wanted to go to, and he remembered me talking about Germany one day, and he said, "Germany." So that's where he was sent.

And through it all Jacquie has been fortunate enough to experience the recognition and the applause reserved for those who give outstanding performances. In 1982 she was selected Teacher of the Year for Robert E. Lee Junior High, and this honor has been the highlight of her teaching career to date. In her words: "This was my proudest moment. The student body gave me a standing ovation that I'll never forget."

When Jacquie Yourist heads for her car each afternoon it is usually quite late. She has supervised several club meetings after school and perhaps led a majorette practice. She is tired, but in all probability she will be returning that evening for some kind of play or debate team rehearsal. Her thoughts as she drives home are not lofty ones — she doesn't think about how she has influenced and broadened her students but about how she will get through tomorrow. The reality is, however, that she has brightened the lives and expanded the horizons of every student she saw during the day. It has been a remarkable performance, and it will be repeated throughout the day tomorrow and the day after.

CONCLUSION

Chapter 2 presented some questions and some answers designed to help you begin to contrast and compare Ruth's and Luberta's elementary classrooms and to see how context in particular might affect teacher thought and action. At the end of Chapter 2 we posed some questions designed to help you think about how individual teachers' personal qualities and beliefs might also affect their classroom behavior. Chapter 3 posed a similar set of questions on the teacher as individual and the context to be used in your own fieldwork.

Now we offer you an opportunity to develop and practice your data-gathering and analysis skills on the three secondary cases just presented. The task is as follows:

1. Look at the questions on the teacher as an individual and on context on pp. 94–95 in Chapter 3.
2. Look through the three secondary cases and try to answer as many questions as you can for *each case* with the available data. (For some of the questions, there will not be data in the case studies.) Put your answers in writing.
3. Once you have notes on the questions for *each case*, answer the following questions:
   a. What are the differences that set the three secondary teachers and their contexts apart?
   b. What are the commonalities that hold these three teachers and their contexts together?
   c. Are there any characteristics of teaching excellence that you believe they share?
   d. Are there any characteristics of teaching excellence that all five teachers share?
   e. What conclusions can you reach thus far about the nature of secondary teaching as it differs from elementary teaching?

By now you may have recognized that this data-gathering and analysis task is more difficult that the one in Chapter 2 for the following reasons: there are three cases instead of two; there are more questions and less specific data; there are no answers listed to help guide you. However, participating in this more challenging exercise is a necessary second step on your way to becoming a skilled participant observer.

DISCUSSION QUESTIONS

The concluding pages of this chapter suggested a lengthy writing and discussion assignment that involves questions on both the individual and contextual dimensions of teaching with each of the secondary school teachers. In addition, there are questions that ask you to compare each of the secondary school teachers with one another. An overarching question regarding the definition of excellence in teaching is also posed with all five of the case study teachers.

The questions that follow focus on the nature of secondary school teaching as revealed by the classrooms of Sandy, Larry, and Jacquie. These questions are the counterparts of those regarding the nature of teaching at the elementary level found at the end of Chapter 2.

1. Using the three case studies what does the day-to-day life of a secondary school teacher look like? What are the principal activities? What are the pleasures? What are the problems?

2. What are the implications for teachers like Sandy, Larry, and Jacquie in terms of their working with different groups of students for short periods of time during the day? Do you think that it is important that as adults they spend most of their working day with adolescents rather than with other adults? How is this different from other professions you might have considered? How is it different from working with students at the elementary school level? What are the advantages or disadvantages of the situation?

3. Think back to your own secondary school experience. What would you have liked or disliked about having Sandy, Larry, or Jacquie as one of your teachers?

4. What do you think is unique, if anything, with Sandy's, Larry's, and Jacquie's teaching that is a result of their working in a secondary versus an elementary setting?

5. To what extent do you think your own views of education and the teaching profession have been shaped by your secondary school experience?

PART TWO

LEARNING ENVIRONMENTS
Physical, Social, Intellectual, and Personal

Part II provides an in-depth and analytic examination of the role of the teacher. The thesis is that to be a teacher is to be responsible for creating physical, social, intellectual, and personal environments for teaching. Chapter 5 discusses how teachers can control the physical space they are given. Chapters 6 and 7 examine the teacher decisions related to the social environment with an emphasis on the establishment of a classroom social system and the use of classroom authority and control. Chapters 8 and 9 focus on the teacher's role in creating an intellectual environment through curricular and instructional decision making. Chapter 10 considers the role of the teacher in developing a personal environment which fosters both student and teacher growth. The analysis is punctuated with concrete examples drawn from the case studies of Part I and concludes with an attempt to define excellence in teaching in Chapter 11. End-of-chapter observation guides extend the analysis into the realm of field experience.

5

THE PHYSICAL ENVIRONMENT FOR TEACHING AND LEARNING

INTRODUCTION

The physical environment of a classroom and of a school plays a significant role in the process of teaching and learning. All teachers must come to terms not only with the community environments that surround them but also with the physical and the social space within their workplaces. Teachers, however, have no control over the design of buildings that house them and the structural subdivision of that space into their classrooms. School buildings frequently span several generations and reflect in the design of each addition the values and curricular innovations popular at the time of construction. Despite these limitations, there are ways that teachers can control elements of their work space to create a more effective environment for teaching and learning.

School buildings and classrooms are such familiar places that people tend to overlook how they may influence what teachers and students can or cannot do. The average student spends 14,000 hours sitting in classrooms by the time he or she completes high school. The typical teacher, if he or she has a career lasting 25

This chapter was written with the assistance of Thomas Cooper, Chief Site Architect, Florida International University. Several of the ideas for activities at the conclusion of this chapter were suggested by Carol Weinstein of Rutgers University.

or 30 years, spends perhaps three or four times that long in classroom settings. Moreover, the basic design and layout of classrooms has changed relatively little over the course of time. A twentieth-century schoolroom looks much like its nineteenth-century counterpart. A contemporary first-grade classroom is not significantly different from a twelfth-grade mathematics classroom, except for desk size. As Smith (1971) has observed:

> For twelve years or more kids inhabit a sequence of virtually identical rooms — teachers change, classmates change, the school changes, courses and teaching methods may change, but not the classroom itself. (p.28)

As a result there is a tendency to become so used to the classroom environment that teachers became insensitive to its subtleties and alternate possibilities.

In order to develop an understanding of the possibilities as well as the limitations of the typical classroom many different factors must be taken into account. The location of the school (i.e., geographical region, type of community, and neighborhood); the design of the building (number of stories, physical materials used in construction, and type of construction); the physical relationship of a classroom to other parts of the school (to the main office, to similar grade or subject

An elementary classroom in St. Louis, 1904

An elementary classroom in St. Louis, 1930

classrooms, and to exits and entrances); the layout and decor of the classroom itself (arrangement of desks, number of windows, and decorations on a bulletin board) are all factors that define what can or cannot be done in the classroom (Delamont, 1983, p. 33).

This chapter examines how some of these physical and social characteristics affect what it means to be a student and teacher. As you read, one overriding question should be kept in mind: Over what elements of the physical environment does the teacher possess or lack control?

SCHOOL BUILDING INFLUENCES ON HUMAN BEHAVIOR

Despite the fact that many people are concerned today with treatment of the natural environment, there is a tendency to pay little attention to the effect of the man-made environment. Relatively little attention is paid to school architecture by either educational theorists or teachers. Yet, how a school building is designed can critically influence the behavior of students, teachers, and administrators. Winston Churchill summarized this matter very well: "We shape our buildings and they shape us" (Hall, 1966, p.106). This is certainly the case in school architecture. The

Luberta's elementary class in St. Louis, 1984

following vignette shows how the design of a school building or classroom shapes the social and cultural experience of those teaching and those who are taught.

Several years ago one of the authors of this text went to visit his father, a principal in a large suburban high school. Before leaving the building for lunch, the author's father took a short walk. The author later reflected on this "short walk."

We walked through the entire building—a considerable distance in a school of nearly two thousand. We talked as we walked along, and I became aware that my father was subtly looking through the windows on the side of each of the doors of the classrooms. Because of the window design, it was easy to see what was going on in the class. It was difficult, however, for the students or the teacher to see out.

Occasionally a teacher at the front of the classroom would look straight out the window and nod in recognition at my father. The students had no way of knowing that we were there. Suddenly I realized how common this type of window is in classroom doors. I thought back to my own high school experience. Instead of a window at one side of the door, there was a large 3′ × 3′ window in the top half of the door. Once again, it was much easier to see in than out of those windows.

After observing my father and questioning him about why and when he took his walks through the building, I realized that the windows on the sides of the classroom doors strongly influenced his administrative behavior. By allowing him to look inside the classroom as he walked around, they made it possible for him quickly to check for problems without interrupting classes. His teaching staff was aware that he was around should a problem arise and that from time to time they were being observed.

I thought about classroom doors at the university. Almost none of them had windows. This fact caused me to wonder whether, in fact, university professors had a stronger tradition of autonomy, or being left alone in terms of their teaching, than elementary and secondary school teachers.

The inclusion of windows in the doors of classrooms may seem a somewhat trivial architectural issue. Yet such features may influence what and how things are taught and learned to a much greater degree than one at first realizes. Certainly the type and placement of windows in doors is related to administrative control. One of the principals in Sandy's high school discussed how he took numerous tours of the very large building, gazing through the slit windows as he monitored the halls. Over the hours, days, weeks, and years of his tours he gained concrete and consistent information on at least one aspect of teacher performance. He simply looked for the number of students with heads on desks — concrete evidence of disengaged potential learners. Some teachers never had heads down. Others had a regular cadre of students in such poses, every hour, every day, every week, every year. The placement of windows allowed him to make continual, unobtrusive evaluations of teacher performance (see Figure 5.1).

THE CLASSROOM AS A PHYSICAL ENVIRONMENT

A school building is a man-made environment. What goes on in it is shaped by not only the educational programs but by the physical features of the school and its classrooms. Such features go beyond walls, windows, and chalkboards. They include everything that an individual can sense or feel. How things are seen, heard, felt, tasted, and in every sense experienced influences both the quality and the quantity of social interaction among students and what they can learn.

Obvious physical components shape the learning environment. The glare on a chalkboard, the noise level of an air conditioner, and the temperature of a room are all important. There are more subtle elements at work as well; the type of floor covering used, for example. The tactile sense provided the students walking on a hard concrete floor or a soft carpet can affect their behavior. Many modern libraries are carpeted, for example, because people tend to lower their voices and to slow down their movements in a carpeted area.

The effects of color determine to some degree how individuals respond to different tasks both physiologically and psychologically. For example, colors at the blue end of the spectrum, such as deep primary blues, stimulate large-muscle activity. Thus a gymnasium from a psychological-physiological point of view probably should be painted blue. A neutral color should probably be used in areas where there is a highly specific task orientation, such as in study halls, libraries, and multimedia laboratories.

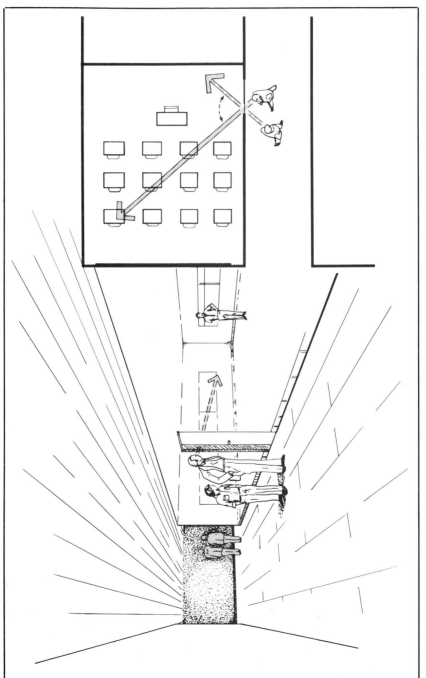

Figure 5.1   Lines of sight provided by a typical classroom door window

Concerns over how the physical environment of the school shapes the learning environment is a science that has just begun to develop. During the 1930s scholars such as Daryl Boyd Harmon began to examine the effects of school furniture and design on the learning process. His introduction, for example, of green, nonglare chalkboards was a major contribution to improving the physical environment of classrooms. The introduction of green chalkboards and their integration with better methods of lighting resulted in a decrease in the number of student eye disorders, and there was even an improvement in student posture.

Such issues are not as trivial as they may at first seem. Educators today, for example, are faced with the question of whether or not the use of computers affects students physically. There is preliminary evidence to suggest that the way a computer is positioned, the color of its screen, the color of the room in which the machine is used, and even the speed at which images are presented on the screen may significantly affect the learning process.

PSYCHOLOGICAL AND SOCIAL ASPECTS OF SPACE

Schools and classrooms are arenas for human interaction. Theorists such as anthropologist Edward T. Hall and psychologist Robert Sommer have recently begun to study the role that space plays in human interaction. The study of what Hall terms *proxemics*—the relationship between human behavior and spatial relations—is probably of significant importance in the process of learning.

The effects of proxemics at work can be seen in any number of learning situations. A teacher who consistently hides behind a lectern and refuses to move into the students' classroom space may be conveying a deliberate message of aloofness and separation. In some cases this may be desirable, in others a serious problem. Similarly, how a teacher arranges the students' seating affects what is or is not done by them. Sandy, for example, very deliberately arranges her students in semicircular seating patterns.

> I set the room up so they're not in rows; they're semicircular. Sometimes they'll move into groups. . . . The thing I found that affects [discussion patterns] is the way they're sitting. If they're sitting in an informal style, they're more apt to discuss than if they're in rows.

Her own position is also deliberate.

> As far as the actual teaching, I always like to see everyone and everything that's going on. I sit on my desk; I never teach from behind a desk; I don't know how that's possible. I always sit on my desk, higher than the rest of the room so I can see everything at all times. It's good for keeping control . . . and also makes you feel like a group, part of each other, not separated by a barrier.

Sandy with students in a semicircle for discussion

Larry echoes Sandy's sentiments that arranging student desks in a semicircle not only allows a teacher to control the environment but also encourages students to discuss things with one another.

> I like to be just one person away from my students, the atmosphere of the semicircle—in two rows—just one person away from every kid. There's no such thing as a back of the room. Everybody is close to the front, wherever the front may be. If I have a small class, I insist they sit in the front row. But on occasions I make seating charts, and I put them where I want to so that they can't be conversing with their neighbor. . . . I want to be in control of the situation, and I'll tell them to sit in the front row and I'll put them where I want them to be. I think physical environment is really important. I've seen other classrooms with rows of chairs and two or three kids in the back of the room, four or five up front. The teacher's up front talking to them and there's no real groupness there. I want my kids to be together as a group and to be working with me as a group and not to have somebody over here who's out of it.

Unfortunately there are few standard guidelines concerning use of space and distance in interpersonal interactions. What is the appropriate amount of space and distance is dependent upon two different factors. The first factor is evolutionary and is largely physiological in nature. As primates we are triggered to assume various postures depending on sensory cues, odors, and temperatures. The second factor affecting personal space is sociological and cultural. We respond, for example, to how people are dressed. A dark, plain tie on a man usually signifies a certain degree of formality, an open shirt a less formal situation. A woman wearing a tailored suit and blouse is more formal than a woman in slacks and a sweater. Think for a moment about how the principal in your high school looked. It is likely that his or her formal dress was used to indicate status, authority, and perhaps a sense of social distance. Then think about the shop teacher and the home economics teacher. Their less formal dress was probably not only functional for their roles but also conveyed less of a sense of formality and social distance. Whether male or female these teachers probably presented themselves according to the roles they were assuming.

In the pictures on pages 164 and 165, who is the principal and who are the teachers? You can usually guess correctly. (Find the answers on page 176.) Why? Not only is dress important but often so is the positioning of the two persons. Height implies a superior position. Recall that Sandy sits on her desk to be higher than the students both to see and to be in a superior position, a position the teacher must occupy. A reversal of heights may also indicate authority and subordination. If one person is standing while another sits in a formal interchange, it is reasonable to assume that the seated person possesses the greater status or social position.

Larry lecturing to students in a semicircle

Teachers with principal

The social role of an individual can often be defined as part of the process of proxemics. In the case of school principals, for example, it is interesting to note how the
design and layout of their offices may be shaped by the expectations of their role.
Think about visiting a principal's office. Typically a visitor must first enter an outer
office, usually a waiting area. A secretary will generally lead the visitor through a
second space to an office complex assigned to the principal. The principal's
secretary usually has a space that must be traversed before it is possible to enter the
inner sanctum of the office. Inside the principal's office the desk is almost never
against a wall. Instead the desk faces out and forms a physical barrier between the
visitor and the principal. A message of power, authority, and control is clearly communicated by this arrangement of space (see Figure 5.2).

The typical architectural pattern of a school isolates the principal's office. One
exception that comes to mind is Luberta's principal, Mr. Benning. His office was
located in a large room together with his secretary's and assistant principal's desks.
Students and teachers constantly entered and left his office. He was extraordinarily
accessible and at the center of the school's action. He was not aloof or intent on
displaying a superior social position. How he arranged his office space said a great
deal about his involvement with his school and his personal philosophy as an
educator. His office arrangement was a mirror of the kind of close, relaxed, supportive interaction he carried on with his faculty members and students.

Clearly, proxemics are extremely important in understanding how schools, administrators, and teachers function. A dramatic example of the role of proxemics in
learning can be seen in the case of the open-school movement in the late 1960s.

Open-Classroom Construction: Problems in the Use of Physical and Social Space

Open-classroom construction achieved widespread popularity during part of the massive construction of elementary and secondary schools in the 1960s. Open construction reflected a major philosophical shift from the traditional to the experimental models of education that characterized the period. It was believed that by removing walls and physical barriers the curriculum could literally be opened, and learning could become more individualized and flexible. Together with innovations such as modular scheduling and team teaching, open-classroom construction was an attempt to redefine the character of American education by redefining the environment in which it took place.

The open-classroom movement was related to the larger open-education movement, although they are not the same. Essentially the open-education movement involves a philosophical position that is child centered. The role of the teacher in open education changed from supervisor and sole instructor to facilitator and co-learner. Straight rows of desks were replaced by activity areas and learning centers. Children were provided flexible schedules and were expected to learn on their own by moving from one activity area, or learning center, to another. Unlike the traditional classroom, open education deemphasized large-group instruction and substituted a focus on small groups, individualization, and learner choice of content.

Underlying the philosophy of open education was the belief that children could

Teachers with principal

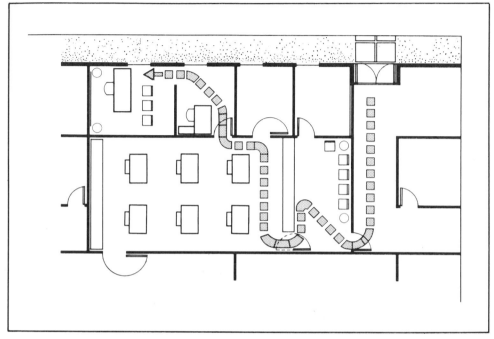

Figure 5.2 The serpentine route to the principal's office

not only accept responsibility for their own learning but that motivation and interest would be greatly encouraged by providing them with a less restrictive
physical environment. Popular figures such as Herbert Kohl (1969) argued that the
open classroom would lead to a new direction and purpose for American education:

> The classroom ought to be a communal center, a comfortable environment in which
> plans can be made and experiences assessed. However, one can open up the classroom
> as much by moving out of it as by changing the life within it. (p. 75)

Classroom environments as *communal centers* were quickly put into place. Open-
classroom construction was seen as facilitating the process of open education.
Perhaps for the first time in the history of American schooling there was the
widespread realization that the physical and social environment in which children
functioned could critically influence the quality of their educational experience.

The construction of open classrooms to promote open education was largely a
failure. Important factors related to the control and use of space as well as to how
people interact in a communal environment were not sufficiently taken into account
before constructing open environments. Noise was a major problem. Noise control
was to have been taken care of by "white noise" and "pink noise" generators—

electronic speakers that generate audible sounds that mask the spoken word. Many of these devices were either eliminated for expense reasons or failed to function adequately. With the confusion of different auditory signals, students and teachers had difficulty concentrating.

In the same way that the auditory environment of the open construction classroom was confusing, so also was the visual environment. Students working independently were frequently distracted by the activities of others. Other problems manifested themselves, too. When a biology class dissected its frogs, for instance, the formaldehyde also pervaded the home economics class adjacent to it.

Most problematic, however, was that whereas openness created possibilities for different types of learning interactions, it also radically changed the possibilities for privacy. Teachers were constantly observed by other teachers and students. Actions that can be performed more easily in private (the disciplining of a student) suddenly became schoolwide events. Deviating from the regular schedule now required that bargaining be undertaken with other teachers. Spontaneity became more difficult to achieve than in a self-contained classroom. This fact is particularly ironic when one realizes that the purpose of open-classroom construction was to facilitate flexibility and freedom in learning.

Smith and Keith (1971) in their analysis of the Kensington School—a classic example of the use of innovative open construction—point out that privacy is a value like openness. Both "are important as antecedents to personal freedom."

Mr. Benning and his secretary in the center of the action

> We have been struck by the too easy generalization that physical openness, that is, an absence of walls, leads immediately, directly or simply to freedom in teaching and learning. A case can be made, we believe, that physical privacy provides some major contributions to freedom. These contributions tended to be minimized in the open space design of Kensington. (p. 196)

Clearly the use of open construction represents a complex problem. Open space redefines the social dynamics of the classroom; proxemic relationships are altered. The result is that the teaching and learning environment is also altered.

Sandy has had experience with an open-space environment. In her fifth year of teaching she joined with one of the authors of this text and two other teachers to create a school-within-a-school alternative program for high school freshmen who were not doing well because of attitudinal and learning problems. The physical setting for the four teachers and 65 or 70 freshmen was a single large room originally designed as a junior high library. Both teachers and students spent their entire day in this room except for physical education class.

One of the major positive outcomes of the program and its physical arrangement was the enhanced collegial interaction among the four teachers. One of the results of the cellular structuring of space into separate classrooms in the typical school is to discourage collegial action and learning from observing other teachers, especially about such core issues as instruction and curriculum. Lortie (1975) has argued that to become more professional, teachers need to develop much stronger collegiality around core teaching issues and to give increased allegiance to sharing methods and insights and to engaging in collaborative experimentation. Sandy's experience in the open environment encouraged collegiality. She recalls this period of her teaching experience as one of tremendous growth, learning about herself, learning from others, and feeling support in trying new methods. Open space brought a greater possibility for collegiality. In this case collegiality was also encouraged by the mutual faculty issue of working with "problem" students in a multidisciplinary team.

However, the physical arrangement also brought some of the problems noted above. Privacy was lost. Visual and noise distractions were encountered. Sandy's team moved in blackboards and other moveable partitions to alleviate some visual distraction. There remained, however, a tension between the positive aspects of teacher collegiality and awareness of important social interactions throughout the day and the negative aspects of loss of privacy and increased distractions.

In many middle and junior high schools today *house plans*, or multidisciplinary teams (consisting of a mathematics, a science, an English, and a social studies teacher), have been developed. These teams or house members share the same group of students. Such organization encourages collegial interaction while preserving the cellular physical structure of the private classroom as the theater for instruction.

There are very few open-construction classrooms functioning today in schools.

Typically space originally based upon open construction has been partitioned into traditional classrooms. In a certain sense these redesigned spaces are a physical manifestation of the failure of open education. One cannot, however, condemn the open-education concept simply because it failed. There is evidence to suggest that the concept of open education may be beneficial in some instances and may even thrive in some traditionally designed settings. The complexity of the physical environment and the deeply ingrained classroom roles and norms to be discussed in Chapter 6 may have made the open-education concept one that was too difficult for many to implement effectively.

A TEACHER'S ROLE IN SHAPING THE PHYSICAL ENVIRONMENT OF A CLASSROOM

Despite the immutable limitations of a school's construction teachers have an opportunity to establish partial control over the physical environment of their classrooms. The general aesthetic quality of the classroom as well as specific furniture and seating arrangements are elements that affect the process of learning and are in large part under the control of the teacher (Weinstein, 1981). Any classroom is defined by the teacher who works in it, as Herbert Kohl (1969) has pointed out.

> The placement of objects in space is not arbitrary and rooms represent in physical form the spirit and soul of places and institutions. A teacher's room tells us something about who he is and a great deal about what he is doing. (p. 35)

Reflect a moment on the earlier discussion of semicircular seating in Sandy's and Larry's classrooms. Kohl's commentary rings true in both cases.

A teacher may or may not be aware of how the environment shapes and influences teaching and the ways in which the environment can be altered to achieve different teaching goals. How a teacher defines the social and learning space of his or her classroom operates on both a *direct* and a *symbolic* level. For example, the arrangement of desks in a straight row can be understood on both levels (Proshansky & Wolfe, 1974). If students are unable to carry on a conversation because it is difficult to hear and see one another, this would be a direct effect. On a more symbolic level, the seating arrangement of rows may suggest that the teacher does not value class discussion and that students are not expected to interact in any significant way—the very antithesis of what Sandy and Larry strive to achieve. A teacher's decisions regarding the physical arrangement of the classroom can be an important direct or symbolic influence on the instructional environment. Look, for example, at the following statement by Ruth:

You need spots where groups can be off a little bit by themselves to work on things . . . [and] a place where I can get everybody's attention if I want to do a large-group thing, and little places to go off where no one can disturb you.

Inherent in her comment is not only a specific philosophy concerning the use of space but also an indication of some of the elements she considers to be important for effective instruction.

Ruth also uses the arrangement of physical space as a real problem for her students to solve. In this she is totally consistent with her orientation that students should confront real problems, wrestle with them, resolve them, and then learn from the consequences of their resolutions. Recall that on the opening day of school she *temporarily* seated her students in assigned desks. At the end of the first day she held a class meeting, and one of the agenda items was a group decision on seating arrangements. Numerous possibilities were suggested. Students decided on islands of two as a pattern, and Ruth asked for names of persons with whom they would like to share an island. This decision process and the spatial arrangement that resulted had both direct and symbolic elements. There was a clear underlying message — You are capable of solving real problems, and I trust you to solve them — inherent in Ruth's resolution of what to do with classroom design. Once again she set the stage for students to confront and resolve a real issue with real consequences.

Jacquie's arrangement of space is quite different from Ruth's. She seats her junior high students in a grid pattern of straight rows. In a beginning language class the dialogue *in the language* must logically be carried on between the teacher and student or students rather than among the students, since they lack a sufficient knowledge and vocabulary base to initiate and sustain a conversation. Jacquie's lessons are a series of rapid-fire exchanges with students. The exchanges alternate between individual verbal responses and choral responses. In essence she is effective in maintaining a continuing dyadic interaction with each student whether the student is actually responding or not. There is constant interaction that draws each student into the activity.

Jacquie's use of classroom space is also different. She moves a great deal. Her pattern includes movement across the front of the room, up and down the side aisles near the windows and wall, and penetration down the rows to about half the depth of each row. She will often address a student across the rows as well as from the front. Eyes stay on her as she moves. Earlier Jacquie was described as an actress on a stage. In her theater, although not arranged in the round, there are only dress-circle seats. There are no back rows, no places to hide or to be uninvolved. The physical seating arrangement suits her own theatrical style of teaching.

It is also probable that seating her junior high students in a grid rather than in a semicircular pattern as Larry and Sandy use for high school students may be a control device. A major agenda for junior high students is to deal with issues of identity, sex role, and appropriate modes of interpersonal exchange. These are learned through practice and trial and error, which may include much note passing, side talk, and giggling in classrooms. Jacquie's seating pattern coupled with her own movements throughout the classroom minimize the kind of disruptions to lessons often interjected into classrooms by the larger personal agendas of students who are learning to become adults. At the same time Jacquie is sensitive to these larger agendas and often incorporates them into the content of her discussion in a foreign language. Her students know that she is tuned in to the personal struggles, joys, and pains that encompass the early adolescent years.

According to Carol S. Weinstein (1981) one of the first decisions a teacher must make in arranging a classroom is to decide whether to organize space in terms of personal territories or functions. Early childhood education and open-education settings often feature functional arrangements; for example, space is divided into interest areas that are available to all students for various activities. In a nursery school these might include the block or play area, the rest area, and the sociodramatic play area. A different rationale for organizing space is based on a concept of personal territory. Arrangements based on this thinking typically occur in the upper-elementary grades where students are assigned their own desks in which to keep their own personal belongings. Functional settings are often most appropriate for classrooms where small groups are engaged in a variety of activities at the same time. The territorial arrangement is particularly well suited to classrooms where instruction is primarily provided to the whole class at once.

Luberta is an example of a teacher who makes particularly interesting use of space in her classroom. Besides providing a rich visual environment in terms of posters on the walls and bulletin boards containing student work, she constantly has her students move their desks around for different types of activities. As students arrive at the beginning of the day their desks are lined up in straight rows, one behind the other. As they break up into reading groups or activity groups they push their desks into semicircles and clusters to work with one another or with Luberta. By having students move their desks into different configurations, Luberta is able to have her students work in both personal and functional settings that suit her needs as well as theirs.

Physical arrangements made by a teacher influence student participation and affect their attitude toward learning. Questionnaire studies concerning territorial organization in the classroom suggest that where students sit is often related to their levels of participation, performance, and attitude. A 1969 study by Walberg, for example, demonstrated that high school students who preferred to sit in the front of the room near the instructor placed a greater value on academics than did students who preferred to sit elsewhere in the classroom. Those students who preferred to sit next to their friends had a greater need for belonging to a social group and also were more sensitive to criticism than other students. Those students who preferred to sit in the back of the classroom or near the windows were more negative about the learning process and were less secure about their ability to succeed as students. A semicircular arrangement of desks, like that used by Sandy and Larry, makes it much more difficult for students either to isolate themselves or to dominate a class.

A study of college students (Becker et al., 1973) focused on the relationship between a current course grade and where a student typically sat in a classroom of typical row configuration. Course grades decreased as a function of the distance of the student's seat from the instructor.

Observational studies of student participation tend to support the findings of the questionnaire and survey research cited above. A 1970 study by Adams and Biddle recorded student participation in 32 mathematics and social studies classrooms arranged in row configuration at the primary and secondary level. Verbal interaction was concentrated in what the researchers labeled *the action zone*, which ran from the center front of the classroom and in a line directly up the room's center. The question arises, of course, as to whether the fact that a student sits front and center is responsible for his or her positive attitude towards participation or whether those students who chose to sit in the action zone are more interested in learning and participating in class. At the present time there is no clear evidence of either being responsible for determining where students decide to sit. Nonetheless Weinstein (1981) concludes that "the weight of the evidence . . . indicates that a front center seat *facilitates* achievement, positive attitudes, and participation for those at least somewhat predisposed to speak" (p. 14). Again, a seating pattern such as Larry or Sandy use totally changes the assumptions of grid seating that underlie most of the research discussed above. Jacquie's deliberate movements also spread the action zone in her classroom to the entire seating area.

After Weinstein (1981) reviewed the available research she suggested that in a classroom where the desks are lined up in rows teachers should:

> (1) move around the room whenever possible; (2) purposely direct comments to students seated in the rear and on the sides; (3) periodically change students' seats; (4) encourage students who normally chose seats in the rear to come forward; (5) not teach to a small group unnecessarily dispersed across a large room; and (6) use a student choice of seat as a clue to his or her self-esteem and liking for school. (p. 14)

Similar research suggests that seating arrangements within small groups can affect patterns of communication and participation.

In classrooms organized by function there has also been evidence that spatial arrangements can affect where children play, what activities they participate in, and their degree of social interaction. According to Weinstein (1981) the research base suggests that teachers would do well to follow these principles of room arrangement in open settings:

(1) interest areas should be clearly delineated or bounded; (2) areas should be located according to the requirements of their respective activities for quiet, protection, and special resources (water, electricity, light); (3) incompatible activities such as block play and reading should be well-separated; (4) all areas should be visually accessible to students; (5) pathways should be clear and should not go through work areas; (6) large spaces that encourage rough and tumble play should be avoided; (7) the teacher's desk should be placed in a corner to encourage his or her movement around the room; (8) materials must be easily accessible and close to work surfaces; and (9) classrooms should contain spatial options — places to be alone, to work in small groups, to be in large groups. (p. 16)

Little research has been conducted on whether aesthetic considerations affect student performance. Two studies (Horowitz & Otto, 1973; Sommer & Olsen, 1980) set in colleges suggest that classrooms specially designed to be aesthetically pleasing and comfortable contribute little to student learning. Nonetheless, in both studies student participation was greater in the more comfortable experimental setting. Thus positive aesthetic settings may indirectly affect student performance, but to what extent is not known.

CONCLUSION

Athough historically there has been only limited attention paid to the ways in which the physical environment can influence teaching and learning experiences, there is now a growing body of research to suggest that the physical environment plays an important role in the learning process. In the future it is hoped more emphasis will be placed on understanding the physical environment of the classroom from a multidisciplinary point of view. Psychologists, physiologists, sociologists, and anthropologists as well as teachers need to explore in greater detail the role of the physical environment in the social and academic process of learning. Until more research is conducted, however, it is largely in the hands of individual teachers to determine how the physical environment can best be used to promote optimal teaching and learning conditions. As this chapter has attempted to illustrate, to be a teacher is to be involved in making decisions that affect not only curriculum and instruction but also the physical environment in which the desired learning takes place.

DISCUSSION QUESTIONS

1. How important is the design and layout of a classroom or school building to the process of instruction? Does the importance of design differ from one type of class to another?

2. If you had the opportunity to design an ideal classroom for a group of first-grade students, what features would you include? If you were to do the same for a high school English class what would you include? What features would elementary school classrooms have in common with high school classrooms? How would they differ?

3. Teachers use space in very different ways. Think about your college instructors: How do they control and use the space in their classrooms? How is their use of space different from or the same as the five case study teachers described in this book?

4. How important is it to present students with an aesthetically pleasing environment in which to work? Is this a luxury or of fundamental importance?

5. In his book *Life in Classrooms* Philip Jackson (1968) contends that although the physical features of classrooms differ their underlying characteristics do not. He asserts that teacher attention given to the physical environment, such as seating arrangements and materials on bulletin boards, is little more than window dressing and does not affect the important aspects of life in the classroom. Think about this position, which differs from that of the authors. How important is physical space, its arrangement, and the visual environment? From your observations in schools and your experience as a student, can you form an opinion favoring one or the other of these positions? You might want to discuss or debate this in class.

ACTIVITIES

1. Draw on a blank sheet of white paper the floor plan for a classroom that you are observing. Be sure to show on your floor plan the location of windows, doors, blackboards, and so forth. Chart with a pencil the teacher's location at the beginning of class. Follow the teacher's movement for a period of 10 or 15 minutes. Consecutively number each spot where each teacher stops, noting the time the teacher remains in one place. Does any sort of pattern emerge in terms of how *the teacher* occupies the space within the classroom?

2. Look at the different public schools in your community. Find out when they were built. If you have buildings that were built in different historical periods compare them with one another. Do school buildings built in different periods reflect differences in construction, aesthetics, and design?

3. Consider each of the following aspects of the room environment for a classroom you are observing and check which ones are satisfactory and unsatisfactory: ventilation; temperature; lighting; acoustics; type of flooring; bulletin boards; storage areas; general cleanliness; general attractiveness; presence of plants, posters, animals, and so forth. Are there other important factors that you can identify? How would you change those conditions that you feel are unsatisfactory?

4. Sometimes the influences of the larger community and the age, structure, and physical condition of a school building seem correlated. For example, an urban school in a lower-socioeconomic area may be either old or modern and either well or poorly maintained. The same is true in suburban and rural areas. Note in Chapter 2 how Ruth's school seems to fit in with its surrounding environment whereas Luberta's does not. In a run-down neighborhood the interior of Jefferson School provides an environment rich with color, inspirational messages, and visual elements. It is a physical and visual alternative to the generally gloomy message of the neighborhood. Look at the school(s) you visit. How are the physical and visual aspects related to the surrounding environment? Note both the exterior and the interior aspects.

QUESTIONS TO GUIDE OBSERVATION

In observing and teaching in classrooms it is helpful to be aware of a number of questions about the physical environment.

1. For what type of instructional approach is the layout and design of the classroom best suited (e.g., discussion, lecture, individualized instruction)?
2. In what part of the classroom does the teacher spend most of his or her time?
3. How does the arrangement of furniture affect the instructional process and more general social interaction that takes place in the classroom?
4. Are seats and desks moveable? If *yes*, are they moved and rearranged? for what reasons? how?
5. How is the room decorated? Do the decorations reflect anything specific about the type of instruction or the students?
6. Is the room used by a single teacher or class or by multiple teachers and classes? How does this affect the room's arrangement, appearance, and so forth?
7. Does the classroom reflect a specific identifiable educational philosophy (e.g., open construction)?

QUESTIONS TO GUIDE TEACHER INTERVIEWS

1. Is the physical environment important to you, or is it something taken for granted?
2. What guides the way you arrange the classroom seating?
3. What would you change about the design of the classroom and the school?
4. What do you feel is most important in creating an effective physical environment for instruction?
5. Do students with special needs (e.g., physically handicapped) have particular problems because of the way that your classroom or school is designed?

REFERENCES

Adams, R. S., & Biddle, B. J. (1970). *Realities of teaching: Explorations with video tape*. New York: Holt, Rinehart & Winston.

Architectual Forum. (1963). See *119* (2) & *119* (5). Both volumes are dedicated to examinations of school architecture in the United States.

Ayres, May. (1917). A century of progress in schoolhouse construction. *American School Board Journal, 54–55*, 23–25.

Becker, F. D. et al. (1973). College classroom ecology. *Sociometry, 36*, 514–525.

Delamont, S. (1983). *Interaction in the classroom*. New York: Methuen.

Hall, Edward. (1966). *The hidden dimension*. New York: Doubleday Anchor.

Horowitz, P., & Otto, D. (1973). *The teaching effectiveness of an alternative teaching facility*. Alberta, Canada: University of Alberta (ERIC Document Reproduction Service No. ED 082 242).

Jackson, P. W. (1968). *Life in classrooms*. New York: Holt, Rinehart & Winston.

Kohl, Herbert. (1969). *The open classroom: A practical guide to new ways of teaching*. New York: Random House.

McClintock, Jean, & McClintock, Robert (Eds.). (1970). *Henry Barnard's school architecture*. New York: Teachers College Press

Proshansky, E., & Wolfe, M. (1974). The physical setting and open education. *School Review, 82*, 557–574.

Smith, D. (1971). On the classroom box. In *Farallones scrapbook* (pp. 28–32). New York: Random House.

Smith, L. & Keith, P. (1971). *Anatomy of an educational innovation*. New York: Wiley.

Sommer, A. & Olsen, H. (1980). The soft classroom. *Environment and Behavior, 12*, 3–16.

Walberg, H. (1969). Physical and psychological distance in the classroom. *School Review, 77*, 64–70.

Weinstein, C. S. (1981). Classroom design as an external condition for learning. *Educational Technology, 21*(8), 12–19.

———. (1982). Strategies for increasing the environmental competence of teachers. *New Jersey Journal of School Psychology, 1*(1), 25–38.

ANSWERS: In the picture on page 164, the principal is second from left; in the picture on page 165, the principal is second from right.

6

THE SCHOOL CULTURE
AND THE CLASSROOM
SOCIAL SYSTEM

INTRODUCTION

This chapter is about patterned regularities in schools and classrooms — social forces, values and beliefs, patterns of behavior, and regular daily events — that are not readily seen. It is about patterns that most practicing teachers themselves typically have not been able to describe explicitly, but ones they nonetheless react to that powerfully shape both their own behaviors and those of their students. Many of the concepts discussed here have not received sufficient attention in teacher education. These concepts, however, can enable you to view the commonplace analytically rather than from the limited common-sense view of a lay person. This chapter will look at two large ideas, schools as cultures and classrooms as social systems.

The chapter begins with a brief discussion of school culture, the powerful set of forces that structure and organize social interactions, purposes, and values in schools. The social system of the classroom, the social microcosm that a teacher must develop and control, is embedded in the larger school culture. Discussion will focus on the interaction of various roles played by both teachers and students and how these roles fit together to create small social worlds. Next the chapter moves to classroom verbal interaction, one dimension of classroom life in which some of the "rules of the game" that guide teacher and student role interaction can be seen.

This chapter will require concentration. You will be asked to view events and patterns that are so familiar that you may no longer see them. You must take an abstract, conceptual, analytical pose keeping in mind that to be a teacher is to live within the culture of the school and to be the leader of a classroom social system.

SCHOOL CULTURE: THE WORLD OF THE MORE OR LESS INVISIBLE

It is helpful to begin by asking why schools, their value and belief systems, cultures and social systems, their patterns of interpersonal interactions and sentiments, have received so little attention. Education has developed within an intellectual tradition that stresses the psychology of the individual; the conceptual lenses that most teachers use to view social reality are psychological. Teachers think, act, and respond to others primarily on the basis of what they believe is going on in others' minds. They attribute the behavior of others to psychological processes.

> [It] becomes increasingly difficult to become aware that individuals operate in various social settings that have a structure not comprehensible by our existing theories of individual personality. In fact, in many situations it is likely that one can predict an individual's behavior far better on the basis of knowledge of the social structure and his position in it than one can on the basis of his personal dynamics. (Sarason, 1971, p. 120)

Philip Schlecty (1976) argues that in a broad sense the field of education suffers from a psychological bias. Seymour Sarason (1971) also asserts that the major professional influences on American education "have been dominated by a focus on the individual and individual differences" (p. 103). Learning theory, for example, is necessarily psychologically based. But learning as it is done in most schools is not something done in isolation. Rather, all schooling including learning occurs in a social or group context. The problem with a strictly psychological view of education is that it is focused on the individual and tends to treat the social context as something to be controlled so that the important individual attributes or results are more easily identified. Schlecty (1976) states the issue succinctly: "Theories about teaching have their basis in the psychology of learning. The practice of teaching has its basis in the social realities of classrooms and schools" (p. 13). The important word here is *social*. A major contributor to the perceived gap between educational theory (learned in colleges) and practice (experienced in schools) is precisely that most educational theory used in teacher preparation is grounded in psychological or individualistic assumptions whereas the reality of practice always occurs in a social context, which theory often minimizes or ignores.

In order to make the world of social structure more readily visible in this and the next chapter the conceptual lenses of sociologists and anthropologists are used, rather than those of psychologists. Anthropologists study cultures; here the focus is on organizational culture, in particular the culture of the school.

Sarason (1971) describes school culture as the structures and patterns by which the settings are organized, the patterns that govern social relationships in the setting. Cultures define the permissible ways in which goals and problems can be approached.

Organizational cultures are powerful. They bind individual behavior; they antedate the presence of any individual; they continue when individuals come and go. They are the essence of "schoolness" that we instantly recognize. But precisely because culture is so pervasive, it is difficult to see. We are so used to following its powerful patterns and structure that we seldom stop to examine the obvious, the world of the more or less invisible.

Looking for Elements of School Culture

Seymour Sarason has developed a device for looking at some aspects of school culture by taking the view of an imaginary being from outer space who, being foreign, can more easily see "behavioral regularities" or commonplace patterns of social behavior. Imagine that a visitor from outer space is parked on an invisible platform high above an elementary school. This being sees everything but does not understand either written or spoken language. It does not occur to the creature that *thinking* goes on in the heads of the creatures being viewed. But the interstellar visitor does have a computer that records and categorizes events or behavioral regularities.

> Our outer-spacer will discern (but not understand) that for five consecutive days the school is densely populated while for two consecutive days it is devoid of humans. That puzzles him. Why this 5–2 pattern? Why not a 4–3 or some other kind of pattern like 2–1–2–1–1?
>
> What if the outer-spacer could talk to us and demand an explanation for this existing regularity? Many of us earthlings would quickly become aware that we have a tendency to assume that the way things are is the way things should be. But our outer-spacer persists. Is this the way it has always been? Is it this way in other countries? Is it demonstrably the best pattern for achieving the purposes of schooling? Does the existing regularity reflect noneducational considerations like religion, work patterns, and leisure time? Is it possible that the existing regularity has no intrinsic relationship to learning and education? (Sarason, 1971, pp. 63–64)

These are penetrating questions. A look into some of the answers makes it clear that many of the behaviors occurring in schools do not arise from individual psychological bases but from deep, often harder to see, social forces.

The 5–2 pattern of attendance at school observed by the space traveler, and the 8:30 A.M. to 3:00 P.M. pattern within the five days are such commonplace aspects of school culture that they are not frequently examined or questioned. But these patterns exert tremendous influence on everything that occurs in school. They are integrated with many of the other organizational elements of the school culture and the classroom social system. They have persisted for many decades and often reflect noneducational considerations like religion, work patterns, and leisure time. Traditional attendance patterns are probably not the best that could be devised if the only purpose of schooling was the maximization of student learning, but on the other hand they do result in achieving one of the major cultural purposes given to schools by the larger social order—custody-control.

Custody-control is another aspect of school culture that often goes unrecognized but exerts a powerful influence on almost everything occurring in schools. The custody-control function of schooling is one of containing and controlling the youth of the society during most of the hours of the normal work week. Put bluntly, an important service the schools perform for the social order is to keep children and adolescents off the streets and out of the job market. Increasingly schooling provides the function of relatively inexpensive child care so that both parents may work outside the home. This custody-control function is strongly related to the cultural pattern of school attendance of both children and adults and limits organizational patterns of grouping teachers and students for instruction. The outcome is the grouping of large numbers of students with a single adult for a long period of time. Given the 5–2, 8:30–3:00 patterns of attendance, there is simply nowhere to send the majority of the class while the teacher works with a smaller group, since the school *must* perform the custody-control function. It is important to understand this parameter, for many of the aspects of the social system of the classroom result from large numbers of people being grouped together in classrooms for long periods of time.

Because there are many students with many different needs in a single classroom with a single teacher over a long period of time, to be a teacher requires being the leader of a social system. If the teacher fails in forming, shaping, and maintaining an effective classroom social system none of the other decisions and efforts concerning curriculum, instruction, and learning are of any avail. The important purposes of schooling cannot occur where there is no order or shared understanding of purpose and acceptable behavior. This task of creating social order is even more difficult because the students whom the teacher must shape and form are generally immature, relatively unsocialized in their earlier years, develop their own competing agendas with age, and in many cases do not even wish to be in the class or school.

To walk into a classroom full of students and stand before them as a teacher is to confront a group and an issue that Willard Waller (1932) described 50 years ago:

> Teacher and pupil confront each other in the school with an original conflict of desires, and however much that conflict may be reduced in amount, or however much it may be hidden, it still remains. The teacher represents the adult group, ever the enemy of the spontaneous life of groups of children. The teacher represents formal curriculum, and his interest is in imposing that curriculum upon the children in the

form of tasks; pupils are much more interested in life in their own world than in the dissected bits of adult life which teachers have to offer. . . . Teacher and pupil confront each other with attitudes from which the underlying hostility can never be altogether removed. Pupils are the material in which teachers are supposed to produce results. Pupils are human beings striving to realize themselves in their own spontaneous manner, striving to produce their own results in their own way. Each of these hostile parties stands in the way of the other; in so far as the aims of either are realized, it is at the sacrifice of the aims of the other. (pp. 195–196)

Classrooms are unusual social settings; they are artificial rather than natural. Typically they comprise a single adult and 20 to 35 children or adolescents. Philip Jackson (1968) has said: "Only in schools do thirty or more people spend several hours each day literally side by side. Once we leave the classroom we seldom again are required to have contact with so many people for so long a time" (p. 8).

The social system of the classroom is not only affected by its grouping structure but also by its social purposes. Waller's commentary recognizes that the reasons for the teacher's presence are to induce learning, to socialize youth into adult roles, and to maintain custody-control. These are all serious responsibilities that point to the preservation of the larger social order as well as the future well-being of individual students. Students, on the other hand, live out many more aspects of their lives in the classroom and the larger arena of school than do teachers. They have intentions of their own, what Waller calls "striving to realize themselves in their own spontaneous manner." Young children are interested in play and fun. As they mature interests include carving out personal, social, and sexual identities. By the time they reach high school a very real focus is learning how to relate to each other through these new found and growing identities, including relationships we call love.

All of these forces, then, are brought together in the classroom, and they affect the social system that develops there. Larger social forces determine how many people are put together and for how long. The teacher carries the social mandates to teach, to socialize, and to control, although individual teachers play out personal variations on these larger themes. Students who enter the classroom also greatly affect the classroom social structure. Their age, experience, background, intentions, and similarity or diversity all contribute to the variations in social systems that may be found in classrooms.

THE CLASSROOM AS A SOCIAL SYSTEM

What is this classroom social system that has continually been mentioned here? The concept of social system is based on the idea that a number of individuals interacting for a period of time is more than a simple aggregate of persons. Rather, within classrooms there develop systems of social interaction, organized wholes constituted of "interacting personalities bound together in an organic relationship" (Hoy & Miskel, 1982, p. 51). Social systems have boundaries. In this case the boundary is easily seen as the physical boundary of the classroom. The system is made up of those who live and work within the given classroom. Thus, the teacher and his or her students are members, but the principal, parents, and other teachers (unless it is a team-teaching situation) are not members.

Roles, shared beliefs, and norms are other components of social systems. *Roles* are composed of the expectations a group holds for the occupants of various social positions. *Teacher* and *student* are the basic roles within the classroom. The specific expectations, rights, and duties attached to these roles will differ somewhat from classroom to classroom. However, general expectations such as the teacher as leader and the student as follower are generally accepted in most classrooms. What will differ are the particular definitions of what it means to lead and follow.

Shared beliefs are composed of perceptions that are held in common by the members of a group. These too will differ from classroom to classroom. Shared beliefs might be about how much a teacher cares for students, the ability level of any student or group of students in the room, a teacher's ability or inability to maintain order, and the reasons for studying a particular subject.

Norms are commonly held expectations for behavior or socially sanctioned rules of conduct. They differ from beliefs because they contain an evaluative component. They reflect what should or should not be done. Like roles and beliefs, norms vary from one classroom to the next. Some norms, such as students should raise their hands to be recognized before speaking out, tend to be general. Other norms, such as what ought to occur if the bell rings and the teacher is still talking, will differ considerably from classroom to classroom. Taken together, then, these elements of the classroom social system form a social web that shapes individual behaviors.

Roles and the Daily Grind of Classroom Life

Philip Jackson (1968) used the phrase "daily grind" to give focus to the myriad "humdrum elements of human existence" that are the overriding reality of classroom life. In discussing the grind Jackson makes visible elements of the world of the more or less invisible.

Because of the custody-control mandate and tradition, students and teachers are arranged in classrooms under very *crowded* conditions. The crowdedness, which teachers are not at liberty to dissipate, creates the need to order and structure many events and interpersonal interactions that would not require conscious structuring were they to occur under different and less crowded circumstances. The need for order and structure is furthered by the fact that in elementary schools the same group of students and their teacher may occupy the same space for most of a day. In secondary schools teachers and students are grouped together in five to seven or more periods during the school day. From these conditions of crowdedness over long durations arises the need to develop social order. Thus, the "packaging" of students and teachers in classrooms and the humdrum events in need of routines all affect the roles, shared beliefs, and norms that constitute the social system of the classroom.

According to Jackson (1968) a teacher may engage in over a thousand interactions in a single day. At the secondary level these interactions may involve over 150 students. All of these interactions require interpretation, and many demand on-the-spot decisions. Good and Brophy (1984) characterize classrooms as exceedingly busy and complex places where the fast pace sometimes prevents a teacher from being fully aware of his or her behavior and its impact on students. Jackson (1968) describes teacher-student interactions as having "a here-and-now urgency and a spontaneous quality that brings excitement and variety to the teacher's work" (pp. 119–120).

The Role of a Teacher   Jackson argues that to be a teacher is to be simultaneously a traffic cop, supply sergeant, judge, gatekeeper of dialogue, and timekeeper in addition to being a curricular and instructional decision maker. One can see nearly all of these roles in the case of Ruth Christopherson on her first day of school (see Chapter 2). Ruth's preparation for the role of traffic cop begins before the students even arrive. She has name tags and individualized folders for each of her 24 students on their newly assigned desks before they enter the room. These actions serve to manage the social traffic when it does arrive, all at once. By placing the

Larry's crowded classroom

One-on-one interaction between Luberta and a student

folders on desks ahead of time, Ruth is preventing both milling around and a sense of being lost. She also engages in the role of traffic cop when she discusses the new departmental structure and the new movement from class to class it necessitates. Taking attendance and lunch count is interrupted to fulfill the traffic cop role once again when the late student arrives, and Ruth directs her to the proper seat. Ruth also exercises this role during her assigned cafeteria duty. At the end of the day she leads her students to the bus line.

Another facet of the teacher role described by Jackson is supply sergeant. Classrooms are environments of scarcity, both of materials and space, so the teacher is charged with judicious allocation of resources. Ruth indicates with a note in the student folders what supplies students are to obtain for themselves and later discusses the issue. During the Cartesian coordinate lesson she distributes grid paper. Although the description of Ruth Christopherson's classroom does not include them, she also undoubtedly controls access in some way to the pencil sharpener, the drinking fountain, and the lavatory. The scissors, the microscope, and the classroom encyclopedias are further examples of the scarce resources that a teacher, as supply sergeant, must manage.

Ruth and other teachers also fulfill the gatekeeper and timekeeper aspects of the teacher role. As the gatekeeper of discussion, Ruth decides who will speak and in what order. Although neither the names of the individual students nor Ruth's method of acknowledging who will speak are described in the Cartesian coordinate dialogue, it is clear that she is managing it in an orderly way. The number and duration of student responses that can be allowed during a lesson are also scarce resources in a large-group setting.

Similarly, a teacher is also a timekeeper who must manage student comings and goings and lesson placement and spacing. Ruth, for example, fits a spelling pretest into the 10 minutes before the end of a period and is charged with getting her students to the gym at the appropriate time for the principal's beginning-of-the-year pep talk. Given these multiple and simultaneous roles, teaching is a profession characterized by what the British educational sociologist Sara Delamont (1983) calls immediacy.

Delamont also maintains that teaching is characterized by privacy and autonomy as well. Whereas teachers are playing all the roles that Jackson describes, they are doing them, in effect, on their own. In Delamont's (1983) words, "There is little time to reflect and none to get a second opinion" (p. 50). Closely connected to the matter of privacy is the issue of autonomy and control. Within the classroom the teacher is alone and *in control*. Teacher control is broad—it encompasses student behavior, instructional activities, and knowledge. When most teachers think of classroom control, they think primarily of management and discipline. They would probably agree with the following definition: "Classroom control refers to the relationship between teacher direction, usually verbal, and high probability of pupil compliance" (Smith & Geoffrey, 1968, p. 67). Teacher control, however, goes considerably beyond the matter of teacher direction and student compliance. It extends to the all-important realm of knowledge. In Delamont's (1983) words, "the teacher's most potent resource is her possession of, access to, and control over knowledge" (p. 50). Within the particulars of a teacher's context, a teacher determines what will and will not be learned.

One of the most obvious ways that teachers control both knowledge and behavior is by doing most of the talking in the classroom. Numerous studies (Galton, Simon, & Croll, 1980; Flanders, 1970; Bellack et al., 1966) suggest that the teacher consistently does most of the talking in the classroom. Flanders (1970), who developed a rating system for analyzing teacher-student verbal interactions, maintains that in a typical American classroom there is 68 percent teacher talk, 20 percent pupil talk and 12 percent silence and confusion.

Studies of classroom questioning similarly reveal that teachers ask the majority of questions. A review of questioning patterns in America from 1912 to 1968 indicate that recitation has persisted despite its recognized limitations (Hoetker & Ahlbrand, 1969). During *recitation* teachers typically ask a lot of factual questions at a rapid pace. Students have little time to reflect before responding and little opportunity to ask questions. Whether teachers are lecturing or conducting a recitation, they are in control of the flow and content of knowledge. During a lecture they are giving the knowledge; during recitation they are asking the students to give it back.

From time to time there have been curricular attempts to alter somewhat a teacher's control over knowledge. However, most of these have been unsuccessful, in part because they seriously alter a role expectation with which teachers are most comfortable and familiar—control over verbal interaction. Delamont cites the Nuffield approach to science teaching in England as a case in point. This curriculum was predicated on a shift in the teacher's role from lecturer and demonstrator to "stage manager" of a guided discovery process. Ostensibly, the idea was well received and exam syllabi were changed to incorporate the Nuffield ideas. Later evaluation of over 100 teachers and 300 lessons revealed, however, that in reality little had changed. Only 17 teachers out of the sample were using the full range of Nuffield techniques, and 25 percent of the sample had not permitted the pupils to design their own experiments. Allowing for student input and control was, of course, central to the new approach. Similar failures in the United States to implement curricula calling for major changes in the teacher's role were the "new" science and social studies of the late 1960s.

Although many factors contribute to the failure of any curriculum effort it is probable that teacher difficulties and/or disinterest in giving up control over knowledge and the flow of verbal interaction was a major source of the problem in the Nuffield project. To relinquish control over knowledge is to relinquish control over students more generally. Teachers need control over student behavior in order to deal with knowledge, but at the same time, control over knowledge enables them to control student behavior. When a teacher is doing the talking—be it lecturing, questioning, or demonstrating—the focus, pace, and direction of classroom activity are in his or her hands. Without such control the role of the teacher is completely changed. Drastic changes in role expectations are apparently quite uncomfortable for most teachers.

In summary, the complexity of a typical classroom is such that control becomes an issue of paramount importance. In the press for on-the-spot responses to the behavior and questions of large numbers of students without opportunities for reflection or consultation, many teachers see as their only strength their overall control of the situation. In effect, then, the factors of privacy and immediacy may cause teachers to feel that autonomy and control are critical preconditions for the instructional process.

Sizing Up the Pupils One way that all teachers approach the issues of control and instruction is to spend considerable time "sizing up the pupils" (Delamont, 1983). In order to respond effectively to students, teachers must have some notion of what their students are like. They must be able to anticipate what students will say and do. Teachers use both their professional knowledge and their practical experience to make judgments and to develop perspectives about their students.

Sizing up the pupils is a continuous process that guides a teacher's actions. Observing students in and out of a classroom setting creates expectations based upon interpretation of those observations. Since teacher expectations often in-fluence pupil behaviors, these observations and interpretations are very important. Unfortunately, teachers' observations often are colored by personal and societal values that lead to unfair stereotyping and labeling.

As do all people, teachers sometimes make erroneous judgments of students based on race, sex, IQ, physical appearance, family situation, socioeconomic class, past per-formance, and reputation. Chapter 3 cited Ray Rist's study that demonstrated how a teacher unconsciously grouped students in ways that reflected the teacher's values as opposed to student ability. Delamont (1983) notes the remarks of a girl from one of her studies who indicates how quickly individual labels can be assigned: "I felt like saying Would you rather it went to the pigs? but you can't rebel against one teacher because if you do all the teachers are against you because you are rebellious!" (p. 64). This student comment is important because it leads to the last point about the teacher role—namely, that teachers are strongly influenced by their peer group and the information it circulates.

The Influence of a Teacher's Peer Group A teacher's colleagues are important at two levels. First, they offer practical advice and help. In interviews from a recent study (Provenzo, Cohn, & Kottkamp, 1985) teachers consistently said that when they need curricular and instructional advice, or simply someone to listen to their problems, they turn first to their fellow teachers. In addition to offering practical assistance, a teacher's colleagues form a reference group that, in turn, helps to shape the teacher's perspective. The importance of perspective to a teacher's work is indicated by the following definition:

> A perspective is an ordered view of one's world—what's taken for granted about the at-tributes of various objects, events and human nature. The fact that men have such ordered perspectives enables them to conceive of their changing world as relatively stable, orderly, and predictable. (Delamont, 1983, p. 60)

In the situation of immediacy, privacy, and autonomy, teachers clearly need a perspective shared by a reference group of colleagues to sustain them.

An example of the importance of the sustaining power of a reference group comes from Sandy's career. For four years she taught in an alternative program for high school freshmen who were having difficulty in accepting the traditional norms, beliefs, and student and teacher roles in the school. In the vernacular these students were considered losers, probable dropouts, and discipline problems because they did not accept the typical rules of the game. The students were assigned to Sandy and three other teachers in a large room for the entire school day. This restructuring of high school into an elementary school configuration was done to increase the teachers' ability to control the classroom social system. The four-teacher team or reference group developed a relatively consistent set of behaviors and expectations designed to help students improve their attitude to school.

The norms, beliefs, and role expectations that Sandy and her colleagues worked to develop were not, however, identical to those of many of the regular teachers. Sandy and her colleagues received many mixed messages from teachers outside the alternative setting. They would hear such comments as, "I'm sure glad *you* have those kids!" but also received criticism for norms of behavior that were "noisier" (more active) than those of teachers outside the program. It was extremely important that Sandy had a supporting peer group, both for structuring a good social and learning environment *and* for maintaining her own sense of purpose and effectiveness in what was a generally hostile external environment.

In sum, to be a teacher is to play a role that is characterized by immediacy, privacy, and autonomy. In order to teach a teacher must maintain certain levels of control and must know the students he or she is dealing with. Although any teacher is essentially alone in this endeavor, he or she frequently draws on colleagues for both a general perspective and practical help.

The Role of a Student The role of a student is dramatically different from that of a teacher because of the power differential. In contrast to a teacher's role, which is characterized by legitimate power and control, a student's role is one of subservience.

> Pupils are expected to learn, and to behave in ways that will facilitate learning, whether this is by sitting quietly absorbing the teacher's lecture, or busy by themselves with work sheets, apparatus, and "resources." They are expected to let their speech, dress, morals and behavior be monitored and corrected, and their state of knowledge constantly examined and criticized. (Delamont, 1983, p. 77)

The subservient role of the student makes sense in light of the control aspect of the teacher role. Roles in organizations like schools must fit together much like jigsaw puzzle pieces if organizational goals are to be met. The most immediate role partner of a teacher is a student. As the puzzle pieces must fit together, the student role must fit with the teacher role. The crowded nature of classrooms and the need for teacher control deeply affects the student role. Jackson's (1968) observations confirm Waller's earlier analysis that many of the aspects of the teacher role function to constrain the individual impulses of a large number of students.

> If everyone who so desired tried to speak at once, or struggled for possession of the big scissors, or offered a helping hand in threading the movie projector, classroom life would be much more hectic than it commonly is. If students were allowed to stick with a subject until they grew tired of it on their own, our present curriculum would have to be modified drastically. Obviously, some kinds of controls are necessary if the school's goals are to be reached and social chaos averted. (p. 13)

Jackson details several student role expectations from his observations of elementary classrooms. One result of a teacher's traffic management, timekeeping, and gatekeeping roles is that students inevitably experience *delay*. In crowds, time and individual attention from a single leader are scarce resources. Thus, one of the more or less invisible expectations of the student role is waiting patiently. Students wait in lines to get drinks, sharpen pencils, prepare for recess and lunch, and board the bus. During classroom discussions they learn to wait in invisible queues. Only one person may speak at a time; typically once a student has been recognized he or she must wait while others have their turn. A student may know all the answers and wave a hand enthusiastically at each teacher question, but it is part of the student role to wait for the next turn.

Students in the lower grades also learn to wait in small reading groups. Those not in the reading group often experience delay when they have questions about seatwork because the teacher is working with others. Students experience delay when the teacher takes attendance, collects lunch money, or deals with a message or other classroom interruption. Patience during many periods of delay is a major expectation of the student role. Recently educators have become increasingly aware of how much student time is consumed waiting. This awareness has resulted in a movement to increase the proportion of total classroom time students spend actually engaging in learning tasks as opposed to waiting. The descriptors associated with this new emphasis are *time on task* and *student engaged time*.

Delay, in turn, results in denial. Not every hand can be recognized, not every request can be granted. The cumulative effect of delay and denial is that students

Waiting in line in Luberta's classroom

Waiting to receive Ruth's attention

cease to expect immediate gratification. They do, however, expect interruptions or distractions. Lessons are disrupted by misbehavior, irrelevant comments, and visitors from outside the classroom. Exciting lessons must end because bells ring. Work is left incomplete, and questions are left unanswered.

Another expectation of the student role is that they learn to ignore those around them, learn to be alone in a crowd. Teachers in lower grades assign seatwork while they work in reading groups or on other endeavors. Students doing seatwork are expected to work on their own, to ignore those around them. The natural propensity for gregariousness becomes a discipline problem in a densely populated classroom where there is a need to maintain social control. In upper and lower grades alike part of the student role involves learning to be silent and to ignore those around you.

Another aspect of the student role is to be evaluated. In classrooms students are constantly the objects of evaluation from varied and often conflicting sources. Teachers are the most obvious and frequent evaluators. To be a student is to be under constant evaluation in terms of one's academic work and progress. Academic evaluation occurs through testing; marking seatwork, homework, and longer, more formal papers presented in the higher grades; comments on boardwork; teacher responses to student answers in class discussions or oral reading groups; and ultimately grades on report cards. Jackson notes that while students are under constant teacher evaluation they must wait patiently, suppressing desires for quick gratification, and not allowing themselves to become distracted by other students. Student motivation is also an object of teacher evaluation. Teachers desire students to demonstrate cooperation and hard work, and they praise or sanction students according to the motivation they perceive.

Students are also under constant evaluation from their peers. These evaluations typically center on personal qualities, and they become increasingly important and powerful shapers of behavior as students progress through school. Student reputations "for being smart or dumb, a sissy or a bully, teacher's pet or a regular guy, a cheater or a good sport" are grounded largely in peer observations and evaluations of classroom behavior (Jackson, 1968, p. 22). Conflicts between teacher and peer evaluations occur frequently. What a teacher praises may earn a student a reputation of teacher's pet among the peer group. Jackson suggests that this conflict is greater for males than females because behaviors associated with institutional compliance are more closely linked to female than to male stereotypes. Thus, the close proximity in which students are held brings ongoing social, behavioral, and academic evaluations.

Although both Delamont and Jackson underscore the generally subservient role of students, anyone who has been in a classroom knows that such subservience is not necessarily a given. In actuality student power is a force that every teacher must confront. Experienced teachers all too often talk of days when "no one will work"; "Martha refused to do her workbook"; "Johnny mouthed off at me in front of the whole class"; and when "no matter what I did I could not get the kids' attention back on the subject."

Consider for a moment the following descriptive notes taken by an undergraduate education student while observing an experienced foreign language teacher in a high school.

Period 4 students came into the room talking and continued to talk after the bell had rung. Miss Johnson gave Stacy and Michelle demerits for being late and told the class to get out their homework. Homework was put on the board. Chris and Pat had problems understanding where to put the negatives. While Miss Johnson was going over the placement of the negative, Theresa and Michelle began giggling. Miss Johnson told Theresa to turn around. After the homework was turned in, several drills were done, changing affirmative sentences to negative sentences. Shelly and Shelby were talking to each other. Miss Johnson reprimanded them for talking. After several other verbal reprimands to Theresa, Miss Johnson instructed her to move her desk to the front of the room. A few minutes later Miss Johnson was explaining how to form an imperative statement. Theresa kept turning around to look at Michelle. Miss Johnson heard the giggles and told Theresa to open the door and place her chair outside the door. Several students laughed. Theresa exclaimed, "Miss Johnson, that's embarrassing!" Miss Johnson replied, "Good, it ought to be!" Theresa moved outside and the explanation continued. While answering questions from students, Miss Johnson noticed Shelly and Shelby talking again. Miss Johnson gave orders: "Shelly and Nicole, change seats." Shelly said, "I was asking her a question about the work." "You should ask me," commented Miss Johnson. When Shelly and Nicole had exchanged seats, the drilling continued. At the end of the period, Miss Johnson commented, "Because we had so many talkers today, your homework will not only be the exercises but you can also take all the sentences on page 30 and put them in the negative. Perhaps tomorrow you will be quieter and more settled." Several moans were heard.

Miss Johnson is attempting to deal with student power. Her response is a rather ineffectual assumption of the role of policewoman. She is forced to deal continually with interruptions and disturbances. She ultimately but narrowly prevails by giving out punishments: demerits, moving Theresa out of the classroom, and assigning extra homework. The fact remains that the students have succeeded in disrupting the lesson. Miss Johnson's response to student power was experienced by all students in the class. Her less-than-optimal method for controlling behavior will create student expectations about her future behavior and about the kinds of behaviors they will be able to exhibit, and their likely consequences.

Almost every day and sometimes within every lesson teachers will encounter students who find their role constraining. Some of these students will develop their own unique role interpretations that are acceptable to the teacher. Others will get into trouble for stepping beyond the role. In addition to personality factors the degree of compliance or deviation from the assigned role can be contingent on a number of situational particulars: the teacher, the lesson, the time of day, the peer group support.

However, it is mainly when students band together because they find their role excessively constraining that they are able to exercise what Delamont calls *pupil power*. Subgroups and cliques that are antischool or antiteacher can pose serious control problems. In some classrooms the norm that gets established with a dominant clique or cliques is to work against rather than cooperate with the teacher. For example, one interviewee in a recent study (Provenzo, Cohn, & Kottkamp, 1985) discussed her problems with a high school chemistry class where six cheerleaders — a solid clique supported by the peer group structure of the entire school — successfully diverted classroom time and interactions toward social pursuits. In instances like this a teacher is in a constant power struggle for control.

Although cliques clearly exist in most classrooms, they do not entirely account for the presence or absence of pupil power. Sometimes, for example, a clique will encourage and support a deviant individual and sometimes it will withhold support. Moreover, sometimes even the worst students are "angels" and sometimes the "goody-goodies" will create problems for the teacher. Furlong (1976) offers an explanation in terms of what he calls the *interaction set*. His argument is that classrooms are dynamic environments that are constantly changing and that as a classroom situation changes, so does student assessment of how to react. Furlong (1976) defines an interaction set as a group that "at any one time will be those pupils who perceive what is happening in a similar way, communicate with each other, and define appropriate action together" (p. 79).

Whether one thinks in terms of cliques or interaction sets, however, the main point here is that subgroups of students united in purpose and action can exercise influence and power. If the group is proschool it can assist a teacher; if it is antischool it can thwart a teacher. Proschool groups who rebel occasionally will clearly be listened to more than antischool groups who consistently rebel. Students who have a high degree of status in their peer group will be in powerful positions to lead the charge either for or against a teacher.

Sizing Up the Teacher In order to determine which teachers can be influenced and manipulated and how, students will invariably both size up and test their teachers. It is central to their role. In sizing up teachers, students first consider their general ability to teach. All students—low and high ability alike—appear to respect a teacher who can create an environment conducive to learning where order, fairness, and clarity of instruction prevail. Students also judge teachers on their personal qualities. Physical appearance, speech, clothing, age, marital status, school status, and information on the teacher's private life are all part of this personal assessment (Delamont, 1983).

In testing a teacher, students are trying to determine whether the teacher can keep order and provide instruction. In addition, they are trying to figure out what is expected in terms of tasks, rules and grades, what can be manipulated, and what their boundaries are. Students want to know what will happen when they break the rules. For example, teachers frequently tell students they must raise their hands if they want to talk, or must behave in certain ways if they want to see a movie, or must be in their seats before the bell if they do not want to be counted tardy. Then in the press of classroom interaction they will sometimes permit students to shout out answers, see the movie despite poor behavior, or slide into the room after the tardy bell. Once students find that these rules are not enforced they generally keep testing for more openings.

The reverse, however, is also true. If students find that they cannot get away with breaking the rules they will usually accept and respect the limits. Consider, for example, the following situation, which was recorded by an undergraduate education student during an observation in a high school.

Today Mr. Stanford revealed himself as someone who really means what he says. He has a policy that three tardies mean suspension from the class. Derek who already has two tardies came into class on time today, but then asked Mr. Stanford if he could leave to get something important from his locker. The dialogue went as follows:

DEREK: Mr. Stanford, can I go to my locker real quick to get
    something. I really need it.
MR. STANFORD: If you can get back here before the tardy bell.
DEREK: I'll run.

The tardy bell rang a few seconds later and Derek was not back. About a minute later Derek dashed in the door and mumbled, "Sorry, Mr. Stanford." Mr. Stanford replied in a very businesslike matter-of-fact tone, "I'm sorry, Derek. Please take your things and go to the office. You are suspended from this class."
The class stared in stony silence. They seemed surprised and so was I.

In this particular instance the observer notes that the message Mr. Stanford was communicating to Derek was also a message to everyone in the class. Kounin (1970), who is interested in classroom discipline, has noted that when a teacher interacts with a single student in a classroom, there is usually *a ripple effect*. A teacher's actions with an individual student ripple through the entire classroom and everyone learns something about the teacher. That was certainly the case with Mr. Stanford—everyone was affected, even the observer.

Licata and Willower (1975) describe a particular student role called *brinkman*. Typically one or more students in a class will engage in brinkmanship behavior, especially early on in the development of a classroom social system. To be a successful brinkman is to test the limits of the teacher's control and behavioral system without getting into serious trouble. The brinkman is constantly probing to find where the *real* behavioral limits are as opposed to the stated ones. The idea of brinkmanship comes from a Native American tradition in which it was considered a greater act to touch but not harm an enemy than to kill him. A student successfully engaging in classroom brinkmanship touches the boundaries of the teacher's rule structure and lives to tell about it. The fact that the whole behavior sequence is public provides a ripple effect for the whole class.

In addition to the testing of rules there is a great deal of student testing of grades. In this area students often attempt to bargain with and to manipulate a teacher. They will try a host of different strategies in their attempts to secure a good grade. Becker et al. (1968) in a study of undergraduates at Kansas University found students trying to impress teachers through apple-polishing. One student described how he used to drop into his professors' offices and talk with them about their interests in an attempt to make a good impression. A part of apple-polishing is, of course, figuring out what a teacher believes and wants from the students and simply giving it to him or her. As one student put it: "It just doesn't pay to disagree with them, there's no point in it. The thing to do is find out what they want you to say and tell them that" (Becker et al., 1968, p. 100).

Delamont (1983) found similar views at a girls' school she studied. A student named Monica told her, "I make it my business to get on with teachers," and a friend of Monica's described her strategy: "[Good pupils] pay attention in class the whole time—suck up—clean boards, et cetera—make suggestions. Monica did that to Mrs. Bruce, and she absolutely adores her" (p. 104).

Delamont (1983) also found, however, that some teachers were not taken in by girls like Monica. Another girl, Claire, told her: "Some teachers can tell when you're trying to be one of their pets—like going up and cleaning the blackboard when you're not told to—some are taken in by that and some aren't" (p. 105).

Sometimes there is pupil manipulation in terms of trying to find out what will be on a test or what criteria the teacher will be using to evaluate students. Carter and Doyle (1982), for example, observed junior high students in a language arts class and found that students employed some rather sophisticated strategies to learn what was considered good work in terms of writing assignments. In the grammar assignments where criteria were clear the students were satisfied, but in the more complex and ambiguous writing assignments the students used various techniques to get clarity, including:

1. "Trying out" answers for assignments, to get teacher reactions
2. "Guessing," to elicit prompts from the teacher
3. Responding incorrectly, to secure answers from the teacher
4. Bringing "work in progress" to the teacher for suggestions and corrections
5. Bargaining as a group for information about accomplishing a task
6. "Contracting" with one student (with a history of success) to get answers from the teacher (Good & Brophy, 1984, p. 39)

Carter and Doyle conclude that when some students are asked to do something new and unpredictable, they will attempt to make the assignment more routine and predictable.

In other instances students use strategies to get good grades with the least amount of effort. In a fifth-grade class that one of the authors studied a girl named Andrea used a very simple but effective strategy to minimize her work load. The class had been assigned a worksheet on the skill of distinguishing between fact and opinion. There were a number of short paragraphs on the worksheet, and students were asked to put an *F* in front of the paragraphs that stated facts and an *O* in front of those that represented someone's opinion. Andrea got every question wrong and so received an *F* on her worksheet, along with a note to redo it. Andrea simply went back to her desk, erased each answer and put the opposite in its place. Then she returned to the back of the room where the teacher was checking the papers of other students. When it was Andrea's turn she got a 100 and a smiling face on her paper. The teacher, in the back of the room surrounded by students, had been too busy to realize that Andrea had not been gone long enough to redo the paper legitimately and, thus, to learn the skill. The author, however, who could see what happened, questioned Andrea. Andrea's response was, "Don't you know anything about fifth graders? We will do whatever we can to get through with our work fast."

In contrast to Andrea's rather simple approach at the fifth-grade level consider the more sophisticated strategy employed by a student at the University of Southern California. Good and Brophy (1984) report that this student successfully manipulated instructors to get extra time to study for exams. The strategy involved contacting instructors and asking to take the exam early. She knew that professors typically prefer that students who need to arrange a different exam time take the exams later as opposed to earlier for test security purposes. The result of her asking to take the exam early would be that the professors would offer to allow her to take the exam late, which gave her additional time to study. Often they gave her the same exam the rest of the class had, so she had the opportunity to find out exactly what was on the test. The icing on the cake, however, was the fact that she often made a good impression on the professors because of her willingness to take the exam early (Good & Brophy, 1984, p. 38).

Clearly, strategies to manipulate teachers range from simple to sophisticated, but the important point is that a major part of the student role, especially early on, is to first size up teachers and their expectations in terms of work and behavior and then to figure out strategies to cope with the tasks and rules. Since students have no legitimate power, they have to work at ways, both direct and indirect, to influence what happens. When students work together to manipulate the situation, they have more power. Similarly, individual students with high status among their peers can more easily generate support either for or against the teacher.

Student Peer Culture: In the Classroom and Beyond Many of the forces that enter a classroom with the students have their origins outside the classroom. The student peer culture, which has its own norms, beliefs, and expectations, is a prime example. Just as teachers are affected by their peers and the collective power of students, so the collective force of student peer culture affects individual students, teachers, and the whole classroom social system. The particular values and the solidarity of the peer culture in any school relates to pupil power and the particular ways that power is exercised. The power and solidity of student peer groups increases in the higher grade levels. Such influences go through rapid escalation when students go through puberty and become increasingly socially aware and self-conscious and invest tremendous energy in defining themselves as individuals within a particular sex role.

The United States Commission on Civil Rights (1967) described the important influence of student peer groups in a cryptic paragraph:

> At Madison Junior High School, if you cooperated with the teacher and did your homework, you were a "kook." At Brighton Junior High School, if you don't cooperate with the teacher and don't do your homework, you are a "kook.". . . At Madison we asked a question, "Are you going to college?" At Brighton the question always is "What college are you going to?" . . . What the pupils are learning from one another is probably just as important as what they are learning from the teachers. . . . It involves such things

as how to think about themselves, how to think about other people, and how to get along with them. It involves such things as values, codes, and styles of behavior.

Since James Coleman's landmark study *The Adolescent Society* (1961), there has been a continuous thread of scholarship describing student peer culture separate from and often at odds with the goals and values of adult society. Coleman, for example, found that the attributes and activities most valued by high school students were antithetical to the central academic and learning goals of the school. When boys were asked how they wished to be remembered in school they ranked three answers in the following order: (1) athletic star, (2) most popular, (3) brilliant student. Coleman also did sociometric analyses based on a question that asked students to list choices of individuals with whom they would like to associate. These responses were used to identify members of the leading crowds, groups whose individuals received disproportionately large numbers of choices. Among boys the athletic stars always received more status than the top scholars, though the athletic-scholar combination received the highest rankings. Similarly, among the girls those heavily invested in visible activities received more status than the top scholars. Coleman (1961) also discovered that the leading crowds were even *less* oriented than the student body as a whole toward what teachers desired of students.

In an earlier work Wayne Gordon studied the adolescent subculture in a school in which he had taught and counseled for 10 years. He concluded that status was more highly associated with participation in highly rated activities such as athletics, band, and certain clubs than with scholastic achievement. He was also able to document that the informal system of friendship cliques was "especially powerful in controlling adolescent behavior, not only in such matters as dress and dating, but also in school achievement and deportment" (Gordon, 1957, p. viii). In other words, the friendship groups, especially those with highest status, had a powerful effect on norms, beliefs, and role behaviors.

In the innovative study *Inside High School: The Student's World,* Philip Cusick (1973), a university professor, at age 32, became a high school student. He attended classes, did assignments, and was rather easily accepted into one of the higher-status, athletic-star cliques composed of seven football players and one basketball player. Cusick's study chronicles high school life from the perspective of membership in the leading crowd. The power of his group vis-à-vis other students, teachers, and even administrators was incredible. Cusick (1973) shows how the clique members and members of other high-status peer subgroups exercised significant influence on classroom situations:

> Those, like Jack, who were popular and who belonged to groups could and did exercise some control over formal classroom situations. It frequently seemed that those who were members of a prestigious group would, if the teacher were not taking strict

charge of the class, just take over with their group. In doing so they would exclude isolates and less popular students from participation. (p. 177)

That only a few students could take over and receive the rewards in class was brutally evident. Once when the teacher opened the session up to a discussion of religion, there were twenty-two students in the class and only five participated. One was Tony, the senior class president; another was Jean, Honor Society, vice-president and number one student; then there was Dick, a leader in almost everything; Mary, Student Council member and cheerleader; and finally Carol, the president of the Student Council. Although this sounds ridiculous enough, it appears even more so when we remember that four of these five were in a tight clique. The rest did not participate. One might say that they did not have any strong opinions, but I cannot accept that. At least some of those seventeen had some opinions, and suggestions about religion, but they kept them to themselves for an entire period while Dick, Mary, Jean, Carol and Tony carried on. (pp. 180–181)

The powerful influence of the student peer group on individual students is also illustrated by Cusick's (1973) experience:

One boy who had recently entered the school told me: "When I first came, I hated it. You know, Phil, I skipped fifty-eight days last year because I couldn't stand to come to school because I didn't know anyone, and when I tried to talk to someone, we would just exchange small talk, never get down to anything. I felt like a real outsider." . . . "Is that the most important thing you do in school, hang around with your friends?" "Like I said, Phil, when I didn't have any friends, I couldn't stand to come." (p. 65)

Cusick asked a number of his "friends" what they would do if they had to choose between flunking an exam and eating alone in the cafeteria. They invariably chose flunking the exam.

Finally, the power of the high-status clique was sufficient to challenge the authority of the assistant principal in charge of discipline, and win. Compare the following incident concerning students with a strong power base rooted in the student peer culture with the incident concerning Derek's tardiness in Mr. Stanford's class.

An incident occurred one afternoon, just prior to Christmas. As vice-president of the student council, Jack was responsible for decorating the building and asked Mr. Rossi [assistant principal] if he could go get a tree with Jim and Greg. Mr. Rossi said, "No."

"We're going anyway," said Jack.

"You do and you'll get suspended."

They went and returned and hour later carrying a large freshly cut tree on top of Greg's car. Mr. Vincent [principal] called them into his office and Jim's version of the confrontation went like this.

"Vincent says, 'This time you guys have gone too far, go see Mr. Rossi.' Then we go in Rossi's office and close the door. He says, 'You boys are going to get a little vacation, about five days' worth.'"

"'Bullshit,' I told him." . . .

"And Rossi yells, 'Don't talk like that.'"

"And Jim says, 'I'll talk any way I want to.' And then Rossi looks at Jack and starts laughing and then Jim starts laughing and then it's all over." (Cusick, 1973, pp. 101–102)

Such is the potential influence and power that high-status students may wield. They do not always wield such power, nor do they always run roughshod over teachers and administrators, but the potential is there.

Classroom Talk: Interacting Roles Although the discussion of student and peer group influence moved beyond the classroom to the larger setting of the school, the focus here is back to the classroom and the argument that the teacher and student roles fit together like pieces of a puzzle. Classroom talk, or the verbal interactions occurring between persons holding the two roles, provides a good illustration of the fit between expectations for the two roles. If, as noted earlier, teachers do most of the talking and questioning in the classroom students will invariably do little more than respond to teachers' comments and questions. This pattern has been observed repeatedly at different classroom levels.

One of the most interesting research projects of this type was conducted by Bellack et al. (1974). Their study involved tape-recording verbal interaction in 15 high school social studies classes in New York City. From the transcripts they concluded that one way to describe what was happening in the observed classrooms was to think in terms of what they called *the classroom game*. They maintained that if one looked closely one could see a language game of a similar type in each of the 15 classrooms. Although there were no explicit rules for this game, or even any recognition that such game was in progress, they found in each classroom studied a set of implicit rules (an aspect of the more or less invisible) that operated "with few deviations." The rules for the role of the teacher were quite different from the rules for the role of the students. What were these rules? According to Bellack et al. (1974) the rules for those who play the role of the teacher were as follows:

1. The teacher will be the most active single person playing the game. This means that he will make the most moves; he will speak most frequently and his speeches will usually be the longest . . . .
2. The teacher is responsible for structuring the form and content of the game. He will specify the subject matter of the game, and the rules for the game. Within any particular setting, as in various baseball parks, there will be specific ground rules. The teacher is responsible for setting these ground rules and for making them explicit to the other players. In addition to setting up the initial structure of the game, the teacher is responsible for launching new topics of discussion and for determining any changes that might occur in the form of play as the game proceeds.

3. The most frequent move of the teacher is called "soliciting." This is a directive move designed to elicit a specific response from the players called "pupils." Frequently, this move will be formulated in terms of a question, but may also be phrased in terms of a direct order, such as directing another player to speak, to open his book, or carry out any other action relevant to this game. . . .

4. After making a soliciting move, the teacher will normally expect a person playing the role of "pupil" to respond. It is then the teacher's responsibility to react to this response. Sometimes, he may react non-verbally, by nodding his head or perhaps by showing approval implicitly by moving to a new solicitation. In most instances, however, he is expected to react in an explicit fashion. Many of these reactions will be evaluative; that is, the teacher is expected either to approve or disapprove of the response made by the pupil player. . . .

5. In addition to reacting to immediately preceding statements, the teacher is also responsible for occasional summaries of larger parts of the discourse. . . .

6. Although either the teacher or the pupil may express "substantive" and "substantive-logical" meanings, it is, primarily, the teacher who is responsible for expressing meanings relevant to instructional processes. . . . (pp. 348–350)

According to Bellack et al. (1974) the rules for those playing the role of the pupil were more restricted:

1. The pupil's primary task in the game is to respond to the teacher's solicitations. This usually involves answering specific questions posed by the teacher, but may also involve following direct orders given by the teacher, such as "Open your book," or "Get up and shut the window." Whenever the teacher makes a soliciting move, the pupil will, if at all possible, attempt some form of response. The response may be right or wrong in terms of the teacher's expectations; it may be relevant or irrelevant to the ongoing game. In any case, the pupil is required to attempt some response to the teacher's solicitation. In extreme cases, the pupil may reply to a solicitation by saying, "I don't know" but this should be used rarely, if at all. The best policy for the pupil to follow in playing the game is "make a response whenever called upon."

2. The pupil does not structure the game; that is, he does not tell the teacher and other pupils what the game is to be about or how to play it. This is the task of the teacher. Occasionally, the pupil is called upon to give a report or to participate in a debate. This is a form of structuring, but pupils make such moves *only* when directed to do so by the teacher. Having fulfilled his assigned structuring obligation, the pupil will not structure again unless the teacher specifically directs him to do so.

3. In general, the pupil will keep his solicitations to a minimum. . . .

4. Even more important than the *don't* solicit rule is the *don't* react evaluatively rule. Under no condition is the pupil permitted to react evaluatively to a statement made by the teacher; that is, the pupil does not tell the teacher he is right or wrong, that he is doing well or doing badly. . . .

5. A corollary of the "don't react evaluatively" rule is the general principle, "within the classroom, teachers speak The Truth." This principle holds by virtue of the teacher's role in the game and the rules guiding pupils' play. Except under extraordinary circumstances, pupils overtly accept the teacher's statements as the spoken truth.

    On the other hand, pupils may or may not speak "The Truth." If one speaks the role of pupil, he must remember that merely uttering a statement does not guarantee that it will be accepted as true. In fact, an important part of the teacher's responsibility is to challenge, though mildly, pupils' statements which he believes to be invalid. In certain classes, pupils may even be challenged occasionally by other pupils.

6. In some classes, pupils are expected to make reactions that carry no explicit evaluative meaning. This will depend upon the ground rules established by the teacher. The only guide one can follow is the expectation of the teacher: does he or does he not expect the pupil to react to other pupils' statements?

7. Finally, a pupil player should remember that his primary task is to respond to the teacher's solicitations and to perform well on the final payoff test. If he fulfills both of these obligations and does not usurp the role of the teacher, then he will most likely play the game successfully. (pp. 350–352)

The findings of Bellack et al. are clear. In the classrooms under study there was a strikingly consistent pattern of verbal interaction in which the teacher was in complete control. The role of teacher was to structure the lesson, to ask the questions, and to react to the students' response. The role of the student was primarily to respond to the teacher's questions. Of course, Bellack et al. by expressing that pattern in terms of the rules mentioned are pointing out how the classroom game *is* played, not how it *should* be played.

Many scholars of classroom interaction bemoan the traditionally normative patterns observed by Bellack et al., and suggest that they do not lead to the highest levels of student intellectual development. These scholars call for change, but classroom verbal interaction does not seem to change. One reason it is difficult to change these language patterns is that they are very functional in maintaining control in a crowded social environment. The teacher role requires control. If students were to control more of the classroom verbal interaction by initiating more of the discussion and talking for prolonged periods, a teacher's ability to carry out other aspects of the teacher role, such as those of timekeeper and gatekeeper, would be diminished. Thus the pattern of verbal interactions continues, and the classroom game as described by Bellack et al. is played and replayed.

Moreover, it is important to recognize that the classroom game does not only apply to verbal interaction patterns. Jackson (1968) and others talk of the *hidden curriculum*—another of the more or less invisible aspects of the classroom—that accompanies the formally acknowledged curriculum. The hidden curriculum arises, in large part, out of the custody-control mandate of the schools. Part of a teacher's role is to establish control through procedural and behavioral norms. In order to achieve that control teachers reward students who comply with those norms. Students do learn the academic curriculum, but they come to understand that part of their role is to learn the hidden curriculum regarding behavior. They eventually see that to do well overall they must play the game of school. In Jackson's (1968) words:

> As he learns to live in school our student learns to subjugate his own desires to the will of the teacher and to subdue his own actions in the interest of the common good. He learns to be passive and to acquiesce to the network of rules, regulations, and routines in which he is embedded. He learns to tolerate petty frustrations and accept the plans and policies of higher authorities, even when their rationale is unexplained and their meaning unclear. Like the inhabitants of most other institutions, he learns how to shrug and say, "That's the way the ball bounces." (p. 36)

Other aspects of the hidden curriculum come more from the larger regional and national culture than from conditions imposed by the local school structure. These aspects of the hidden curriculum include sexism, racism, and classism, and the degree to which they exist varies widely from school to school and often from class to class. Careful scrutiny of the more or less invisible will indicate that these factors are embedded in the norms, shared beliefs, and roles of the social system.

The discussion in Chapter 3 of Ray Rist's analysis of Mrs. Caplow's kindergarten class is an example of how classism was part of the hidden curriculum in her class. Students with middle-class values were grouped together in a higher or fast-learner group whereas students coming from lower-socioeconomic family backgrounds were put in two slower groups, regardless of their objectively measured abilities. Part of the hidden curriculum was to learn that middle-class students are fast and lower-class students are slow learners. To the degree that racial or ethnic background also correlated with socioeconomic status or became a subconscious criterion for grouping in Mrs. Caplow's class they then also became part of the hidden curriculum learned in kindergarten. Another aspect of the hidden curriculum is sexism. To the degree that teachers encourage girls to play with dolls and boys to play with blocks they are contributing to sex-role stereotyping. At the secondary level this element in the hidden curriculum often comes out in official and informal counseling of young women to take home economics and to avoid higher math while young men are often counseled in just the reverse.

The variation from school to school and classroom to classroom in the degree of classism, racism, and sexism inherent in the hidden curriculum is related to a number of factors. The textbooks used are often an unrecognized source for supporting or challenging racial, ethnic, and sexual stereotypes. The values and beliefs of an individual teacher, a Mrs. Caplow contrasted with Luberta Clay, Jacquie Yourist, or Larry Wells, makes a tremendous difference in what is taught and learned in a more or less invisible way in the classroom. The amount of support or antagonism an individual teacher's belief system receives from the teacher peer group and principal in the school also affects the strength of particular messages inherent in the hidden curriculum. For example, when there are shared beliefs among all adults in a school either that all students can learn or that only certain kinds can learn, the strength of this aspect of the hidden curriculum is much greater. Thus, just as student outcomes related to the formal curriculum vary from school to school and room to room, the outcomes related to the hidden curriculum — messages about control and "appropriate" ways of viewing the self — also vary.

CONCLUSION

To be an insightful classroom observer as well as teacher is to be aware of the hidden curriculum, the classroom and school games, and the specific rules, norms, and role expectations for teachers and students. To be an effective teacher you must be able to understand the school as a culture and the classroom as a social system; to see the patterned but more or less invisible regularities; and to recognize the well-defined roles of the teachers and students. But to be a teacher is also to be in a position to direct the social system in a way that allows for some personalization and creative interpretation within the role. Chapter 10 will argue that to be a teacher also involves putting oneself into the role. That chapter will also illustrate through the five case study teachers that it *is* possible to deviate from the more negative aspects of roles, norms, and beliefs typically found in schools.

DISCUSSION QUESTIONS

1. Carefully reread the sections of Chapters 2 and 4 that contain the descriptions of classroom interaction and behavior in Ruth's, Luberta's, Jacquie's, Larry's, and Sandy's classes. What elements of student and teacher roles, shared beliefs, and norms do you see in those descriptions? Do these five teachers approach their work and structure their classroom social systems in ways that are not totally in alignment with the general descriptions of classroom social structure in this chapter? Do Ruth, Luberta, Jacquie, Larry, and Sandy do things to mitigate some of the more negative aspects of typical classroom social system structure? Your observations about the case study teachers may yield new possibilities for developing a classroom social structure. Can you find any of these alternatives in classrooms you observe?

2. What can happen when teacher and student expectations for role behavior differ? In what kinds of settings or under what conditions is such basic disagreement likely to occur? What can a teacher do in circumstances of essential conflict between his or her expectations and those of the students? Have you observed such situations in a classroom?

ACTIVITIES

1. Listen to student conversations while attending several sequential classes. What can you learn about their perceptions of the student role and the teacher role?
2. Interview some students about classroom rules and the roles of teacher and student. Ask them what the norms of the class are and how they know. If they have more than one teacher try to get them to contrast them. This is not an easy project but one you may learn a great deal from.
3. Develop a simple language interaction analysis form that counts the frequency of teacher and student talk. See if you can find classrooms that deviate significantly from the norms that research specifies about teacher and student talk. Look for how these classrooms differ from the typical classroom in other ways.
4. Find a classroom in which traditional recitation is a dominant pattern of teacher-student interaction. Also, find a classroom where a less traditional form of interaction occurs frequently. Alternative patterns might include individualized work, small-group discussion or projects, and inquiry approaches in large or small groups. Attend carefully to the verbal interaction in both settings. Can you detect the rules of the game described by Bellack et al. in the traditional setting? Can you find the same rules in the less traditional setting? If you cannot identify Bellack's rules, can you discover an alternative set from observing the interactions?

QUESTIONS TO GUIDE OBSERVATION

1. Does the teacher act as a traffic cop? supply sergeant? judge? gatekeeper of dialogue? timekeeper? Look for specific behaviors that fit each role.
2. What kind of on-the-spot decisions does the teacher make?
3. Does the teacher control knowledge as well as behavior? Who does the most talking in the classroom? Who asks the most questions in the classroom?
4. How much time do students spend waiting for the teacher? Do they experience denial, interruptions, disruptions? Do they have difficulty ignoring students around them?
5. In what ways does the teacher evaluate students? In what ways do peers evaluate students?
6. Are there student cliques? Do they exercise pupil power?
7. Do individual students play the brinkman role?
8. What evidence is there of apple polishing on the part of students?
9. Do students use a variety of strategies to size up and manipulate the teacher?

10. Do teachers and students participate in the classroom game as described by Bellack et al.?
11. What other roles and games are teachers and students playing?
12. What is the hidden curriculum of the classroom? What evidence is there of classism? Racism? Sexism?

QUESTIONS TO GUIDE TEACHER INTERVIEWS

1. What norms do you try to establish, and what expectations do you hold for student behavior?
2. What is your approach for getting appropriate norms established, and how do you respond to those who fail to live up to expectations?
3. What are the biggest control problems you face?
4. How do you size up students?
5. What kinds of student cliques do you encounter? How do you deal with them?
6. Do you feel that your work is characterized by immediacy? privacy? autonomy? Explain.
7. Do you encounter any students who try to manipulate you? How do you respond?
8. Do you worry more about control of student behavior or about curriculum and instructional issues?

REFERENCES

Becker, H. S., Geer, B., & Hughes, E. C. (1968). *Making the grade: The academic side of college life*. New York: Wiley.

Bellack, A. et al. (1966). *The language of the classroom*. New York: Teachers College Press.

Bellack, A. et al. (1974). The classroom game. In R. T. Hyman (Ed.), *Teaching: Vantage points for study* (2d ed., pp. 347–354). Philadelphia: Lippincott.

Carter, K., & Doyle, W. (1982). Variations in academic tasks in high and average ability classes. Paper delivered at the annual meeting of the American Educational Research Association, New York.

Colman, J. S. (1961). *The adolescent society*. New York: Free Press.

Cusick, P. A. (1973). *Inside high school: The student's world*. New York: Holt, Rinehart & Winston.

Delamont, S. (1983). *Interaction in the classroom*. New York: Methuen.

Flanders, N. A. (1970). *Analyzing teacher behavior*. New York: Addison-Wesley.

Furlong, V. John (1976). Interaction sets in the classroom. In M. Stubbs & S. Delamont (Eds.), *Explorations in classroom observation*. Chichester: Wiley.

Galton, Maurice, Simon, Brian, & Croll, Paul. (1980). *Inside the primary classroom*. London: Routledge & Kegan Paul.

Good, T. L., & Brophy, J. E. (1984). *Looking in classrooms* (3d ed.). New York: Harper & Row.

Gordon, C. W. (1957). *The social system in the high school.* Glencoe, IL: Free Press.

Hoetker, J., & Ahlbrand, W. P., Jr. (1969). The persistence of the recitation. *American Educational Research Journal, 6,* 145–168.

Hoy, W. K., & Miskel, C. G. (1982). *Educational administration: Theory, research, and practice* (2d ed.). New York: Random House.

Jackson, P. W. (1968). *Life in classrooms.* New York: Holt, Rinehart & Winston.

Kounin, J. S. (1970). *Discipline and group management in classrooms.* New York: Holt, Rinehart & Winston.

Licata, J. W., & Willower, D. J. (1975). Student brinkmanship and the school as a social system. *Educational Administration Quarterly, 11*(2), 1–14.

Provenzo, E. F., Jr., Cohn, M. M., & Kottkamp, R. B. (1985). *Teacher work incentives and rewards: A twenty year perspective.* National Institute of Education Research Project.

Schlechty, P. C. (1976). *Teaching and social behavior: Toward an organizational theory of instruction.* Boston: Allyn & Bacon.

Smith, L. M., & Geoffrey, W. (1968). *The complexities of an urban classroom.* New York: Holt, Rinehart & Winston.

U. S. Commission on Civil Rights. (1967). Racial isolation in public schools. Washington, D.C.: U. S. Government Printing Office.

Waller, W. (1932). *The sociology of teaching.* New York: Wiley.

7

CLASSROOM AUTHORITY
AND CONTROL

INTRODUCTION

When a teacher enters a classroom for the first time he or she will be greeted by 20 to 35 eager and not-so-eager faces. Neither the teacher nor the students will have had any part in choosing each other. Some of the students will prefer not to be in the class, or even in school, and may even be willing to make the point forcefully. Unless the teacher establishes authority and control early, no organized learning will occur. This first-day confrontation with reality is scary for most new teachers. Even veterans, if honest, will admit that they feel increased anxiety on the first day of a new school year.

For the past two decades the Gallup Poll has conducted an opinion survey on public education from a scientifically selected sample of adults across the nation. For the last five years, *lack of discipline* has been the first choice of this sample from among a list of perceived school problems. Clearly, the beginning teacher is not the only one concerned with the issues of authority and control.

The focal point of this chapter is the expectation that teachers control small social systems populated by immature and only partially socialized individuals—students in classrooms. This issue of authority and control will be analyzed primarily through the conceptual lenses of anthropologists and sociologists. Both of these disciplines focus on human interaction in groups or social contexts rather than on isolated individuals. This chapter is closely linked to the previous one since authority and control are a part of any social system. In fact, it is difficult to separate a discussion of authority and control from that of a social system. It is done in this book only for purposes of analysis. Although there will be some reference to the aspects of classroom life raised in Chapter 6, these will be discussed from a different perspective and through new concepts.

Classroom control is simply a visible aspect of the larger issue of authority and control that pervades American education. Although teachers are acutely aware of a need for discipline many are only subconsciously aware of larger authority and control issues. Such issues include the role of the school principal, school district organization, local, state, and federal governance sources, and extralegal influences. These broader aspects of authority and control will be reserved for Chapter 12, where their discussion will put the issue of classroom control within a larger perspective.

This chapter begins with a careful definition of authority, an important concept and something that every teacher needs to understand. Authority is popularly confused with both power and authoritarianism, which are different concepts and not very useful in effective teaching. After comparing these terms the chapter discusses the link between teacher authority and classroom control using the familiar concepts of social system, roles, expectations, and norms. The influences of the teacher, students, and the larger school and community setting are all tied to the development of teacher authority and control within the evolving classroom social system. Discussion then shifts to specific teacher management behaviors that research studies have shown to be associated with high teacher authority and effective classroom control. The chapter concludes with concrete examples of teacher management behaviors, authority, and control taken from observations of and interviews with the case study teachers.

This chapter asserts that authority and control are neither mysterious nor developed through a bag of tricks and gimmicks. Rather, they are inextricably bound up with all other aspects of excellence in teaching. In order to gain this perspective keep these questions in mind: What are the most important types of authority for a teacher to possess, and how are these earned? How are authority and control related to teacher management of the physical setting and the classroom social system and to a command of curricular content and teaching methods?

POWER AND AUTHORITY

Power is social control. Put simply, "one who possesses power gets what he wants despite opposition" (Hage, 1980, p. 54). Power is a broad concept encompassing control through means ranging from direct coercion to gentle suggestion. The coercive end of the spectrum is not very useful for accomplishing the goals of schools (Etzioni, 1975). Coercion, applied to students or teachers, typically results in alienation and psychological, if not physical, withdrawal.

Authority is a more limited but a more useful concept. Authority does not involve coercion and is not to be confused with authoritarianism. Authority is the probability that specific commands will be obeyed by a group (Weber, 1947). It differs from power in three ways. In authority relationships, the followers: (1) give voluntary compliance to legitimate commands; (2) suspend their own criteria for decision making in a particular situation and instead accept the criteria of the leader (Simon, 1957); and (3) create a group norm legitimizing the actions of the leader (Blau & Scott, 1962). Thus, authority is a narrow but legitimate subset of power. To possess authority is to possess social control with the consent of those controlled. *Authority is exactly what every classroom teacher desires!*

Weber (1947) describes three types of authority. *Charismatic authority* arises from devotion of group members to a particular personality who inspires trust and a personal following. The subject of authority is a person, and such authority is not transferable to others. Administrators, teachers, and students may possess charismatic authority among a particular group. Teachers may follow the directive of a principal or students the directives of teachers because of a particular mystique about them. Such charismatic authority can be put to good use in teaching because it makes classroom control much easier. However, not all teachers possess charisma.

The second type of authority suggested by Weber is *traditional*. This authority is based on a group norm of giving allegiance to a particular organizational role or position, such as to teachers, and has its origins in tradition. A teacher possesses this sort of authority to the degree that students believe teachers should be obeyed simply because they are teachers, a belief that was passed on as part of the traditional family outlook. Another example of traditional authority is the natural deference of the very young to older persons. This too is supported by traditional family and societal norms. Elementary teachers receive more traditional authority than do secondary teachers, but at no level can it be demanded of students. In general, the traditional authority base for teachers has declined over the past decades as the educational level of parents has risen and as traditions of all kinds have given way to change. However, the granting of traditional authority differs among various ethnic and cultural groups.

The third type of authority is *legal-rational*. This authority is based in social contract or law. Obedience is related not to a person or a position, but to abstract agreements and principles. A teacher, for example, owes compliance to a principal in certain areas because in accepting employment in the school he or she entered into a social contract in which the principal is granted the authority to carry out such organizational tasks as scheduling classes, disciplining students, and evaluating the teacher's work. Students grant legal authority to teachers when they accept a teacher's enforcement of attendance, grading, or dress-code policies. All teachers have access to some legal authority, although in itself it is a rather restricted basis for social control and one that is not necessarily recognized as legitimate by every student.

There is another way of analyzing the concept of authority. Robert Peabody (1962) differentiates between formal and functional authority. *Formal authority,* similar to Weber's legal-rational authority, is established in positions, rules, and regulations. This is the authority base teachers receive when they are hired because of the implicit social contract with their students. This type of authority "comes with the territory." All teachers receive it when they accept jobs. The problem with formal authority is its narrow, nonexpandable base. Everyone who is a teacher receives roughly the same amount.

Functional authority is both expandable (or contractable) and variable from teacher to teacher. The sources of functional authority are competence and personal characteristics. This type shares some of Weber's idea of charismatic authority, but the idea of competence is new. Unlike with formal authority, teachers can increase their functional authority and thereby can increase the degree of student compliance.

Research shows that the personal characteristics of teachers influence their classroom authority. Students grant more respect and authority to teachers with the personal attributes of cheerfulness, friendliness, sincerity, emotional maturity, and good mental health and personal adjustment than teachers lacking such traits. In addition, teacher *ego strength* has been associated with good classroom management. From ego strength flows the basic self-confidence that allows a teacher to remain calm in a crisis, to listen actively without defensiveness, to avoid placing students in win-or-lose situations, and to maintain a rational, problem-solving orientation rather than nonproductive (e.g., punitive, withdrawal) emotional states (Brophy & Putnam, 1979, p. 188).

Competence is the other basis of functional authority and it too is tied to observable classroom behavior. Teachers' functional authority will probably increase if they know their subject matter; maintain high expectations for learning and behavior; organize groups effectively; ask good questions and lead effective discussions; defuse tense situations before they explode; teach exciting lessons and use varied approaches; find ways to help all students learn; are adept at forming a classroom social system; and manage or orchestrate the flow of classroom activity smoothly. Sound utopian? Perhaps; but good teachers are perceived by their students as behaving in these ways. Leaf through Chapters 2 and 4; look for these attributes in Ruth Christopherson, Jacquie Yourist, Larry Wells, Luberta Clay, and Sandy Snodgrass. What is important to remember about functional authority is that it grows as teachers gain experience.

On the other hand, a teacher's functional authority can contract, with disastrous results. Again, authority is granted by followers, students in this case, and legitimized by group norms of acceptance. A teacher may also behave in ways that the majority, or even a vocal minority, of students in a classroom view as incompatible with the teacher role. Such interpretations of a teacher's behavior might include: bias toward particular students; lack of knowledge; lack of confidence; fluctuating or inconsis-

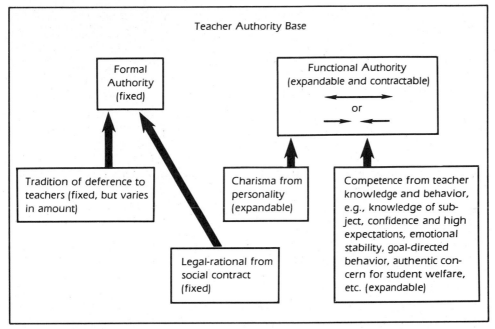

Figure 7.1   Sources of teacher authority and student voluntary compliance

tent emotional orientations; inability to keep reasonable order; lack of fairness; a consistently boring approach to lessons; assignment of much busy-work; demands for learning unaccompanied by a reasonable rationale; and attempting to win over students by becoming like them. Such behaviors probably lead to the loss of functional authority. When this happens a teacher is left with only a formal or legalistic base of authority, a very narrow and inadequate base of operation. Teachers with only formal authority are ineffective. The various types and sources of teacher authority are shown in Figure 7.1.

The importance of voluntary compliance and legitimizing group norms as the basis for authority is especially apparent in multicultural classrooms or classrooms in which the teacher is from one cultural background and the students from another. Under these circumstances the types of behavior the teacher assumes to be acceptable may not be so to the students. For example, most teachers from middle-class backgrounds consider it a sign of respect for the students to look the teacher in the eye when he or she is being disciplined. Students who look down or away exhibit body language implying disrespect. It says to a middle-class teacher, "I am not listening." However, if this teacher demands that a student from any one of a number of minority groups look him or her in the eye, the teacher stands to lose a good degree of respect, especially if the situation occurs in a classroom filled with students from the same minority group. In some cultures the behaviors to display respect and deference are *reversed* from those of the middle-class mainstream, and to look down shows respect (Weiss & Weiss, 1977). Multicultural settings call for careful attention to the behavioral basis of authority. They also remind people of the important fact that authority is granted by the followers.

The old saw, You can't demand respect; you have to earn it, condenses this whole discussion of authority into a single sentence. *Authority* as defined in this chapter is similar to *respect*. Both terms imply voluntary compliance. Authority that can be demanded is very circumscribed and only legal or formal in nature. A teacher cannot be effective on that basis alone. Authority that can be earned is largely functional and, to a lesser degree, charismatic. In this sense the more teachers invest in improving their teaching skills, the better they will become, the fewer discipline problems they will face, and the more fun they will have.

CLASSROOM CONTROL

All teachers must concern themselves with classroom control. Effective veteran teachers are noticeably less self-conscious about this issue than are novices. This fact is understandable, for being able to control a class of students is one of the major factors that determines whether a first-year teacher's contract is renewed. Classroom control is one of the major criteria by which not only administrators but also teachers judge the effectiveness of their peers (Lortie, 1975).

As noted earlier, Smith and Geoffrey (1968) define classroom control as "the relationship between teacher direction, usually verbal, and a high probability of pupil compliance" (p. 67). Interestingly this definition is a paraphrase of Weber's general definition of authority. Thus can be seen the link between teacher authority and classroom control; they are, in a sense, the same. When teachers possess real authority—functional as well as formal—they are in control. This is a very positive circumstance since the control is granted to them and legitimized by those they are controlling.

The concepts of roles, norms, and social systems introduced in Chapter 6 are useful in understanding the evolution of an authority-control relationship between a teacher and his or her students. A *role* is a set of behaviors expected of an individual occupying a given position in a group. These behavioral expectations can be seen as privileges, obligations, responsibilities, and powers.

The primary roles in a classroom are teacher and student. Examples of role expectations for teachers include: freedom of movement around the room (privilege); maintenance of order; initiation of student learning and reporting student achievement (obligations and responsibilities); invoking sanctions and rewards; making decisions concerning sequences of lessons and their content; and choosing particular students to fill specific roles such as paper monitor or crossing guard (powers). Examples of role expectations for students include: raising a hand to be recognized before speaking; completing assigned work; following teacher instructions; waiting patiently when the teacher is working with another student (obligations and responsibilities); deciding whether to volunteer answers; and controlling energy flow into schoolwork (rights and privileges). Clearly, for students, the responsibilities and obligations predominate whereas teachers have a more balanced set of both privileges and powers and obligations and responsibilities.

Role expectations for teachers and students do not come preset and do not automatically constitute a functional social system. Such roles are established in the hands of competent teachers, teachers who are authority figures in the social microcosm of the classroom. As the authority figure the teacher is the major source of expectations and norms, and it is in the process of developing and nurturing the social system that the teacher solidifies authority and classroom control.

Norms are rules specifying appropriate and inappropriate behaviors that have become accepted by group members. Thus, norms contain expectations for the interactions among various roles. For example, in one classroom it may be the norm for a teacher to employ specific sanctions before students stop talking among themselves, whereas in another classroom a gentle reminder may be sufficient to achieve the same result. The different sets of teacher-student interactions have become normative in the two classrooms.

A social system is the pattern of normative, behavioral relationships that exist among members of various roles. Put another way, the interaction of roles, role expectations, and norms constitute a social system. The following section looks at the development of a functional classroom social system, one in which the teacher has solid authority and in which the purposes of schooling are accomplished. See Figure 7.2 for a diagram of this process.

DEVELOPING A SOCIAL SYSTEM WITH TEACHER AUTHORITY AND CLASSROOM CONTROL

All classrooms exist within larger contexts, and people or groups in those contexts have expectations for the type of teaching and control that a teacher will pursue. Important extraclassroom sources of expectations are other teachers in the school, the principal, the superintendent, central office personnel, parents, and taxpayers. The expectations of these groups affect the social system developed within the classroom. Some degree of congruence must exist between these external sets of expectations and a teacher's classroom. For example, if a teacher is working in a school where the expectations are minimum basic skills achievement, tight teacher control, teacher-directed lessons, diagnostic teaching, and a great deal of time-on-task behavior, trouble will arise if the teacher attempts to develop a classroom environment characterized by emphasis on social adjustment, student participation

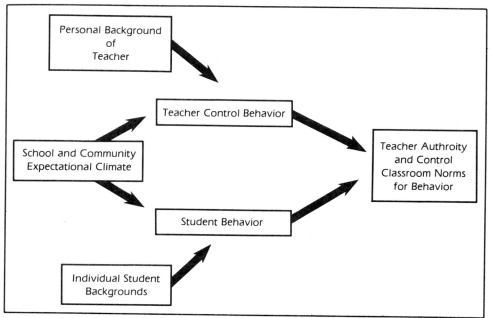

Figure 7.2   Classroom control and social system development

in decisions about curriculum and classroom control, and much general discussion. The expectational climate surrounding teachers, then, puts limits on the kinds of control they can hope to establish. However, this external expectational climate will also support a teacher's efforts to develop control if those efforts are congruent with community values.

Interacting with the expectational climate is a teacher's personal philosophy of teaching. As discussed earlier teachers come to their work with varying orientations. Assuming reasonable congruence between the outside expectations and the teaching goal, teachers' attempts at classroom control should match their teaching objectives. For example, a teacher who emphasizes discussion and independent study in order to develop critical reasoning and student initiative might also have students develop, critique, and internalize their own rationale for classroom order. In this case control procedures might deemphasize rule enforcement since the goal is to have the class recognize the need to develop and enforce behavioral norms. Here a teacher plays the role of facilitator more than that of director. This view of control will not work in all cases and will fail in many. If, for instance, a teacher confronts a class with a history of disruption, in which the expectational climate is one of order and quiet and the educational goals are those of basic skills mastery, then a much tighter system of teacher control is needed. In short, the establishment of an effective classroom control system and of desired behavioral norms will result in part from the interaction of a teacher's own purposes and the expectational climate in the school.

Students enter the classroom subject to the same two categories of influence (expectational climate and personal purpose) as their teachers. The expectational climate affecting students comes from their parents, their general expectations of school climate as interpreted through their previous classroom experiences, and, increasingly with advancing age, the expectations of their chosen friendship groups — peer group pressure. Recall Luberta's comment that many of her students come with different ideas of control from home and other teachers and therefore initially see her low-key manner as weakness. In addition, students have their own purposes for being in school, some of which are shared and others of which are individual.

Except in the case of kindergarten or first-grade teachers, incoming students will have been socialized into one or more classroom control systems in previous years. These students will expect a viable control system. This expectation is further supported by the desire of almost all human beings to live under reasonably predictable conditions. All groups develop predictable patterns of interaction and norms to support them. This is true whether the group is the board of directors of a multinational corporation, players on an athletic team, or members of a street gang. In short, students enter the classroom with past experiences of classroom social systems and a general expectation that some predictability and control will be established in their new classroom.

Nash (1976) carried out a study among English students designed to answer the question of exactly what students expected of their teachers in the way of classroom behavior. He found that students expected effective management, and he isolated six themes. Students expected teachers to keep order; teach effectively; explain things satisfactorily; and be interesting, friendly, and fair. If teachers acted in these general ways the students tended to grant them authority and compliance. If teachers did not act according to these expectations students tended not to like them or to go along with them. Note that Nash's research findings overlap greatly with the personal attributes and behaviors associated earlier with functional authority.

Nash's study shows that teachers who avoid setting limits and imposing a workable structure for the social system run into trouble. Experienced teachers understand the need to invent the wheel anew each time a new class is formed. Teachers cannot safely assume that students know the roles, role expectations, and the norms they wish to establish and that students will automatically act accordingly. Every new classroom is a new group, and every new group must go through the process of establishing those roles, expectations, and norms that constitute the social system. So unless the teacher wishes to create an authority-control vacuum that the students will quickly fill with their own rules because of their need for predictability, a teacher must move quickly to establish a social system.

Kounin (1970) conducted a major series of studies concerned with effective classroom management and control. Original attempts to focus on how teachers coped with and handled discipline problems once they occurred were generally unsuccessful in differentiating between successful classroom managers, those with smooth running rooms, and unsuccessful managers, those with chaotic, confusion-filled rooms. Looking at what teachers did after discipline problems erupted did not explain much. However, looking at what teachers did that prevented discipline problems in the first place proved to be of major importance in explaining the difference between successful and unsuccessful teachers. Classroom control, thus, appears more related to preventative management than to the disciplining of students once trouble occurs. Kounin coined the term *withitness* to describe a major attribute of effective managers. With-it teachers are constantly monitoring classroom activities, are always aware of what is happening, and are sensitive to situations that may develop into trouble.

Teacher classroom management has been defined as "planning and conducting activities in an orderly fashion; keeping students actively engaged in lessons and seat-work activities; and minimizing disruptions and discipline problems" (Brophy & Evertson, 1976). Good managers plan effectively; their lessons are interesting. They have needed materials readily at hand. They plan meaningful work that is matched to their students' levels. They minimize delays, disruptions, and interruptions of lessons. They create appropriate rules, and they often use capable students to help the others. They spend little time disciplining individual students (Brophy & Evertson, 1976; Good & Brophy, 1978). They perform at a high level the various teacher roles. Thus, the lesson content, the objectives, and the actual learning activities all contribute to the effectiveness of a teacher's classroom control. In short, competent teachers are effective managers who have functional authority.

Trouble will erupt periodically in the best-managed classrooms. Throughout this chapter the contention has been that prevention is the best approach to trouble. Specific little hints and tricks for discipline have not been discussed because a solid understanding of the classroom social system and authority system is more useful than tricks that only work in particular circumstances. There are, however, a number of specific approaches to classroom management, control, and discipline that have been developed over the past several decades. Although this introductory text does not detail these various approaches, references with brief annotations are presented at the end of the chapter. These approaches should not be viewed as isolated tricks or gimmicks but rather as a means of developing norms in a social system and functional authority through competence in managing classroom behavior.

A CONTINUUM OF CLASSROOM CONTROL SYSTEMS

After observing the classrooms of 15 teachers for a full school year, Mitchell, Ortiz, and Mitchell (1983) describe four points along a continuum of classroom control systems. At one pole the classroom has essentially no rules, is often in chaos, and is a setting in which little learning occurs. At the other pole the classroom is orderly, students accept and internalize the rules, and the teacher is granted a great deal of authority. Four points along the continuum will be described, beginning with the least and ending with the most desirable control system. These four positions are illustrated in Table 7.1.

The worst case, at Point 1, is the classroom in which there is essentially no visible rule structure and the teacher possesses little authority. Students simply choose not to comply with teacher directives. These classrooms continually totter on the brink of chaos. The methods by which teachers in such classes attempt to maintain order include: shouting, threats, repetition of requests, and repeatedly sending students to the principal. Little teaching occurs. Teachers in these classes spend large amounts of time addressing individual student behaviors—telling individuals to stop talking, stop hitting others, stop moving around the room, get a pencil, or move to another location. These teachers are not good managers. They seem to build in delays and interruptions in lessons; their classes lack a smooth flow of purposeful work, and students often ignore them. Such teachers have little or no understanding of the concepts developed in this chapter. They completely lack functional authority, and their attempts to evoke formal authority (e.g., sending students to the principal) also fail. New teachers who show such lack of control usually do not have their contracts renewed. Some tenured teachers, however, persist in this mode year after year. The human cost in such classrooms is very high.

The somewhat better Point 2 along the continuum is the classroom in which rules exist but are viewed by the students as arbitrary, capricious, or lacking in fundamental purpose. The rules are often enforced by overt power strategies. Since the students do not "own" or have a stake in the rule system, the teacher must hover over the classroom like a police officer on surveillance. Teachers in such classes have some functional authority based on their ability to wield coercive strategies. Learning may occur as long as the teacher is present, but a climate of tension and conflict pervades the setting, which reduces the learning potential.

Next comes Point 3 where explicit rules exist that students have accepted as the norm. Teachers in these classrooms take pains to make the rules quite explicit, often by discussing them with their students and offering rationales for their existence. Rules may be as simple as: (1) no inappropriate talking; (2) remain seated

Table 7.1   Points along a continuum of classroom control systems

| | Growth in Functional Authority of Teacher | | | |
	Point 1	Point 2	Point 3	Point 4
Rule Structure	No visible rule structure	Explicit rules exist but are seen by students as arbitrary or lacking in purpose	Explicit rules exist and are accepted by students as useful	Rules have become internalized, normative, no longer explicitly discussed
Teacher Authority Base	Formal authority only	Formal authority backed by functional use of coercion	Functional authority in addition to formal	Broad functional authority in addition to formal
Teacher Behaviors	Ineffective requests, pleading, threatening, shouting, or showing resignation; dealing with individuals rather than creating a social system with appropriate norms	Adept use of power and coercive strategies; constant vigilance	Effective explication of rules and public praise to celebrate desired behaviors; private or public reprimand for offenders; frequent responses to help make rules visible and normative	Rules accepted well enough that control is exercised by giving directions to keep student behaviors on track
Student Behaviors	Often ignore teacher attempts to create order; much inattention to lessons; many discipline problems	Orderly when teacher is present to enforce with coercion; order breaks down when teacher is not present	Generally orderly behavior	Orderly behavior based on thorough acceptance of norms

SOURCE: D. Mitchell, F. Ortiz, and T. Mitchell, *The Cultural Basis of Teacher Rewards and Incentives.* University of California, Riverside, 1983.

unless permission is given to do otherwise; and (3) no name calling or hitting. Rules such as these are generally accepted by students as reasonable and legitimate to provide safety, order, and the channeling of energy into learning activities.

Rules are important, but it is possible to develop too many of them and make them too specific. Rule systems tend to be more effective when the rules are fewer in number and flexible enough to allow a teacher to adapt them to specific circumstances. Large numbers of extemely specific rules may actually ensnare a teacher, and they are also difficult for students to remember. Lists of dos and don'ts are best avoided. Rather, positively stated guides to desired behavior provide general directions that apply to a broader array of circumstances and provide a teacher with more flexibility of interpretation (Brophy & Evertson, 1976, pp. 196–197). Student input into the rules can also be helpful to a teacher. If students have a proprietary interest in the rules and norms they are more likely to act in accordance with them.

An example of a classroom control system at this point on the continuum is that of William Geoffrey, who was discussed in Chapter 3. Recall the concept of grooving, where he initially bombards his students with structure. As he moves through the stages of I-mean-it, follow through, and softening the tone, the rules explicitly put forth in the initial grooving episodes become the norm for his students.

Effective teachers at this third position often use praise of desired behaviors to help establish them as the norm. Elementary teachers may develop little ritual celebrations that they invoke when individuals or whole classes behave in desired ways. Sanctions for inappropriate behavior are often private, in contrast to public praise for desired behavior and may take the form of reminding the offender of the appropriate rule and the reasons for it. Teachers in this position, however, sometimes use public shame as a means of enforcing rules. In some cases, breaches of the rules are even dealt with in a public forum with the students helping to formulate the response to the rule offender. Such proceedings provide a stage for presenting the rules and discussing the reasons for them.

Teachers who obtain this position on the continuum of social system development usually demonstrate considerable functional authority. They are adept at presenting simple but meaningful rules, using positive responses to reward appropriate behavior, differentiating times when private rather than public sanctions for rule breaking are most appropriate, and doing all of the little things that help develop a set of supportive norms. Their students soon grant them voluntary compliance, and the classroom social system runs in a way that facilitates learning.

The Point 4, and most desirable, social system is found among teachers who start the school year with overt references to explicit rules but progress throughout the year to a position where they are able to maintain an orderly and effective classroom by giving directions rather than referring to the rules. Students internalize the rules to such an extent that they become norms that are so strongly held that specific reference to their origins are no longer necessary. In such classrooms teachers guide students by providing suggestions and giving directions. When this condition is reached virtually all student activities provide an occasion for teaching.

An incident in Sandy Snodgrass's low-ability social studies class provides an example of this kind of higher-order authority and control system. At one point she hears a familiar rustle of paper, which her with-it sixth sense tells her is the subtle announcement of a paper airplane about to be hurled. Without breaking stride in the classroom dialogue she is leading she simply announces, "The airport is closed today." No airplane or missile follows. She uses humor to remind the potential transgressor of the rules without making explicit reference to them. She is on top of everything going on in the classroom. Her students respect her for it and accord her much functional authority through their voluntary compliance.

In classrooms where the highest type of classroom control system exists it is difficult to discover the rules that underlie student behavior. For example, in the airport incident from Sandy's class it is likely that an outside observer may have missed the meaning of her comment completely, even though her students understood it perfectly. In such classrooms the rule structure can only be discovered through inference from student behavior patterns. Classrooms like these are a joy to visit. The teachers are imbued with vast amounts of functional authority. Students simply defer to them and follow their directions. These teachers are so skillful and seem so natural in their work with students that it is often difficult to see them employing their skills. One has the sense that they know what they are doing, that the students are very willing to follow their lead, and that their classrooms are places of real learning.

A major factor in moving from control by rules to control by enculturation and direction giving seems to be a teacher's skill in monitoring student behavior, spotting potential trouble quickly, and intervening by redirecting student behavior back toward expectations. If you are lucky enough to find yourself in one of these classrooms, strain your observation skills to their limits. The insights you will gain by careful attention are worth the extra effort.

EXAMPLES FROM THE CASE STUDIES

All five of the case study teachers are at Point 4 on the continuum of control systems described. In none of the classroom observations did these teachers raise their voices, and there were no instances of real discipline problems. All of the classrooms were of the sort where an observer would have to look carefully to see the control system. It is obvious that each of the teachers possesses a great deal of functional authority.

Both Luberta and Ruth believe that nothing is important enough to interrupt the work or learning activities of the classroom. Both communicate this attitude to their students in numerous ways. Implicit in Luberta's Power of Knowledge pledge is the message: If you are here to learn and empower yourself through knowledge, you are not here to mess around because that only gets in the way of your purpose. The pledge is a major symbol of purpose and a means through which Luberta sets the normative expectations of the classroom. When her children recite the pledge, which they take very seriously, their enculturation into the norms is solidified.

The comment "No time was devoted to discipline problems— there simply were not any" was used in Chapter 2 to describe Luberta's classroom. She describes her approach to classroom management in these terms:

> They have to be comfortable with whatever rules we have in here—they'll have to see the need for allowing each other to hear and to give each other a chance to talk—we just work at it—if someone gets a little pushy, we just say, "Hey, wait, it's not your turn," and we can be pretty brisk if we have to. . . . but on the whole we don't have to.

Luberta keeps the flow of events occurring so smoothly and communicates her expectations so strongly and directly that complying with them seems the only reasonable thing to do. As they move from one subject to another Luberta simply asks, "Is it reasonable to expect to be able to hear a pin drop now?" and her students answer Yes. She continues: "Okay. I'll expect to hear the pencil sharpener but nothing else." A simple, direct statement of expectations.

Chapter 2 also illustrated Ruth's similar approach to control. Like Luberta she keeps students highly involved and expects them to behave properly. The description of Ruth's classroom shows how far she is able to get toward the fourth level of the control continuum on the very first day.

Ruth uses a technique of ignoring improper behavior whenever possible but telegraphing expectations for proper behavior through positive statements. When the overweight girl entered the classroom late and some students made rude remarks, she simply attended to the new student in a polite and respectful manner by helping her to her seat. The unspoken message to the rest of the students was: Everyone in this room is treated with respect.

Ruth has been teaching in the same school for a long time and has a reputation that precedes her.

> After you've taught for a while you have a reputation in the school that helps. I think letting them take part in the planning and evaluating of the things that go badly is important. They need to look at things that don't work well, realize that things are not going to work well all the time, be able to look at things that are not going well and do something about it. And I think if you involve them in these kinds of decisions, you don't really have to be a strict authority figure. You don't come across as a strict authority figure. I think basically kids want a peaceful, smooth working environment where they can do what they're supposed to do.

Ruth solidly establishes her reputation on the first day of school:

> It has to be all of us working together. You know, I once had a student named Charlie—Charlie had a lot of tricks. If I said go out, he went in; if I said go in, he went out; if I gave him crayons to draw with, he would eat them. I think I know all of the tricks, but if you come up with any new ones, I'll tell you.

The anecdote is funny, but the unarticulated message about the rules that apply in her classroom is clear: I am no wet-behind-the-ears novice or pushover substitute; I have been around. I know the ropes, and now you know I know them too!

Ruth is also direct about giving other indicators of her expectations. While the class is filling out the student surveys she announces, "At the bottom put down your suggestions for handling problems—although I don't think we'll have to deal with any. I like to take care of problems as soon as they arise. What are some ways we can handle problems?" She is consistent with her stated intentions. She states her expectations and immediately involves the students in solving class problems. As with Sandy and the airplane incident, Ruth also uses asides in the midst of running dialogue. For example, in the middle of a discussion of not being embarrassed about asking questions she interjects: "Also, I do not have patience with people who do not pay attention because that makes my job harder—so if there's going to be a problem we'll have to do something. I hope it's not a problem." She is grooving the children. She gives a great deal of information in a few words. She gives the rule; she gives the rationale for the rule; and she gives her expectation for student behavior. Granting her functional authority is the only conceivable response from the students.

Jacquie, Sandy, and Larry have students for only one-hour periods at the secondary level yet still manage to establish Point 4 control systems for each of their classes. All of them move around the room, are in touch with everything that is going on, and telegraph this to the students. Sandy acknowledges her sixth sense of anticipation:

> I think you intuit it [trouble] . . . you know when their eyes do something, or when you hear the rumblings of whispers that things are going to start to happen, or when you hear the crumple of paper you know that an airplane is going to be sailing . . . and the movement of bodies, restlessness setting in. You can hear the chairs beginning to move, things like that.

CONCLUSION

Schools are arenas in which power, authority, and control are major concerns. Coordination and control are necessary to keep classrooms moving toward a set of learning goals. Control is most effectively exercised through authority in which subordinates willingly comply with the directions of superiors. Although power may be used for control it builds resentment and, in the end, is ineffective in schools.

The formal authority that comes with the position of teacher is really too limited to form a base for effective leadership and coordination. Effective teachers expand their authority base by developing functional authority. This base of authority grows from student recognition of a teacher's knowledge, ability, caring, and interpersonal effectiveness. In short, students recognize good teachers and grant them authority and respect.

The relationship between classroom control and student learning is well documented. The reason that Point 4 on the continuum of classroom social systems is the most desirable is because it provides the *greatest potential for learning*. Whereas learning the designated curriculum is unlikely in the chaos of Point 1, by the time Point 4 is reached, a teacher is almost totally free to attend to the teaching-learning process.

DISCUSSION QUESTIONS

1. Recall effective teachers you had from primary school through college. Can you identify particular authority bases they possessed (e.g., charismatic, traditional, legal-rational, functional)?
2. Read one or more of the specialized sources on management, control, and discipline in the annotated bibliography. Do the specific systems fit within the larger concepts of authority discussed in this chapter?
3. Discuss in class or in small groups your findings from the interview and observation activities suggested at the end of this chapter.
4. Does the information learned by answering Questions 1–3 raise any questions or discrepancies?

ACTIVITIES

1. Observe a school and community setting for expectations of behavior of students or children, expectations about control in families, and assumptions of how school should manage and control students.
2. Observe an elementary or secondary classroom at the beginning of a school year or a one-semester secondary class at the beginning of a new semester and look specifically for the forces involved in the developing social system as depicted in Figure 7.2.
3. Observe a classroom for the purpose of placing it along the continuum of classroom control systems found in Table 7.1. Look particularly at how the rule structure and teacher behaviors seem to be related to student behaviors.
4. Observe a classroom for several hours or days. Look for the relationship between teacher classroom management behavior and instances of behavior and discipline problems. This is difficult. Essentially you will need to look backward from the point where a discipline problem surfaced. What was the teacher doing prior to the incident? Was there an interruption in the lesson? Were materials not readily at hand? Were directions not clear for individualized work? Did some problem originating outside the classroom arrive with the students? Was the lesson interrupted by an intercom announcement, a messenger, or a tardy student? Do you see relationships between breakdowns in teacher management behaviors and discipline problems?
5. Conduct an interview with an individual student or a group of students, preferably from a classroom you have observed. The purpose of the interview is to gain the students' perspective on their teacher's authority base and

classroom management and control system. Using your own words try asking questions like:

> Why do (or do not) you and your classmates listen to and follow this teacher's directions?
>
> Do you see the room as orderly or is there a lot of confusion and misbehavior? What does the teacher do that contributes to this condition?
>
> What are the key words that come to mind when you describe this teacher?
>
> What does the teacher do to make you think about him or her in these ways?

You may also find it helpful to get the students to compare their teacher with others they have had. Comparisons may help students see important points and may help you understand their meanings. You may also want to try similar interviews with both young children and adolescents. What perceptions are similar? What perceptions differ? You may want to share your results with other class members.

QUESTIONS TO GUIDE OBSERVATION

1. What kinds of explicit statements or rules and expectations does the teacher express?
2. Is the teacher consistent in upholding rules and expectations?
3. Does the teacher groove or remind the students of rules and expectations in many different ways?
4. What methods does the teacher use to deal with those who transgress the rules or fail to live up to behavioral expectations?
5. Does the teacher display withitness? how?
6. What personal attributes, demeanor, emotional states, and attitudes does the teacher exhibit? How are these related to the kind of classroom management he or she maintains?
7. What kind of flow and interest level does the lesson have? How many interruptions, gaps, or dead spaces occur in activities?
8. Is there any evidence of student brinkmanship or testing the teacher and the rule structure?
9. How do students interact with each other before the class begins?
10. How do students respond to teacher's rules and expectations during class?
11. Can you perceive the forces involved in developing the classroom social system?

QUESTIONS TO GUIDE TEACHER INTERVIEW

1. What methods do you use during the first few weeks of class to establish control in the classroom? (Probe for specifics if the answers are very general; ask about what rules are established; how students are informed of them; what expectations the teacher holds for students; what expectations the students have.)
2. How is the flow and content of a particular session related to student behavior?
3. What kinds of forces or events coming from outside the classroom make management and control difficult? Are they periodic or continual problems? What do you do to counter such forces?
4. How do the total school climate, other teachers' behaviors and attitudes, and the attitudes and behaviors of the principal affect your classroom management?
5. How do you monitor student behavior?
6. What kinds of outside classroom supports are available to you if there is a student whose behavior is consistently unacceptable? How effective are these supports? How is a teacher who occasionally requests help with a student perceived by peers? students? administrators?
7. How have your beliefs about establishing and maintaining management and control changed over the course of your career? What accounts for these changes?
8. What are the problems associated with teachers who lack adequate classroom management and control?
9. What problems do beginning teachers have in this area of teaching? What advice do you have for a new teacher?

REFERENCES AND SOURCES

Blau, P., & Scott, R. W. (1962). *Formal organizations: A comparative approach*. San Francisco: Chandler.

Brophy, J. E., & Evertson, C. E. (1976). *Learning from teaching: A developmental perspective*. Boston: Allyn & Bacon.

Brophy, J. E., & Putnam, J. G. (1979). Classroom management in the elementary grades. In D. L. Duke (Ed.), *Classroom management: The seventy-eighth yearbook of the National Society for the Study of Education*. Chicago: National Society for the Study of Education.

Etzioni, A. (1975). *A comparative analysis of complex organizations* (2d ed.). New York: Free Press.

Good, T. L., & Brophy, J. E. (1978). *Looking in classrooms* (2d ed.). New York: Harper & Row.

Hage, J. (1980). *Theories of organizations.* New York: Wiley.

Kounin, J. S. (1970). *Discipline and group management in classrooms.* New York: Holt, Rinehart & Winston.

Lortie, D. C. (1975). *Schoolteacher: A sociological study.* Chicago: University of Chicago Press.

Mitchell, D. E., Ortiz, F. I., & Mitchell, T. K. (1983). *Work orientation and job performance: The cultural basis of teaching rewards and incentives.* Final Report. (Grant No. NIE–G–80–0154). (ERIC Document Reproduction Service No. ED. 237 488). Riverside, CA: University of California.

Nash, R. (1976). Pupils' expectations of their teachers. In M. Stubbs & S. Delamont (Eds.). *Explorations in classroom observation* (pp. 83–98). New York: Wiley.

Peabody, R. L. (1962). Perceptions of organizational authority: A comparative analysis. *Administrative Science Quarterly, 6,* 463–482.

Simon, H. A. (1957). *Administrative behavior.* New York: Free Press.

Smith, L. M., & Geoffrey, W. (1968). *The complexities of an urban classroom.* New York: Holt, Rinehart & Winston.

Weber, M. (1947). *The theory of social and economic organization.* (T. Parsons, Ed.; A. M. Henderson & T. Parsons, Trans.). New York: Free Press.

Weiss, M. S., & Weiss, P. H. (1977). *Taking another look at teaching: How lowerclass children influence middleclass teachers.* (ERIC Document Reproduction Service No. ED 137–223).

Sources for specific methods of classroom control and management

Canter, L. & Canter, M. (1976). *Assertive discipline: A take charge approach for today's educator.* Seal Beach, California: Canter and Associates. Canter and Canter have developed an approach to classroom control which they call assertive discipline. The approach is built upon principles from assertion training and maintains that both teachers and students have basic rights. Teachers, for example, have the right to establish optimal learning environments, and to determine, request, and expect appropriate behavior from students. Students, on the other hand, have the right to have teachers who help them control their inappropriate behavior, provide positive support for appropriate behavior, and give them the opportunities to choose how to behave with full understanding of the consequences of their choices. The Canters believe that these rights are best met through assertive discipline in which the teacher clearly communicates expectations to students and consistently follows up with appropriate actions, but never violates the best interests of the students.

Curwin, R. L., & Mendler, A. N. (1980). *The discipline book: A complete guide to school and classroom management.* Reston, VA: Reston. A broad source that includes discussion of more specific approaches detailed in these references including discussions of teacher self-awareness; awareness of students feeling expression; preventative approaches; social contracts; school-wide discipline; use of resource persons; and working with parents. Useful exercises and a bibliography are included.

Duke, D. L. (Ed.). (1979). *Classroom management: The seventy-eighth yearbook of the National Society for the Study of Education*. Chicago: National Society for the Study of Education. A scholarly work containing various specialized chapters concerning classroom management and discipline. This work provides a good introduction to the research in this area and contains many references.

Glasser, W. (1969). *Schools without failure*. New York: Harper & Row. Grounded in what he calls *reality therapy*, Glasser's approach to discipline problems rests on his belief that misbehavior stems from feelings of failure that arise when students are not involved in important school processes. He would have teachers involve students in meaningful activities such as formulation of rules through the vehicle of class meetings, where the stress is on behavior and commitment to appropriate behavior. This approach deals with individuals in the context of the social system of the class.

Good, T. L., & Brophy, J. E. (1978). *Looking in classrooms* (2d ed.). New York: Harper & Row. This work contains two helpful chapters on classroom management. The first, following Kounin's work, stresses preventing problems and the second deals with coping approaches once problems exist. Useful guides for observing classrooms are included.

Gordon, T. (1974). *Teacher effectiveness training*. New York: Wyden. An outgrowth of earlier work on parent training, this approach focuses on communication as the key to classroom discipline. Gordon's model of effective communication centers around the concepts of active listening, I-messages, problem ownership, and negotiation. This approach includes focus on both the individual student and the classroom as a social system.

O'Leary, K. D., & O'Leary, S. G. (1977). *Classroom management: The successful use of behavior modification*. New York: Pergamon. Based on general social learning theory, behavior modification rests on the concepts of rewarding desirable behavior and extinguishing or punishing undesirable behavior. These ideas were popularized by B. F. Skinner. This work presents a clear explanation of the principles of behavior modification. The approach focuses on control of behavior through external means.

8

TEACHERS AND THE CURRICULUM: MACRO AND MICRO ISSUES

INTRODUCTION

The various physical arrangements and social systems that teachers create in their classrooms all have a central purpose: to enable them to teach content or subject matter. Students are in schools to learn, and teachers are in schools to teach, first and foremost, content. The term *curriculum* is generally used to describe the overall content of a school program. Sometimes educators talk in terms of disciplines, and speak of the mathematics curriculum or the English curriculum. At other times they talk more generally of the elementary curriculum or the secondary curriculum. In either case they are referring to the *intellectual content*, that is, the knowledge and skills that are purposely taught to students in different subjects.*

Many people, however, define the school curriculum more broadly to include all experiences that are purposefully arranged for students such as the ways in which the content is taught as well as the values, social experiences, and extracurricular activities sanctioned by the school. We tend to prefer this broader definition because we believe (1) the social and moral goals of the schools can be as important as the intellectual ones; (2) students may learn as much from informal experiences as they do from formal ones; and (3) teaching and learning are holistic experiences

---

*The term *intellectual content* includes the formal vocational and personal development courses which contain a knowledge base and skills.

that cannot be readily subdivided into different categories. Nonetheless, for purposes of clarity this book takes a more narrow view which separates curriculum from instruction and other school experiences. This chapter defines and focuses on curriculum as the intellectual content, the *what* that is formally taught to students in courses. Chapter 9 will focus on instruction or *how* that content is taught.

Since these two areas are so closely related some of what is discussed in this curriculum chapter will overlap with material in Chapter 9 on instruction, and vice versa. The absence of distinct boundaries between chapters should not cause a problem, however, because it is the two chapters on *what* is taught and *how* it is taught that, taken together, comprise the intellectual environment of the classroom.

In discussing the academic curriculum our primary interest is on the classroom or *micro* level, particularly the amount of control teachers exert over the curriculum on a day-to-day basis. Major curricular decisions, however, are often influenced by forces at the *macro* or larger societal level and implemented at the state or district level. In this sense, teachers are often the "last to know" about curriculum matters. In spite of the fact that many curricular decisions originate outside the classroom, individual teachers can generally exercise considerable control over what is actually taught in individual lessons. These daily lessons, in turn, can eventually have some effect on the larger society.

In order to understand the nature and scope of a teacher's curricular role, this chapter begins at the macro level with a historical overview of the societal forces that have influenced curriculum, a brief statement on curriculum as it exists in schools today, and some discussion of recent efforts at national curriculum reform. Next it considers the role that a classroom teacher can play in shaping the curriculum he or she is given to teach. Finally, the influence that individual teacher curricular decisions can have on society is discussed. In effect this chapter comes full circle and demonstrates how a classroom teacher's role in curriculum decision making is necessarily interactive with the influences imposed by the larger society. As you read this chapter, look for the ways in which both macro and micro influences affect teachers' curricular decision making.

SCHOOL CURRICULUM: THE MACRO LEVEL

A Historical Overview

The history of school curriculum in America is largely tied to the history of America itself.* As the country developed and grew, educational goals and school curricula were adapted to respond to the nation's emerging needs. In the process major disagreements as to the fundamental mission of schools and long-term strug-

---

*We are indebted to Ernest L. Boyer for this overview, which is based heavily on his historical account in *High School* (1983).

gles to achieve both educational excellence and equity have developed.

In the beginning the mission of schools was limited and clear. The goal of the Boston Latin Grammar School founded in 1635 was to prepare young men for Harvard (Boyer, 1983). This idea has been reformulated in a number of ways throughout the past 350 years, but it still represents the notion that the fundamental purpose of schools is academic and that the major goal of schools is to prepare students for higher education.

As America grew, however, it was inevitable that the schools would have to broaden their mission. In 1751 Benjamin Franklin established a secondary school in Philadelphia that focused on more practical skills, such as letter writing and accounting. Franklin's school served as a model for the academies that flourished in the 1800s. Although privately controlled the academies differed from earlier private institutions in that students came from different socioeconomic classes and additional support often came from communities and state governments. Most importantly, the curriculum was designed to meet both academic and vocational interests. At Gould's Academy in Bethel, Maine, for example, there were "different courses of study for those fitting for college, teaching, or the countinghouse" (Boyer, 1983, p. 44). Latin, Greek, English, French, and mathematics were available alongside business and commercial subjects, sewing, and agriculture. This mixed curriculum indicated that the purpose of school was also vocational and that a major goal must be to prepare students for the world of work.

In 1821 the first public high school was established in Boston, and in the early public institutions both academic and vocational subjects were present. In 1827, for example, Massachusetts passed a law requiring every town and village of 500 or more families to establish a school to teach American history, surveying, geometry, and bookkeeping along with the common primary subjects. Towns of 4,000 people were to have schools that included general history, rhetoric, logic, Latin, and Greek (Boyer, 1983, p. 45). In the mid- to late 1800s, however, some geographically related differences in goals and curriculum began to emerge. The curriculum was often highly classical and academic in urban areas and more practical and applied in rural regions.

In the late 1800s Calvin Woodward, a Harvard-trained mathematician working in St. Louis, launched a campaign to make the public schools less academic. Claiming that the curriculum was failing to meet the nation's changing economic and vocational needs, Woodward argued for manual training to be an equal partner with the broad general curriculum for everyone. Woodward received much support from the business world, and his efforts firmly established vocational education as a major goal of public education.

With America's industrial expansion, however, more and more students tended to gravitate toward vocational offerings, and a backlash came in the form of a committee appointed in 1892 by the National Council of Education. This prestigious committee, known as the Committee of Ten, was dominated by college professors who argued for renewed emphasis on academics and mental discipline for all students. The committee maintained that higher education is the best preparation for life and recommended the following core of academic subjects in high school for everyone: Latin, Greek, English, French, mathematics, natural history, physical science, geography, history, government, and political science.

The arrival of great masses of immigrants at the turn of the century, however, brought additional pressures upon the schools to help Americanize the newcomers. Courses were developed to teach them the fundamentals of English, health, sanitation, nutrition, and citizenship. In 1918 another blue-ribbon committee appointed by the National Education Association issued a report entitled "The Cardinal Principles of Secondary Education" and explicitly added to the mission of public schools "health, citizenship, and worthy home membership" (Boyer, 1983, p. 50). This new emphasis on citizenship, in effect, indicated that the purpose of schools was also political and that a major goal was to prepare all students to become active and informed citizens. The accent on health and nutrition laid upon the schools a new physical goal: to help students develop and maintain healthy bodies. The notion of "worthy home membership" had personal and moral overtones to it.

During the same years the philosopher John Dewey was formulating a social purpose for the schools. Dewey, who was the father of what is known as the Progressive Movement in education, argued that industrialization and urbanization were eroding the traditional American institutions of home, community, and church. His recommendation was that schools begin to teach the whole child and to foster social learning.

With these multiple and ambitious goals—academic, vocational, political, physical, personal, moral, and social—the schools increasingly served more and more students. By 1950, 65 percent of the age group eligible was enrolled in public high schools, and the majority of America's adolescents were completing high school. As youngsters from minority populations became part of this cohort, entrance requirements were changed to allow completion of elementary school to be the basis of high school admission. This completed the transition of high school from an elite institution to one that would serve the masses. High school had become "the people's college," and a new national goal—universal high school attendance—was in place (Boyer, 1983).

From the 1950s to the 1980s there have been varying ideas about how to reach this goal of education for all. Major societal events and trends have shifted first in one direction and then another and pushed the country into a long-standing excellence-equity debate.

In the late 1950s, for example, the launching of the Soviet satellite Sputnik sparked a major revolution toward educational rigor in America. Earlier in the 1950s there had been curriculum reform efforts to prevent a lowering of standards related to the increasingly diversified high school population. With Sputnik, however, curriculum reform became a national priority. Determined not only to match but to overcome the Soviets' supremacy in space, the government passed the National Defense Education Act in 1958, which allocated large sums of money for improvement in math, science, and foreign language curricula. In 1959 James B. Conant, a scientist and former President of Harvard, undertook a study of American high schools and among his numerous proposals was a reiteration of the need to strengthen math, science, and foreign language education. The goal for the schools once more was academic rigor but this time with an eye toward preparing America to compete internationally.

By the mid-1960s the schools had accepted yet another goal: social justice. The 1954 *Brown vs Board of Education* supreme court decision, which declared separate was not equal, pressed schools for racial balance and compensatory education. The federal government gave massive support for the effort through Title I programs offering remedial curricula and programs for the poor and underachieving. Equity with the new educational byword.

The Vietnam War brought protests and confrontations to city streets and calls for academic relevance in schools and colleges. "Progressive" approaches were more prevalent as educators sought to allow students more freedom, choice, and control over their own learning. Many elementary schools opted for open education, and many secondary schools lowered requirements and increased student options through minicourses, electives, and alternative schools.

A serious backlash to these humanistic ideas of freedom and choice was, however, in full swing by the mid-1970s. In response to evidence of dropping SAT scores, grade inflation, increasing enrollments in nonacademic courses, and economic hard times a back-to-basics movement developed that emphasized academic standards and discipline. This movement was not merely a renewed call for academics. Efforts to make the schools accountable through minimum competency tests were an integral part of the new backlash. These notions of accountability through testing can be traced in large part to the federal government's use of the Planning, Programming, and Budgeting System (PPBS) to evaluate programs in all agencies and departments, including the Department of Health, Education, and Welfare (HEW). At HEW this system was used to measure the efficiency of Title I programs for the poor and underachieving in cost-benefit terms. The assumption was that one could define a *production function* as the relative effectiveness of specified inputs in reaching stated objectives. Ideally this meant that educational programs could be compared in terms of test-score results and that the government could ultimately mandate the most efficient programs and methods through legislation (Wirth, 1983). This belief that there was a clear, direct, and knowable relationship between educational inputs and outputs and that tests could be used to measure that relationship gained enormous acceptance. The commitment to testing moved quickly from the federal to the state and local levels, and by 1978 nearly 40 states had adopted minimum competency tests to assess whether students had learned enough to be promoted or graduated (Ravitch, 1983).

Back-to-basics accountability and competency tests prevail today. In elementary and secondary schools there is an emphasis on covering the text and measuring the information learned through criterion-referenced and standardized tests. Teachers are being held accountable for low test scores. Still, the loudest cry for educational reform since post–Sputnik days has been heard within this back-to-basics movement. Blue-ribbon commissions and prestigious foundations in recent years have bombarded the public and professional educators with reports calling for major changes in the school curriculum. In the following sections this chapter will give an overview of the present curriculum and will examine some of the latest efforts to alter it.

At this point, however, it is necessary to underscore the fact that although there has never been a national set of educational goals, historically the expectation has been that the schools will assume the changing goals of the larger society. This chapter's brief historical overview clearly documents that as each societal problem arose, the schools took on a corresponding educational goal. It also suggests that as each new educational goal appeared others inevitably were set aside. When the country went too far in one direction, there was invariably a press toward the opposite direction. The history of American education has been a struggle to meet the original and primary academic goal for all students in the face of other legitimate and competing societal goals. Within this struggle the educational pendulum has often swung between the traditionalists who argue that schools should focus on student intellectual development and the progressivists who argue that schools should educate the whole child, that is, the intellectual, social, personal, moral, physical, and vocational dimensions.

THE EXISTING CURRICULUM

The Elementary Curriculum

Although individual states and, to some degree, local districts can mandate subject-area offerings, both elementary and secondary school curricula are remarkably alike countrywide. At the elementary level an academic curriculum generally consists of (1) a combination of English, reading, and language arts, (2) social studies, (3) mathematics, and (4) science. Physical education (and possibly health), art, and music usually round out the program. Despite this similarity of offerings throughout the country, there are variations that can seriously affect what Goodlad (1984) calls students' "access to knowledge" (pp. 130–166).

The first distinguishing variation is the amount of time devoted to each subject. On page 55 one can see the amount of time Luberta Clay at Jefferson School allocates to each subject area. John Goodlad's (1984) recent study of schooling examined the curriculum of 13 elementary schools. By comparing the teachers' estimated instructional time in different subject areas he demonstrates the amount of variability that exists. In addition, his figures, which can be seen in Table 8.1, show considerable variability in total time spent in an instructional setting. The table reveals that the average hourly allocation per week is 7.5 for language arts and 4.5 for mathematics. The variation in language arts is from 6.4 hours per week at Atwater, Palisades, and Laurel to 8.8 at Bradford. Similarly, there is a range in mathematics from 3.8 hours at Vista to 5.5 at Manchester. Since the amount of time spent on a subject should have some effect on how much knowledge is gained, these differences seem highly significant.

Another feature of elementary curricula that can affect students' access to knowledge is the presence or absence of ability grouping. In elementary schools it is common to group students in reading and in math. The amount and type of material covered in the various groups can differ considerably. Students in high groups generally do more qualitatively and quantitatively than the lower-group counterparts. Moreover, these groups are established at the beginning of the year, often as a result of the teacher's judgment and/or test scores (recall the case of Mrs. Caplow), and usually remain stable throughout the year. According to Goodlad (1984), the stability of group membership relates to the reality that the work of the higher and lower groups becomes more "sharply differentiated with each passing day" (p. 141). It becomes increasingly difficult for students in a lower math group, for example, to catch up with the advanced sequence of those in the higher group as a school year progresses. Goodlad (1984) therefore maintains that "it is not uncommon for a child in the most advanced group to have progressed five times as fast as a child in the least advanced group over the course of a year" (p. 141). Furthermore, he claims, "By the fourth grade children at the bottom and top can differ in reading achievement by as much as six grades" (p. 141). His research suggests the possibility of a self-fulfilling prophecy as well as a genuine difference in curricula for students in different ability groups.

A third variation is whether the elementary teacher is a generalist or a specialist, or some combination of the two. In some elementary schools all subjects are taught by one teacher to one class. In other elementary schools one teacher is responsible for all academic subjects for one class, and specialists are hired to teach physical education, art, and music. In still others different teachers are responsible for different academic subjects and specialists are hired for physical education and fine arts. Luberta Clay represents the second type of teacher, who teaches all the subjects to her class except for physical education, art, and music. Ruth, who teaches math to several classes and English, reading, and language arts to her homeroom, represents the third type of teacher.

The Secondary Curriculum

At the secondary level the four core academic subjects are generally present with the addition of a fifth—foreign language study. Typically within each academic

Table 8.1   Elementary teachers' estimated instructional time in subject areas—Mean hours spent per week and percentage of total estimated instructional time

	Overall	English/ Language Arts	Math	Social Studies	Science
Vista	19.7	7.5 38%	3.8 19%	2.2 11%	2.1 11%
Crestview	19.1	7.6 40%	4.5 23%	2.1 11%	1.3 7%
Fairfield	24.7	7.9 32%	4.7 19%	2.5 10%	2.2 9%
Rosemont	22.4	6.8 30%	4.4 20%	2.3 10%	1.6 7%
Newport	18.6	8.4 45%	4.1 22%	1.8 10%	1.1 6%
Woodlake	22.5	8.7 38%	4.5 20%	2.9 13%	2.1 9%
Atwater	19.6	6.4 33%	4.0 20%	2.4 12%	1.6 8%
Palisades	22.1	6.4 29%	4.5 20%	2.9 13%	2.4 11%
Laurel	25.7	6.4 25%	4.4 17%	3.7 14%	3.0 12%
Manchester	26.0	8.1 31%	5.5 21%	3.4 13%	3.0 12%
Bradford	20.7	8.8 42%	5.4 26%	1.9 9%	1.6 8%
Euclid	22.5	7.4 33%	4.4 19%	2.6 12%	2.3 10%
Dennison	27.5	6.7 24%	4.3 16%	5.3 19%	5.3 19%
AVERAGE NUMBER OF HOURS	22.4	7.5	4.5	2.8	2.3
AVERAGE PERCENT		34%	20%	12%	10%

SOURCE: Goodlad, *A Place Called School*, McGraw-Hill, 1984, p. 133. Reprinted with permission.

area there is a range of choices. Expanded physical education and fine arts programs are taught, as well as a range of nonacademic requirements and choices including vocational education programs.

Frequently what distinguishes one secondary school from another is the amount of credits required in each academic subject area to graduate; the variety and nature of choices within and outside the academic offerings; and the way in which student tracking is handled. In terms of offerings and choices, Goodlad (1984)

Table 8.1 (continued)

Art	Music	Drama	Dance	Foreign Languages	Physical Education	Total Academic
1.2	1.2	0.2	0.3	0.0	1.2	15.7
6%	6%	1%	1%	0%	6%	80%
1.2	1.0	0.0	0.2	0.0	1.2	15.5
6%	5%	0%	1%	0%	6%	81%
2.0	1.4	0.3	0.4	0.2	3.2	17.5
8%	5%	1%	2%	1%	13%	71%
1.5	1.2	0.2	0.4	1.6	2.6	16.6
7%	5%	1%	2%	7%	11%	74%
1.1	0.7	0.0	0.1	0.0	1.2	15.5
6%	4%	0%	1%	0%	6%	83%
1.6	1.1	0.2	0.1	0.0	1.3	18.2
7%	5%	1%	0%	0%	6%	81%
1.6	1.3	0.3	0.4	0.0	1.5	14.4
8%	7%	1%	2%	0%	8%	74%
1.5	1.2	0.4	0.4	0.1	2.4	16.2
7%	6%	2%	2%	0%	11%	73%
2.2	1.3	0.4	1.2	0.0	3.0	17.5
9%	5%	2%	5%	0%	12%	68%
1.6	1.5	0.0	0.4	0.0	2.6	19.9
6%	6%	0%	2%	0%	10%	77%
1.3	0.7	0.1	0.1	0.1	0.7	17.7
6%	4%	1%	0%	0%	4%	86%
1.2	2.7	0.0	0.2	0.0	1.6	16.7
6%	12%	0%	1%	0%	7%	74%
1.3	2.0	0.0	0.5	0.0	2.0	21.7
5%	7%	0%	2%	0%	7%	79%
1.5	1.3	0.2	0.4	0.2	1.9	17.2
7%	6%	1%	2%	1%	8%	77%

maintains that one way to get a sense of the curriculum in a particular high school is to examine the allocation of courses and teachers in academic and nonacademic choices. Table 8.2 reveals the variations across the high schools in Goodlad's sample. What is striking here beyond the variability is the resource allocation in vocational education. These figures show that when there is a limited number of full-time teachers one goal, academic preparation for higher education, may suffer at the hands of another goal, preparation for the work world.

Table 8.2   Percentages of full-time teacher equivalencies (FTEs) in subject areas: Senior high schools

	Total N of Teachers	N of Subject Teachers	English		Math		Social Studies	
			N	%*	N	%	N	%
Vista	84	80.0	16.0	20	10.0	13	9.0	11
Crestview	44	44.0	9.0	20	6.0	14	6.0	14
Fairfield	57	53.2	9.2	17	5.0	9	4.8	9
Rosemont	121	118.6	26.2	22	16.0	13	15.6	13
Newport	85	70.2	13.7	20	8.0	11	7.7	11
Woodlake	57	54.8	11.8	22	5.0	9	7.0	13
Atwater	25	23.6	5.0	21	2.2	9	4.0	17
Palisades	68	63.8	10.0	16	9.4	15	10.0	16
Laurel	18	20.0	3.0	15	4.0	20	3.0	15
Manchester	114	111.0	25.0	23	15.0	14	17.0	15
Bradford	63	50.0	8.0	16	8.0	16	6.0	12
Euclid	24	14.5	2.0	14	1.3	9	1.0	7
Dennison	11	8.5	1.0	12	1.0	12	1.0	12
AVERAGE		54.8	10.8	18	7.0	13	7.1	13

SOURCE: Goodlad, *A Place Called School*, McGraw-Hill, 1984, p. 202. Reprinted with permission.
*Percentages based on total FTEs in subject areas only—other teaching (e.g., special education) was excluded.

What distinguishes one student's program from another (within a single high school) is the choices he or she makes with regard to the academic and nonacademic offerings. A student's access to knowledge can vary widely depending upon these choices, which are not always freely made. In many schools, students are advised to take or actually assigned to particular tracks or courses that are more formalized and sophisticated versions of the ability groups in elementary schools.

To give a more concrete flavor to the issues of choice and tracking, Larry Wells's school, Hillsboro High, serves as a case in point. For many years Hillsboro High School has had three tracks leading to three different diplomas. Each track has a different set of requirements. Until recently graduation from the lowest track required one year of math and of science, two years of social studies, and three years of English. The science requirement could be filled by taking general science, and the math requirement by something called functional math, which focused on the basic operations of addition, subtraction, multiplication, and division. Thus students could choose to graduate from high school without any advanced work in mathematics or science. Although three years of English seems a reasonable standard, students in the lowest track were required because of previous poor performance to take a particular sequence: the first two courses focused exclusively on

Table 8.2 (continued)

Science		The Arts		Foreign Languages		Vocational Education		Physical Education		Total Academic	
N	%	N	%	N	%	N	%	N	%	N	%
10.0	13	9.0	11	3.0	4	18.0	23	5.0	6	48.0	60
4.0	9	4.3	10	1.2	3	10.6	24	3.0	7	26.2	59
5.0	9	1.6	3	1.0	2	22.6	42	4.0	8	25.0	47
17.6	15	6.0	5	5.0	4	25.0	21	7.2	6	80.4	68
7.0	10	7.7	11	6.7	10	9.2	13	10.0	14	43.2	62
5.0	9	4.0	7	2.0	4	15.0	27	5.0	9	30.8	56
2.0	8	2.0	8	1.0	4	5.0	21	2.4	10	14.2	60
8.0	13	7.4	12	5.0	8	8.0	13	6.0	9	42.4	66
3.0	15	2.0	10	0.0	0	3.0	15	2.0	10	13.0	65
14.0	13	4.0	4	6.0	5	21.0	19	9.0	8	77.0	69
6.0	12	6.0	12	3.0	6	7.0	14	6.0	12	31.0	62
1.3	9	1.5	10	0.3	2	6.0	41	1.0	7	6.0	41
1.0	12	0.5	6	0.0	0	3.0	35	1.0	12	4.0	47
6.5	11	4.3	8	2.6	4	11.8	24	4.7	9	33.9	59

grammar; the third course continued to emphasize grammar with the expectation that students would learn how to write sentences. Thus, once relegated to this track students could graduate without ever having to write a paragraph in English.

Although most high schools across the country offer only a single diploma, the existence of three tracks—academic, general, and vocational—is commonplace. The academic track is the most rigorous in terms of core courses, and the students in this track aspire to college. Typically, students on the academic track will take four years of English, three years of social studies, two or three years of mathematics and science courses, and a foreign language.

The general track is often characterized by few academic requirements and many electives. A United States Department of Education study of high school transcripts revealed that this track has recently become extremely appealing. According to the report, students in the general track composed 12 percent of the student body in the late 1960s but by the late 1970s the percentage had risen to 42.5.

The vocational track prepares students for work immediately after high school. The curriculum usually includes a core of academic requirements and five or six vocational courses. Whereas more than 75 percent of all students typically take at least one vocational course as an elective, about 11 percent choose the vocational track. Vocational students usually specialize in one of the following areas:

Agriculture

Distribution and marketing
Health
Business and office occupations
Industrial arts
Trades and industry
Consumer and homemaking.

Students in the vocational track are frequently those who have had difficulty in academic courses.

Given these splits among academic, general, and vocational tracks, one can readily see that there is considerable variability within a single high school curriculum. A high school diploma is not necessarily an indication of what students were taught. Moreover, since minority students and those from the lowest socioeconomic groups are disproportionately represented in the less academic tracks, the question of equity in relation to access to knowledge is a serious one (Goodlad, 1984). Recently, some of these problems surrounding choice and tracking have prompted major criticisms of secondary schools as well as comprehensive efforts at curriculum reform.

Efforts at Curriculum Reform Today

The 1950s and 1960s were times of great ferment in American education, particularly in the area of curriculum development. An already mounting concern in the 1950s regarding the rigor of American education reached crisis proportions when the Soviet satellite Sputnik was launched in 1957. The prevailing belief was that America was behind in the space race because the public schools were not preparing young people for careers in science and mathematics. Because it was thought that America's national defense and international reputation were in jeopardy, the federal government for the first time allocated large sums of money to education in the areas of curriculum development, teacher education, and research. In 1960 at the height of federal involvement and concern over school curriculum, a psychologist, Jerome Bruner, published a book entitled *The Process of Education* in which he outlined a different approach to curriculum development. Bruner argued that disciplines like mathematics and the sciences ought to be studied in terms of their *structure*; that is, in terms of their key concepts and methods of inquiry. The idea behind this approach was to help students understand fundamental principles rather than learn particular facts. With an understanding of principles, students could become independent learners who could themselves discover meanings, solve problems, and apply the concepts to other areas. This approach had great impact at a time when new ideas were desired and needed. Math, science, and foreign language curricula were developed along this notion of structure, and remnants of these still exist in elementary and secondary schools today.

The years 1983 and 1984 will also be recorded as milestones in the history of American school reform due to a number of major reports that critiqued the public schools and offered sweeping proposals for change. Table 8.3 gives a sense of the focus for and data base of some of these reports.

Table 8.3   **A summary of national reports**

Report	Author	Focus	Data Base
A Place Called School	John I. Goodlad	Public schools only, K–12	38 schools in 7 states using 8,600 parents, 1,350 teachers, 17,000 students, 1,000 classrooms
High School	Ernest L. Boyer (President of the Carnegie Foundation for the Advancement of Teaching)	Public high schools as educational institutions	Case studies of 15 high schools using 25 observers; 2,000 hours in schools plus Goodlad's database and James Coleman's data in High School and Beyond
A Nation at Risk	Eighteen-member National Commission on Excellence in Education, Department of Education	To assess quality of time and learning, makes comparisons with other advanced nations; defines problems to be overcome if we are to pursue excellence	Commissioned papers, public testimony offered both orally and in writing and panel discussions
Horace's Compromise	Theodore R. Sizer	High schools, public and private	Observations and interviews in 11 public and 4 private high schools.
Action for Excellence	Task Force on Education for Economic Growth (41 business leaders, educators, governors, and legislators)	K–12 education, national economy, and international competition	Task-force deliberations and commissioned papers
The Paideia Proposal	Mortimer Adler and Paideia Group (22 educators and scholars)	Public schools K–12	Group deliberations
Making the Grade	Twentieth Century Fund (11 educators)		Task-force deliberations
Educating Americans for the Twenty-first Century	Commission on Pre-College Education in Mathematics, Science, and Technology (20 educators, scientists, government officials, and leaders from business and industry)	Mathematics, science, and technology education at elementary and secondary level	Hearings

One common denominator of these reports is that they all called for major curriculum reform. As one might expect, however, each had a somewhat different conception of what kinds of changes are in order. Four of the most prominent reports will be examined here along with their prescriptions for improving curriculum in American schools. (Because these reports concentrate on high schools, this discussion has a secondary school emphasis.) In addition, a response to these reports by a group of educators critical of some of the recent proposals for change will be examined.

A Nation at Risk In 1983 under the Reagan administration, Secretary of Education Terrell Bell assembled a National Commission on Excellence in Education. This 18-member commission included academics, state officials, school board members, business men and women, and four school people: a superintendent, two principals, and one teacher. Their task was broad:

> to generate reform of our educational system in fundamental ways and to renew the nation's commitment to schools and colleges of high quality throughout the length and breadth of our land. (*A Nation at Risk*, p. 6)

The process included 18 months of hearings, commissioned papers, and task-force deliberations. The final report was strong and dramatic in tone:

> Our nation is at risk. Our once unchallenged preeminence in commerce, industry, science, and technological innovation is being overtaken by competitors throughout the world.
>
>   This report is concerned with only one of the many causes and dimensions of the problem, but it is the one that undergirds American prosperity, security, and civility. We report to the American people that while we can take justifiable pride in what our schools and colleges have historically accomplished and contributed to the United States and the well-being of its people, the educational foundations of our society are presently being eroded by a rising tide of mediocrity that threatens our very future as a nation and a people. What was unimaginable a generation ago has begun to occur—others are matching and surpassing our educational attainments.
>
>   If an unfriendly foreign power had attempted to impose on America the mediocre educational performance that exists today, we might well have viewed it as an act of war. As it stands, we have allowed this to happen to ourselves. We have even squandered the gains in student achievement made in the wake of the Sputnik challenge. Moreover, we have dismantled essential support systems which helped make those gains possible. We have, in effect, been committing an act of unthinking, unilateral educational disarmament. (*A Nation at Risk*, p. 5)

The ensuing report in the form of an open letter to parents focuses upon four aspects of the educational process: content, expectations, time, and teaching. By *content* the commission meant "the very stuff of education, the curriculum." The commission found the secondary school curricula to be "homogenized, diluted and diffused to the point that they no longer have a central purpose." Citing the previously mentioned statistics related to the large number of students in the general track and to the fact that within this track students often elect nonacademic or remedial courses, the commission recommended:

> that state and local high school graduation requirements be strengthened and that, at a minimum, all students seeking a diploma be required to lay the foundations in the Five New Basics by taking the following curriculum during their four years of high school: (a) four years of English; (b) three years of mathematics; (c) three years of science; (d) three years of social studies; and (e) one-half year of computer science. For the college bound, two years of foreign language in high school are strongly recommended in addition to those taken earlier. (A *Nation at Risk*, p. 24)

In the Commission's view "a high level of shared education in these Basics, together with work in the fine and performing arts and foreign languages, constitutes the mind and spirit of our future."

In addition to prescribing the number of years to be devoted to each basic subject, the commission set out specific recommendations to implement the requirements. In English, for example, the commission specified:

> the teaching of English in high school should equip graduates to (a) comprehend, interpret, evaluate, and use what they read; (b) write well-organized, effective papers; (c) listen effectively and discuss ideas intelligently; and (d) know our literary heritage and how it enlivens imagination and ethical understanding, and how it relates to the customs, ideas and values of today's life and culture. (A *Nation at Risk*, p. 25)

This entire report received tremendous media attention and its dramatic and emphatic language succeeded in arousing lay people, educators, and politicians alike. The response to the curricular recommendations was particularly positive. Almost immediately state legislatures began enacting statutes to raise graduation standards.

High School Several months after A *Nation at Risk* appeared, a major study of secondary education was released by the Carnegie Foundation for the Advancement of Teaching authored by its president, Ernest L. Boyer. Boyer is a former United States commissioner of education and the former chancellor of the State University of New York. The Carnegie Foundation report, entitled *High School*, is quite different from the government report. Based on case studies of 15 different secondary schools, *High School* is a much more descriptive and analytical look at the problems and possibilities of secondary education. The focal point of the report is the curriculum, and Boyer (1983) begins from the premise that over the years the schools' central mission has been muddied.

Since the English Classical school was founded over 150 years ago, high schools have accumulated purposes like barnacles on a weathered ship. As the school population expanded from a tiny urban minority to almost all youth, a coherent purpose was hard to find. The nation piled social policy upon educational policy and all of them on top of the delusion that a single institution can do it all. (p. 57)

The solution according to Boyer is for American high schools to define "a clear and vital mission" and to develop a new curriculum that will accomplish that mission. The mission that Boyer (1983) proposes has four essential goals:

1. To help all students develop the capacity to think critically and communicate effectively through a mastery of language.
2. To help all students learn about themselves, the human heritage, and the interdependent world in which we live through a core curriculum based upon consequential human experiences common to all people.
3. To prepare all students for work and further education through a program of electives that develop individual aptitudes and interests.
4. To help all students fulfill their social and civic obligations through school and community service. (p. 67)

To meet the first goal, Boyer (1983) proposes an English proficiency test prior to high school entrance and, if necessary, remediation in the summer term before high school or during the first year. During high school all students should complete one unit of basic English with an emphasis on writing and one-half unit of speech. His rationale is clear and unwavering:

Language defines our humanity. It is the means by which we cope socially and succeed educationally. The advent of the information age raises to new levels the urgency, the need for all students to be effective in their use of the written and spoken word. The mastery of English is the first and most essential goal of education. (p. 93)

To achieve the second goal, Boyer (1983) recommends a core of common learning:

a study of those consequential ideals, experiences, and traditions common to all of us by virtue of our membership in the human family at a particular moment in history. These shared experiences include our sense of symbols, our sense of history, our membership in groups and institutions, our relationship to nature, our need for well-being and our growing dependence on technology. (p. 95)

Boyer (1983) translates these ideas into a core curriculum for all that includes courses in literature, the arts, foreign language, history (United States, Western, and non-Western), civics, science, mathematics, the impact of technology, health, and the meaning of work. The capstone of the core is a senior independent project that would ask students to complete "a written report which focuses on a significant contemporary issue, one that draws upon the various fields of academic study that have made up the student's program" (p. 115). Table 8.4 shows the courses that comprise the proposed core for *all* students and the academic units attached to each.

In order to reach the third goal, Boyer proposes that a program of elective clusters be developed for each student. A cluster would be five or six courses that might involve advanced study in certain academic subjects for the college bound, exploration of career options, or some combination of the two. It is within these elective clusters that students for the first time are exposed to separate and individualized school experiences. Boyer recommends that the last two years of high school be thought of as "a transition school" where students spend half their time completing the common core and the other half in elective clusters.

Finally, to reach the fourth goal Boyer proposes an extracurricular program whereby students would complete a service requirement. This requirement, which Boyer labels a new Carnegie unit, involves students in volunteer work in the com-

Table 8.4 Proposed core of common learning

	Academic Units
Language, 5 units	
Basic English: writing	1
Speech	$\frac{1}{2}$
Literature	1
Foreign language	2
Arts	$\frac{1}{2}$
History, $2\frac{1}{2}$ units	
U.S. history	1
Western civilization	1
Non-Western studies	$\frac{1}{2}$
Civics, 1 unit	1
Science, 2 units	
Physical science	1
Biological science	1
Mathematics	2
Technology	$\frac{1}{2}$
Health	$\frac{1}{2}$
Seminar on work	$\frac{1}{2}$
Senior independent project	$\frac{1}{2}$
TOTAL	$14\frac{1}{2}$

SOURCE: Boyer, *High School*, Harper & Row, 1983, p. 117

munity and at their schools. Students could earn this unit on weekends and eve-
nings during the school year or in the summer. The proposed four-year curriculum
is shown graphically in Figure 8.1.

A Place Called School A third report, which has already been cited a number of
times in this chapter, is *A Place Called School*, by John I. Goodlad, a former dean of
the Graduate School of Education at the University of California, Los Angeles.
Goodlad studied 38 elementary and secondary schools in seven states, visiting over
1,000 classrooms. He and his coresearchers surveyed 1,350 teachers, more than
17,000 students, and 8,600 parents.

   In addition to revealing the nature of the current curricula, Goodlad's data show
that all constituencies—parents, teachers, and students—want the schools to pursue four types of broad goals: academic, vocational, social (civic and cultural), and
personal, but Goodlad (1984) concludes that "Curricula and pedagogy appear not
to reflect adequately the expectations implied in our goals for schools" (p. 358). As
noted earlier, Goodlad's examination of the curriculum in his sample shows inequities both among and within schools with regard to opportunities for access to
knowledge. Moreover, Goodlad (1984) found that the variation grows greater as
one moves from elementary to secondary school.

> It appears that children at Newport Elementary spend about 70% as much time on
> learning as the children at Laurel Elementary and distributed that time across subjects
> quite differently. And if the distribution of teachers can be taken as a significant
> criterion, the junior and senior high schools of our sample placed markedly different
> values on the importance of the several subjects. The school a child or youth happens
> to attend determines the curriculum available and likely to be taken—and there are, it
> appears, substantial differences in what is available. (pp. 157–158)

   The fact that there is such inequity and that "at least some of these differences
in opportunity to learn, it appears, were differentially associated with economic
status and racial identification" (p. 160) led Goodlad (1984) to recommend, at the
high school level, a curricular balance that would divide a student's program into: 18
percent for literature and language; 18 percent for mathematics and science; 15 percent for society and social studies, the arts, and the vocations; and up to 10 percent
for physical education. The remaining time would be for individual but guided
choices. Within each of these five domains about two-thirds of the students' programs would be common—the choice would come from a limited array of electives.
The result would be a common core, but Goodlad argues against a common set of
topics as the basis of the core. Instead he proposes "a common set of concepts, principles, skills and ways of knowing" (Goodlad, 1984, p. 298).

   Goodlad (1984) sees the best hope for assuring a coherent and substantial curriculum coming from the establishment of major centers for curriculum develop-

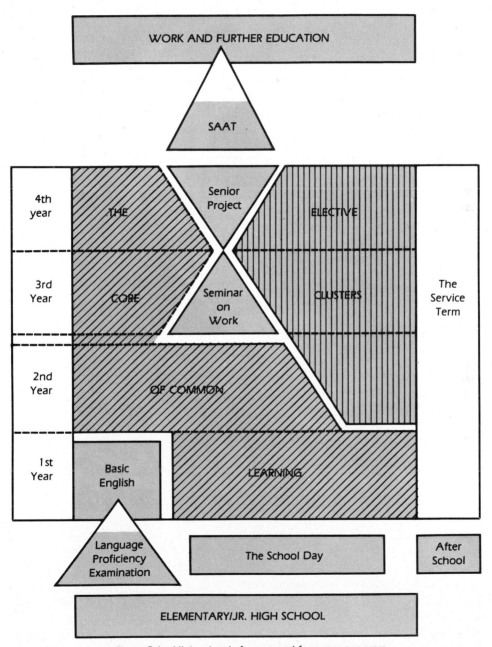

Figure 8.1 High school: A proposed four-year program

ment, which would address a district's curriculum, kindergarten through twelfth grade. He also maintains that ability grouping and tracking must be eliminated.

> Students should be assigned to classes randomly in a way that assures heterogeneity. Only in this way can we have some assurance that grouping practices alone will not lead to different subject matter, different expectations and different treatment of students. Students should not all be treated alike, but the variations should be based on a teacher's deliberate judgment that this rather than that practice serves the student better. Classes of randomly assigned or heterogeneous students appear to offer the most equity with respect to gaining access to knowledge while still preserving the more advantageous content and teaching practices of the upper tracks. (pp. 298–299)

Horace's Compromise A fourth report on secondary education that has received considerable attention is one written by Theodore R. Sizer entitled *Horace's Compromise*. Sizer, a historian, is a former dean of the graduate school at Harvard University, former headmaster at Philips Exeter, and the current chair of the education department at Brown University. Sizer begins with the observation that high schools today suffer from a "mediocre sameness" rather than diversity and fragmentation. In his words, "Today we need no new consensus, but, rather, an agreement to help our adolescents break out of our existing mediocre harmonies." In Sizer's (1984) view, "Tacit agreement exists as to the purpose of high school and how it is to be accomplished" (p. 6), and it is that agreement that needs to be changed.

The change that must take place, he then argues, is that high schools must "narrow their mission." The Seven Cardinal Principles set forth by the National Educational Association in 1918 were appropriate for a "newly modernized state," but Sizer (1984) believes that the question to ask today is "what special role schools should play among the extraordinary sets of educating influences around and available to the modern American adolescent" (p. 84). The answer he arrives at is twofold: "One purpose for schools—education of the intellect—is obvious. The other—an education in character—is inescapable" (p. 84).

Regarding the intellect Sizer maintains that the complexity of the times and the fact that no other institution in the culture is solely devoted to the development of mental power dictates that the focus of the high school curriculum be the training of the mind. This means concentrating on teaching students how to use information rather than simply giving them information. Once students know how to use their minds they can teach themselves much of what has traditionally comprised the comprehensive high school curricula. Concerning the goal of character Sizer argues that in schools, as in all institutions, issues of conduct—of rights and responsibility—naturally arise and that by sensitively confronting these a school can help to develop a student's character.

Sizer (1984) believes that the state should mandate only certain essentials for all students. The essentials are limited to *literacy, numeracy,* and *civic understanding.* He defines literacy as more than the ability to decode words:

It means the ability to comprehend and to understand ideas and arguments to a degree that allows an individual to use them. Literacy implies clear thought; that is, one must read easily and sensitively enough to comprehend at least the basic arguments presented by contemporary political and social life. Without that ability and the correlative ability to present such arguments oneself orally and in clear writing, a citizen cannot fully participate in a democracy. Any community that expects collective, affirmative government requires a literate citizenry. (p. 86)

Equally important is the concept of numeracy, according to Sizer (1984):

Numeracy means the ability both to use numbers, arithmetically and algebraically, and to understand the concepts, relationships, and logic embedded in mathematical thought. A modern citizen cannot make critical judgments without these skills. (p. 86)

Civic understanding refers to a grasp of the basis for democratic government, a respect for its processes, and acceptance of the restraints and obligations incumbent on a citizen.

Sizer believes that for the state to mandate beyond these essentials would be an encroachment on the freedom of the individual. A core curriculum of subjects might be available to all, and certain kinds of diplomas might be available to those who voluntarily choose to take such a core, but a long list of required subjects should not be compulsory. Another basic premise of Sizer's (1984) is that "less is more":

I believe that the quality of mind that should be the goal of high school needs time to grow and that they develop best when engaging a few, important ideas, deeply. Information is plentiful, cheap; learning how to use it is often stressful and absolutely requires a form of personal coaching of each student by a teacher that is neither possible in many schools today nor recognized as an important process. (p. 89)

In effect Sizer is arguing against the current emphasis on covering a large amount of content in many different subject areas. Instead he recommends that the entire curriculum be divided into four areas that blend traditional subjects: inquiry and expression, math and science, literature and the arts, and philosophy and history. Each student would progress at his or her own rate. Instead of electives there would be opportunities to pursue personal interests within these categories.

What would students learn in each of these areas? Sizer endorses the three key spheres that Mortimer Adler (1982) recommended in yet another report, *The Paideia Proposal*. The first sphere involves the acquisition of skills, and the following skills are cited by Sizer: reading, writing, speaking, listening, measuring, estimating, calculating, seeing, and modes of imagining and reasoning.

The second sphere is acquisition of knowledge—what a student needs to know. Since the extent of things worth knowing is infinite, the critical issue is how to select. Sizer says that there should be no choice until the students have met standards in the essentials. Thereafter Sizer recommends that the students, their families, and their teachers have the chance to pick their preferences from the available choices. Sizer (1984) believes choice of subject matter should "support the students' learning of skills" and should "lead somewhere in the eyes and mind of the student"; it must "connect to wherever that student is rooted—his experience," and it must "promise to take him toward an important place" (pp. 111–112). This is another way of saying that all subject matter should whet the intellectual appetite.

Sizer's (1984) third sphere is "understanding the development of discrimination and judgment" (p. 116). This is the kind of judgment required to decide whether one novel is better than another, or whether capital punishment an effective way to deter crime.

Education for a Democratic Future In some respects *Education for a Democratic Future* (Berlak, 1985) is a response to the previously mentioned reports. It was developed and supported by a broad base of concerned educators and citizens, known as the International Committee of Correspondents for Democratic Schools. The report begins with the premise that many current proposals for change encouraging more course requirements, more homework, tougher grading, and more tests actually threaten popular democracy and increase existing problems. It offers an alternative vision of democratic public schools in which students:

1. gain the knowledge and develop skills and interests to enable them to pursue individual goals as well as to enter fully into the lives of their communities.
2. are stimulated to think, use their imaginations, and cultivate their talents.
3. are actively engaged in the process of their own learning. (*Education for a Democratic Future*, 1985, p. 4)

This report describes a democratic curriculum as one that fosters:

Critical literacy. This goes beyond the ability to read and write to include the motivation and capacity of individuals to be critical of what they read, see, and hear; to probe beyond the surface appearances and question the common wisdom.

Knowledge and understanding of the diverse intellectual, cultural and scientific traditions: we refer not only to the more familiar academic disciplines and traditions of high-culture, but the histories and cultural perspectives of those people, including women and minorities, traditionally excluded from formal study.

Ability to use knowledge and skills to: pursue one's own interests, to make informed personal and political decisions and to work for the welfare of the community. (*Education for a Democratic Future*, 1985, p. 7)

In addition the report emphatically states that curriculum decisions need to be made by *teachers* in conjunction with students and citizens. Teachers need to be given the time and resources to create their own curricula and to develop their own pedagogical strategies. Over time, the report argues, more top-down controls drive out thoughtful teachers who want to exercise their initiative and creativity and "deskill" those who stay. It also argues that children "almost never participate in curriculum decisions, ask few questions in class, and rarely are expected to take the initiative for their own learning" (*Education for a Democratic Future*, 1985, pp. 15–16). Because a passive role does not prepare students for democratic decision making, the report recommends more student involvement in curriculum.

These recommendations stem from the committee's belief in the strong interconnections between schools, local communities, and society in general, as well as from the committee's concern for equity. The report states that:

> the practice of democracy depends upon a system of public education that educates all children in the basics of reading, writing, and mathematics to the very highest standard regardless of gender, cultural, racial and social class backgrounds. Excellence in a democracy is not for the favored few but for all. We reject outright the belief that children from any cultural group or socio-economic class have limited potential because of their parents' educational history, social background or values. Second, in a democracy every person has the right and the responsibility to participate directly in the control and reform of their institutions. Democratic control and management is as essential in schools as it is in all aspects of our work, community, and political lives. (*Education for a Democratic Future*, 1985, p. 3)

This belief in turn leads the committee to a single, overarching recommendation for local control of curriculum and schools.

> People in each community must develop their own agendas and specific programs for reform. This requires the formation of coalitions of parents, teachers, counselors, librarians and other school-based specialists, working in concert with local educational and political officials. Together they would examine existing practices and institute changes. (*Education for a Democratic Future*, 1985, p. 6)

This recent report brings the discussion right back to the historical overview of school goals and curricula and to the long-standing tension between excellence and equity. Just at the time when the traditionalists are bombarding this country with recommendations that advocate academic excellence in the form of more requirements and higher standards, the voice of the progressive movement is raised once again through calls for attention to democratic and equity issues. Thus the debate continues, and for good reason. The stakes are high in a democratic society that knows its survival depends upon educational excellence that is equally available to all citizens. The goals framed and the curricular decisions made for schools relate directly to the society future generations will inherit and to the knowledge and skills they will have to confront it.

This last report also gets to the core of this chapter — the role of the teacher in curriculum development and selection. *Education for a Democratic Future* argues that it is teachers who should be developing the curriculum, not curriculum specialists outside classrooms. Some of the other reports seem to suggest that the role of a teacher is more implementator than developer. The next section considers how much control classroom teachers can exert in relation to the curricula they teach.

A TEACHER'S ROLE IN DETERMINING
CURRICULUM: MICRO ISSUES

This chapter now moves from the macro level of societal needs and national reports to the micro world of individual classrooms, particularly the classrooms of the five case study teachers. It considers their curricular decision-making roles and their thoughts about curricular issues. Next the chapter considers general factors that seem to affect the amount of control or influence teachers have regarding curricula. This section concludes with a consideration of some curricular dilemmas and decisions all teachers confront consciously and unconsciously. While reading this material look for the interplay between the nature of an individual teacher's curricular decisions and the decisions made outside the classroom.

The Five Case Study Teachers:
A Sense of Curricular Control

Recommendations on curriculum from national commissions or foundations eventually find their way to state legislatures and to local school districts. Sometimes a state sets graduation requirements; sometimes a school district does. Whatever the case, the local school district is ultimately responsible for the particulars in terms of curriculum guidelines and objectives. The case study teachers work in districts of varying size and populations. Still all five claim to have considerable control over the curriculum in their individual classrooms.

Ruth Christopherson and Larry Wells work in relatively small districts and both experience considerable freedom to select the content of what they teach. Ruth, for example, has seen the curriculum pendulum swing from very structured, skill-oriented programs, to open classrooms where curriculum decisions were left to children, and back to a more structured basics curricula. When Ruth worked in the St. Louis Public Schools there was more curricular control imposed upon her than in the county, but she still believes that in almost any setting and in any time period a teacher can exercise some control over the curriculum. At Conway, she certainly feels such control.

> Teachers determine curriculum in their classrooms here. What's written down on paper is often gathering dust on the shelf rather than being applied. I think basically the teacher has control over what is going on in that classroom.

Larry, who teaches in a much smaller school district, feels almost total freedom to determine curriculum and might, in fact, prefer a little less.

> I feel here at Hillsboro we have an unusual situation. It's a small district, and we make a lot of the decisions. In our department, we pick our own textbooks. If you are forceful in the department, then you can have an awful lot of say about what textbooks you use. As far as what classes we are going to teach, we have a lot of say in that because the curriculum we have right now was essentially created by the teachers in the department. And there's not really a formal way of getting those kinds of things approved, which I think is somewhat of a problem. I think there should be a curriculum process—there's not much now.

A case in point is a course that Larry saw a need for seven years ago, created, and now teaches entitled Senior Survival. The course deals with love, marriage, family, children, consumer education, community involvement, and citizenship. The process for approval, as Larry tells it, was simple and informal:

> I simply presented it to the department, to the principal, and it became a class. I don't know how usual that is with small districts. I would think with larger districts that is pretty unusual to have that kind of a say. If I were principal, I'm sure it wouldn't be quite that easy to create a class and to put it into the curriculum. I'd have to look at a lot of other things.

In addition to a curriculum process for course approval, Larry believes there needs to be more district coordination and direction. Instead, the elementary, the middle, the junior high, and the senior high schools develop their curricula independently. Still, he is generally glad that he has the freedom to put his own ideas into action.

What might be surprising to Larry and others is the fact that the case study teachers in larger systems also feel they can directly influence what is taught in their classrooms. There is, however, a fairly wide range within that sphere of influence. At the extreme is Sandy Snodgrass, who feels that she is basically free to make her own decisions. She says that over the years she and many of her colleagues have written their own curriculum, and they are "pretty much left alone to use that—pretty much free to do what we want." One exception to Sandy's basic freedom is the class she teaches for students who have not passed the social studies section of the state's competency test. In this instance, the test is the curriculum.

Somewhere in the middle is Jacquie, who is handed objectives created by the district curriculum personnel but then is free to determine how she will reach them. In her words, "Nobody bothers us." According to Jacquie, the only monitoring of what she has taught is the informal assessment by the high school teachers. As long as her students are prepared to continue their language study in advanced courses, she can control what she teaches. Foreign language study in the past, however, has not been considered as important as other areas of the curriculum she maintains. Today, under the press for excellence, it is receiving more attention, and she expects more external control in the future. At the present she feels curricular choice is primarily up to her.

Even Luberta, who works in a large urban system with a high degree of bureaucracy and is at the low end of the continuum of curricular influence, maintains that she can make important choices. She is comfortable with both what she is given and what she can contribute in terms of selection and emphasis.

> I think the curriculum is fine. We have a curriculum which teaches each subject matter, science and health, reading and language, math and social studies, but how you handle this is your particular job and concern. There are objectives they want us to cover. Okay, this has to be done, but how we do it or how much importance we give to certain areas of it is left up to the teacher's judgment. . . . In reading, for example, I try to touch on all the skills but stress and focus more on the ones that I think are extremely important. I think the skills of drawing conclusions and inferences are tough ones for the children, and I don't hesitate to make one of these reading skills a part of math. . . . Also the textbooks today are well chosen. . . . There are just too many of them, but here again . . . we can select.

Larry and Sandy talk about writing and creating their own curriculum, and by that they mean developing courses or units within a course that are unified wholes. Larry talks about his curriculum development this way:

> What a person is essentially doing when he teaches a class is verbally writing his own book. In order to create a good course and good units, you've got to have a beginning, a middle, and an end. You've got to know where you're starting and where you're going.

Ruth and Luberta create curriculum units and experiences as well. Ruth is extraordinarily skilled at creating projects in science from which students can learn from their own research. To teach energy, for example, one year she started not with the textbook but with a very basic question, What is energy? Then she helped students try to answer the question through a series of experiments, after which they recorded their observations. The result? Ruth describes it as:

> a "Rube Goldberg" machine that started with a gravity thing and ended up lighting bulbs and photoelectric cells, and the whole thing was just woven together. You could light a candle at one spot. What did it do? It melted a piece of wax, and it dropped something on a lever . . . it just went all around.

Ruth also is masterful at involving the students in curricular decision making. Her curricular priority is teaching basic skills, particularly the skill of thinking, and she maintains that these skills can be taught through almost any content. Whenever she can she allows the students to pick the topic or content because they are simply more interested.

> Topic-wise, I think it would be nice if the student had control because you can teach basic skills with any topic, and if you have a topic that they're interested in, then you get more effort and output than input. . . . Just feeling that they have a part in the decision making changes their attitudes toward the material.

In sixth grade, for example, Ruth has capitalized on the students' interest in the Olympics in order to teach math skills, reading skills, and mapping skills. Students read and examine previous records, and they predict what athletes might do in the future; they use mapping skills to figure out how far Los Angeles is from St. Louis; they read books about the Olympics and famous athletes. Similarly, in first grade, Ruth has asked the students what they want to learn about this week. If the class decides on dinosaurs, then they read about dinosaurs; they write about dinosaurs; they add and subtract dinosaurs; they draw pictures of dinosaurs; they learn to spell the names of different dinosaurs.

Luberta, in contrast, puts much effort into making concepts and ideas come alive by taking students outside the classroom and by bringing experts into the classroom. To get ideas about what is available she is always enrolling in different workshops. Financial cutbacks at school are sometimes a problem in terms of field trips, but she has learned how to make use of the available free resources in the community.

> Our city is a marvelous place, I guess most cities are. We have outreach programs which will come to you. I took the time to find out a lot about them this summer. The places to which we were going have education programs—the Art Museum and Shaw's Garden have education departments, and they have a variety of tools for people. If you can't come to them, you can arrange for them to come to you. I also found out the Gateway Arch has a traveling exhibit. It's coming to our class in February. That's Black History Month, and both Jefferson Memorial and the Missouri Historical Society are sending me a terrific kit in February. These two items are coming with interpretive material so I can use them immediately. It has been good to learn that these people will come to you—very, very helpful! We've already had one of the ladies from the Missouri Historical Society come in and she did a nice presentation on early pioneer life.

The Balance Between the Macro and the Micro

Clearly all of these teachers exert control over the curriculum either by selecting what to present or what to emphasize or by creating the materials and presentations themselves. All teachers, no matter where they teach, can do some of the same. No prescribed curriculum can meet all needs or work equally well in all groups. An individual classroom teacher with intimate knowledge of his or her own students is in the best position to make certain curricular decisions, adaptations, and changes. Ruth found this to be the case even with an extremely well-written, highly successful mathematics curriculum entitled the Comprehensive School

Mathematics Program (CSMP). This program is a highly prescriptive curriculum developed by a regional research laboratory with a teacher's guide that gives step-by-step teacher plans and questions. A central tenet of the curriculum is that lessons be conducted with an entire class so that slower students can learn from brighter students. Ruth, however, began to sense that the bright students were "carrying the class too often." She took steps to make some significant alterations in grouping arrangements and in the kinds of questions posed. Without question a classroom teacher must be more than an implementor of curriculum. To be effective a teacher must evaluate the given curriculum and then select or emphasize certain aspects of content, or create materials that will be appropriate within a particular classroom situation.

This book advocates teacher control and influence over what is taught in the classroom, but it also recognizes the dangers inherent in excessive curricular independence. If every school or classroom teacher had complete curricular flexibility there could be a serious lack of continuity and cohesiveness in the nation's public schools. Larry Wells worries about this problem in his district. It is possible for students in a school or a district where there are no overarching curricular guidelines to receive too much of some content and not enough of another. Similarly, where there is no nationwide consensus on broad curricular goals there will be an absence of a common core of understanding that unites citizens in a democracy. All learners have simultaneous ties to their individual and local interests and to larger societal interests, and the curriculum must address both needs.

In addition to the issue of developing curriculum that reflects individual and common concerns is the matter of available expertise and resources for curricular development. The CSMP curriculum can serve as an example once again. This highly effective curriculum is one that few individual classroom teachers working alone or in a team could produce. The developers of CSMP were creative mathematicians with the time, skills, and resources to conceptualize and pilot this course of study until it was perfected. If teachers fail to make use of such external expertise because they want to create their own curriculum, they may be short-changing themselves as well as their students.

The issue to be addressed then is not simply teacher influence but teacher influence that is meaningfully interactive with events, needs, and materials at the macro level. Hereafter teacher influence or control in the classroom will refer to influence that involves broader and external factors as well as individual classroom considerations.

MICRO FACTORS THAT AFFECT TEACHER CONTROL AND INFLUENCE

There are a number of factors at the classroom or micro level that can affect the amount of influence teachers can exert on a curriculum. These can be divided along individual and contextual dimensions.

The Individual Teacher

Knowledge of Subject Matter Probably the most important individual factor that can affect teacher influence on the curriculum is the teacher's own knowledge base. Unless teachers have a firm grounding in the subjects they teach they will be highly dependent upon existing materials or a text, regardless of its quality. Larry Wells explains how knowledge of his field is central to his curricular decision making:

> What influences actual decision making in determining curriculum in my courses is my background more than anything. I teach a class in the Civil War of the United States and slavery. My educational expertise determines that. . . . If I'm not that versed on a particular aspect of a subject, like some parts of world history, I'll find myself not covering that quite as well, not as deeply, not as intensely. I'll try to get over that as fast as I can, which is not necessarily good . . . but which also is not easy to avoid. . . . In world history I'm expected to know everything that's ever happened in the world—technically. And there's no way anybody can do that—no way.

Still Larry tries. He reads as many books and journals as he can to stay knowledgeable in his field. One of his frustrations is that he doesn't have the time to do more.

> If I had extra time, I would spend it reading and doing some scholarly research. It might sound really silly to say that, but I don't have enough time to do as much research and to keep up with it as well as I could.

Another of Larry's frustrations is that some high school teachers do not ever try to stay abreast of their field and that others will teach a subject in which they have the most minimal preparation.

> It's so funny. Teachers want to call themselves professional. That's great, that's right. But how many history teachers in this country get the American Historical Association's journals? Who gets *The Mississippi Valley Review?* Too many high school teachers don't do that. . . . I'd say a third of the people who teach social studies, seventh through twelfth grade, really shouldn't be teaching it because often you have a coach who has a minor, 15 hours in history, and he's in there teaching without a text-book. Because he has very shallow knowledge, he might show a lot of films. It's happened here at this school; no wonder people think their kids aren't learning anything. They're not.

State departments of education as well as departments and schools of education in most universities have certification requirements that far exceed 15 hours. According to the state of Missouri's standards, for example, teachers must complete 40 hours to teach social studies in high school. This includes 12 hours in American history; 8 hours in European history; 3 hours in economics; 6 hours in some combinations of sociology, anthropology, or psychology; 3 hours in geography; and 2 hours of electives. Even with this much coursework Larry Wells did not feel prepared to teach, and he earned a master's degree in history before looking for his first teaching position. But, as Larry has pointed out, someone hired as a coach in a particular school can end up teaching social studies. Those who are unprepared to teach in the field to which they are assigned are forced, at best, to rely completely on the existing textbook or curriculum guide and, at worst, as Larry puts it, "to show a lot of films." Larry and all the case study teachers are grounded well enough in their fields to make intelligent decisions to create, select, or emphasize certain aspects of their classroom curriculum.

Closely related to a teacher's knowledge of subject matter is a teacher's understanding of the structure of the discipline itself. In a foreign language or in mathematics, for example, where concepts or principles build logically upon others, there is less opportunity for selection than there is in literature and social studies. Teacher influence, therefore, must be related to the content itself.

A Teacher's Concept of Self A second individual variable affecting teacher influence on the curriculum is a teacher's confidence and self-esteem. It takes initiative and belief in self to question a textbook, a district's guidelines, or existing departmental curriculum. All five case study teachers clearly exhibit such self-esteem. They are thinking, questioning human beings, and they are confident that they have the capacity, the knowledge, and the right to seek and to find answers that will be beneficial to their students. When they see the results of their efforts they are further encouraged, and their trust in self and satisfaction in their work grows.

School Context

Administrative Trust and Encouragement Teachers who are knowledgeable in their subject matter and who have high self-esteem and initiative can do much to influence curriculum, but unless there is administrative support for such influence teachers can find themselves in positions that are subversive or antagonistic. On the other hand, if administrators support teachers as central decision makers in the instructional process, they can make significant contributions to the curriculum. All of the five case study teachers felt they had such support from their administrators. Three of our teachers spoke to this issue directly. Sandy, for example, attributes her freedom to make curriculum choices to board and administrative trust.

> I think that from school board down, the powers that be feel that staff is pretty competent. They're not worried about radical kids out of college anymore, which years ago was sort of a concern. I'm guessing the average length of service of teachers here is around 20 years. They trust and respect us. We're evaluated, so they know what we're

doing. The district has a good reputation; they pretty much know that it's because the teaching staff has come up with the curriculum. We do make changes now and then, but we're basically pretty free.

Both Luberta and Larry talk about the positive effects of having the administration trust you and encourage you to experiment. Larry remembers fondly his first principal who encouraged him to recognize that through experimentation and changes he could grow. Luberta also recalls an assistant superintendent who encouraged her to innovate rather than to accept existing curricular materials.

He was assistant superintendent where I was working and he decided that he would start an innovative program and simply label it an *enrichment program*. I was chosen to be one of the teachers in this pilot program and I am so glad I was. . . . When he asked me if I wanted to be in his program, I dared not say no—he was the assistant superintendent—I said yes, but I did have sense enough to ask him what was expected of me, and he said really nothing. Now how can you refuse getting into a program where nothing is essentially wanted of you. . . . He said, "There are no guidelines, I'm not going to structure it for you. All I'm going to do is make sure that you have select students, not gifted, but average and maybe slightly above average students, but they're going to be firmly average." Well, that sounded ideal, so I said great. He said, "That's what I'm going to do for you, but the program you devise, you come up with, will be yours." He said, "I'm also going to give you any support I can. If you get any great ideas I'm behind you." And that's what happened. I worked in that program. I had these marvelous little human beings. Now when I said they were average or above average, I don't mean that they were performing in this manner. They weren't necessarily performing like this, but they had the ability. They had been tested. They had mental ability. For one reason or another, probably they were not doing their very best. They weren't getting top performance out of themselves. And I started there. The kids were so dynamic that they just inspired you and from then on I think I've come into a classroom and said wow, we can do it, because those children reached such heights.

Although she remembers that experience as a special time when she planned "all the activities I had ever dreamed about," Luberta also thinks of her current principal as one who encourages her to give her own shape to the prescribed curriculum: "He is willing to experiment with something that could have good results—he is willing to let people with something worthwhile come in." Thus, in Lindbergh High and Jefferson School, schools within large districts, teachers can bring their own expertise to the curriculum as can teachers in the smaller districts of Ladue and Hillsboro. One key appears to be administrative confidence and trust in teachers' ability.

Opportunities to Participate in School and District Decision Making A related contextual issue is the role teachers are asked to play in purchasing external materials or in writing district curricula. School and district decision makers can adopt textbooks and curriculum packages and write curriculum materials without involving the classroom teachers who will be told to use them, or they can involve teachers in the initial decision making. It would seem that to use a teacher's expertise would make more sense. In many schools, teacher committees are formed to devise goals and to review existing curriculum packages or texts for possible adoption. These committees weigh the advantages and disadvantages of existing materials and then select the ones that seem most appropriate for the goals. If nothing suitable exists they will take on the task of creating materials. This process, of course, requires allocating time and money for teachers to do this work.

Involving teachers in district and school curricular decision making has a number of advantages. First, teachers can select the existing materials that come closest to their standards. Adapting these materials to their own needs may then require minimal time and energy. Second, if teachers know about the wide range of materials available they can make intelligent initial decisions as well as accumulate resources to supplement their final choices. Third, teachers who are involved in the process of decision making will probably feel more committed to and satisfied with the final choice.

Teacher Decisions on the Nature of Knowledge: The Macro within the Micro

The argument has been made that teachers can and should influence curriculum through selection and emphasis of content as well as through creation and organization of new materials. Factors that can foster the degree of influence a teacher exerts in these directions have been considered. This discussion now turns to some of the individual decisions teachers make, consciously or unconsciously, that convey to students certain attitudes and understandings about the nature of knowledge and that have larger societal implications. Ann and Harold Berlak's *The Dilemmas of Schooling: Teaching and Social Change* (1981) serves as the basis for the discussion.

The Berlaks' book addresses some important links between everyday schooling behavior and broader social, economic, and cultural change. It builds upon the earlier work of researchers such as Pierre Bourdieux, Basil Bernstein, and a group of British sociologists known as the New Sociologists who have been investigating the connection between schools and society. Bourdieux, for example, focuses on the idea of "cultural capital," which refers to "high status knowledge, dispositions, and skills which are acquired and/or reinforced within the institutions of society, particularly schools" (Berlak & Berlak, 1981, p. 16). At the individual level this concept means "the inherited and acquired linguistic and cultural competence that facilitates achievement in school and provides access to prestigious and economically rewarding positions in society" (Berlak & Berlak, 1981, p. 16).

What Bourdieux contends is that students come to school with certain advantages or disadvantages related to academic achievement and that schools reinforce these, thereby recreating existing social inequities. In effect he argues that upper-class children are largely destined to stay at the top of the social ladder by virtue of the type of education they receive whereas lower-class children will remain at the bottom because of the education available to them. Recall that earlier this chapter noted Goodlad's data on the broad range of achievement within a given class and the role of tracks and ability groups in reinforcing discrepancies in student achievement. Bernstein's work also focuses on social inequities, and he attempts to connect what is taught (curriculum) and how it is taught (instruction) to the inequities of British social class, with the idea that analysis can lead to change.

Researchers like Bourdieux, Bernstein, and the New Sociologists have their counterparts in the United States: Michael Apple, Henry Giroux, and the Berlaks, to name a few. They share the beliefs that those who control curriculum content can influence the nature of the culture and that the current idea of what being educated means needs to be questioned. Also, they stress people's more active, creative aspects and believe that individuals can bring about change in the existing order, thereby exerting control over their own lives.

The Berlaks, drawing upon the ideas of the social psychologist George Herbert Mead, view teacher behavior as potentially *minded*, or *reflective*, activity. Mead uses these terms to suggest that people are capable of examining or reflecting upon a problem from multiple perspectives and then developing their own unique solutions. In this way people can be active changers as well as transmitters of society. To explain further the way change can be brought about the Berlaks invoke Karl Marx and the Marxist critical social theorists. The Berlaks argue that whereas human beings are deeply affected by the prevailing society, they are also aware of some contradictions within the status quo. The Berlaks cite, for example, the fact that although the prevailing capitalist ideology is that hard work and individual initiative and ability will be rewarded regardless of social and economic class, there are inevitably some people whose experience shows this ideology to be untrue. As some individuals become aware of these kinds of contradictions they may begin to see alternative interpretations or explanations. The Berlaks maintain that it is this kind of awareness that can eventually lead to change.

Based upon these ideas and their observations of teachers in British primary schools, the Berlaks have conceptualized a set of 16 schooling dilemmas that capture some of the contradictions within people and society. As teachers become aware of these dilemmas, reflect upon and resolve them in different ways, they can work consciously to transmit or to transform the existing culture.

The Berlaks (1981) divide their dilemmas of schooling into three sets—control dilemmas, curricular dilemmas, and societal dilemmas. The curricular dilemmas describe and inquire into how "teachers through their schooling acts transmit knowledge and ways of knowing and learning" (p. 144). To give some sense of the formal substance of the curricular dilemmas, three are briefly discussed below: personal knowledge *vs.* public knowledge; knowledge as content *vs.* knowledge as process; knowledge as given *vs.* knowledge as problematical.

Personal Knowledge vs. Public Knowledge This dilemma represents two positions regarding worthwhile knowledge. As in all the dilemmas, teachers are usually drawn in both directions. On the one hand teachers believe that "worthwhile knowledge consists of the accumulated traditions of the ages, traditions which have a value external to and independent of the knower" (Berlak & Berlak, 1981, p. 144). Public knowledge is the body of formal and informal skills and ways of knowing that have stood the test of time. It is the common core that Boyer and Goodlad advocate.

On the other hand teachers also believe that the value of knowledge is established through its relationship to the knower. Implicit in this position is the belief that the worth of knowledge cannot be judged apart from its relationship to the knower. Knowledge is useful and significant only in so far as it enables one to make sense of experience. Sandy Snodgrass, who in psychology tends to build upon the students' experience with drugs, alcohol, and anorexia, seems to be drawn to a personal knowledge resolution. Similarly Ruth, who tries to start with and incorporate students' personal interest, like the Olympics, seems to value highly personal knowledge. She consistently asks students what they want to know, and their topics become the content. Luberta, on the other hand, interested in helping her students to be more successful than their parents, stresses acquisition of public knowledge the parents do not have.

Knowledge as Content vs. Knowledge as Process This dilemma captures the conflict of whether to view public knowledge as "organized bodies of information, codified facts, theories, generalizations, on the one hand, or as a process of thinking, reasoning and testing to establish the truth or adequacy of a body of content or set of propositions on the other" (Berlak & Berlak, 1981, p. 47). Ruth frequently resolves this dilemma in terms of knowledge as process. She is interested in teaching thinking skills, and she says that almost any topic will suffice. Larry, Jacquie, and Luberta, on the other hand, focus much of their energy on teaching students particular content.

Knowledge as Given vs. Knowledge as Problematical This dilemma expresses "the pull toward treating knowledge as truth 'out there' and the alternative pull toward treating knowledge as constructed, provisional, tentative and subject to political, cultural, and societal influences" (Berlak & Berlak, 1981, p. 148). The emphasis on knowledge as problematical asks students to look critically at what they think are "givens."

An example of each approach can be seen in the different ways two social studies teachers might choose to handle Custer's Last Stand. The teacher who sees knowledge as given might require students to learn the basic facts of the Battle of the Little Bighorn—the date and place of the battle, the principal characters, and the traditional explanation as to why it was "necessary" for Custer to attack the Indians. The teacher who sees knowledge as problematical might ask students to consider what took place from two perspectives—Custer's and the Indians', and in doing so, to examine critically the assumptions of their text's interpretation. Whether or not the students agree with the textbook, the teacher's goal of critical examination has been achieved.

Larry Wells has actually posed similar questions regarding the topic of Custer's Last Stand, and Ruth in her approach to mathematics has students check the theories of mathematicians to see whether they hold up. Both at times seem to stress knowledge as problematical. Luberta and Jacquie by virtue of what they are teaching—basic reading, writing, and math skills and a foreign language—seem more often to emphasize the "given" nature of knowledge.

In order to clarify the various pulls within each dilemma this chapter has used examples from the case study teachers that illustrate certain positions. It is important, however, to emphasize that because these are genuine dilemmas that pull teachers simultaneously in two directions, each of the teachers has exhibited behaviors on both sides of the dilemma. A resolution in a particular instance sometimes seems connected to the individual philosophy of the teacher; at other times it seems related to the classroom context or to the subject matter.

Still, some teachers like Ruth, for example, tend to resolve dilemmas in a consistent way, and that consistency or pattern in turn transmits to students a particular way of viewing knowledge. A specific example in Ruth's teaching emphasizes this point.

Ruth gave her homeroom students an assignment in which they were to select a controversial issue, to interview certain adults regarding the issue, and to write a report highlighting the views of the interviewees and their own conclusions on the issue. The issues included the death penalty, the practice of copying cable TV movies, alcoholism, the appropriate penalty for drug pushers, and the relationship of smoking to cancer. Most of her students got personally involved in their topics, and Ruth describes one who made highly personal connections to his own family situation.

> One kid wrote a report on drinking. He called it "The Dynamic Drinking Dilemma." As we were going over these reports in class and discussing our findings, this boy poured out his whole story about his father being an alcoholic and how he is now recovered after going to AA. But he described to all of us his feelings of how scared he was when his friends would come over. They would go hide in the basement if his Dad would get mad. Can you imagine how tough it is for a kid living like that?

This one assignment and one student's reaction to it illustrates how Ruth often resolves the three curriculum dilemmas. This assignment starts with students' personal interest and lets them share the personal knowledge they gained from their research. Further, the emphasis is not on any particular topic or content but instead focuses on the processes or skills of gathering data, drawing conclusions, and writing. Finally, the assignment presents knowledge as something open-ended and problematic with different positions and conclusions possible. In all subject areas Ruth generally emphasizes personal knowledge, knowledge as process, and knowledge as problematic, although sometimes she takes the other positions as well. These emphases encourage her students to think critically and to question that which others might simply accept. It encourages them to become active and skilled problem solvers. It imbues them with a sense of confidence and trust in themselves as constructors and critics of knowledge, as persons in control of their own lives.

Teachers who are aware of curriculum dilemmas can consciously choose the view of knowledge they want to convey to students. They can then transmit that view through their classroom behavior. In this sense, all teachers have inherent influence over curriculum. Furthermore, in a broader sense, a teacher's views transmitted in the classroom can have some effect on the larger society. If, for example, teachers consciously worked toward conveying that public knowledge in certain instances can be questioned, they could conceivably produce a generation of citizens who feel a sense of control, who have the potential and inclination to determine what in the society is worth conserving and what is in need of change. In this way the acts of individual teachers can have a major effect upon the larger social order.

CONCLUSION

This chapter began with the notion that the school curriculum is influenced to a large extent by issues at the macro level of society. The content that is taught in schools is in part externally influenced and developed at the national, state, and district level. The chapter then focused on the micro, or classroom, level and argued that individual teachers can, nonetheless, make decisions that influence a given curriculum. The five case study teachers, who often exert curricular control by selecting what to present and emphasize and by creating their own units and materials, served as examples. Individual and contextual factors that affect the degree of teacher influence were considered. Finally, following the Berlaks, this chapter maintained that there are curriculum dilemmas that all teachers can consciously resolve in ways that can influence how young people perceive the nature of knowledge. These student perceptions can become adult views that can lead, in turn, to social change at the macro level.

Whereas the focus throughout has shifted from macro to micro and back to macro, the aim has been toward a single target: to convey that the role of a classroom teacher in the area of curriculum is highly connected to the events and forces of the larger society. To be a teacher is to make curricular decisions in the classroom that both reflect and shape the nature of society. Such decisions, therefore, must be given careful consideration.

DISCUSSION QUESTIONS

1. Historically changes in society have shaped and influenced curriculum content in the schools. Can you recall societal changes that influenced or shaped what you learned as a student? Think for a moment about the Civil Rights movement, the Vietnam War, and the Women's Rights movement. How have they affected curriculum content in recent years?
2. Compare and contrast the various national proposals for reform in terms of (a) their diagnoses of the problems of education and (b) their prescriptions for curricular reform. Which report is most convincing?

ACTIVITIES

1. Create your own proposal for curricular reform in high schools.
2. Form a panel within your university or college class in which students role play John Goodlad, Ernest Boyer, Theodore Sizer, Terrell Bell (secretary of education who commissioned A *Nation at Risk* report), and Harold Berlak (secretary for the network that wrote *Education for a Democratic Future*). Those role playing the writers of the reports should first state their proposals for curricular reform and then discuss among themselves their differences and similarities. Other students in the class should have opportunities to question them regarding similarities and differences in their positions.
3. Education is a process of changing individuals. In turn, those individuals affect the social order. All curricula have inherent assumptions about the nature of a good individual and a good society that would result if their goals were successfully attained. Examine the traditionalist and progressive orientations toward education to understand the nature of a good individual and a good society as defined by each position. Toward which of the positions are you inclined? As a next step investigate the major assumptions about the desired individual traits and the social order inherent in reports such as *A Nation at Risk, High School, A Place Called School, Horace's Compromise,* and *Education for a Democratic Future*. How would you characterize the assumptions inherent in each of these documents and their blueprints for the future of education? How explicit are the assumptions and visions of a good individual and a good society in each of the documents?

4. Use a combination of observation and interview methods to ascertain the relative influences of various forces on the daily curriculum. Consider the following: macro (national) forces filtered through state regulations and district policies; teacher knowledge of subject; teacher self-concept; teacher personal philosophy; administrative orientation; district curriculum committees; parental and taxpayer orientation; and student interests.

5. Examine the resolutions a teacher makes on the three curricular dilemmas posed by the Berlaks. Is there a consistent pattern of resolution or does the teacher seem to be pulled toward both poles of the dilemmas with about equal frequency? Careful observation followed by short interviews to test your hypothesis is probably a good strategy. To go further with this exercise choose another teacher who you believe has a very different philosophy and approach to teaching. See whether the second teacher's resolutions of the dilemmas differ markedly from the first. What are the implications of differences you may see for the students experiencing the different teachers?

6. Use your experience of reading this chapter, observing one or more teachers, and discussing issues with classmates and your instructor to clarify your own views of the major controversies embedded in making decisions about the curriculum your future students will experience.

7. Look carefully for evidence of the tension between the goals of educational excellence and equity. Does one of the concerns seem to dominate? Are the teachers, administrators, and others in the setting explicitly aware of the potential tension, or does it seem to go unrecognized? How might you account for the way it is in your setting?

QUESTIONS TO GUIDE OBSERVATION

1. What is the basic content of the course(s) or subject(s) taught by the teacher?

2. What kinds of materials does the teacher use: direct sources; text, curriculum package developed by external sources; curriculum package developed by the district, by the school, by the classroom teacher? How many different kinds of materials are used?

3. Do the content and materials seem appropriate in terms of students' knowledge level, skill level, interest level? Is there evidence of sexism, racism, or classism in the materials?

4. To what degree do current societal forces seem to influence curriculum? Is there, for example, a strong back-to-basics push? Are there new requirements aimed at excellence?

5. Does the teacher exercise control through selection of materials? through emphasis of certain content over other content? through creation of materials?

6. Does the teacher appear to have a strong background and grasp of the subject being taught? Is there any evidence of interdisciplinary teaching?
7. Does the teacher appear to have a strong sense of self in terms of the ability to influence the curriculum?
8. How does the teacher resolve the following dilemmas (use teacher behaviors as the basis of observation)?

> Personal knowledge *vs.* public knowledge
> Knowledge as content *vs.* knowledge as process
> Knowledge as given *vs.* knowledge as problematical

In Elementary Schools

9. Is the teacher a generalist or specialist?
10. How much time is given to each subject? Are there significant differences in time allocation? What does the variability suggest in terms of school or teacher priorities?
11. Do ability groups exist? If so, in what subjects? Do students appear able to move from one group to another? How much difference is there in terms of content in the different groups? Is the teacher's attitude toward content and students different in the various groups? Is there any evidence of student reaction to groups?

In Secondary Schools

12. What are the requirements for graduation?
13. How many full-time faculty are there in each subject area? If there is considerable variability, what implication does that have for student learning?
14. What kinds of choices and options are available to students?
15. Are there explicit or implicit tracks that sort students on the basis of ability and/or interest? If so, who chooses the track? What percentage of the student population is in each track? What is the ethnic background and socioeconomic status of those in each track?

QUESTIONS TO GUIDE TEACHER INTERVIEWS

1. How much curricular control do you feel you have? Would you prefer more or less?
2. To what degree do you feel that curriculum is imposed from outside? How do you keep knowledgeable in your field?
3. How do you think about the following curriculum dilemmas? (Teachers do not usually talk in these terms, and so the interviewer will have to explain the dilemmas.)

Personal knowledge *vs.* public knowledge
Knowledge as content *vs.* knowledge as process
Knowledge as given *vs.* knowledge as problematical

4. What do you know and think about the curriculum reform efforts of the 1980s? Do you agree with the proposed raising of standards and increase in requirements?
5. What kind of administrative support do you think you have to develop curriculum or make changes regarding selection or emphasis?
6. What opportunities do you have to participate in district or school departmental curricular writing or selection of materials?
7. What do you feel about the existing curriculum in your school?
8. How do you feel about grouping students according to ability (in elementary school) or tracking (in secondary school)? What are the advantages of ability grouping and tracking? What are the disadvantages?
9. What past curriculum reforms, if any, have you experienced? How have they affected your teaching?
10. Do you believe the school can achieve the twin goals of excellence and equity?
11. To what degree is your curriculum today influenced by pressures for high test scores?
12. What will happen to slower or disadvantaged students after graduation requirements are raised?

REFERENCES AND SOURCES

Adler, J. J. (1982). *The paideia proposal: An educational manifesto.* New York: Macmillan.

Apple, M. (1979). *Ideology and the curriculum.* London: Routledge & Kegan Paul.

Berlak, A., & Berlak, H. (1981). *The dilemmas of schooling: Teaching and social change.* New York: Methuen.

Berlak, H. (1985). *Education for a democratic future. Equity and excellence: Toward an agenda for school reform.* Public Education Information Network, Box 1183, Washington University, St. Louis, MO.

Bernstein, B. (1973). Class codes and control (vol. 1). *Theoretical studies toward a sociology of language,* London: Routledge & Kegan Paul.

Bernstein, B. (1975). Class codes and control (vol. 3). *Towards a theory of educational tranmissions* (2d ed.). London: Routledge & Kegan Paul.

Boyer, E. L. (1983). *High school: A report on secondary education in America.* New York: Harper & Row.

Bruner, J. S. (1960). *The process of education*. Cambridge, MA: Harvard University Press.

Goodlad, J. I. (1984). *A place called school*. New York: McGraw-Hill.

National Commission on Excellence in Education. (1983). *A nation at risk: The imperative for educational reform*. United States Department of Education, Washington, D.C.

Ravitch, D. (1983). The educational pendulum. *Psychology Today, 17*(10), 62–71.

Sizer, T. R. (1984). *Horace's compromise: The dilemmas of the American high school*. Boston: Houghton Mifflin.

Tom, A. (1970). *An approach to selecting among social studies curricula*. St. Ann, MO: Central Midwestern Educational Laboratory.

Wirth, A. (1983). *Productive work in industry and schools: Becoming persons again*. Washington, D.C.: University Press of America.

9

THE INSTRUCTIONAL
ROLE OF THE TEACHER

INTRODUCTION

This chapter is at once a continuation and a departure. It is a continuation in the sense that it builds and expands on the preceding chapter on curriculum and the teacher's role in deciding *what* is taught. It presents an externally developed supplemental television curriculum for upper-elementary students entitled *ThinkAbout* (Sanders & Sonnad, 1982) and illustrates how two teachers use the same curriculum quite differently.*

To understand why the two teachers initially chose to use the curriculum and then how they selected which parts of it to use, we refocus briefly on some of the micro curriculum decisions raised in Chapter 8. To look at the overall process of lesson planning and the specific teacher decisions related to lesson objectives, strategies, and evaluation practices in implementing the *ThinkAbout* curriculum, we move from curricular decisions about *what* is taught to instructional decisions about *how* the curriculum is taught.

The teacher as instructional decision maker is our primary focus, and our basic premise is that teachers have enormous control over the domain of instruction. We use the two teachers' differing approaches in working with *ThinkAbout* to demonstrate (1) the complexity arising from the countless choices open to teachers, (2) the difference in the nature of those instructional choices, and (3) the

*Permission to include excerpts from *ThinkAbout* was granted by the Agency for Instructional Television.

effect that differing choices can have upon student learning and the intellectual climate of the classroom.

This chapter is different in the sense that it departs from the practice of using only the five case study teachers as exemplars. In order to demonstrate as sharply as possible differences in alternative instructional decisions and approaches, the chapter introduces two new teachers using the same *ThinkAbout* curriculum. Since none of the case study teachers use the same curriculum, excerpts from a participant observation study of three teachers using the *ThinkAbout* curriculum will be examined (Cohn, 1982). This chapter begins with a focus on two of the three teachers who represent dramatically different approaches to instruction and then moves to a more general discussion of instructional decision making.

CURRICULAR AND INSTRUCTIONAL DECISION MAKING: COMPARING TWO TEACHERS

The ThinkAbout Curriculum

The *ThinkAbout* curriculum is a series of sixty 15-minute television programs that are, according to the series guide, intended to "help fifth and sixth graders acquire and use the skills they must have to be independent learners and problem solvers." More specifically, it is to aid in their learning to "(1) effectively express themselves, (2) manage their own learning, (3) reason systematically, and (4) think flexibly" (Cohn, 1982, pp. 1–2).

The general format of the *ThinkAbout* series typically involves a problem-solving episode that is presented to the students. Young actors, the same age as the students watching the program, confront and solve specific problems of the sort the students might easily encounter themselves. A teachers' guide provides not only an outline of the program, but also the key teaching points that should be emphasized in each program. In addition there are suggestions for introducing the programs and for follow-up questions and activities. Depending upon the arrangement of the individual school district, the program is either broadcast at a specific time of day or available on a video cassette.

The chapter first introduces Ms. Church and the way in which she used *ThinkAbout*; it follows with Mr. Cartwright's approach to *ThinkAbout*. In reading the accounts of Ms. Church and Mr. Cartwright compare and contrast the methods of each instructor and the various kinds of responses that they elicit from their students. Ask yourself the following questions:

1. How does the use of the *ThinkAbout* curriculum differ in each class?
2. How does each teacher prepare for and follow up on the possibilities provided by the curriculum?

3. To what degree does each teacher appear to facilitate students' learning and understanding of the key ideas and development of thinking skills?
4. What seems to be the expectations of each teacher?
5. In which class would you prefer to be a student? Why?

Ms. Church and ThinkAbout

Ms. Church is a fifth-grade teacher at Glenview Elementary School in the suburb of Forest Hills. Forest Hills is a large and thriving suburb of a large and not so thriving midwestern city. Twenty-five years ago, one-room schoolhouses served a predominantly rural clientele, but today some of the nation's largest, most modern, and luxurious school buildings serve what one of the teachers working at the school labels "a very fast urban middle class."

Racial difficulties thus far have been minimal in the district. A relatively small black population is scattered throughout much of the community, so that in most schools the black children make up 8 to 10 percent of the total school population. Forest Hills is an almost exclusively Christian community. The Catholic church is dominant, although there are prominent Protestant groups as well.

The Forest Hills School District has been influenced by recent national trends in education. Teacher militancy, back-to-basics, and declining enrollments have all been important issues in the school district. The back-to-basics movement, however, has unquestionably had the most pervasive and far-reaching effects. At the time the observations were conducted the district had adopted a fundamental-skills program that permeated every aspect of school life, particularly at the elementary level. Students who did not achieve a score of 80 percent or better in the areas of communication, mathematics, science, and social studies were not promoted to the following grade level at the end of the school year.

Ms. Church has taught at Glenview for 10 of her 13 years as a teacher. She leads a rich and varied life outside of the classroom. She is a leader in the local teachers' union, belongs to a sorority, and works with a church-related youth group.

Ms. Church has 22 students in her fifth-grade class. On Tuesdays and Thursdays she includes the *ThinkAbout* curriculum as part of the day's activities. Before the students arrive each morning she writes the schedule on the chalkboard. Today, October 30, the day's schedule looks like this:

9:00	Pledge, etc.
	Spelling
	Language
	Reading
11:15	Lunch
11:45	Story time, rest room
	Math

> 1:00 *ThinkAbout*
>   Finish math
>   Snack, rest room
>   Social studies (or science)
> 2:45 P.E.
> 3:15 Summary
> 3:20 Announcements
>   Dismissal

The time is 12:55. Ms. Church looks up from the math lesson she has been conducting with a group of students and says, "Who's supposed to get the TV?" Two students leave. The math lesson continues while the TV is being set up. Within a few minutes the television is turned on. Across the screen is written:

PROGRAM 13
THE BIGGER PICTURE

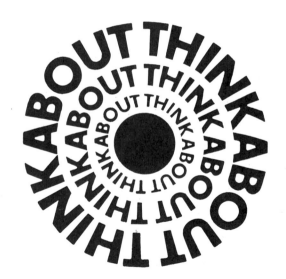

As the program begins Ms. Church says:

Boys and girls, this program is talking about context. We've talked about context before, haven't we? This morning on the playground, some kids asked me what *blanks* meant. At first I didn't know what they were talking about, but when I finally figured out they meant on their report cards, then I could answer them.

Below is a program summary of "The Bigger Picture."

The Bigger Picture

Danny is running away from home because he thinks his mother wants to get rid of him. Since his father died, Mom has to work long hours, is often worried about money, and never wants to do things, like go to the movies, with Danny. On the bus the runaway meets a young man named Carpenter to whom he tells his story: Mom was taking care of the monthly bills at the kitchen table one evening when Danny came in to show her his new model airplane and accidentally upset her tea. A bad scene ensued, and even though Mom apologized, Danny hears her tell her boss when he calls about working overtime: "But I have my problems too. Danny for one, and he's not going to go away either."

Carpenter admits that sounds bad, but he suggests that the statement has been taken out of context. To illustrate, he reads Danny a sentence about pentode tubes from his book. Danny has no idea what the sentence is about until Carpenter shows him the book's title, *Basic Radios*. Once he knows the context, he can get some meaning from the passage. Then a man named Jones walks by and begins a series of put-downs with Carpenter. Danny is convinced they hate each other until Carpenter assures him they are friends. With that information, Danny sees the bigger picture and realizes they were kidding.

At his destination, Danny uses the book incident and the Jones incident to rethink his own situation and try to get the bigger picture. He remembers his mother saying on the day his father was buried: "Things will be different now, Danny. Things may get difficult. But whatever happens, remember this: You mean more to me than anything else in the world." Danny buys a ticket back home and finds Mom waiting on the front steps, very glad to see him.

The class then proceeds to watch the program. There is some occasional fidgeting and fussing. One student complains that she has already seen the program at home the other day; another pulls out his electronic calculator and plays with it. As the program continues, however, the students are drawn into it and begin to watch it attentively.

After the program there is the following discussion:

MS. CHURCH: *(Reading from the teachers' guide)* What did the man mean — it's hard to get the meaning without context?

STUDENT: It depends on the situation.

MS. CHURCH: Do we sometimes take things out of context?

STUDENT: Yeah.

MS. CHURCH: Can you think of any examples?

STUDENT: Kids on the playground say, "You dummy, you can't catch the ball"—they're just teasing.

STUDENT: Sometimes you make fun of people when they make a mistake.

MS. CHURCH: How did it help Danny's relationship with his mother when he started to see the bigger picture?

STUDENT: Until he got the picture, what she said sounded bad.

MS. CHURCH: What did he understand?

SAME STUDENT: That his mother was having a bad time.

MS. CHURCH: So he uses it to explain that she had things that were important to her too. When she said, "Danny is a problem and he isn't going to go away either," what do you think she meant?

STUDENT: She had to buy clothes for him.

STUDENT: She has to have time for herself.

STUDENT: She could cook while he paid the bills.

MS. CHURCH: What about the reverse? I'm for women's liberation. If both work, should both work around the house? How many of you have two parents working?

MALE STUDENT: I cook.

MS. CHURCH: Are you a good cook?

MALE STUDENT: I can cook lamb chops.

MS. CHURCH: Do you think it's important for boys to know how to cook?

FEMALE STUDENT: If the mother passes away——

MALE STUDENT: What if you're married and your wife is at work and you are at home and the kids say, "I want something to eat?"?

MALE STUDENT: Sometimes my dad will fix himself a hamburger. I can cook too, I can bake a cake and——

FEMALE STUDENT: When my parents used to live together, my dad would go to work early and be at home 2:00. My mother doesn't get home until 4:00, so he cooked—but not so good.

FEMALE STUDENT: My uncle can't cook—his hard-boiled eggs come out bad. If a wife passes away, a man should know how——

MALE STUDENT: My brother goes crazy with instant things, he likes cooking everything from scratch.

The discussion ends with Ms. Church announcing, "I want to see the last math group—the Mathematical Menaces."

Viewing Patterns

Ms. Church's students saw almost every one of the 60 *ThinkAbout* programs. They viewed them sequentially as they were aired on the local educational channel, and the only event that interrupted the regular Tuesday and Thursday afternoon schedules (other than school holidays) was a two-week set of rehearsals with another class for a spring assembly program. Ms. Church termed the consistency of their *ThinkAbout* viewing a habit.

> There are several other programs I used to watch, but I haven't this year. But I still consistently watch *ThinkAbout* — it's sort of a habit I got into. The kids won't let me forget now. We just do it.

Before the Program: Teacher Preparation

Ms. Church did nothing in the way of advance preparation for using the *ThinkAbout* series. In fact, one of the reasons she gave for her frequent use of instructional television in general was that it required no prior planning: "I don't have to spend a lot of time playing with it, and I can use it and go on from there." She also explained, however, that she expected explicit directions in the teachers' guide:

> When I use TV I like it to be right there for me. I like it to let me know exactly what to do. If they have a suggestion for a game or something that will bring a point up, I want it written. If I have to come up with all those ideas on my own, then it's just as easy for me to use the textbook or to use a film or something. So the immediacy of it is very important to me.

Before the Program: Student Preparation

Although Ms. Church did not prepare herself for viewing, she was obviously committed to the idea of preparing the children, if only in a most cursory way. Often amidst the noisy chair moving and above the sound of the *ThinkAbout* musical theme she would read directly from the teachers' manual the suggested *guide question*. She only allocated one or two minutes for preparation. Therefore, when the guide called for a preliminary discussion or activity, she either ignored or abbreviated it. Her brief remarks on context in the "The Bigger Picture" transcript cited above were her response to the manual's directions to *discuss* context with the children.

The *ThinkAbout* series was designed around cluster themes. This thematic approach was described in considerable detail in the teachers' manual that accompanied the series. Despite this fact, in her introductions, Ms. Church focused only on the individual program that was being viewed, never trying to relate one program to the larger cluster of which it was a part.

On at least two occasions, when introducing new *ThinkAbout* programs, Ms. Church quickly glanced down at the teachers' guide and inadvertently read the introductory remarks for another program. The children, however, didn't seem to notice or mind. Her apology on one occasion brought a flippant student remark, "Who cares?"

During the Program

While each program was in progress Ms. Church alternately watched the screen and scanned the "After the Program" suggestions included in her teacher's guide. The children, on the other hand, rarely took their eyes off the screen. During almost every one of the programs the children consistently sat totally engrossed, laughed (and sometimes even cheered) at appropriate places, and often sighed in disappointment when they were over.

After the Program

Ms. Church was as religious about discussing the *ThinkAbout* programs as she was about introducing them. The students were often restless in the discussions that followed the airing of the program. Following the teachers' guide Ms. Church usually posed a series of questions to which many of the children would eagerly respond. Unfortunately a number of interactive factors often made their verbal responses difficult to understand and assess. First, since the children exhibited far more interest in having a turn to talk than listening, their answers often did not even address the question. Second, their answers were often brief, mumbled, or incoherent. Third, Ms. Church never probed these limited responses or asked for the clarification of ideas. Finally, on some occasions either Ms. Church or the students would take the discussion far afield before it was clear there was understanding on prior points. Looking at the content of the previously cited dialogue transcript, it is difficult to determine the extent to which the students actually understood the material that was presented to them.

An example of this last point can be seen in the student's response to Ms. Church's request for instances "when we sometimes take things out of context." One student responded, "Kids on the playground say: 'You dummy, you can't catch a ball'—they are just kidding." Another student responded to the request, "Sometimes we make fun of people when they make a mistake." On the surface the first child seems to have a general grasp of the concept, whereas the second child does not. Ms. Church does not attempt, however, to get clarification of the students' ideas.

Similar difficulties arise when one examines the two answers to the question, "When she said, 'Danny is a problem and he isn't going to go away either,' what do you think she meant?" On the one hand, these responses ("She has to buy clothes for him." "She has to have time for herself.") could mean only that they can see some of the mother's difficulties. On the other hand one or both of these children could be trying to communicate their recognition of a picture that is bigger than a mother not having time to take her son to the movies. Without probing, however, it is almost impossible to know the children's level of understanding.

One final noteworthy aspect of "The Bigger Picture" discussion was the lack of closure. Ms. Church cut off the tangential interchange regarding male cooking with the announcement, "I want to see the last math group—the Mathematical Menaces." Rather than summarize, generalize, or relate any of the program's concepts to the rest of the day, Ms. Church frequently stopped when she felt it was time to move on, and thus the entire *ThinkAbout* process came through as a 30-minute break during math time. Even when the *ThinkAbout* program was dealing primarily with the mathematical concepts of estimation and approximation, there was no connection to math groups.

"The Bigger Picture" transcript is illustrative of several characteristic aspects of the after-the-program discussions, but there were others as well. The following discussion transcript from one of the children's favorite programs—"the one about the UFO"—reveals two of the most salient.

TEACHER: Let's review the program. How did Pete and Marty solve their problem?

STUDENT: They researched and found out what UFOs are.

TEACHER: Let's go over that step by step. What did Marty do?

STUDENT: He talked to people in the neighborhood.

TEACHER: What did Pete do?

STUDENT: He went to the library and used the card catalogue.

TEACHER: What did he discover about a lot of the books?

STUDENT: Too old.

TEACHER: Pete then got help from the librarian. What kind of help did she give him?

STUDENT: Groups and associations.

TEACHER: What was Pete going to do when he found the numbers?

STUDENT: Call them.

TEACHER: Why didn't he do that?

STUDENT: It was too expensive.

TEACHER: Then he was going to do what?

STUDENT: Write, but it would take too long.

STUDENT: He decided to call on one that was real close.

TEACHER: How was the meeting helpful?

STUDENT: It showed him it was a hologram.

TEACHER: Do you know what that is? What could we do to find out what a hologram is?

The lesson ended with several children looking up the word in different dictionaries and an encyclopedia and Ms. Church noting that it was not in some of them because it was a relatively new term.

The most obvious feature of this teacher-pupil interaction is that it is a recitation rather than a genuine discussion. Most of the observed discussions were essentially a two-stage process that began with a similar series of recall questions requiring only brief factual answers and ended with a sharing of personal experiences.

A somewhat less obvious but far more significant feature of the UFO discussion is that it does not explicitly focus upon the key point of the program—that it is important to consider as many different *sources* of information as possible. Although in their recitation the students recalled different steps pursued, there was no indication that they saw these as a variety of different sources for collection information. (The word *sources*, in fact, was never used.) An indication that they did not see or at least remember these, however, did manifest itself exactly two weeks later when Ms. Church assigned oral reports on Christmas customs. After the assignment was made, the following interchange occurred:

TEACHER: What are some of the possibilities you can think of?
STUDENT: Russian customs.
STUDENT: Different names.
TEACHER: Yes, it could have different aspects. Where are you going to find information?
STUDENT: Encyclopedia.
STUDENT: School library.
STUDENT: Bookmobile.
STUDENT: Public library.

These sources certainly do not suggest much variety.

The fact that Ms. Church missed the mark in the *ThinkAbout* discussions was pervasive throughout the observation period. In a program about estimation, the follow-up discussion never focused explicitly on the key teaching point, which was that estimations are different from wild guesses because they are based on knowledge and past experience. In the discussion following a program on *approximation*, Ms. Church stopped in confusion and admitted, "I'm not sure that we know what *approximation* is." After a program aimed at exploring the complexities involved in designing and interpreting time capsules, the discussion that followed centered on student visits to historical sites.

The explanation for Ms. Church's almost consistent failure to hit the key points in the guide appeared to be related both to a lack of preparation and to a lack of questioning and discussion skills. The practice of following the program and scanning the guide simultaneously frequently caused Ms. Church to pick up only parts of the key idea. Then her inability to pose and sequence appropriate questions and respond to incorrect answers often seemed to block key ideas from coming across.

Long-Range Teacher Follow-Up

Ms. Church had at least three different options for follow-up to her *ThinkAbout* sessions: (1) using the *ThinkAbout* activities in the *Weekly Reader*; (2) assigning special tasks and problem-solving situations that involve practice of *ThinkAbout* skills; and (3) connecting *ThinkAbout* skills and ideas to the rest of the curriculum. She chose, however, to exercise none of them.

Mr. Cartwright and ThinkAbout

Mr. Cartwright is a sixth-grade social studies and science teacher at Baker Middle School in Lyon Heights, a relatively small but highly sophisticated suburb on the edge of another large midwestern city. In one resident's view, "It is the only really integrated community and the most cosmopolitan in the entire metropolitan area." A more diverse community is in fact hard to imagine. Whites, blacks, Orientals and other ethnic groups, university professors, blue-collar workers, highly paid professionals, senior citizens, and college students for differing reasons find Lyon Heights an attractive place to live.

Educational excellence is a community value, but there are sharp disagreements as to how to achieve it. Eighth-grade students in Lyon Heights recently scored low on a statewide competency test, and the newly hired superintendent has committed himself to raise the test scores through a return to the basics. Elementary teachers are being required to teach certain curricula and to cover certain textbooks.

Baker Middle School is a relatively recent development in the Lyon Heights School District that utilizes two buildings in the eastern part of the community — a former elementary school and a former junior high in the midst of one of the community's more affluent residential neighborhoods. Occasional reproductions of African art and bulletin boards of student art break up the drabness of the long corridors of lockers in both buildings. The general lack of attention to decor suggests that teacher and administrative effort goes in other directions. When the bell rings and countless numbers of active adolescents surge into the halls, it appears that most adult effort is probably aimed at getting and keeping the attention of this vibrant, mostly black group of young people. Their energy seems to explode in every direction as they shove, shout, strut, and sing their way through the buildings. In contrast to the raucous and mostly good-natured banter and activity of the blacks, the white students appear passive and quiet as they congregate in their small cliques.

Control is indeed the watchword of Baker, and the principal who was hired several years ago to turn things around appears to have achieved it. In addition to a counselor, who works with disruptive students in each building, the principal supervises student behavior in the main building while the assistant principal supervises in the annex.

Although Mr. Cartwright speaks of teaching as stimulating, exciting, and rewarding, his decision to become a teacher was neither a casual nor a quick one. It came after the completion of his A.B. in psychology and sociology, several years of travel, and a year of odd jobs. Once he reached the decision he accumulated a variety of educational experiences in a relatively short time. For the past six years he has taught in three different schools and at almost every elementary grade level.

Mr. Cartwright concentrates almost all of his time and energy outside school on classroom preparation. Pulling on a variety of sources and his own creativity he develops unique lessons in great detail and then internalizes them so completely that he never uses a note. He purposely avoids school politics and teacher organizations because he "would rather put the time into developing a curriculum and teaching." The extraordinary amount of time given to planning seems to be appreciated by his students. According to most of them, Mr. Cartwright is their favorite teacher.

The social studies curriculum is a series of large units that incorporate both district expectations and Mr. Cartwright's personal beliefs. He is comfortable with the curriculum and feels considerable freedom to develop these units in any number of ways. Although the seventh-grade social studies teachers are required to correlate their curriculum with the state's eighth-grade competency test, he and the other sixth-grade teachers have thus far escaped such outside influence.

Because Mr. Cartwright has a strong commitment to the development of thinking skills and to the use of media as a teaching tool, there was nothing unusual about his decision to incorporate *ThinkAbout* into his social studies curriculum. At times, however, the particular manner in which he chose to do so seemed unusual.

Viewing Patterns

Rather than view the *ThinkAbout* series sequentially and in its entirety, Mr. Cartwright decided to select only those programs that directly related to his students' needs. During November and December Mr. Cartwright defined students' needs in terms of general thinking and study skills for improved academic performance. Toward that end he selected four programs. Although there were always connections to ongoing or previous classroom work, these four programs were in essence a problem-solving strand that was separate from the content of the ongoing social studies curriculum.

In January during a unit on communication, Mr. Cartwright's approach to *ThinkAbout* clearly changed. After looking through the guide and discovering programs directly related to the unit at hand, he reconceptualized student needs in terms of comprehension of the unit goals. When his focus was on human characteristics, he showed a program entitled "People Patterns." When his focus moved more specifically to the communication process, he found programs entitled "What's the Meaning?" "Communication Patterns," and "Meaning Is More Than Words" relevant. These programs were interspersed wherever sequentially appropriate among a variety of other classroom activities and media, and students were held responsible for them on the unit evaluation. Throughout January *ThinkAbout* became an integral part of Mr. Cartwright's communication unit rather than a separate exercise in study or thinking skills.

Before the Program: Teacher Preparation

In Mr. Cartwright's view *ThinkAbout* requires considerable teacher preparation:

> I think it's essential in the *ThinkAbout* series that the teacher have a lot of input into it and a lot of preparation for it, especially in follow-up, because it is, as I see it, more entertaining for the kids. If the teacher doesn't pull out the facets of the program that he wants to be taught or covered and specifically work with those, the students will not become conscious of them.

Although he did not preview the programs because of time constraints, Mr. Cartwright prepared extensively for each *ThinkAbout* session. First, he carefully read the summaries in the teachers' guide to select the program to view and then he read the "Before the Program" and "After the Program" suggestions of his selection. The third and final step was the creation of his own before and after activities, which from an observer's perspective also took "a lot of time and work to pull off."

Before the Program: Student Preparation

The preprogram activities that Mr. Cartwright invariably prepared for students differed considerably in format; there were, however, some commonalities as well. A look at the lead-in to two of the programs reveals some of the core elements.

One of the programs was entitled "You Can Remember" and the other was "People Patterns." Below is a program summary of each.

You Can Remember

It's Peter's first day on the paper route and police officer Johnson's first day on the patrol, and both worry about remembering everything. When veteran officer Wayne stresses the importance of committing scenes to memory, Officer Johnson uses her mind like a camera to take a mental picture of a jewelry store.

Peter's predecessor, Erica, assures him that if he learned his multiplication tables he can learn the paper route—even the "maze" of multifamily dwellings. She accompanies him along the route, showing him where the papers go and pointing out special things to remember (like being sure Miss Phillips' dog, Alfonse, does not get out).

Remembering that he learned his mulitiplication tables a little at a time, Peter determines to learn one section of his route each day, draws a map to help, and mentally groups the houses. He groups the number of papers that go to each of the first seven houses with a phone number, and easily memorizes it. Alfonse is harder to remember.

The next week Officer Johnson stops a robbery of the jewelry store because she remembered (as a result of her mental picture) that the curtains were not usually closed. As she and Peter chat about it afterwards, Erica walks up with the captured Alfonse. Officer Johnson suggests that Peter take a mental picture of the problem dog behind the screen door of Miss Phillips' house.

People Patterns

Richie's class is studying people patterns. Two of his classmates make a graph on world population in which Richie sees these patterns: the number of people in the world is increasing, and it is taking less time for the population to double. Linda, another classmate, gives a slide presentation about an experiment she did at a bus stop. She found that the people usually stood about a meter apart.

At home Richie talks to his family about patterns and gradually becomes aware of a neighbor's pattern. Every day for two years he has passed Mr. Harper at the same time in the hallway of their apartment building. When Mr. Harper does not appear as usual one afternoon, Richie is worried. A call to the apartment manager and an investigation saves Mr. Harper's life.

Richie's mother spots a pattern shared by Richie and his dad and wants them to change it. She connects the tiredness both feel around lunchtime and Richie's headaches with the pattern of not eating an adequate breakfast.

Before "You Can Remember" Mr. Cartwright's introduction to the first program on memory tips was actually a five-step procedure. First, students were asked if they could remember the exact number of hostages released from Iran (they could not). Next, the students were asked if they could remember five telephone numbers (they could) and how they memorized them (mostly from using them). Third, students were given the following set of directions to remember until the end of the class period:

> I want the person that I will call on at the end of the period to get out of your seat and come up here to the front of the classroom. From here I want you to go over to the shade, pull down that yellow shade, continue on to the back of the room and knock on the piano three times and then two times. It will be like a code—one, two, three, one, two. Then you will come up to the front of the room and you will have a piece of paper on the TV set here; take this piece of paper and put it on the chalk lying here, like that. You may have to hold it in order to get it there. Then I want you to turn on the cold water faucet, come back out to the middle of the room, turn around once and then go back to your desk again. Okay, no more for now, forget about that for a while.

Fourth, students were given a choice of six lists of 10 items each to memorize in three minutes (some could and some could not). Fifth was this rationale and introduction to the specifics of the program:

> Okay, now what we are going to do is see a TV program that is going to give you some advice on how to remember things. As most of you are aware of and have been aware of for the last five and a half years, teachers in your class often require you to memorize lists and to memorize an awful lot of things. So this TV show should be helpful to you on how to remember things, not just in the classroom but in your jobs.

The story is about two people. One is a young boy, sixth or seventh grade, and he has just gotten a job on a newspaper route and he is on a trial period. That means he has one week to learn the newspaper route, and if he doesn't learn it quickly, he doesn't get the job. He tries to memorize that route using a particular technique. Now the other person is a policewoman. She is just new on the job also and she uses another technique to remember things to do her job well. All we are going to do is simply watch the program and then we can do some more experiments afterwards and see what tips you have picked up from the program on memorizing.

Before "People Patterns" Mr. Cartwright began by announcing the need for five volunteers, and when they came forward he handed each a marker and directed them toward a large yellow piece of paper that was covering the chalkboard. The first four were told to draw a triangle and the fifth was told to draw a circle. Then he called for five more volunteers to whom he gave the same tasks, and then five more. Afterward, the yellow paper looked like this: △ △ △ △ ○ △ △ △ △ ○ The dialogue went this way:

MR. CARTWRIGHT: If we were to fill up the whole sheet, what would we be doing?

STUDENT: Repeating the pattern.

MR. CARTWRIGHT: What is the pattern?

STUDENT: Four triangles and a circle.

MR. CARTWRIGHT: You can tell it's a pattern because it always repeats itself. Does the different color of some of the triangles make a difference?

STUDENT: No.

MR. CARTWRIGHT: This is a lead-in to today's lesson, which has something to do with patterns. Can you give me a definition of *patterns*?

STUDENT: Something you follow.

MR. CARTWRIGHT: What would be an example?

STUDENT: Football patterns.

MR. CARTWRIGHT: Okay. (*He draws some football diagrams on board*)

STUDENT: A series of steps like you follow to figure out a murder.

MR. CARTWRIGHT: Okay. What we are going to do now is to follow a pattern on a *ThinkAbout* show that has to do with behavioral patterns. What are *behavioral patterns*?

STUDENT: How people behave.

MR. CARTWRIGHT: Right. The diagram on the board deals with physical characteristics, but this program is about behavior. This idea of patterns is important in life. I haven't forgotten the homework; it will tie in. (*On board he writes, "pattern = something you follow—something that repeats itself"*)

General Preprogram Characteristics A close look at these two introductions reveals a few striking commonalities. Each, in one way or another, includes a general rationale and a specific reason for watching the program, numerous opportunities for student participation and "discovery," and an explicit focus on the key concepts and points of the program. These core elements were prevalent throughout the observation period and on most occasions they appeared to enhance student interest and understanding.

During the Program

Mr. Cartwright used a variety of media selections in social studies, but *ThinkAbout* was clearly the most engrossing. Whereas some of his other choices appealed more to one group or another, all of the students, even those who were generally difficult to control, watched *ThinkAbout* intently. Occasionally because of some unrelated preprogram incident a student would initially turn or look away in hostility, but after a few moments he was invariably drawn in.

Mr. Cartwright also watched the programs intently. During the viewing he took notes on what points he wanted to emphasize after the program. He would sometimes interrupt the programs to pose a question or emphasize a point. On one occasion, after he stopped a program three times, some students expressed annoyance. He responded with annoyance of his own:

> Look, I'm teaching you, and I want to make a point. This is not entertainment like it is at 7:00 at night at home. I'm trying to teach you, and I still think you'd rather see it this way than listening to me talk all the time!

After the Program

In addition to several minutes of questioning to quickly assess comprehension after each *ThinkAbout* program, Mr. Cartwright always assigned either an in-class or homework follow-up activity.

In-Class Follow-Up Activities Because of the lengthy introduction to *ThinkAbout*, the usual classroom interruptions, and the 45-minute time limit, in-class follow-ups were necessarily brief. Nevertheless, within the 10 minutes or less remaining after each program Mr. Cartwright consistently attempted to provide practice on at least one of the featured skills. The most clearly focused in-class follow-ups were those that he directly linked to preprogram activities. After "You can Remember," he gave students lists of items to memorize that were similar to the ones they attempted before the program. The directions afterward were, "See if you can memorize these lists quicker, within two minutes, by using the tips from the program."

Homework Follow-Up Activities Mr. Cartwright's homework follow-up activities stood in clear contrast to the in-class variety because they provided extended opportunities for students to apply *ThinkAbout* skills and concepts to their own lives in school and out. The *ThinkAbout* homework assignment that followed "People Patterns" required students to look for behavior patterns among their teachers, friends and relatives, and within themselves. In addition they were to recognize that certain patterns inevitably occur in certain places and to identify patterns at school, home, and a place of their choice. A worksheet with marked spaces to record the patterns of four different people and three different places was given to each student in order to clarify the assignment and organize the data collected. This homework assignment and many others seemed to serve essentially the same function—to provide genuine opportunities for students to develop *ThinkAbout* skills and concepts through meaningful application and practice.

Long-Range Teacher Follow-Up

Connecting ThinkAbout Skills and Ideas to the Rest of the Curriculum In the month of January *ThinkAbout* programs were completely woven into the fabric of the communication unit, and at all other times they were explicitly connected to in- or out-of-school problem solving. The memory tips were linked to academic tasks in social studies and science. "Estimating" was tied to sixth-grade camp; "Where Should I Go?" (for information) and "Collecting Information" were presented as preparation for a forthcoming research project, and "Stereotyping People" was an introduction to a religion unit.

In addition to these broad connections Mr. Cartwright also frequently incorporated specific *ThinkAbout* terminology and concepts into other lessons and contexts. The concept *patterns* is a case in point, for after "People Patterns," he inserted the term *patterns* wherever appropriate. Immediately after the program, for example, he referred to an earlier assignment on Eskimos as a search for human patterns. The next day he asked students to watch for patterns in a fishbowl discussion with the counselor, and two days later he instructed students to look for communication patterns in the family. These repetitions in different contexts seemed to clarify and further reinforce some of the key *ThinkAbout* points for students.

DIFFERENT INSTRUCTIONAL DECISIONS: MS. CHURCH AND MR. CARTWRIGHT

One way to compare and contrast Mr. Cartwright and Ms. Church in their use of *ThinkAbout* is to evaluate them in terms of their effort and skill. Mr. Cartwright appears to spend a lot more time and to be a more skilled teacher than Ms. Church.

Another way, however, to consider their differing approaches is to identify the kinds of instructional decisions they each made and to examine the implicit or explicit assumptions about the teaching-learning process that underlie their decision making. This section will focus on the instructional decisions involved because they can shed light on the nature of the teaching act. First, however, some preliminary curriculum decisions will be considered.

What to Teach

As noted in Chapter 8 teachers in both large and small districts can exercise a considerable amount of curricular control. Ms. Church and Mr. Cartwright each teach in districts that feature central office curricular decision making and relatively prescribed curricular goals. Yet both were free to choose whether or not they wanted to weave *ThinkAbout* into their existing programs. They both gave as reasons for using *ThinkAbout* the fact that it teaches valuable problem-solving skills and that students always enjoy instructional television. In addition Ms. Church hinted that television in the classroom made life a bit easier for her, and Mr. Cartwright saw some of the *ThinkAbout* programs as important additions to existing curriculum units.

Generally the choice of what to teach is closely aligned with the values of the teachers. Both Ms. Church and Mr. Cartwright believe that problem-solving skills are as important as content in the fields of math, English, social studies, or science. Toward the end of the semester, however, Mr. Cartwright stopped using *ThinkAbout* in order to have time for another television series on values that he thought might be more beneficial for students. In the earlier part of the year, when he was committed to using *ThinkAbout*, he decided to select only those programs that met the needs of his particular students. The decision to use a limited number of segments instead of the whole series of 60 programs and to pick certain programs and reject others were subsets of the larger decision to use the series in the first place. Thus Ms. Church and Mr. Cartwright held in common the decision to use *ThinkAbout*, but Ms. Church opted to use the series in its entirety, and Mr. Cartwright chose a limited number of programs at the beginning of the year and eliminated it altogether at the end.

How to Teach It

Once a teacher has made decisions regarding what to teach there are numerous decisions involving instruction, or *how* to teach the *what*. Teachers will differ, of course, in the way in which they make such decisions. One format and sequence for instructional decision making used in Washington University's School-based Teacher Education Program (STEP) is presented here. It provides a vehicle for demonstrating the numerous decisions that teachers make regarding instruction.

To add clarity and concreteness to the format and sequence, we cite examples from the five case study teachers as well as from Ms. Church and Mr. Cartwright.

Planning for Instruction: Selecting a General Approach

To teach most concepts, a teacher can choose to present a lecture, conduct a discussion, arrange an experiment, create a role play, organize group or individual projects, show a slide presentation, construct programmed materials or individual worksheets, or combine a number of these approaches. In using the *ThinkAbout* curriculum, Ms. Church chose not to plan at all. Instead she relied totally on the discussion topics suggested in the teachers' guide for questions and then attempted to conduct a discussion. Her approach never varied. In contrast, Mr. Cartwright usually planned thoroughly and creatively and selected different strategies for different concepts or skills. Sometimes he conducted a discussion; other times he arranged preprogram experiments, activities, and role plays; other times he devised individual research projects.

In addition, within the number of available approaches, a teacher can choose to arrange a lesson so that it is either *deductive* or *inductive*. A deductive lesson is one in which the teacher starts out with a generalization and then supplies the specific information or examples necessary for students to substantiate it. When Ms. Church first gives a definition of context and then shows the program to illustrate the definition, she is proceeding in a deductive way. When Larry Wells is teaching the concept of mercantilism, he first tells the students in a number of ways that it involves the strict regulation of the economy by the government; he then asks questions and uses examples from the students' own experience to make the concept clear and meaningful. Similarly, when Jacquie teaches verb conjugation she may first show the students how to conjugate a particular verb and then give them sentences on the board and at their desks for them to practice applying the correct ending. In these instances Larry and Jacquie are also teaching deductively.

An inductive lesson is one in which a teacher starts by giving students certain examples or information from which they can discover or figure out the generalization. In *ThinkAbout* when Mr. Cartwright has students repeatedly put on the chalkboard four triangles and a circle so that they can come up with the definition of the word *pattern*, he is working inductively. Similarly, when Ruth starts a unit on energy with the question What is energy? and then arranges a number of experiments in which students can begin to figure out the concept, she is proceeding inductively. Finally, when Sandy has students experience two different kinds of communication before they start examining the concept of communication, she is hoping that through an inductive approach the students will begin to discover some characteristics of the communication process.

The decision to lecture rather than discuss or to proceed inductively rather than deductively must be made by the individual teacher in each particular instance because, to date, there is no evidence that there is one best way to teach or any single strategy that is appropriate for all kinds of subject matter or all kinds of students. In their book *Models of Teaching* (1972) Bruce Joyce and Marsha Weil make this point explicitly:

> Although the results are very difficult to interpret, the evidence to date gives no encouragement to those who would hope that we have identified a single reliable, multipurpose teaching strategy that we can use with confidence that it is the best approach. (p. 4)

On what basis do teachers make such decisions? Sometimes teachers base their decision upon their particular philosophy or theory of learning. There are those, for example, who strongly believe that meaningful learning cannot occur unless students are actively involved in the process. These teachers will tend, whenever possible, to teach inductively and to choose discussion, group projects, role play, and inquiry as instructional strategies. Consciously or unconsciously they subscribe to learning theorists such as Jean Piaget and Jerome Bruner.*

Piaget argues that learning is active information processing that results from exploration and discovery. Learning is what individuals *do*, not just what they see or hear. Bruner agrees and maintains that each individual organizes and constructs knowledge in his or her own way. Bruner argues that learning through discovery enables one to understand knowledge and to apply it to solve one's problems.

According to Lauren B. Resnick (1982) there is actually an emerging consensus on the nature of learning that supports some theories of active learning. Referring to research in what she calls *cognitive science*, she maintains that there is now evidence that "learners construct understanding. They do not simply mirror or reflect what they are told or what they read" (p. 3). Teachers like Ruth, who for years have intuitively but consciously chosen active approaches that encourage students to construct their own meaning and make discoveries on their own, should feel strongly validated by such research findings.

There are other teachers, however, who subscribe to theorists such as David Ausubel and B. F. Skinner. Ausubel argues for *reception*, or deductive, learning as opposed to discovery learning. In reception learning as defined by Ausubel (1969) "the entire content of what is to be learned is presented to the learner in final form. The learning task does not involve any independent discovery on his part" (pp. 249–250). Skinner is a behaviorist who sees humans controllable and therefore

---

*Our references to the learning theories of Piaget, Bruner, Ausubel, and Skinner are much too brief and simplified to do them justice. You will undoubtedly meet them and examine their theories in the depth they deserve in courses in educational psychology and in learning theory. In this instance, we are merely trying to make the point that there are multiple theories of learning and many teachers consciously or unconsciously subscribe to one over another. A teacher's commitment to one of these theorists rather than another can, in turn, affect teacher behavior greatly.

teachable through reinforcement that is contingent on their behavior. He favors programmed instruction featuring positive reinforcement for correct responses, which he maintains can shape learning behavior. Teachers who consciously or unconsciously agree with the Ausubel or Skinner positions will tend to teach deductively and will select a lecture format or programmed materials whenever possible.

Often, however, teachers make their instructional decisions on more immediate and practical grounds. Their decision may be based upon what they like to do or feel they do best, upon what they think their students like or seem to handle best, or upon what seems to be most appropriate for the content being taught. For Ruth, a major consideration is whether the content is knowledge or a skill. If it is a skill she asks herself, "What do they need to bring to this situation before they can function at the level I'm designing the lesson for?" Then she attempts to identify the children who are not at the necessary skill level and makes some effort to "fill in the gaps for them—so that when the lesson is presented they'll be able to catch on." Thus, delineation of what is being taught and diagnosis of student background are important parts of Ruth's general planning process.

Larry also first thinks about what it is he is teaching, for, in his view, "some subjects lend themselves to teaching by differing methods." His second step is to think about "how to keep their interest. Simply telling students something and having them go to sleep on you is not education."

Interest is also important in Sandy's preliminary decision making, and she uses herself as a baseline: "If something doesn't interest me, it's not going to interest them." In terms of a particular method, she too says it "depends on the content. If it's something they don't have an opinion on, such as schizophrenia, I will lecture about the various kinds. That does not lend itself to discussion . . . but wherever possible I try to combine methods." Luberta and Jacquie, as we have seen, also will use several methods and activities within a single class period or segment of the day.

Planning for Instruction: Developing a Specific Lesson Plan

After teachers decide upon a general approach they think makes sense given the content and the background and interests of the students, they generally make a more specific lesson plan that outlines step by step how they will proceed in the lesson. Each step involves important and difficult decisions. Most effective teachers, beginning and experienced alike, write these plans out, but some highly experienced teachers develop and keep them in their head rather than on paper. Still they have planned carefully and made decisions every step of the way.

Phase 1: Specification of Goals The first phase of a lesson plan usually involves specifying the goals the teacher aims to achieve through the lesson. Goals can be thought of as *long-range goals* and as *instructional objectives* for a particular lesson. In

Mr. Cartwright's lesson "People Patterns," for example, his long-range goal is student understanding of the communication process. Mr. Cartwright selected this program because it added a useful dimension to the communication unit in progress by showing how people can communicate nonverbally. The long-range goal of a lesson, then, is the broader domain toward which an individual lesson contributes.

In contrast, instructional objectives are goals for a specific lesson. Instructional objectives indicate what the students should learn or know as a result of that day's lesson. In this case, Mr. Cartwright's instructional objectives might have been:

1. The student will be able to define *pattern* and give several examples.
2. The student will be able to explain the meaning of *people patterns* and give examples.
3. The student will be able to identify people patterns in familiar places — school or home.
4. The student will be able to explain how knowledge of people patterns aids the communication process.

Each teacher for each lesson needs to think through and decide what instructional objectives to pursue. Regardless of the decision, however, there are a number of important characteristics of well-written instructional objectives. First, they are written in terms of what the *student* will be able to *do* or know at the *end* of the lesson (Mager, 1962).

Instructional objectives say what the student, not the teacher, will do or know, and whenever possible they specify a student behavior — such as *define, explain, identify* — that the teacher can observe at the conclusion of a lesson. Teachers who specify observable behaviors should be able to assess whether the objective has been reached. If students cannot exhibit the desired behavior, then teachers can choose to reteach the lesson or alter the objective. The point of instructional objectives is that they force teachers to think clearly and to pinpoint exactly what they are trying to achieve and then provide a basis for assessing the results.

A second important point about instructional objectives is that they can be formulated to tap various levels of student thinking. According to Benjamin Bloom (1956) there are six different levels of objectives to choose from within the cognitive domain. The kinds of objectives teachers decide to formulate can greatly influence the intellectual climate of the classroom.

The first level of objectives is *knowledge*, which involves *recall* of specifics and universals; methods and processes; and a pattern, structure, or setting. An example of a knowledge objective is: *Students will list in chronological order the major battles of the Civil War.*

The second level is *comprehension*, which represents the lowest level of understanding. Finding the main idea, summarizing a selection, or translating from one symbolic form to another are types of comprehension. A comprehension objective is: *Students will translate verbal statements into appropriate algebraic equations.*

The third level is *application*, which involves the use of abstractions in concrete situations. It is putting knowledge to use. For example, after students had studied ways to do a research paper the teacher might formulate the following application objective: *Students will prepare for the schoolwide seminar and debate on the United Nations by writing research papers on different aspects of the organization.*

The fourth level is *analysis*, which involves breaking down a communication into its component parts. Such an objective is: *Students will identify what persuasive techniques are being used in the following advertising campaigns.*

The fifth level is *synthesis*, which involves putting together various pieces to form a whole unique communication. An example is: *Students will compose an original TV advertising campaign to sell our school as a product.*

The sixth level is *evaluation*, which involves making value judgments based upon criteria established by the student or criteria given by the teacher. An example of an evaluation objective is: *Students will select six men or women who made outstanding contributions to America's technological growth and explain the criteria used to make their selections.*

Since different cognitive objectives tap different levels of thinking, teachers need to choose a variety. The level of cognitive objectives that predominates can determine the intellectual quality of a classroom. Reliance on knowledge or comprehension objectives alone, for example, might indicate a classroom in which little or no higher level thinking takes place.

In the *ThinkAbout* cases the kinds of questions Ms. Church asked indicate that her students were operating primarily on a knowledge or comprehension level whereas the kinds of assignments that Mr. Cartwright developed were aimed at getting students both to apply and to analyze.

Phase 2: Specifying the Procedure In this part of a lesson plan a teacher outlines the different steps of the general approach chosen to achieve the objective. If there is to be a lecture, for example, there might be notes or key topics for the lecture. If there is to be a discussion, then there might be a list of the teacher's questions. If there is to be a role play, there might be notes on the situations and a method for choosing participants. If there is to be a reading skills lesson, there will be the key points in activities to be covered. This section then is the core of the plan, the specific steps a teacher has decided to take to carry out the approach.

The first step in effective lesson plans is usually some statement or activity that will arouse interest and focus students' attention on the learning task. In Ms. Church's handling of "The Bigger Picture," the few introductory remarks on context serve this function. In Mr. Cartwright's handling of "People Patterns," his activity at the chalkboard with triangles and circles was his effort to arouse interest and focus on the learning objectives. Although in this instance his longer introduction is more effective than her shorter one, length is not necessarily a factor. One or two sentences or questions well phrased can set the stage for a lesson. Sandy, for example, frequently begins a lesson with brief but effective attention-getting and focusing remarks. Sometimes it is a few questions: "How many of you have heard of *anorexia*? Well, what do you know about it?" After the students tell her what they know she responds with, "Well, let me tell you what I know," and then the lecture begins. In other cases, particularly when she thinks there is low interest, she will start by telling them why they need to pay attention: "I think it's important that you really pay attention because we are talking about mental illness. One out of four of you may seek help some day." Then she launches into more statistics or related topics. In some teacher education programs these introductory remarks for interest and focus are called *set inductions* (Cooper, 1977). In others they are called *anticipatory sets* (Hunter, 1979b). Whatever the label, most effective lesson planning involves thinking about and deciding upon the most appropriate way to focus and interest the learner at the outset.

After the set induction the rest of the procedure in a lesson plan is usually outlined. Because she did no lesson planning, Ms. Church relied on the procedure in the teachers' guide. Mr. Cartwright, on the other hand, decided to compose his own questions for brief discussion during and after the program and his own longer follow-up assignment to give students extended opportunities to apply concepts, and practice skills. The fact that Mr. Cartwright chose to plan activities that required students to learn by doing reflects his implicit commitment to the learning theories of Bruner and Piaget.

As teachers decide upon and write down the steps they will follow with activities, they usually also include some checkpoints along the way. They may decide to pose questions or to give some brief exercises that will tell them whether students are comprehending the lesson. The last step in a procedure is a closure statement. This is usually a sentence or two in which the teacher decides either to summarize or ask the students to summarize what has been done or learned. As noted earlier Ms. Church omitted closure. Mr. Cartwright's closing statement in "People Patterns" was a transition to the homework assignment. He told the class, "Now that we have watched an example of a people pattern, I'm going to ask you to look for others around you. The program showed how important and useful it can be to recognize the behavior patterns of others, and this assignment will give you practice in observing these patterns." He then passed out and explained the assignment in detail.

Phase 3: Evaluating What Students Have Learned The evaluation of student learning has always been a key aspect of teaching, but today it has become a pervasive and controversial issue in education. In recent years an aroused public, disturbed by declining SAT scores and by evidence that some high school graduates cannot read, write, or compute, has been demanding a return to the basics and accountability for teachers and students. One response to the call for accountability has been the competency test movement. Most states today have mandated competency tests that students must pass before they graduate. In addition the chief criterion by which effective schools are judged today is the improvement of test scores.

There are many arguments pro and con related to the new emphasis on testing. The point here, however, is that within this broader context of accountability and prescribed tests, an individual teacher still has important decisions to make regarding the evaluation of daily lessons. Both Ms. Church and Mr. Cartwright work in districts where testing is highly emphasized. In Ms. Church's district students who do not get scores of 80 or above on a series of subject matter tests each year are held back. Still, Ms. Church as well as Mr. Cartwright could decide how to evaluate a supplementary curriculum like *ThinkAbout*. Ms. Church decided not to do any evaluation. She viewed *ThinkAbout* as falling between subject matter areas and therefore felt no inclination to assess whether students were actually developing problem-solving skills. The teachers' guide actually suggested activities by which a teacher might assess growth in problem solving, but since Ms. Church never read the guide thoroughly she did not initially notice them. When they were pointed out she maintained that they were too time-consuming.

Mr. Cartwright chose to hold students responsible for *ThinkAbout* programs, although he too ignored the suggested activities for assessment. On the test covering the communication unit, for example, he asked questions related to the *ThinkAbout* programs on communications. In addition, he gave students some exercises and homework assignments that tested their ability to use some of the memory techniques covered in certain programs.

Ruth Christopherson comments upon the importance of giving students feedback on their learning in these terms:

> I think it's important for kids to know what they're expected to know. Sometimes I'll have a folder with a check list in it. It might say something simple like *I can add two numbers*, and when they think they can do it, I'll check it off, give them a little evaluation. I think it's important that the kids get feedback and know what they're supposed to learn, how they're going to learn it, and how we're going to know they have learned it. I keep records of the basic skills, especially.

Phase 4: Materials Teachers who want to be sure that they are organized and ready for instruction will jot down in their lesson plan the materials they need to make the lesson work. This is a check point rather than a decision point but it is noteworthy because it can be central to the success of any lesson. It is a painful experience for teachers to reach in vain for materials they forget to duplicate or to search for a portable chalkboard that they failed to move into the classroom. Equally important to consider, of course, is the quality of the necessary materials. In every lesson teachers need to decide what materials will be appropriate to accomplish their aims. One focal point for observation, then, is both the quality and accessibility of materials for any given lesson.

I. Goals
    A. Long-range Goal: Student understanding of the communication process.
    B. Instructional Objectives:
        1. The student will be able to define the word *pattern* and give several examples.
        2. The student will be able to explain the meaning of people patterns and give examples.
        3. The student will be able to identify people patterns in familiar places—school or home.
        4. The student will be able to explain how knowledge of people patterns aids the communication process.

II. Procedure.
    A. *Set Induction:* Call on volunteers to make a pattern on chalkboard. Elicit from students the word and definition of *pattern*. Relate to program.
    B. Watch "People Patterns"—stop where appropriate and ask questions to check understanding.
    C. After program, ask further questions to test understanding.
    D. *Closure:* Link program to students' lives—people patterns everywhere.

III. Evaluation of Student Learning: Assign individual research project; pass out work sheet.

IV. Materials: cassette, videoplayer, markers, yellow sheet, worksheet for assignment.

V. Self-evaluation.

Figure 9.1 Sample lesson plan for "People Patterns"

The lesson plan format that we have considered reveals the number of decisions that teachers must make just in the planning stages. Deciding upon what kind of daily and long-range objectives to formulate; what kind of overall strategy and specific activities to arrange in order to achieve the objective; and what kind of set induction, closure, and evaluation is appropriate is both time-consuming and complicated (see Figure 9.1 for a sample lesson plan). These kinds of decisions that can be made prior to the classroom instruction Philip Jackson (1968) labels *preactive decisions*. There are, of course, a number of decisions that must be made on the spot, or in what Jackson calls the *interactive stage*. Whether to stop a particular line of discussion or allow it to continue, whether or not to call on nonvolunteers, whether or not to interrupt the plan of a lesson for a discipline problem, whether to quicken or slow the pace are but a few of the decisions that need to be made during a lesson. The following section looks more closely at some of the decisions to be made during the process of teaching and learning.

Decisions during Teaching

A consideration of some of the pedagogical decisions made by Ms. Church and Mr. Cartwright during their *ThinkAbout* lessons reveals some sharp differences. On the one hand, Ms. Church's decision not to plan for *ThinkAbout* forced her into the practice of looking through the teachers' guide during the program to prepare for questions afterward. This, in turn, meant that she could not pay close attention to the program itself, and the result was that she sometimes missed the key point of the program. Moreover, since she had not chosen clear objectives earlier she frequently wandered off the main point. Even when she knew the main point she found it difficult to phrase clear, well-formulated questions. Finally, when student responses were unclear she did not probe for well-developed answers. A lack of skill in questioning techniques was clearly evident and because of this lack many of her lessons appear to be of dubious value. Mr. Cartwright, on the other hand, chose to watch each program intently and to stop the program to pose a relevant question to make a point. He had a definite objective for each program, and he chose to keep the students focused on that objective by interrupting the programs periodically with appropriate questions and by following the programs with focused application activities.

The rather rote and superficial exchange between Ms. Church and her students is much more the norm in classrooms accross the country than the clearly focused activity-oriented classroom of Mr. Cartwright. Within the 1,000 classrooms that his research teams visited, Goodlad (1984) found a pervasive passivity among students who mostly listened to teachers, did worksheets, and took tests and quizzes. The teacher was the dominant figure in classrooms, not the students. The questions that teachers asked primarily involved recall of facts, and thus there was little intellectual stimulation. His recent descriptions and findings are reminiscent of Bellack's classroom game findings mentioned in Chapter 6. Goodlad (1984) states:

> We do not see in our descriptions much opportunity for students to become engaged with knowledge so as to employ their full range of intellectual abilities. And we wonder about the meaninglessness of whatever is acquired by students who sit listening or performing relatively repetitive exercises, year after year. Part of the brain, known as Magour's brain, is stimulated by novelty. It appears to me that students spending twelve years in the schools we studied would be unlikely to experience much novelty. Does part of the brain just sleep, then? (p. 231)

Not in the classrooms of the five case study teachers. Part of what makes all five of these teachers excellent is that they do precisely the opposite of what Goodlad found to be the more general case. If Goodlad had visited their classrooms he would have seen teachers who plan a variety of quickly paced activities and ask a lot of high-level and probing questions. He would also have observed students who actively participate, make decisions, solve problems, and think critically and creatively.

In Jacquie's classroom, for example, Goodlad might see four or five activities in a single class period where the pace is lively and students interact well with her, showing great interest throughout the class period. When they try to answer a question superficially in a word or two, she insists, "You have to give me more information." They go out of the classroom singing a chorus of "Alouette."

In Larry's classrooms Goodlad might find him using very different methods with the same content. Recognizing that there are multiple ways to teach the same content, Larry pays some attention to the learning styles of the students and then varies his instructional strategies accordingly. To Larry, having multiple methods in one's repertoire is the hallmark of a good teacher.

> When I first began, just trying to decide how to teach a subject was a real problem. And I was nervous. I think that I became a good teacher when I figured out that I could teach a lesson three or four different ways. There are all kinds of ways to teach—whatever is right works well with you and works well with those kids. Some kids love to be talked to—love to take notes. Other kids don't. And if you've got a pile of kids that are one way in one classroom, you can deal with that. If you've got them all mixed up, then you've just got to play by ear and do the best you can.

Whatever method Larry chooses, he will always be interacting with students, pushing them to think by asking questions and using analogies. Sometimes Larry actually reads the text with the students so they will do some deep processing of the ideas. They will read a paragraph and then discuss it thoroughly.

> I can read with them, and they can see the words. We can talk; we can stop at a paragraph and we'll discuss it for a while. I never thought I would teach that way. I'm almost embarrassed to teach that way sometimes, but it works. The kids—we interact back and forth—their brains working on the same wavelength as mine. It works. And nobody falls asleep generally. If they do, I hop around the room and ask them a question or two to get them to thinking about why this is relevant and go from there.

Student participation, high levels of thinking, and variety also abound in Ruth's and Luberta's elementary classrooms. Luberta's students thrive on a variety of material and activities. When students do computation problems, they are expected to think them through and apply them to real situations. Compare, for example, the math transcript in Luberta's classroom where she probes and pushes for meaning and understanding with Ms. Church's superficial questions after "The Bigger Picture." Recall as well Ruth's classroom, where students figure out patterns, discover relationships, and make significant decisions that affect their classroom life.

What John Goodlad saw and has reported, however, seems to be more generally true. A recent case study of a high school conducted by the Carnegie Foundation for the Advancement of Teaching reported a similar picture of instruction (Cohn & DiStefano, 1982). Still, it is important to remember that there *are* teachers like Mr. Cartwright and the five case study teachers who make instructional decisions that can create stimulating intellectual environments for students.

CONCLUSION

Through the vehicle of the *ThinkAbout* curriculum, this chapter showed both the number and kinds of instructional decisions that are left to classroom teachers and how different decisions can affect the quality of intellectual life in a classroom in dramatic ways. Although teachers have only partial control of the curriculum, they have extraordinary control in the realm of instruction. There is a wide area of decision making and control in both the preactive and the interactive stages of teaching. Even, as in the case of Ms. Church, when one chooses not to decide, that in effect is an important decision. This chapter concludes with a word about *postactive* decision making.

Teachers who decide to put time into reflecting about instruction immediately after teaching are in an excellent position to assess their decision making and teaching behavior. In teacher education programs throughout the country, student teachers are asked by their supervisors or instructors, "If you were to teach this lesson again, what would you do differently?" In some programs student teachers are expected to write their responses in a self-evaluation phase of their lesson plan. (See Figure 9.1.) The answers to this question can often lead novices to different and possibly better preactive and interactive instructional decisions the next time around. For all teachers, experienced and inexperienced alike, instructional decision making is a complex and powerful process that requires constant reflection for growth and development. To be a teacher is to be an instructional decision maker who is willing to reflect upon content, students, pedagogy, and oneself as a practitioner.

DISCUSSION QUESTIONS

1. What might account for the passive and monotonous instructional patterns that Goodlad found to be the norm in his study?
2. In what ways are the instructional decisions and behaviors of the five case study teachers alike, and how do they differ? Use the lessons in the case studies in Chapter 2 and Chapter 4 for comparison and contrast.

ACTIVITY

1. Ask the teacher in your field setting if you can plan and teach a lesson to the class or to a small group within the class. Plan a lesson, teach the lesson, evaluate student learning, and finally reflect upon and evaluate your own instruction.

QUESTIONS TO GUIDE OBSERVATION

1. Is there evidence of carefully planned lessons? What kinds of lessons does the teacher tend to plan: lecture, discussion, experiments, role plays, group or individual projects, media presentations, combinations of these?
2. Is there variety in overall strategy or is there a similar structure to each day's activities?
3. Does the teacher tend to arrange deductive or inductive lessons or vary them?
4. Do the approaches the teacher takes vary according to the particular content of the day or week?
5. Does the teacher appear to have a written lesson plan?
6. Can the observer or learner discern clear objectives for the lesson? Does the teacher state the objectives of the lesson to the students? What cognitive levels do the objectives attempt to reach?
7. Is there a set induction that arouses student interest and focuses students on the lesson?
8. Do the specific strategies or learning activities the teacher has planned seem appropriate for the lesson objectives?
9. Is there closure to the teacher's lessons?
10. How does the teacher evaluate student learning during and after a lesson?
11. Are the materials needed for the lesson accessible and appropriate for the objective?
12. What is the nature of teacher-student interaction during the lesson? Who does the most talking? Who asks the most questions?
13. Are students active or passive?
14. What kinds of activities are students involved in during a lesson? Do they appear interested and engaged in the lesson? What kind of questions do teachers ask? Do they ask students to recall information or to think on higher levels? What kinds of responses do students give?
15. Do teachers probe students for well-developed answers?
16. What is the overall pace of the lesson?
17. Do students appear to be intellectually challenged and to be learning?

QUESTIONS TO GUIDE TEACHER INTERVIEWS

1 How do you go about planning a lesson or a unit? How, in particular, do you decide how to teach a particular concept or skill?
2. Do you favor a particular strategy or a variety of strategies according to content?
3. What are the most difficult on-the-spot decisions you have to make during the lesson?
4. Do you have a particular theory about how students learn that guides your lesson planning and decision making?

REFERENCES AND SOURCES

Ausubel, D. P. (1969). *Reading in school learning.* New York: Holt, Rinehart & Winston.

Bloom, B. et al. (1956). *Taxonomy of educational objectives.* New York: Longmans Green.

Bruner, J. S. (1960). *The process of education.* Cambridge, MA: Harvard University Press.

Cohn, M. (1982). *ThinkAbout: Teacher use and student response in three classrooms. Volume II, research on the introduction, use and impact of ThinkAbout instructional television series.* Bloomington, IN: Agency for Instructional Television.

Cohn M., & DiStefano, A. (1985). Ridgefield high school. In V. Perrone & Assoc. (Eds.) *Portraits of high schools.* Princeton, NJ: Princeton University Press.

Cooper, J. (Ed.). (1977). *Classroom teaching skills: A handbook,* Lexington, MA: D. C. Heath.

Goodlad, J. I. (1984). *A place called school.* New York: McGraw-Hill.

Hunter, M. (1979a). Teaching decision making. *Educational Leadership, 37,* 62–64, 67.

Hunter, M. (1979b). Diagnostic teaching. *The Elementary School Journal, 80,* 41–46.

Jackson, P. (1968). *Life in classrooms.* New York: Holt, Rinehart & Winston.

Joyce, B., & Weil, J. (1972). *Models of teaching.* Englewood Cliffs, NJ: Prentice-Hall.

Mager, R. F. (1962). *Preparing instructional objectives.* Palo Alto, CA: Fearon.

Resnick, L. (May 1982). A new conception of mathematics and science learning. Presentation at the National Convocation on Precollege Education in Mathematics and Science, National Academy of Sciences and National Academy of Engineering.

Sanders, J. R., & Sonnad, S. R. (1982). *Research on the introduction, use, and impact of ThinkAbout instructional television series.* (Vol. 1). Technical report. Evaluation Center, Western Michigan University.

Skinner, B. F. (1961). *Cumulative record.* New York: Appleton-Century-Crofts.

Wadsworth, B. J. (1978). *Piaget for the classroom teacher.* New York: Longman.

─── 10 ───

PUTTING THE PERSON
INTO THE ROLE

INTRODUCTION

Throughout Part II this book has argued that to be a teacher is to be a decision maker. Every time a teacher walks into a classroom he or she is faced with innumerable decisions regarding the physical environment, the social system, authority, curriculum, and instruction. What any individual teacher should or should not do in a particular classroom setting can never be entirely predetermined. According to the educational philosopher Maxine Greene (1973):

> There are no final answers, nor are there directives to govern every teaching situation. If he is to be effective, the teacher cannot function automatically or according to a set of predetermined rules. Teaching is purposeful action. It must be carried on deliberately in situations never twice the same. (p. 7)

To be a teacher, then, is to be constantly confronting countless physical, social, and intellectual situations. Even more than that, to be a teacher involves creating a relationship between teacher and students that builds upon the unique personalities within the two roles.

Roles are enacted by individuals who can interpret them in an almost infinite number of ways. Many actors, for example, have played Hamlet, but Maurice Evans's interpretation is not the same as Sir Laurence Olivier's or Richard Burton's. Similarly, each of the principal actors in the drama of classroom interaction will play the assigned role somewhat differently. It is these personal interpretations that enable teachers and students to abandon periodically the superficial dimensions of the classroom game and to define, instead, meaningful and purposeful relationships within the context of the classroom. What is important for teachers and prospective teachers to realize is that there is "wiggle room," room to create within the role, but that this room must be gained by the individual—like functional authority, it does not just come with the territory.

One illuminating way to examine and describe the nature of classroom interaction is to consider the extent to which teachers and students can move beyond their assigned, more or less stereotypic roles and relate to one another as persons. This chapter focuses on the personal interaction and interpretation involved in the instructional process. It begins by looking at some background assumptions on human interaction in general as discussed by the social psychologist George Herbert Mead and by considering a classroom application of those assumptions by Sara Delamont. Next it introduces the concept of dialogue as a way of describing and understanding interactions in the classroom that go beyond the prescribed roles. It concludes with examples of dialogue from the classrooms of the five case study teachers. As you read this chapter, try to formulate your own working definition of dialogue and try to recall teachers you have had who were able to establish a dialogue with you.

BACKGROUND ASSUMPTIONS ON HUMAN INTERACTION

George H. Mead was mentioned in Chapter 8 because the dilemma framework of Ann and Harold Berlak is based in part on the Meadian notion of minded or reflective activity. According to Mead all human beings possess a self and are self-interacting. This means that people think about what they do and that their thinking plays a crucial part in their actions. Every individual construes the world in a particular way and then acts according to his or her construction of reality.

Mead divides human interaction into two categories: symbolic and nonsymbolic. Nonsymbolic interaction is essentially biological in nature and manifests itself in such reflex actions as blinking, sneezing, or pulling away from a flame. The vast majority of human actions, however, are symbolic in nature and involve interpretation. When two individuals are talking with one another each one is continually interpreting his own actions and comments and those of the person with whom he or she is talking. For example, in a classroom conversation about a math problem between a teacher and a student the teacher will react differently, depending upon the signs that he or she picks up from the student. If the teacher notes a puzzled look or hears the student say, "I still don't get it," the teacher will respond differently than if he or she perceives a look of genuine understanding.

Sometimes, of course, human interactions involve a large number of individuals participating in a joint action because they all have a shared interpretation of what it is that is taking place. Crowd behavior at a rock concert or a World Series game, or laughter by all of the members of a classroom as the principal walks in, are examples of joint action.

Sara Delamont applies George Herbert Mead's approach to human interaction to the classroom. In doing so, however, she highlights the concepts of authority and power. For Delamont (1983) the notion of power is central to understanding the dynamics of the classroom, or for that matter any human situation. As she explains:

> In any area of human life some participants may have more power than others and so may be able to enforce their definition of the situation upon others. . . . It clearly makes nonsense of many social situations if the power element gets lost. (p. 27)

Delamont maintains that teachers and students enter classrooms as unequal part-ners in the teaching-learning process and that inequality in terms of power greatly affects their interpretations and behaviors. Because the power relationship is an unequal one, for example, a teacher inevitably has more opportunity for creative interpretation than the students. Nonetheless, the ways in which students respond to the teachers' initiatives greatly influence the teachers' subsequent actions. In light of this perspective Delamont (1983) views the relationship of teachers and students

> as a joint act—a relationship that works and is about doing work. The interaction is understood as the "give and take" between teachers and students. The process is one of *negotiation*—an ongoing process by which everyday realities of the classroom are constantly defined and redefined. (p. 28)

The quality and nature of this relationship is ultimately determined by the teacher. The way in which teachers develop that relationship depends, in turn, upon their assumptions concerning human nature and potential. Many of one's assumptions are hidden—even from oneself. Before any teacher can fully realize his or her potential as an educator, these assumptions must be recognized and understood. Moreover, individuals are defined or created by their relationships with others. For a teacher this process of definition and creation of self is partly the result of the "dialogue" between student and teacher.

DIALOGUE—THE FOUNDATION OF BEING AND TEACHING

Dialogue is crucial in creating successful relationships between teachers and their students. Rather than being a one-way process in which a teacher imposes his or her point of view on the students, teaching involves an interchange or dialogue.

The idea of teaching as a process of dialogue has been part of educational thought since the ancient Greek philosopher Plato. In the late nineteenth century the educational philosopher John Dewey recognized that education involved a process of dialogue, and he sought to achieve it. In the experimental school that Dewey founded at the University of Chicago, the notion of dialogue between student and teacher was perhaps the single most important part of the curriculum.

Dewey intended his school to be a community of teacher and student learners. The idea behind this design was that in order to encourage reflective thinking two conditions were necessary. First, there needed to be a sense of community that respected individuality, which in turn would stimulate creativity. Second, there needed to be a quality of communication that fostered dialogue.

> The final actuality is accomplished in face to face relationships by means of direct give and take. Logic in its fulfillment refers to the primitive sense of the word: *dialogue* in which ideas are communicated, shared, and reborn in expression. (Dewey, 1927, p. 218)

The German philosopher Martin Buber (1957) has articulated the concept of dialogue with additional depth and meaning. According to Buber, human beings cannot achieve fulfillment in isolation; they need human interaction. Buber maintains, however, that there are different kinds of human interaction. Sometimes individuals interact with others as objects; sometimes individuals interact with others on a person-to-person level. Dialogue can only occur when individuals communicate on a person-to-person level. It cannot exist when individuals interact with others as objects or communicate only through their roles. When individuals engage in dialogue, they come to know themselves as well as others and they are, in fact, altered or transformed by the process. The teaching profession, when it works well, achieves this dialogue, this interaction of person with person. Through their interactions with students, teachers come to know not only the selves they instruct but themselves as well. They are transformed and fulfilled by the process of being a teacher.

More recently, the Brazilian educator Paul Freire has written about dialogue, stemming from his efforts to teach reading to illiterate peasants. Freire's view of education is based upon his image of what it means to be a human being: "a human being face to face with the world . . . *in* it, *with* it as a being who works, acts and transforms the world" (Freire, 1974, p. 154). For Freire the purpose of learning is ultimately linked to the idea of "becoming more fully human." When Freire applies this notion to teaching illiterate peasants or children to read he concludes that the way in which they are taught will have a fundamental effect upon what they will become. Either they will learn to read in a way that helps them to see themselves as active participants in the process or they will learn to read in the sense of giving correct answers to the teacher who is the authority and expert (Wirth, 1983, pp. 192–193). In reflecting upon the failure of Brazilian peasants to learn from agricultural experts Freire distinguished between the teaching methods of monologue and dialogue. With dialogue there can be "education for the practice of freedom," but with monologue education becomes only "a form of technical aid or assistance."

Education for the practice of freedom according to Freire is liberating for the teacher as well as the student. The underlying assumption of teaching as technical aid is that knowledge can be packaged and given to the learner or receiver. In a monologue the student is treated as a depository, an object or a thing. In contrast, education that liberates involves an ongoing relationship between teacher and student, both of whom are subjects, in which the teacher "permanently reconstructs the act of knowing." As the educational philosopher Arthur Wirth (1983) has written in reference to Freire:

> "To be more fully human" means to have a relation of *integration* as opposed to *adaptation*. Integration results from the capacity to adapt oneself to reality *plus* the critical capacity to make choices and transform reality. When we lose our ability to make choices and are subjected to the choices of others; when decisions are no longer our own because they are imposed by external prescriptions, we are no longer integrated. We have "adjusted" or "adapted." We have become *objects* instead of integrated active, human *subjects*. (p. 193)

According to Freire a positive learning situation is one in which teachers and students jointly work to solve problematic situations. Effective teaching almost always involves some type of problem-posing situation in which teachers ask *how* and *why* questions rather than *who* or *what* questions. In these kinds of encounters teachers seek to raise the level of understanding concerning life issues both they and their students share.

> Teachers who engage in this kind of action "re-enter" problem situations and in so doing find new roads opened for themselves as well as their students. This is how and why teachers continue to learn. They experience the growth of personhood that emerges from the dialogue of communication. (Wirth, 1983, p. 195)

Arthur Wirth in his book, *Productive Work in Industry and Schools* (1983), focuses upon the special need in the 1980s for dialogue in the workplace and the school. Wirth's book is subtitled "Becoming Persons Again," and this subtitle builds in turn upon the statement of the philosopher Martin Buber that "the great task of our time is to become persons again."

Wirth's thesis is that American society including the institution of education has been influenced negatively throughout the 1960s and 1970s by what he calls a *technocratic ideology*. In a technocracy, according to Wirth, the machine is the metaphor that defines the culture. Human work is made analogous to machine work. Scientific methods are given greater credence than human insight and intuition. Production, both human and mechanistic, is evaluated strictly in quantifiable terms. Work tasks can be reproduced and broken into constituent components and the worker reduced to a gear or cogwheel within a larger machine. This ideology, according to Wirth, has manifested itself in the schools primarily through the accountability movement. The unquestioned assumption is that human teaching and learning can be improved through a more scientific process that measures input and output in the form of test scores. The accountability movement is, in his view, an inadequate technological fix that is unable to confront complex human problems such as those faced by teachers in their classrooms. Wirth (1983) does not necessarily believe that the arguments for competency or the need to learn basic skills is wrong, only that they are being addressed inappropriately.

> Believers in the new technocratic ideology hold to a faith that a systems analysis approach which produces airplanes will also produce efficient child learning; and to belief in a crude form of behaviorism which assumes that behaviors will occur if it is specified that they shall occur. They assume that the principles of a mechanical model of production and cost/benefit economic principles can be transferred to education. The intention is to conceive of instruction as a management system. This requires the existence of a science of education analogous to the sciences of mechanical production. Serious problems arise when such a science of education does not exist, yet policy makers create prescriptions for educational practice as if it did. (p. 120)

Wirth (1983) believes there is no evidence to demonstrate that "engineered education is superior to, or as good as the creative work of committed professionals" (p. 124). There is, however, evidence that engineered education can in actuality be highly destructive. Wirth (1983) writes:

> the continual use of the machine as model in educational engineering efforts makes teachers unwittingly carriers of a technological consciousness . . . marked by mechanisticity, anonymous social relations, fragmentation of learning and experiencing of selves in a partial and segmented way. (p. 126)

If Wirth is correct, then during the final years of this century there may be significant forces at work in the schools that will limit the opportunities for students and teachers to engage in the process of dialogue that is essential not only to being a teacher but also to maximizing one's human potential, or as Freire puts it, to "becoming more fully human." We conclude that in the decades ahead to be a teacher will involve increased effort and energy in terms of putting oneself in the role. It is, however, a challenge that must be confronted.

To speak of fulfilling or defining oneself through one's interactions with others, of moving beyond one's role to relate to others as persons, or "becoming more fully human" is to speak in highly abstract terms. The following section attempts to clarify these ideas through examples from the five case study teachers.

THE PERSON IN THE ROLE: FIVE EXAMPLES

One thread that holds the five teachers together is their inclination and ability to establish genuine dialogue with students. Each of them has developed relationships with students that transcend the teacher role definitions in the classroom game.

Dialogue in the Elementary Classroom: Ruth and Luberta

Ruth brings to her classroom at least three related assumptions that enable her to establish dialogue with students. The first is that students are active, thinking individuals who can contribute significantly to the teaching-learning process. This assumption can be seen in action during her first day of school. For example, when some students are having trouble she responds in this way:

> Never be afraid to say I don't understand—we need to clear that up quickly. Sometimes you feel embarrassed—I used to be that way—tell me privately, if necessary, but please tell me.

The message that comes through here is: Your role is to be active and to take responsibility for yourself as a learner.

This expectation is repeated a number of times on the first day as well as throughout the year. On the first day the students are actively involved in figuring out how Descartes developed the Cartesian Coordinate System and in applying what they learned in a game format. Later they are asked to recreate for themselves the major mathematical discoveries of Eratosthenes. In small groups they work actively to figure out whether Eratosthenes' findings regarding prime numbers mesh with their own. The overall approach she uses is to arrange lessons and ask questions that encourage students to discover patterns. Once a student experiences the I-did-it feeling it is hard to keep him or her still. Students then became active participants rather than passive recipients in the instructional process.

In addition Ruth believes that students should substantially contribute to curricular and procedural classroom decision making. Whenever possible she encourages students to pick the topics they want to study and to decide how their classroom should operate. At the close of the first day, for example, she asks her homeroom students to decide how they should govern themselves, what the arrangement of desks should be, and who they want to sit near. In almost every facet of classroom life Ruth finds similar opportunities in which she can share with students some of the control that is usually reserved for the teacher.

A second major assumption that lies beneath Ruth's behavior is that students are human beings to be treated with dignity and respect. This assumption leads her continually to consider school situations from the students' perspective. On the first day, for example, aware that the temperature is over 90 degrees outside and that her homeroom students will be hot and perspired after gym class, she prepares cold towels for their return to her classroom.

The message "I know how you feel" and "I respect you as a person" comes through in other less obvious ways. At times it is just a spontaneous phrase: "Sometimes you feel embarrassed—I used to be that way." On other occasions, it is a more deliberate effort:

> I am asking you to fill out your activity schedule so I can take it in consideration when I assign homework. Anybody have early morning swimming or soccer practice? I know you're busy. I usually have a policy of no homework on the weekends . . . We will have homework—which night is best?

A third assumption that appears to guide Ruth's behavior is that each student is a unique individual to whom the teacher should respond in personal ways. Ruth expresses this belief from the very beginning. The first thing that each student finds as he or she enters Ruth's classroom on the first day is a folder with a personal handwritten note. To the students she knows from other years there is some shared memory recalled. To the new students there is a personalized wish. Throughout the year she works very hard at getting to know each individual better.

> Oh, you work at it. It might start with talking about a hobby you have, and then they start telling you about their hobbies. You have to lay yourself on the line a bit and then they'll start opening up to you. But then you have to remember all they share with you. You have to have a good memory so you can remember everything and respond. The kids really appreciate this.

In addition to working toward developing her relationship with individual students, Ruth also attempts to help individuals relate to the classroom group.

> I like to look at each child and find some way that I can give that child status in the group. Sometimes you have to search a lot to be able to do this. But I like to do this for everybody at least once in the first weeks so that they feel good about their place in the group and that they have something to contribute to the group.

Ruth's accent on the individual student is academic as well as social. As noted earlier, during language arts she distributes individual assignments—tickets—with a set of activities designed for individual needs. Some have a personal word of encouragement or direction: "Let's try for 100 percent." "TV story was very nice." "Copy story in neat handwriting."

Having established so many personal contacts with individuals and with the students as a group, Ruth clearly comes across as more than the teacher—she is the special "Mrs. C." Ruth creates the warm personal environment that characterizes her classroom due to the assumptions she holds and the behaviors that exhibit them. If Ruth had made different assumptions—(1) that students are passive beings to be filled with the teacher's wisdom, (2) that students are raw materials to be processed, and (3) that because there is so much curriculum content to cover there is little time for individuals—her classroom would be a dramatically different place.

Luberta, like Ruth, relates to her children as persons rather than as subservient students. She never forgets that they have feelings and frustrations just as adults do. Her own feelings generally serve as a barometer. "If you respond to what you're feeling, they're feeling practically the same thing...." Sometimes when her students have been sitting for a long time she gives them an opportunity to stand up and stretch; other times, she expresses encouragement and empathy: "I know it's been a long morning, but if you can stay sharp for 15 minutes, you'll get a nice break." Luberta is equally sensitive to psychological discomfort. She recognizes, for example, that the children do not like to be put on the spot any more than she does, and she responds accordingly.

To Sean, who reads a number incorrectly "42 thousand, 5 hundred *and* 59," she acknowledges as part of her correcting comment that others frequently make the same mistake: "A lot of people do that, but when you're trying to be very correct, don't do it." To Tiffany who is silent after being called on, Luberta responds: "Tiffany, maybe I was unfair. Are you ready? You didn't have your hand up and I pounced on you. All right, you want me to pass on?" To Leekesha, whom Luberta calls on after Tiffany, she jokes: "You're thinking—well, I didn't have my hand up either." To the whole class, after asking if anybody was able to get down to the Arch to see the president of the United States, she adds: "If you didn't get there, don't feel bad. I didn't either."

Another way in which Luberta steps beyond the traditional role is by empowering students while, at the same time, acknowledging the fallibility of the teacher. In Luberta's classroom the teacher is not always right. If, for example, a student appears confused, Luberta will typically assume some responsibility: "It's probably my fault. I probably was not clear as I should be—let me repeat it."

In Luberta's classroom, the teacher is not all-powerful. Rather, Luberta has great authority, in part, because she shares responsibility with students. They help each other, and they help Luberta. When, for example, a student has a question about a math problem Luberta refers her to others: "Who else has finished number 2?— Melissa. Go check with Melissa. If two or three of you get the same answer it's probably a good answer." Luberta also strongly believes in the ability of the children:

> My children believe they can do anything and many of them can do much.... Children can be terrific in teaching each other. They seem to know that magic word to say to each other while I might stand all day to try to make a point.

And if they believe in themselves, it is because she keeps telling them how great they are. Sometimes it's a simple statement on her part: "You all have had so many words, I don't know how you remember them all." Sometimes it is a unison recitation of the Power of Knowledge pledge. Whatever the format, they get the message—I can do anything I want and am willing to work for. Over and over each day she personally reinforces the school motto: Believe, Work, Achieve.

As with Ruth, Luberta's special classroom environment is the way it is because *she* makes it that way. She does not take either an easy or a conventional way out. She does not do exactly what her students expect from their past experiences. In the early part of the year there is, in fact, a tension between the atmosphere, norms, beliefs, assumptions, and interpersonal dynamics she works to create and the backgrounds of her students. Her gentle and caring manner is often perceived as weakness by children who are used to being ordered around. But eventually they come around. As she puts it: "If you persist, and they find out that you're for real, they accept it."

In both Luberta and Ruth's elementary classrooms there is a genuine interchange, or dialogue, between teacher and students. With the age, size, and power differential in elementary classrooms, there clearly exists the possibility of total domination by the teacher. In these cases, however, one can see selective sharing of responsibility as well as sincere concern for the children's perspective. Genuine authority rather than naked power and domination characterize both Luberta's and Ruth's classrooms.

In their dilemma framework the Berlaks (1981) talk about "Teacher Control versus Student Control" in terms of time, operations, and standards. The control over time dilemma refers to who will control when students begin activities and the duration of time to be spent on a particular activity. Control over operations involves the amount of control teachers or students exert over what students are to do or how they are to behave in the various learning activities. Control over standards refers to who will set and monitor the standards by which work is to be done and evaluated. Both Luberta and Ruth at different times give students some control over these areas. Ruth, for example, gives students tickets for their morning work, but the order and time spent on the task is theirs to arrange within the confines of the morning time period.

The Berlaks' (1981) Child as Person versus Child as Client dilemma captures varying attitudes that teachers have toward the students with whom they work.

> The Child as Person pull is towards relating to the child as a fellow human being, acknowledging the common bond of humanity between teacher and child. The alternative pull is toward teaching the Child as a Client, as a receiver of professional services—time, energy, knowledge, skills—that fulfill the child's needs. (pp. 155–156)

Luberta and Ruth typically resolve the dilemma in terms of the child as person, but each teacher's individual personality and each teacher's social setting makes the interpretation of that resolution somewhat different. Moreover, the way in which their students respond to that interpretation has affected who Ruth and Luberta are as persons and as teachers. Each has defined a relationship with students that works and that centers on doing work. In each classroom the instructional process is a joint act.

Dialogue in the Secondary School: Sandy, Larry, and Jacquie

At the secondary level the fact that students are adolescents usually means that they have perfected the classroom game. They see considerable payoff in playing according to the rules of the game, and they have also had years of practice. Still there are many secondary teachers like Sandy, Larry, and Jacquie, who in varying ways create meaningful relationships with students. The approaches that these three case study teachers take toward reaching beyond traditional teacher and student roles have some similarities and some differences.

If you leaf back through Chapter 4 you will notice that Sandy Snodgrass and Larry Wells have several things in common. Although Sandy teaches in suburbia and Larry in a rural setting, they are both high school social studies teachers, and they both attended the same state college, though at different times. The physical arrangement of their classrooms is also similar but different from the norm for secondary school classroom layouts. Both teachers seat their students in a double layer semicircle. The typical high school seating arrangement is a grid pattern of five or six rows each five or six desks deep. Chapter 5 discussed the meaning of space and seating arrangements from both a direct and symbolic perspective. One direct effect of a semicircular seating pattern is that students are able to carry on conversations among themselves because they can see and hear each other. The grid pattern makes both seeing and hearing difficult for many students. Symbolically a semicircle suggests something about the way the teacher defines the student role. This arrangement suggests that discussion among students is expected or wanted. The teacher is still at the front of the semicircle, which suggests that he or she is still the center of the classroom, but a heightened expectation for student participation is suggested by the semicircle. Larry and Sandy have roughly the same number of students to place into the same physical space as most teachers, but they arrange that space and the group differently. It seems a reasonable speculation that their classrooms do not have the degree of teacher-dominated verbal interaction that the research generally shows. Students are likely to have a larger, more active role.

In fact the description of Sandy's psychology class contains a low proportion of teacher talk. On the day of observation her class was engaged in an experiment for comparing circle and wheel communication patterns. Her students move rapidly from the semicircle to several small groups for the duration of the period. Sandy's comment that the problems encountered during the experiment would be discussed tomorrow, the questions that the students were asked to think about for the next class, and the high interest level generated by the experiments and the small-group arrangement all suggest that the next class is likely to contain a lively discussion among the students.

Sandy works hard to establish a personal relationship with each student. After years of teaching she has come to believe that she teaches students more than subject matter, and she goes out of her way to respond to individuals.

> A lot of kids will say that this teacher, the whole semester, never said anything to them. I try to make it a point—if I see one of my students in the hall—I always say hello or kid around or talk to them, just little things like that. If I walked down the hall and saw one of my students, and they didn't say hello, it would really hurt my feelings. And I think it works both ways. And seeing them in public—I live close enough to the community—I'm around. A lot of it works on the fact that they know you don't look down on them.

And clearly Sandy does not look down on students, even the ones who typically give teachers a rough time.

> I had a kid the other day who's quitting school, moving to another state, and I said, "I'm really going to miss you; I enjoyed having you in class," which wasn't exactly true, but he said, "You're the only teacher who said that to me today." But some of these kids know they're not the kind of kids teachers like: they never do their work, they skip school, they're always in trouble. I let them know that maybe I don't like them as a student, but as a person, they're all right.

Not surprisingly Sandy's students respond openly and warmly in return. They seek her out for advice on personal problems and her greatest satisfaction is when she is helpful in these one-on-one encounters.

Sandy has yet another vehicle by which she alters the traditional teacher-student roles: her keen and unpredictable sense of humor. In class she teases and jokes. The class on group communication is a case in point. During the exercise when the students could not talk, she broke the silence with, "Oh, I love the quiet, I wish we could do this every day." To the group that could not organize itself, she quipped, "Force is a nice way to decide." To the group with the lowest score she teased, "I wouldn't go into space with you." Outside class she is a lot less subtle—she tells outrageous stories and plays tricks.

Sandy also establishes meaningful relationships with students because she participates in extracurricular activities. Currently she is head of the pompon squad and finds that outside the classroom and regular school day schedule there is even more opportunity to respond to students on a person-to-person basis.

Larry Wells and Jacquie Yourist also find participation in extracurricular activities an excellent way to establish dialogue with students. In Larry's work as sponsor of the student council and in his position of cosponsor of the yearly trip to Washington D.C., he interacts with students when both he and they are outside their traditional roles.

Jacquie, as coordinator of student activities, has even more extracurricular responsibility than Larry. In addition to being responsible for student council she is in charge of all social and charitable activities and the student newspaper. Through these activities she gains an outlet for her creativity, an opportunity to get to know students beyond an academic situation, and special respect from students. Her extracurricular activity has, in fact, become a principal source of teaching satisfaction in a difficult urban environment.

Like Sandy, Jacquie also uses humor to establish dialogue with students. She surprises first-year students by talking only in French from the first day of class, and she seems to be able to accomplish this feat by her lively pace, warm smile, and good humor. She banters with students, feigns great disbelief or joy with exaggerated facial expressions, and teases about boy-girl relationships in the class. She also forces everyone to get involved. She moves briskly from one student to another, pressing them, usually with humor, until they respond.

Students clearly enjoy responding to Jacquie in class, but they also like to talk with her in private. Each morning before school as she is organizing herself for the day several students invariably drop by just to talk. On the days surrounding the Alvarez trial, some of the boys admit openly to being frightened by the real possibility of violence. Jacquie acknowledges the danger, but calms them as well.

Larry also establishes dialogue with the students in the classroom and with individuals privately. During every class period Larry succeeds in getting students actively involved in the teaching-learning process. Knowing, for example, that many parents work in automobile factories, he relates the concept of tariffs in Colonial America to taxes on Japanese cars: "Do you think that if we said to your fathers that we ought to put a $2,000 tax on these Hondas and Toyotas that they would like it or not?" When students say they would be in favor of such a tax, he then asks what the Japanese response might be. Soon all the students are involved, discussing that tariffs are neither a simple nor a clear-cut matter.

Larry also gets involved in helping individual students with nonschool problems. When a student whom he counseled about family and boyfriend problems the previous year came in to thank him for his understanding and help, he was clearly moved: "You have situations like that which make it [teaching] satisfying. If I were a meat cutter someplace or an accountant someplace, I wouldn't have that. That's different."

Why do students talk openly in private and in public with Sandy, Jacquie, and Larry? Probably it is because they are open to person-to-person relationships between individuals that are invariably based on caring. Larry expresses well the concept of caring and its implications:

I have a key word, and that is the word *care*. And the emphasis here is on legitimate care. Kids can quickly read through a smoke screen. You can say all you can about how you care about them, this, that, and the other. But if you don't, they know it. They know by your voice inflection, your body language, and everything else. You've got to really relate to them on such a personal level that they realize you really do care about them and they will return that. The teachers that are cared for by students are the caring teachers. Kids just flock to them. And those teachers that are more interested in something else, can hardly wait for the bell to ring, can hardly wait for the year to be over. The students know them, and instead of caring there is friction.

Within Larry's explanation of caring a single yet powerful statement stands out: "The teachers that are cared for by students are the caring teachers." It is significant because it establishes at once the interactive, reciprocal nature of the teacher-student relationship and still places the responsibility for initiating such a relationship with the teacher. Sandy comes to the same conclusion independently: "I think a lot of teachers' problems are that they are teachers first and people second, and they treat the kids that way. They make their own problems."

One very important way of demonstrating care is by really listening. Sandy talks about relating to students through listening.

I don't know how you can learn to relate to them. I guess if you know what's important to them . . . when I first started teaching, things that amazed me were like if a couple would break up before prom, they'd still go to the prom together. They still do that, now that's something as an adult I can't understand. But you have to just get in there and try to understand how they think. The way they look at things. Drunken driving is something I will never agree with them on, but at least I know what they're saying. I'll listen to them. I will say to the girls, "Well, if I am with a guy—even if it's my husband—and he's had too much to drink, I will insist on driving or I won't go." And the girls' answer is always, "That would really hurt his feelings." That's their main concern. Or take the matter of having sex and not using any kind of birth control. The girls will say, "If you plan it, it's dirty; if it happens, it's love." That's another thing as an adult, I don't understand. So I try to listen to them without saying, "that's stupid," even though I'm thinking, "that's stupid." So I don't always agree with them, but I can probably tell you what they will say, even though I will violently disagree. That comes from just listening to them a lot. They'll come and tell you things, and if they think you don't care or if they think you don't understand, they don't come back again.

This caring relationship that Larry and Sandy talk about is not present in all the daily interactions of the five case study teachers, but it does typify the overall approach of each one of them. It takes effort, but it works.

It is important, however, to distinguish between caring and lowering standards, or forgetting who is ultimately in charge. Larry says:

There is simply a thin line, and you must know when not to cross that line. In the classroom, and in the school you still have to be the teacher. I've had to make some tough decisions about my students—scholastic or academic decisions that I didn't want to make but had to. I mean if I've got a kid I just love and he makes an *F*, then he makes an *F*. That's all there is to it. It hurts, yes, but I can't help it. I simply refuse to let my personal feelings play any part in my evaluation of a student. Also, I'm going to teach what I teach because of what I think needs to be taught, not how I feel about how the kids are going to react to it.

Jacquie agrees:

> They always know how far they can go with me with joking and kidding around. There's always a certain point they know they have to stop outside class, and they also know there's a certain point in class. I let it be known that my primary reason for my being there is to teach them. They can only go so far. I won't let friendship or fooling around interfere with the primary purpose. Occasionally they will try to take advantage of friendship, and I confront them with it. The student council president or one of the officers in my class will sometimes think that I will give them special treatment because they're officers. So, I have to talk to them and say, "You know, it's a different type of situation; you're in the classroom, and I can't show favoritism," although obviously there are students I'm going to like better than others.

For Larry, Sandy, and Jacquie, caring is not being soft; it is simply respecting the students as human beings. Larry recounts his handling of students who seem to step over the bounds of propriety in their display of love and affection:

> If I see two kids hugging a little too closely in the hallway, I will talk to them or make a comment or come up to them in such a way that won't embarrass them terribly. Some other teacher might grab them and take them to the office. . .but I won't do that. I am hoping they get the message that I care for them and that rather than get them in trouble, I just want to get this solved. In effect, I'm saying to them, "You stop this and let's go on." Hopefully, the next time they see me coming down the hall, they will realize that they know they shouldn't be doing that.

Larry, Sandy, and Jacquie are three secondary teachers who care and whose students care for them. They are successful teachers because they enjoy rather than battle with their students. In the process they have grown and defined themselves as human beings. Being a successful teacher has made each of them a more successful person.

Jacquie maintains that through teaching she has learned that she is "probably a frustrated actress." Once a very shy person, she now enjoys "being in front of a group and having an audience." The change that has occurred still surprises her, but she is quick to add that the change is still closely tied to teaching. As she puts it: "I'm a totally different person at school than anyplace else."

Larry talks of his personal growth in terms of confidence and communication skills:

I think I've grown as a person from extracurricular and curricular activities. I'm a better speaker. I have more deep confidence as a human being. In those two respects, I think I'm better. I can speak to the whole school or in assembly with a thousand kids there and I enjoy that. Ten years ago, I would have been scared to go out there and talk in front of all those people.

Sandy also believes that becoming a teacher has affected her significantly. Teaching has kept her young.

I'm 35, I have two children, yet I don't feel old. I feel younger now than I did at 25. I think you sort of keep a youthful outlook from being around kids. You're aware of the music, the dress, the things that are going on in the world of youth. In my neighborhood I find that teenagers are interested in me . . . they come to me, and they talk about school and their schedules. I think you just sort of keep a youthfulness about you.

Teaching has kept her openminded.

For me it's important never to be closeminded. I think when you stop letting yourself be open to new ideas is when you really quit growing as a person. You can keep growing as a person until the day you die, and I think teaching has provided me with that— being open to other points of view. You have to compromise a lot when you're a teacher. Not give up your beliefs, but just to make it through the day you make a lot of little compromises—you're more flexible—that's important for me. Teaching has provided me with a means for keeping an open mind.

Teaching has also helped her to learn how much she enjoys children.

One thing I have really learned is I really do like children. There are a lot of teachers who don't like kids . . . I went through a period where I thought not only did I not like kids, but I didn't really want any of my own. Now I'm sorry I got started so late that I couldn't have a couple more. I really enjoy children. We always have a houseful of kids. We have two, but there usually are six or eight at home, and I enjoy it.

But perhaps most importantly teaching has given Sandy a sense of self-worth.

A lot of times when you teach, you think, "I really couldn't do anything else," or "Are the kids really getting anything out of it?" I think I do affect people's lives. With some kids you can really make a difference in which direction they go. So I've come to attach more importance to my role as a teacher. . . . There are times when I will say, "Boy, if it weren't for me, this wouldn't have happened to her or him," and I think that's really neat—I am really worthwhile and important. A lot of people in their jobs feel that they're "just there," that they really don't make a difference and that anyone could do the job—now I don't think anyone could do the job that I do. I think I have special qualities that someone else coming in wouldn't have. For example, I'm very proud of what we did for Mary who was autistic. I don't think other people could have done that in our school. I think about what we did for her and what she did for herself with our help. But I only see it now—I didn't see it at the time. I thought at the time, "Oh, God, we're curling up in odd positions to talk to this autistic girl and for what? She's not getting anything out of it." But now I can look back and see her out of college, engaged, and think, "Wow, we were partially responsible for that," and that really feels good.

CONCLUSION

This chapter has introduced the concept of dialogue as a central aspect of teaching and then has attempted to explain the idea more concretely through examples from the case study teachers. The examples show that dialogue involves academic and social as well as personal dimensions. Dialogue is much more than just caring about children, or wanting to make them feel good about themselves. It has as its goal providing the intellectual, social, and personal means necessary for students to act on their world.

In helping students reach their potential teachers in turn reach theirs. When teachers personalize the teaching role and make it their own they move beyond a hollow stereotype. This cannot be done if a teacher sees a student as an object or client upon whom knowledge is to be imposed. Teaching must be seen as a dialogue—a two-way process between teacher and student. The teacher as the most powerful individual in the relationship usually bears the responsibility to initiate this dialogue. The fact that the teacher has the power to set the dialogue in motion adds an important moral and ethical dimension to his or her work (Tom, 1984).

Obviously, every act involved in the process of teaching cannot include a dialogue. Much of the day-to-day teaching world is mechanistic, routinized, and bound by externally imposed rules. There are, however, moments in every teacher's day when he or she can reach beyond the routine to respond to students as people. Think for a moment about some of your own elementary or high school teachers. How many of them were able to establish genuine dialogue with you? In all probability only a few, and the reason is quite simple. To establish genuine and meaningful dialogue with students is not an easy task. It requires that a teacher have knowledge of subject matter, pedagogy, and human nature; the ability and inclination to see beyond the daily routines of classroom life; a value system that places people above role or status; and the motivation to override environmental influences that discourage such an orientation. Although difficult to achieve, dialogue is at the core of what it means to be a teacher.

DISCUSSION QUESTIONS

1. What are the barriers to establishing dialogue in the classroom?
2. How much dialogue occurs in college or university classrooms? Why?
3. If a teacher regarded genuine dialogue with students a top priority, what implications might that have for his or her curricular and instructional decisions?

ACTIVITY

1. Compare a teacher with whom you have shared a genuine dialogue with the stereotypes of teachers depicted in literature as cited in Chapter 1. Do the depictions of assumptions and behaviors of teachers engaged in dialogue ring true in your own experience?

QUESTIONS TO GUIDE OBSERVATION

1. What is the nature of the human interaction in the classroom?
2. What evidence is there of negotiation between teacher and student? What kinds of issues get negotiated? How?
3. Is the classroom characterized by monologue or dialogue? How does the teacher establish dialogue with students? Cite examples where teachers and students step out of the prescribed roles of teacher and student.
4. How does the teacher resolve the dilemma *child as person vs. child as client*? In what instances and types of activities are students treated as persons; in what instances and types of activity are students treated as clients?
5. How does the teacher resolve the dilemma *teacher control vs. student control*? In what areas does the teacher exercise control; in what areas do students exercise control?
6. Do students appear empowered or passive recipients of knowledge?

QUESTIONS TO GUIDE TEACHER INTERVIEWS

Teachers rarely talk in terms of establishing dialogue; they simply do it. None of the five case study teachers, for example, used the word *dialogue*, yet they talked about and exhibited clear instances of dialogue. As you talk to teachers, try to convey the *sense of dialogue* rather than to use the term *dialogue*.

1. What assumptions do you hold about students as persons?
2. Do you consciously think about ways in which to relate to students as persons?
3. How do you think about and resolve the dilemmas *teacher control vs. student control; child as person vs. child as client*?

4. What problems can arise from moving away from the prescribed teacher role where all the authority and control rests with the teacher? What problems can arise from staying within that role?
5. What outside pressures do you feel for staying detached from students?
6. Do you feel that you have changed and grown as a result of being a teacher? Explain how.

REFERENCES AND SOURCES

Berlak, A., & Berlak, H. (1981). *Dilemmas of schooling: Teaching and social change.* New York: Methuen.

Buber, Martin. (1957). *I and thou.* New York: Scribners.

Delamont, S. (1984). *Interaction in the classroom.* New York: Methuen.

Dewey J. (1927). *The public and its problems.* Chicago: Swallow.

Freire, P. (1974). *Education for critical consciousness.* New York. Seabury.

Greene, M. (1973). *Teacher as stranger: Educational philosophy for the modern age.* Belmont, CA: Wadsworth.

Tom, A. R. (1984). *Teaching as a moral craft.* New York: Longman.

Wirth, A. (1983). *Productive work in industry and schools: Becoming persons again.* Washington, DC: University Press of America.

11

TOWARD A DEFINITION OF EXCELLENCE IN TEACHING

INTRODUCTION

From the very beginning this book has described the five different case study teachers as excellent, and yet the term has never been defined explicitly. As noted earlier, these teachers were not chosen on the basis of objective criteria of excellence. Instead, subjective judgments were made based on the authors' collective experience in classrooms and knowledge of teachers and teaching. These subjective judgments were then validated by others in the schools where the teachers worked.

The way in which Part II is organized, however, reveals an implicit set of criteria. To be a teacher is to make decisions that enable one to create a positive physical, social, intellectual, and personal environment for learning. Excellence in teaching arises from the effectiveness of decisions and behavioral follow-through made to reach these multiple and complex aims.

Further, this view of excellence implies that teacher thought and action lead to learning that is both measurable and immeasurable. Because this book focuses on the teacher rather than on the learner, it has not discussed learning outcomes such as student test scores, knowledge acquisition, and skill development. The book's assumption is, however, that if teachers create positive physical, social, intellectual, and personal environments, such environments will result in learning, growth, and development. Indeed, in every one of the five case study teachers' classrooms there is continual evidence of student learning.

323

The chapters in both Parts I and II have sought to illustrate how these different teachers think about and act upon the various situations they confront. Because they are different individuals working in different contexts, their classroom thoughts and actions are understandably different. Each teacher creates a positive but unique physical, social, intellectual, and personal environment for learning. Excellence comes in many varieties.

Reflection upon their different approaches to achieving similar aims, however, shows there are some underlying characteristics that bring greater clarity and understanding to the definition of excellence. These characteristics start with both explicit and tacit assumptions about students and the teaching-learning process that guide their decisions and actions. Furthermore, each teacher is imbued with personal attributes, knowledge, and skills that enable him or her to actualize these assumptions and decisions. Finally, each of these teachers has the capacity and inclination to be self-reflective, to examine continually his or her own assumptions, decisions, and actions.

ASSUMPTIONS: BASES FOR ACTION

All five teachers assume that students are capable of achieving high levels of thought and inquiry. They assume that real learning is an active process involving a partnership in which the teacher's responsibility is to set the stage and initiate the action, or to give enough information to provoke thought and response from the students. It is the students' responsibility to take in the skills and basic knowledge that provide a foundation for thought, to ask questions, to seek help when something does not make sense, and to define meaning through interaction with the teacher and peers. Luberta describes part of this process as follows:

> I find I have to, at the beginning of the year, help them open up. I say to them, "Let's open up a little bit." Of course I don't mean open up in the sense that we are going to violate good behavior, but open up to the extent that we are going to listen, going to be interested, and honestly say, "We don't know." That is a hard thing to get the children to admit: "I don't know." It's hard for me, too. It's hard for all of us in front of a crowd. But I would like to think that they feel free enough and comfortable enough to say, "I don't know that."

The five teachers assume that every student they teach has the potential to be highly successful, "to be a winner." Implicit in this view is their belief that they as teachers can help their students succeed in one form or another. It is almost as if they hold a key that allows them to unlock the potential found within every one of their students. Simply put, they believe that every student is important and worthy of their attention. Sandy describes how she has a particular interest in her quiet and withdrawn students. It is this kind of student whom she is most interested in drawing out.

> I go for the kids who are very quiet and withdrawn, particularly if they're intelligent — maybe I see myself. In high school, I was very quiet and withdrawn, and I go for them. I love to try to draw them out, and a lot of times the fact that you recognize the fat, ugly girl with the stringy hair sitting in the corner makes her want to discuss, or talk, or kid around, or joke, or whatever.

Ruth expresses a similar statement.

> I like to look at each child and find some way that I can give that child status in the group. But I like to do this for everybody, at least once in the first few weeks in school, so that they feel good about their place in the group and that they have something to contribute to the group. They may not be superior mathematicians, but they may be superior artists. . . . The days that I find most frustrating are the days that I am asking myself, "What could I have done to help this child do better in this situation?"; the days when I have not been able to find the time to devote as much attention to that one to get him over humps so that he can feel good about it.

Each of our teachers assumes that what he or she is doing is very important and that somehow he or she makes a difference in the lives of students. Luberta explains that "if I have a strength, it's probably commitment to the job. I really feel that education is important, and because I feel it's so important I'm willing to work at it."

Ruth sees herself as:

> building up the foundation for people who are going to have to solve the serious problems that are out there. I think that the biggest gift we can give is to turn out a body of people who are not apathetic. People who are concerned, who know the skills and techniques to solve problems that we cannot even imagine now. My ideal is that we have an elementary school curriculum that focuses on thinking skills, where the subject matter flows from the interest of the students. . . .

What Ruth expresses in the above quote is what all of these teachers believe and demonstrate, that a critical part of the curriculum involves *process*; that is, the process of critical thinking and problem solving. This does not mean that they do not believe in basic skills and knowledge as content, but it does mean that knowledge and skill must be meaningful to be learned. Basics are essential but only if used in a meaningful way and as building blocks for higher-order thinking processes and problem solving.

Each of the five teachers assumes that the classroom is a real part of life, not an artificial or contrived environment. The outside world inevitably makes its way into the classroom through the consciousness and experiences of the students. Recall that one of Ruth's students wrote about drinking and "poured out this whole story about his father being an alcoholic and how he is now recovered after going to AA." For Ruth's students her classroom is not only a setting for talking about real problems from home but also a place to work through social problems that arise in the classroom.

> I think letting them take part in the planning and evaluating the things that go badly is important. I think they need to look at things that don't work well, realize that things are not going to work well all the time, be able to look at things that are not going well and do something about it.

To help students realize that they live in a less than perfect world and to encourage them to solve their problems as well as they can is highly important. This makes the classroom a genuine part of life.

Each of our teachers has a clear and overarching sense of mission that gives purpose and meaning to the content that he or she teaches. Some of these missions overlap; others are different. Jacquie explains:

> I hope that I teach them a little about other people and other cultures, civilizations, so they can develop an idea of their own world in perspective . . . an appreciation of people with different cultures and different backgrounds.

For Larry, it is his desire to "open the window [and] let the light come in . . . to see things that they have never seen before." His purpose in opening windows is to develop citizens for democracy, to take them beyond the confines of the rural community in which they live, and to lead them to the awareness that they are part of a larger nation and people.

> The world is not all black and white, . . . the world is various shades of grey—and other people because they don't agree with us does not necessarily mean that they have the wrong idea. You must appreciate other people's values, other people's cultures, and understand why they think the way they do.

Ruth's goal is "motivating a child to function on his own, to experience the joy of discovery and to give him or her the feeling of accomplishment." Luberta expresses her goals in terms of success for each student.

> I want him to have a good life for himself. I want the child to expand himself as much as he possibly can and to get to know that what he will be is not necessarily what the kid sitting beside him is going to be . . . [and] to do the very best he can do.

Each teacher assumes that a solid base of subject content is essential for effective teaching and that he or she must spend the time and energy to stay current in whatever field is being taught. Larry, for example, continually strives to stay current in his field. He started teaching with a master's degree in history and can't imagine how others can teach with less. His grasp of the content of history gives him the confidence to teach well.

Sandy keeps revising her psychology curriculum to include current research on topics of serious interest to today's adolescents—anorexia, bulimia, and adolescent suicide. Jacquie, who is extremely proficient in the French language, looks for workshops to keep up with her methodology. Luberta, by her own admission, attends every possible workshop she can in search of knowledge and resources.

Each of the five case study teachers assumes curriculum is not something that comes completely constructed or is given to teachers ahead of time. The curriculum also includes the meanings students establish in interaction with content through the process of individual thought and classroom interaction. Curriculum is based on rich subject matter information available from printed and other media and from a knowledgeable teacher. But teachers must create, invent, and recast curricula in the process of teaching, in attending to the meanings students make or fail to make as instruction and activity moves forward.

Larry exemplifies this assumption in his long metaphor contrasting a colleague, the tour guide on the Delta Queen, going in a straight line with Larry's "not teaching in a straight line" but having his students in canoes experiencing the river in a deeper sense, hitting the rapids, sometimes turning over. The tour guide's curriculum is written down, is presented over a megaphone. Larry's curriculum goals exist before he begins, but the curriculum itself is created in a zig-zag course attending to student responses as the lesson unfolds, checking for meanings, and story-telling rather than lecturing.

Rather than treating language curriculum as vocabulary lists she must get through, Jacquie's curriculum is really interaction in the language, even in the first year. When her classroom is interrupted by a visitor she simply shifts the conversation in French to the interruption, knowing intuitively that the interruption has distracted the students and that plowing ahead with a predetermined course of discussion would only result in losing them. With great agility she adjusts the subject of discussion so that the meaning derived through using the language remains central.

Sandy talks about growing into the sort of orientation Jacquie exhibits.

One thing I've learned as the years have gone by, is if something comes up, don't dismiss it as not relevant to what we're talking about. When you first start teaching, you're very organized, you want all your classes to stay together at the same point, and if you have a kid come and say, "Did you hear so-and-so committed suicide?" you're apt to say, "Well, that is a shame, but let's get back to this." The thing I've learned the most is to roll with the tide. If they come in and are upset about something, that's probably going to be more important to them in their lives . . . than maybe what we were going to talk about that day.

Sandy intuitively makes the curriculum relevant to her students. Suicide is curriculum when it comes into the classroom, especially when the students know the victim. Reality takes precedence because a preplanned curriculum would simply fall on deaf ears.

The case study teachers assume that they are in control of their classrooms and that they are knowledgeable professionals with an obligation to make decisions in the best interest of the learners. Although they are affected by external influences, they also assume it to be their responsibility to maintain essential control over events in the classroom and to work to counteract or to gain support from external forces when it is necessary in order to support or defend their professional decisions.

Luberta works conscientiously within the spirit of the time-on-task monitoring system, an influence from beyond the classroom. But she is willing to deviate from mechanical adherence to a schedule in order to achieve her essential purpose. She, not a technocratically based accountability system imposed on her in a systemwide effort to improve her less professional peers, remains in control of classroom events.

If a film Sandy believes is an important base of information and a springboard for discussion has been censored, she works with other teachers to convince school officials that her decision to work with the film is sound. Through discussion she achieves a compromise and thereby retains control over her classroom. She is willing to fight external influences because she believes in her own professionalism and she works in the best interest of her students.

Finally, as discussed at some length in the preceding chapter, each of these five teachers assumes that teaching involves establishing genuine dialogue with students. These assumptions are by no means exhaustive, but they give a sense of the shared belief system that seems to underlie teaching excellence.

PERSONAL ATTRIBUTES, KNOWLEDGE, AND SKILLS: COMPONENTS OF INDIVIDUAL TEACHING

Another of the common threads that holds the five case study teachers together is the fact that they possess the knowledge, skills, and personal attributes to implement their assumptions. In fact, there is congruence between what they assume and say and what they do. They blend thought and action in a consistent way.

The combinations of attributes, knowledge, and skills differ with each of the teachers. The varied combinations arise both from the unique individuals and the unique settings in which they work and result in the distinctive styles the teachers possess. You have been introduced to these styles in almost every chapter. Following is a brief recap of the most outstanding attributes of each teacher.

Jacquie's style is characterized by incredible energy and movement. Her humor is revealed in quick banter focused on aspects of her students' personal lives, exaggerated facial expressions, and a genuine enjoyment of acting in the classroom. The pace of her lessons is lively, and the content varied from beginning to end. Her commitment to student development finds outlets both within the classroom and within the extracurricular program. Jacquie exudes creativity and refuses to make her work anything less than fun for herself and for her students.

Ruth's style is characterized by skills for eliciting higher-order thinking and for setting the stage for learning in such a way that real problem solving seems inevitable. Her sense of humor is characterized by playing tricks on the kids. She has a deep capacity for empathy and is skilled in seeing the world through the eyes of children. Ruth elicits and uses detailed information about the interests, the motivations, and the family circumstances of each student. She has a proclivity for and skill in building group cohesiveness in her classroom.

Larry's style is steeped in historical knowledge and excitement about his subject. He tells stories, asks provocative questions, and connects historical ideas with the contemporary experiences of his students. He actively involves students and attempts to pull them to a new level of understanding of important social issues. He invests great energy developing leadership abilities in his students, both in the classroom and in extracurricular activities. He is a role model of an active, informed citizen of democracy. Larry has incredible skill in reading messages conveyed by student body language. He spins complex metaphors and develops multiple analogies in pushing for higher-level student thought. He has a deep conscientiousness about his work and feels secure in the ways he pursues his goals.

Luberta's style is characterized by calm reassurance and a gentle manner that underlie her tenacious belief in her students' ability to learn and become. Her lessons are characterized by clarity, variety, concern for the individual, and a commitment to make every part of the curriculum meaningful. She empowers her students and turns the classroom into a family and the students into believers in themselves. She never lets up on the basic skills, but at the same time she makes her classroom a rich physical and cultural environment that facilitates moving beyond basics. Luberta takes her students out of the classroom and brings much of the larger culture surrounding them into it. The manner is gracious and gentle. The presence is direct and forceful. Her humor stems from an understanding of the foibles of the human condition.

Sandy's style is characterized by concern for the individual, especially the underdogs, be they learning disabled or social isolates. Her banter and teasing convey a perspective of seeing the world through teenage eyes with a hint of higher-level wit used as much for her own entertainment as that of her students. Sandy breathes meaning into the curriculum through her combined knowledge of content and ability to understand human nature and perceive the world from her students' point of view. Her empathy elicits openness from the children and she is able to guide their problem solving. Her teaching success is bound up in her effective interpersonal relationships.

The thread that runs through these different styles is, quite simply, that all these teachers enjoy teaching, love children, and employ friendliness and humor in their classrooms. Their references to acting and to being on stage are pertinent. They all act and entertain, but they also engage their audiences in authentic dialogue.

SELF-REFLECTION: AN INDISPENSABLE INGREDIENT

All of the case study teachers are self-reflective. Each carries on some kind of internal dialogue concerning assumptions and decisions about teaching. In addition they all have the capacity to see the students' perspective, to observe their own behavior from the student viewpoint.

Earlier the concept of minded, or reflective, activity was introduced, which was developed by social psychologist George Herbert Mead, who both influenced and was influenced by his colleague John Dewey. The kind of self-reflection the five case study teachers exhibit is closely related to Mead's idea of being able to view "oneself as an *object*. . . . To view oneself as an 'object' is to see oneself from the point of view of another" (Berlak & Berlak, 1981, p. 115). The high degree of congruity between the thoughts and actions of our teachers is obviously related to their penchant for self-reflection. Recent attempts to improve professional behavior among educators and other professionals have been built on the idea of identifying discrepancies between assumptions and beliefs, thought and behavior or action (Argyris & Schon, 1975; Kottkamp, 1982). The teachers followed throughout this book possess a natural talent for such self-reflection. Recall Larry's statement:

> I'm always thinking. I take a shower in the morning and I'm thinking. There will be times when I'll be sitting at my desk, I've got to walk from my desk up to the podium and I'm still thinking: How am I going to introduce this?

As Larry is thinking about how to introduce a topic, he is carrying on a reflective process in which he is visualizing his own behavior at the podium as if he were one of his own students. This internal dialectic helps him to modify his intended behavior so that his message will most effectively inform or provoke thought from his students.

Ruth's self-reflection needs no interpretation. Her statement is elegant in its simplicity.

I play with ideas and talk to myself and try to role play how the children are going to respond, what their answers might be, what my responses are going to be, so there won't be put-downs and yet will kind of guide their thinking.

In planning curriculum Sandy puts herself into the perspective of the students and attempts to capture their responses to her even before she begins teaching.

As far as taking a body of knowledge and going into the classroom, my feeling has always been if something doesn't interest me, it's not going to interest them. I have chopped out areas that other teachers go into because I just can't make it interesting, and I don't think it's important. There are times when something might be a little slow, but I think it's important they know it. So I will go through it then, and anything I think isn't interesting, or drags, or if this theory isn't that vital to the lesson—I throw it out. So I weed and sort a lot, and do that every semester I teach the class. So kids will say, "Well, we didn't do that last semester,"and I'll say, "No, we didn't, but I'm doing it now."

Sandy obviously reflects on the results of her teaching and those reflections do influence her subsequent planning.

Luberta consciously monitors her own emotional state and uses it as a gauge for knowing where her students are: "If you respond to what you're feeling, you'll find they're feeling practically the same thing. I know they are." Luberta's advice to a novice teacher also indicates her self-reflection. She suggests internalizing as much material as possible beforehand so that the teacher becomes a "walking lesson plan." When teachers are able to store the guide points in their heads, they are then freed up to reflect on what occurs during the act of teaching and to modify their actions if necessary.

CONCLUSION

Part II ends by presenting a concept of excellence in teaching that attempts to go beyond ephemeral definitions. This point of view was developed through a synthesis of educational theory and five excellent models of classroom practice. It is not a simple checklist. Rather it is a fairly abstract way of looking at teachers that goes one step beyond what has gone before. Each of the preceding chapters has presented a way of looking at classrooms that, taken together, suggest that excellence in teaching stems from teacher decisions that lead to the establishment of a positive physical, social, intellectual, and personal environment for learning. Although specific decisions and teacher behaviors may differ, there seem to be some underlying characteristics that ultimately will help teachers establish a positive overall environment for learning. These characteristics involve: (1) a particular set of assumptions about students, teaching, and learning, (2) the knowledge, skills, and personal style to turn these assumptions into action, and

(3) the inclination and ability to reflect analytically upon one's actions and one's assumptions.

This analysis is based specifically on five teachers. Many more teachers should be observed closely to continue the search for a definition of excellence. Through your own participant observation in schools and perhaps through your own teaching you will continue the pursuit of excellence in teaching, in terms of both a theoretical definition and practical action.

DISCUSSION QUESTIONS

1. As noted earlier in Chapter 8 there has been a long-standing tension between excellence and equity. How might equity issues impinge on the analysis of excellence given in this chapter?
2. Think about the different styles of the five case study teachers. Which one most nearly represents the style you might want to develop? Why?

ACTIVITY

1. Think back to excellent teachers you have had. In what ways does this chapter's analysis of excellence fit with your experience of excellent teaching?

QUESTIONS TO GUIDE TEACHER INTERVIEWS*

1. Ask the teacher what he or she thinks about or reacts to the following assumptions:

   - Students are capable of achieving high levels of thinking.
   - Learning is an active process in which students have responsibility for asking questions, seeking help, and figuring out meaning on their own.
   - Every student has the potential to be a winner.
   - What a teacher does is very important and will make a difference in the lives of the students.
   - Knowledge and skills must be meaningful to be learned and are building blocks for higher-order thinking processes and problem solving.
   - Classrooms are a part of life and activities should reflect this.
   - Teachers must have a clear and overarching sense of mission.
   - A solid knowledge base in one's subject area is essential for effective teaching.

*You will notice that in this chapter the interview questions precede the observation questions. With the content of this chapter it is advisable to first interview the teacher to determine his or her assumptions and then observe to determine whether those assumptions manifest themselves in teacher action.

- A solid understanding of pedagogy is essential for effective teaching.
- Teachers must contribute to curriculum development.
- Teachers, rather than administrators, are in control of classrooms because they are knowledgeable professionals who are in the best position to make curricular and instructional decisions.

2. How much time do you give to reflecting upon your performance in the classroom?
3. Do you think of teaching as acting?

QUESTIONS TO GUIDE OBSERVATION

Observe the teacher to see if his or her behavior appears to be based upon the above assumptions. In other words, look for congruence between teacher thought and action. In addition, consider the following questions:

1. What skills does the teacher need to act on his or her assumptions?
2. What is the teacher's style?
3. Is humor a part of the style?
4. Does the teacher appear to enjoy his or her work?
5. Does the metaphor of teaching as acting seem to fit the teacher?

REFERENCES AND SOURCES

Argyris, C., & Schon, D. A. (1975). *Theory in practice: Professional effectiveness.* San Francisco: Jossey-Bass.

Berlak, A., & Berlak, H. (1981). *Dilemmas of schooling: Teaching and social change.* New York: Methuen.

Kottkamp, R. B. (1982). The administrative platform in administrative preparation. *Planning and Changing, 13*(2), 82–92.

PART THREE

BROADER CONSIDERATIONS

Organizational, Professional, and Educational

Part III moves outside the classroom and examines some of the external influences that affect the daily lives of teachers and one's decision to become a teacher. Chapter 12 considers how the school as an organization and local, state, and federal policies impinge upon the work of a classroom teacher. Chapter 13 examines the special career and work rewards of those who join the teaching profession. Chapter 14 discusses the process of becoming a teacher and includes the reflections of two prospective and three first year teachers. As in Part II, the theoretical issues raised in Part III are related to the practical experiences of the five case study teachers described in Part I.

—————12—————

GOVERNANCE AND LIFE
WITHIN SCHOOL
ORGANIZATIONS

INTRODUCTION

Parts I and II of this book have attempted to examine what it means to be a teacher in America by looking carefully at not only what goes on in classrooms and schools but also at the lives and experiences of five excellent teachers. Chapter 8 dealt with the role of the teacher in terms of curriculum and showed that external social and political forces impinge upon the day-to-day life and activities of the teacher. This chapter extends the discussion of the external forces that significantly affect classroom teachers. It will consider the governance of schools, the organizational and bureaucratic structure of schools, and how schools and teachers are shaped by the interaction of social, political, and economic forces.

The discussion of these issues will not be exhaustive. Rather, it will center on the perspective of the classroom teacher. The issues are presented to illuminate their effects on teachers and their struggle to maintain control of classroom decision making. Forces outside the classroom that ultimately affect the teacher, the students, and their interaction in the classroom social system are examined.

The chapter begins with the issue of schools as complex organizations requiring control and then moves on to issues of school governance at three different levels: federal, state, and local. Next it examines how these three tiers of governance combine to shape the experience of the case study teachers. Finally, the chapter focuses on local school districts and the role of bureaucracy in terms of coordination and control. In doing so this discussion emphasizes the role of the principal and the effect he or she has upon teachers in terms of the instructional process.

As you read this chapter, look for: (1) the different types of control that the federal, state, and local levels exert on teachers; (2) the ways in which they interact to influence teachers in general and the case study teachers in particular; and (3) the way in which the principal of a school can positively or negatively influence what goes on inside the classroom.

THE NEED FOR CONTROL IN THE COMPLEX ORGANIZATION OF SCHOOLS

Schools are organized for the purpose of socializing and educating the young. They are a relatively new publicly supported undertaking. The schools of today evolved because of the rapid changes in the economic, social, and political structure of the Western world. As the social order became more complicated, social organizations became increasingly large and complex, usually taking on some form of bureaucratic structure. As complexity in the social order grew, complexity and specialization also occurred within school organizations. Whereas a century and a half ago the technical and work socialization of youth was entrusted to the informal structures of the home and the slightly more formal structures of religious organizations, today such modes of education and socialization are inadequate to prepare citizens for the social order. The transition to formal education on a mass level was carried out first in small, simple schools such as the one-room schoolhouse. With continuing changes in the social order schools grew into large, complex, bureaucratically structured institutions.

Federal Governance Role

The framers of the Constitution consciously limited the powers of the new government. As an example, the Constitution contains no mention of public education. Further, the reserved powers clause of the Tenth Amendment reserves to the states and the people "the powers not delegated to the United States by the Constitution, nor prohibited by it to the States. . . ." Thus, major power to create and to govern public education is reserved to the individual states.

However, the role of the federal government has been more complex than turning education over to the states. The Constitution also contains a general welfare clause (Article I, Section 8) that gives Congress authority to tax to provide for the defense and general welfare of the nation. Over the course of the nation's history the Constitution has proved to be a rather elastic document, and it is the general welfare clause that has provided Congress entree into public education. This clause has been interpreted and upheld by the Supreme Court as giving the legislature taxing power for broad social purposes, such as education. Thus, the federal legislature has a direct route through which to influence school governance.

The earliest federal role in education was in the form of land grants provided to support public schools in the Northwest Territory. A 1-square-mile lot out of every 36-square-mile township was reserved for the support of schools. Following 1850 admission requirements for new states stipulated even greater land grants for support of education. The Morrill Act in 1862 provided land grants in each state to support at least one college, thus the origin of the term *land grant college*. The Nelson Amendment of 1907 extended the purposes of these colleges to teacher training.

The growth of direct federal influence in education was slow, however, until about 1950. The Smith-Hughes Act of 1917 provided support for vocational education. Various acts of depression legislation provided for construction and repair of public buildings, including schools, and for training and employment of youths through their early 20s. The United States Office of Education was created by Congress in 1867, but its minor role is indicated by two reports that showed that by 1950 only 1 percent of the total federal education expenditure was channeled through it as compared to 81 percent through the Veterans Administration, largely for GI Bill payments that provided college financial support for returning World War II veterans (Allen, 1950; Quattlebaum, 1951).

Thus, during the early history of the nation the federal role in education was limited. But as the social order grew more complex, as communication and transportation improved, as America became a world power, and in the aftermath of World War II and the advent of the Cold War, the interest of the federal government in public education grew. Rapid and broad expansion of direct federal influence in education occurred in the decades between 1950 and 1970. Some aspects of this expanded influence are mentioned here.

The National Science Foundation was established in 1950 to provide progress in science. The Cooperative Research Program, begun in 1957, supported university and education agency research on education. The National Defense Education Act of 1958 contained provisions ranging from college student loans; to fellowships to prepare college teachers; to support for guidance, language, science, and vocational education; to research on instructional media and collection of educational statistics. The Civil Rights Act of 1964 was aimed at public school desegregation and the guarantee of nondiscrimination in federally assisted programs, and the Economic Opportunity Act of the same year was an antipoverty bill aimed in part at improving the educational opportunities of low-income children through programs such as Head Start.

Probably the most significant single piece of federal education legislation to date was the Elementary and Secondary Education Act of 1965. This omnibus support bill was amended several times until it contained nine titles. Perhaps the best known, Title I, funded assistance to local schools with concentrations of children from low-income families. Title II funded library resources and textbooks. Title III supported supplementary education centers, guidance, and counseling. Title IV supported research and training. Title V provided funds for state and local educational agencies. Title VI supported education for the handicapped but has been replaced by the Education for All Handicapped Children Act (Public Law 94–142). Title VII funded bilingual education. Title IX prohibited sex discrimination against both students and employees of programs receiving federal funds.

To this point focus has been on the legislative branch of the federal government. The executive branch also affects public education. The president has frequently used his power and prestige to influence legislative action. Examples of executive influence include the passage of the Elementary and Secondary Education Act of 1965, one of the key bills in President Johnson's ambitious War on Poverty, and President Carter's creation in 1979 of the Department of Education, which established a cabinet-level executive department concerned solely with education. The executive branch may also use its powers to enforce actions of the legislative or judicial branches. A dramatic use of executive power to affect education was President Eisenhower's decision to nationalize the Arkansas National Guard during the desegregation of Little Rock's Central High School. The secretary of education, head of the Department of Education, influences policy both through setting guidelines for departmental decisions and functions and through direct influence on the president as a cabinet officer.

The federal judiciary, particularly the Supreme Court, has had a major role in education, especially since the 1954 *Brown* v. *Board of Education* ruling, which set the precedent for overturning state statutes and judiciary decisions supporting segregated schools. Federal judicial influence in education has come through interpretations of a small number of provisions of the Constitution. Especially important have been cases appealed to the Supreme Court on grounds of abrogation of civil rights guaranteed in the First, Fifth, and Fourteenth Amendments. The First Amendment guarantees of freedom of speech, religion, press, assembly, and petition have been the basis for deciding cases concerned with conflicts between religious groups and state public education laws and the permissibility of certain kinds of symbolic protests in schools. Fifth Amendment protection against self-incrimination has been the basis for dealing with loyalty oaths and teacher testimony.

A single sentence in the Fourteenth Amendment has provided the means through which many state laws and court decisions have been overturned:

> No state shall make or enforce any law which shall abridge the privileges or immunities of citizens of the United States; nor shall any state deprive any person of life, liberty, or property, without due process of law; nor deny to any person within its jurisdiction the equal protection of the laws.

The equal protection clause was the basis upon which the Supreme Court reviewed the *Brown* v. *Board of Education* case and cases concerning inequities in state school funding formulas said to deny equal protection. A discussion later in the chapter will show how litigation based on the equal protection clause in the Eighth Federal Circuit Court in St. Louis directly affected three of the case study teachers. The due process clause of the Fourteenth Amendment has been the basis for judicial review of cases concerning disciplinary treatment of both students and teachers.

With even this brief look it can be seen that the federal role in educational governance is complex. Although primary powers for educational governance are reserved to the states, direct federal influence has grown greatly since about 1950 through the vehicles of legislative enactment and judicial review, both with bases in the Constitution. The general growth of executive power since Franklin D. Roosevelt has also been evident in the sphere of education. One way in which federal influence has grown is that once a state or local school district accepts federal aid it is bound to abide by other federal regulations or lose the aid. Thus, for example, schools that accept federal aid are bound not to discriminate on the basis of race, creed, national origin, age, and sex. Although the federal government supplies only about 7 percent of public school revenues (Plisko, 1984, p. 44), federal influence in governance is considerable, and most teachers and their students are affected by it directly and indirectly.

State Governance Role

The state role in educational governance is also complex and has changed over time. Presented here is an outline of the general pattern of state control of education. There are exceptions in one or more states to almost any statement made concerning state governance. Your instructor will point out where your state deviates from the general pattern.

Having been left primary responsibility for education by the Constitution, most states by the 1820s had at least minimal provisions for protection and encouragement or direct establishment of schools in their constitutions or statutes. In this early period state legislatures were usually the locus of school governance. Schools were organized simply at this time, and most operating functions were delegated to local districts, which were legal subdivisions of state government (Campbell et al., 1985, pp. 51–56).

Beginning in the mid-1800s, states began to develop special governmental bodies for education. By 1837 Michigan, Kentucky, and Massachusetts had established permanent state superintendencies, and by 1900 all states had a chief state school officer, though the titles and means of election or appointment varied considerably. Beginning in 1825 with North Carolina, all states except Wisconsin have instituted state boards of education composed typically of laymen and appointed or elected variously (Campbell et al., 1985, pp. 54–55). State departments of education are the professional arm of the chief state school officer and the state board of education. They have grown considerably since 1960 largely because of growing federal assistance. Chief state school officers have considerable influence because they typically are professional educators in a position to recommend policy to lay state boards of education that meet only occasionally and because they head growing state departments of education.

General state governments have by no means relinquished control of education to the special governmental bodies created by them. Governors exert influence, and state legislatures pass the bills that fund public education. In most states education is the largest single item in the state budget. In 1982 the state share of total public elementary and secondary school revenues averaged 47 percent across all states, up from an average of 38 percent a decade earlier. However, the variation in 1982 state portion of funding ranged from 7 percent in New Hampshire to 90 percent in Hawaii, which has only one statewide district (Plisko, 1984, p. 44). Increases in state proportions of school funding rose in part from the fact that schooling costs in the decades from 1960 to 1980 rose considerably faster than the rise in the gross national product and in part from an increase in costs that citizens in local districts were unwilling to fund. Another issue influencing increased state shares of funding was litigation over equalization formulas designed to provide more state funds to less wealthy districts and less to more wealthy districts. Many states increased funding to education through the institution of or increase in state income taxes (Campbell et al., 1985, pp. 56–59).

In recent years the role of the state in governance of education vis-à-vis that of federal and local influence has been growing. The Nixon and Carter administrations suggested a decreasing federal and increasing state role in education; the Reagan administration has moved to make that shift a reality. Further there appears to be some shift of control traditionally exercised by local school districts back to the legal origin of that control by the state. The recent shift has been supported by increases of state proportions of total educational revenues, court mandates to improve funding equity, accountability demands, and the increasing power of teacher organizations that cannot be countered effectively at the district level (Campbell et al., 1985, pp. 56–59). Governors, state legislatures, and their special organs of school governance have begun to take more initiative and flex more muscle.

States such as New Jersey and Florida have taken direct action by mandating minimum basic skills competency tests and new teacher education and certification requirements. New Jersey has sent state department monitors into local schools to assess compliance with state provisions and has developed a noncollege alternative certification system for teachers in conjunction with local districts. The Commissioner of Education in New Jersey has withheld state funding from districts that do not comply with the minimum 180-day school calendar because they dismiss high school seniors for the last week of school. In Florida the state government has mandated merit pay systems, increased the minimum daily minutes of classroom instruction, and created more rigorous high school graduation requirements. State legislatures and governors across the country have responded to the recent national reform proposals with a rash of recommendations and enactments, many of them based on the technocratic and accountability ideology discussed in Chapter 10. Clearly, state governments are quite active in ways that affect the daily functioning of local schools and teachers.

Local Governance Role

The third realm of governance influencing schools and teachers is the local lay board of education and its hired officers. The tradition of local control of schools grows, in part, out of the colonial experience of distrust of distant governing power and the exigencies of life in isolated agricultural settlements where citizens had only themselves and their neighbors to rely upon. The tradition of local control remains strong, although some see it as more dysfunctional than functional in a society as complex and interconnected as today's (Lieberman, 1960).

Most school board members are elected, although in some states members are still appointed by mayors or city councils, and most serve without pay. Roughly four out of five board members are male, and membership generally tends toward white middle-class professionals. Minorities, including women and those from the lower social strata within individual district boundaries, tend to be underrepresented, hence their interests are often underrepresented. Membership on a school board is also often the first step in a political career because it gives public visibility (Campbell et al., 1985, pp. 177–184).

School districts and their lay boards are legally subdivisions of state government at the local level, just as teachers are technically state employees. Boards have two general control obligations to fulfill: (1) as the link with the local public they translate public will into action, and (2) as the policy making and overseeing body they direct the management of the local educational enterprise. Further, boards have both mandatory and discretionary powers and obligations. Their mandatory powers include building and staffing schools; setting and enforcing attendance boundaries; and transporting children. They have an obligation to perform these duties within the letter and spirit of state and federal law; for example, to provide for student safety and to abide by court decisions. Board discretionary powers include actions to carry out desirable objectives rather than those mandated by law. These may include participating in federally funded programs, raising district graduation requirements beyond state minimums, adding central office positions, and appealing legal rulings. However, with the growth of federal influence in education since 1954 and the recent resurgence of state-level activity, local school control is declining (Campbell et al., 1985).

Local boards typically hire a superintendent or chief executive officer for the district, although some small districts have no such officer. Hired as an educational expert and leader, the superintendent's role is to manage the total educational enterprise in a professional manner, one through which he or she carries out board policy. In reality, however, the superintendent often has great influence in setting district policy he or she is hired to carry out. Like the chief state school officer, the superintendent is a professional educator working with a lay board, members of which often defer to the informational base and judgments of the executive in policy deliberations.

The relationship between the board and superintendent often sets the stage for the direct impact of the board on teachers. Board-teacher relationships or those with the teacher bargaining agent may range from smooth to rocky. Several kinds of board behavior appear particularly galling to teachers: direct intervention into teaching, learning, and curriculum rather than influencing these areas through policy executed by administrators; actions perceived as petty politics, favoritism, or educationally unsound; and activities that strain board-teacher association relations further than necessary during collective negotiations.

Sandy, for one, thinks of her local school board positively. Recall her statements:

> From the school board down, the powers that be feel that the staff is pretty competent — they trust and respect us. We're evaluated, so they know what we're doing. The district has a good reputation; they pretty much know it's because the teaching staff has come up with the curriculum.

Almost the opposite view of a school board is expressed by one of the other case study teachers.

> They don't think of teachers as professionals. We're hired hands. Get us as cheaply as you can. Keep those kids in line, and shut up, and let's get a good coach. They've got a staff here of really well-educated, caring people. They don't always show that they think they've got that. More often they show that we're just employees. And they keep hiring good faithful substitutes who haven't got many brains, but they show up when they are called. They're not looking for good teachers; they're looking for docile employees. That irks me. That's not professional, not good education. It's just politics.

School board meetings, with the exception of executive sessions to decide personnel matters, are open to the public. Attend one or more such meetings as an observer. You will learn even more if you attend several different board meetings in different kinds of school districts.

Extralegal Influence

In addition to the legally constituted bodies discussed so far that have formal roles in school governance, there are numerous extralegal influences active in the actual control of schools. Extralegal influences come from individuals, informal groups, and formal organizations who exert control over schools, school employees, or students without formal legal basis. Such diverse organizations as the Parent-Teacher Association (PTA), including its national congress; the National Association for the Advancement of Colored People (NAACP), and the two major teacher organizations, the National Education Association (NEA) and the American Federation of Teachers (AFT), regularly influence educational policy and actual control at all three levels.

At the national level organizations such as the NAACP have the resources to maintain professional lobbyists whose job it is to influence educational and other types of legislation. The Civil Rights Act of 1964 and the Elementary and Secondary Education Act of 1965, for example, both received tremendous lobbying effort from the NAACP. The same organization has financed a number of important federal court cases aimed at the desegregation of schools.

At the state level the most powerful lobby able to exert political influence in educational matters is typically the predominant teacher organization, the state affiliate of either the AFT or NEA (Aufderheide, 1976). In other ways groups such as professors in state colleges and universities often have input into deliberations concerning teacher certification requirements and other related matters. Groups as diverse as the National Association of Manufacturers, the John Birch Society, and organizations representing ethnic and racial minorities and religions of various persuasions are involved in attempts to promote or block certain textbooks in states where adoption lists are maintained. Moreover, the influence that statewide text adoption has on publishing companies can spread from state to state. Recent reports by national commissions, foundations, and academics advocating educational reform such as those discussed in Chapter 8 have had visible impact on the activities of state governors and legislatures.

Much extralegal influence is often attempted and achieved at the local level. Both superintendents and school board members are open to attempts to influence their decisions. Parents and PTAs are reported to be the most frequent source of pressure on both kinds of office holders. When it comes to tax issues to support schools, parents are most likely to demand revenue for schools whereas members of local municipal governments most frequently oppose increases, for which they apparently believe citizens will hold them responsible (Gross, 1958). Most communities have informal power elites, typically composed of middle-class business executives and other influentials. Case studies have shown that such groups can

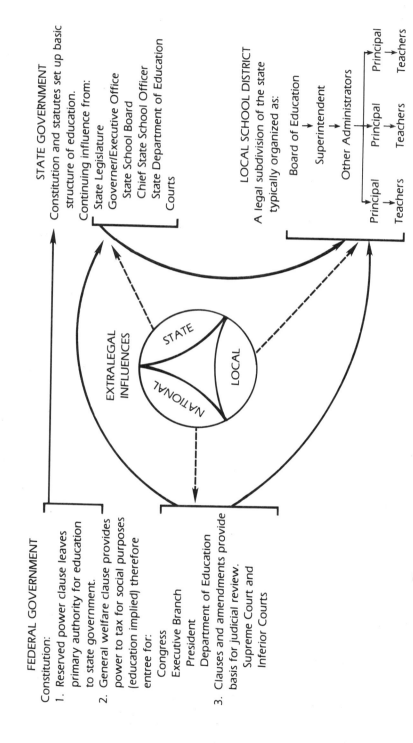

FEDERAL GOVERNMENT
Constitution:
1. Reserved power clause leaves primary authority for education to state government.
2. General welfare clause provides power to tax for social purposes (education implied) therefore entree for:
   Congress
   Executive Branch
   President
   Department of Education
3. Clauses and amendments provide basis for judicial review.
   Supreme Court and
   Inferior Courts

STATE GOVERNMENT
Constitution and statutes set up basic structure of education.
Continuing influence from:
State Legislature
Governer/Executive Office
State School Board
Chief State School Officer
State Department of Education
Courts

EXTRALEGAL INFLUENCES

STATE
LOCAL
NATIONAL

LOCAL SCHOOL DISTRICT
A legal subdivision of the state typically organized as:
Board of Education
Superintendent
Other Administrators
Principal   Principal   Principal
Teachers   Teachers   Teachers

Figure 12.1   Governance and extralegal influences related to control in local school districts

346

have more influence on important decisions than formal and legally constituted organizations (Kimbrough, 1969). In some districts particular religious, ethnic, or ideological groups may have considerable influence. When collective bargaining comes to impasse or strike, state level teacher groups will sometimes pressure target districts using statewide resources in an attempt to influence the outcome and set precedents for future contract disputes throughout the state.

These illustrations by no means exhaust the categories of influence exercised by extralegal groups and individuals. As with the legal dimensions of school governance, extralegal influence is very complex. Figure 12.1 depicts the interplay of the four kinds of influence in the governance and control of public education.

GOVERNANCE AND EXTRALEGAL INFLUENCES: EXAMPLES FROM THE CASE STUDIES

Federal Influence

The simultaneous influence of the three levels of policy and governance has been experienced by each of the five case study teachers.

Luberta, Sandy, and Ruth have been directly affected by a voluntary desegregation plan that finally arrived after years of litigation in the Eighth Federal Circuit Court in St. Louis. The background is unique. The St. Louis Public School District's boundary is coterminous with the political boundary of the city. Unlike most cities, however, St. Louis is not situated in a county. The St. Louis school-aged population is approximately 80 percent black, and meaningful desegregation is not a possibility within the city limits. St. Louis County, which completely surrounds the city, is predominantly white. During the desegregation suit evidence was presented indicating that county districts had consciously sought to continue segregation and racial bias illegally following the 1954 *Brown* v. *Board of Education* decision. Since the court seemed to have sufficient evidence to force a compulsory city-county desegregation plan in the long run, there was enough impetus for the named county districts to engage in a voluntary city-county desegregation plan while they could still have significant input into the agreement rather than being forced to comply with a later court dictated plan. The resolution included a busing plan that moved city students into county districts and specialized magnet schools that, for the most part, moved county students into city schools.

The Ladue School District and Conway School where Ruth teaches are recipients of black students transported from the city. The Lindbergh School District where Sandy teaches is also a participant in the voluntary desegregation plan. The plan continues on an increasing scale with more and more city students being transported to county schools each year. There are roughly 150 city students attending Lindbergh High School, which has a population of 2,500 students. Sandy has city students in all of her classes. Her response to the plan is positive. Although she recognizes and feels frustrated that the city students often have not had the kind of solid educational background they would have received from teachers like Luberta Clay, she has great admiration and respect for these students. School is of critical importance to them; they see it as a way to a better life. They choose to spend tremendous effort for the opportunity. Sandy acknowledges that many of these students wake at 5:30 A.M. to wait for a 6:30 A.M. bus that transports them to a school day that begins at 8:00 A.M. On Fridays many of them stay until 10:00 P.M. in order to attend basketball games. They have that much school spirit. She has also been pleasantly surprised by the positive attitudes and behaviors of the Lindbergh students, parents, and fellow teachers in accepting the city students. However, not everyone at Lindbergh High is as positive about the desegregation plan as Sandy, who by her own admission has throughout her life tended to favor the underdog.

Not all St. Louis City students have an opportunity to participate in the voluntary desegregation agreement. Jefferson School, where Luberta teaches, is completely black and a nonparticipating school. However, as noted earlier, from an attempt at another kind of equity, Jefferson receives additional funds in a "school of emphasis" program for science enrichment. The school receives a richly provisioned science laboratory with a full-time science instructor who helps students engage in scientific inquiry. Luberta is very excited about the program because she sees her students receiving knowledge and resources she could never offer in her classroom.

Thirty-five miles away in Hillsboro, Larry Wells is not directly affected by desegregation plans implemented by the federal government. However, Larry as well as Jacquie, Luberta, Sandy, and Ruth is affected by education legislation. All the schools of our five teachers are under Public Law 94–142, which mandates a least restrictive environment for handicapped students. This law has meant that wherever possible handicapped students are to participate in regular classrooms. Sandy, in particular, works with many handicapped students who are "mainstreamed" into her classes.

Students in Luberta's school receive both free or reduced-price breakfast and lunch as part of a federal assistance program, a service that provides them the basic nutrition necessary for a day in school. Jacquie's school also participates in this federally supported program. She, more than any of the other teachers, is directly affected by a liberal federal immigration policy. Her students include Haitian and Cuban immigrants, as well as native-born blacks, Hispanics, and whites.

State Influence

State influence is also felt by these teachers. Four are directly affected by Missouri legislation and executive branch action. All Missouri students must take the Basic Essential Skills Test (BEST) in the eighth grade. If they do not pass the test they must retake it yearly until they do. One of Sandy's social studies classes is tutorial and teaches the basic skills and information necessary for passing the BEST. Of the constraints put on her and the real help this test might be to students, Sandy says:

> I'm real ambivalent toward [the BEST]. I can see that in some cases there are things that all people in our society should know. But there are also kids with learning difficulties and learning disabilities, and I feel that the test doesn't measure the subject matter. It measures their reading ability. They may know the material, but they can't read the test.

Larry is acutely aware of the potential negative effects on his district of changes in state funding formulas. Hillsboro has essentially no local industrial or commercial tax base. Local taxes must come from residential property. His district is highly dependent upon state funds. Should the legislature reconstitute the funding formulas, for example, to improve the support of schools like Luberta's attended by the urban poor, Larry's school might receive significantly lower funding. As a social studies teacher and a Hillsboro city council member, Larry is cognizant of these issues and the political process through which they will be hammered out. An indirect effect of the St. Louis City-County voluntary desegregation plan on Hillsboro and all other Missouri districts was the need for funds to transport the students attending Conway School, Lindbergh High, and other county schools. State funds were inextricably part of the solution to the problem that arose through St. Louis County district's noncompliance with federal court decisions three decades ago. State funds that might have made their way to Hillsboro were spent instead on the implementation of desegregation plans.

Jacquie has been directly affected by a number of Florida legislative mandates and executive branch decisions. Recent revision of high school graduation requirements, which include passing a minimum competency test, resulted in increased course requirements in English and foreign language. The new emphasis on language at the high school level fuels interest at the junior high level, thus affecting the number and quality of students Jacquie finds in her classes. It may also have an indirect effect on her job security. The Dade County Public Schools have also had to work out local applications of recent state requirements for merit pay incentives and performance-based evaluation. These have had a direct impact on Jacquie.

Local Influence: Formal and Extralegal

Each of our teachers experiences local influences filtered through the policies of the lay school board. Different kinds of influences are discussed here in order to show the scope of possibilities, which in turn is largely dependent on issues and circumstances.

Luberta is affected, even somewhat constrained, by the St. Louis School

System's monitoring of student instructional time, which is calculated to the minute. There is an inevitable tension that runs through a situation in which a capable and highly professional teacher is constrained by a well-intentioned mechanism to improve instructional quality. An observation of Luberta's classroom shows this tension.

> The students are working on math seat work. Luberta announces: "Everyone tighten up, you have *eight more minutes to go.* We will be moving to spelling. Sorry about that, *we have to move,* but don't rush and make mistakes! If you don't finish, you will be able to finish later. I want you to be correct. This is not a timed test—I just *have to start spelling.*" [emphasis added]

In a later discussion of the rigidity of the instructional time calculations, Luberta commented that it does look "cold and hard." However, she goes on to say and to demonstrate through her "flowing back and forth" between subject areas that she does not let herself become "stifled by a program like that." She does not, but a weaker teacher might. Luberta is extremely conscientious in following the *spirit* of the instructional time-monitoring program although she sometimes deviates from the *letter* of program mandates in order to fulfill its spirit. The tension is there between professional decision making and compliance with district policy. However, Luberta is able to resolve it to the benefit of her students and her own image of herself as a teacher.

Ruth works in a district with one of the oldest merit pay systems in the nation. She has prospered under this system and believes that it is a legitimate means of evaluation. However, she cannot escape the tension that surrounds the yearly evaluation that has direct consequences on her salary.

Sandy at one point experienced some censorship of the birth control unit of her psychology class, an instance of extralegal influence. A parent of one of her students complained on religious grounds about a film on birth control, which included abortion. After a two-year discussion with school officials, Sandy and other teachers resolved to show the film up to the point of the abortion discussion and then turn it off.

TENSIONS ASSOCIATED WITH MULTIPLE INFLUENCES

Further examples could be given of direct influences on teachers and their teaching from all three levels of governance. However, the point has been made and illustrated. All three levels affect teachers simultaneously, and the particular school or district in which one teaches matters greatly in terms of specificity of influences. The various influences both provide support for teachers and their goals and produce tensions, sometimes simultaneously. Many of them, like Title I, bilingualism, and affirmative action, are means for fulfilling larger social responsibilities. Yet at the same time they complicate teachers' lives and potentially dilute some of the important goals they are pursuing. Instruction of non-English-speaking students, for example, is a major social responsibility but also greatly increases the complexities of teaching. Feeding children who would otherwise be without good nutrition is important to learning, yet breakfast and lunch programs drain the time and effort of principals, create more paperwork, and force districts to add and pay for more school personnel and central office administrators.

The dilemma of increasing multiple influences was raised years ago by Arthur Bestor (1953):

> The idea that the school must undertake to meet every need that some other agency is failing to meet, regardless of the suitability of the schoolroom to the task, is a preposterous delusion that in the end can wreck the educational system. (p. 75)

Chapter 8 discussed the evolution of the curriculum. Both Boyer's and Sizer's reports on high schools call for a more limited purpose in schooling, in essence a withdrawal from increasing influences. Boyer (1983) writes:

> Today's high school is called upon to provide the services and transmit the values we used to expect from the community and the home and the church. And if they fail anywhere along the line, they are condemned.
>   What do Americans want high schools to accomplish? Quite simply, we want it all. (p. 57)

Sandy, Larry, and Jacquie at the secondary level and Ruth and Luberta at the elementary level all work under these circumstances. Each resolves the tensions that arise from multiple or conflicting demands in a personal way. To be a teacher is to work amidst the multiple and changing influences of external forces. Resolutions of tensions are temporary; new problems always take the place of ones that have been successfully resolved.

LOCAL SCHOOL DISTRICTS: BUREAUCRACY, COORDINATION, AND CONTROL

Growth in the complexity and specialization of all organizations in this century brought with it the dilemma of increased needs for coordination and control. Without such counterbalancing forces schools, like other organizations, would lose any purposeful thrust and dissolve into smaller groups of individuals simply pursuing their own interests. In the one-room schoolhouse there was little need for formal mechanisms of coordination and control; they took place as a result of face-to-face interactions between the board and a single teacher. The intentions of the governing body were easily and directly conveyed to the teacher and then to the students. Today, boards have become more distant; specialization of subject matter and teaching technologies have increased; and the world for which students are prepared has grown more complicated. Coordination and control to maintain unity of effort and purpose is a major need in schools, as in other organizations.

Bureaucracy is the predominant structure American organizations, including school districts, have assumed in an attempt to provide coordination and control. The word *bureaucracy* often evokes negative emotional responses and images of red tape and impersonality. Bureaucracies can produce these as unintended consequences, but the primary intention of this structure is coordination and control for reaching organizational goals in an efficient manner.

Ideally, bureaucracies consist of hierarchically arranged positions that constitute a chain of command. Officeholders are hired to complete particular portions of the organization's work. When an officeholder is unable to solve a problem on the basis of organizational policy, rules, or his or her base of expertise, the problem is passed up to a higher level where, it is presumed, greater competence resides. The lower official is then expected to comply with the superior's decision. This is, of course, an idealized conception, but one that underlies the structure of most local districts.

The chief executive of a school district is the superintendent of schools hired by the lay board to administer, coordinate, and lead the work of the whole organization. Below the superintendent are, depending on district size, various associate or assistant superintendents, directors, coordinators, and other central office personnel. The next layer of the bureaucracy is typically found within the individual schools. A principal serves as the chief executive, coordinator, and leader within the school. The various teachers and other certified and uncertified personnel report to the principal. It is through this chain of command that external federal, state, or local influences enter the school system and filter down to the classroom teacher.

The superintendent is the most important decision maker in the hierarchy and, in practice, often the one who originates policy through his or her ability to "suggest" courses of action to the lay board. However, the individual teacher is not likely to realize a great deal of direct influence from the superintendent because the bureaucratic organization operates to channel decisions to teachers through their immediate superiors, principals.

The need for coordination and control and the bureaucratic organization that has arisen to provide it, however, stands in conflict with teacher desires to be recognized as professionals. There has been a long debate over just how professional teachers are (Howsam et al., 1976; Lieberman, 1956; Lortie, 1975). One thing is certain, teachers do not pursue their work in the same context as classical fee-for-service professionals such as physicians, attorneys, and architects. Unlike these professionals who have their own practices, teachers do their work as employees of complex public bureaucracies. Because of the governance system of local boards of education and the accepted view that the schools "belong" to the local citizenry, the very purpose of public educators' work is constrained by local and state control. Power, authority, and control are major issues for teachers as well as students because teachers practice within complex bureaucracies that are creatures of local and state political systems and that exert direct control over their work.

THE PRINCIPAL: COORDINATOR, CONTROLLER, AND INSTRUCTIONAL LEADER

Teachers have lived with one certainty: there is always a principal. It is important to focus on the role of principal because the principal is the direct supervisor of the teacher. Teachers often have a rather shallow understanding of the role of principal in the bureaucracy of a school district. In part the misunderstanding stems from the fact that teachers actually see a very limited part of what principals do. For example, teachers seem fond of expressing a particular wish: "If the principal would only go back to the classroom for a year. She has just forgotten what it is like to be a teacher." What is implied, but less often stated is, "Then she would act less like a principal and more like a teacher." Therein lies the problem. If a principal thinks and behaves like a teacher, then he or she is likely no longer a principal. Teachers may desire such a state of affairs, but the principal's superiors would not

The sign at the entrance to Luberta's school

be thrilled by the prospect. A principal's role in general terms is to be the educational leader in the building, and there are numerous definitions of what this means. In fact, to say that principals exert educational leadership is a rather idealized statement of what they do. The following discussion of principals begins by examining what principals must accomplish in order to keep their jobs.

Coordination and Control

Principals are middle managers in a bureaucracy. That means they manage or supervise subordinates—teachers—but are in turn accountable to their superiors in the central office. In this relationship they are within their own school buildings like a captain of a ship, responsible for everything that occurs there. Put bluntly, every time someone messes up, every time a teacher does something wrong, the principal's head is on the block. With increased numbers and specialization among teaching personnel comes the increased need for coordination to prevent a school from pursuing divergent goals. Most simply, a principal's task is to coordinate and control aspects within the school building that keep the school moving in a definite direction with the fewest number of problems.

As a middle manager a principal receives at least three role expectations: (1) The board-superintendent-central office expects that general policies will be carried out in coordination with all other school units, that order will be maintained and trouble avoided, and that mandates passed down from higher state and federal authorities will be implemented. In many districts the central office also genuinely expects the principal to exert instructional leadership. (2) Teachers, the principal's subordinates, expect the principal to buffer them from irate parents and the central office—including the paper work that often comes with external mandates, to provide discipline, to invite their input into the implementation of policies mandated by the central office, and to be pleasant and hand out praise to the faculty (Lortie, 1975, pp. 196–200). (3) Parents want good education, but they may also want special consideration for their children. These special requests, of course, are at cross-purposes with standard policies advocated by the board, the superintendent, and the teachers' own needs to maintain uniform student classroom expectations and behaviors. The principal is, literally, in the middle.

Sandy recognizes this status of the principal. In the midst of a discussion of conflicts with administrators over disciplining of students she says:

> From the principal's perspective, I think they have to account to everyone, and teachers don't. So [in disciplinary situations] they need to do something that is satisfactory to the teacher, to please us; for the student, for the student's well-being; for the parents; for the administrators over them; and for the school board. So they've got a lot of people to please. I try to keep that in mind when I get irritated with them.

Gertrude McPherson (1979) gives us further understanding of the relationships between principals and teachers:

> The teacher, in filling her role, views the principal as a free agent, able to act in her interest, to protect her from parents, to support her against students, and to act as a partner in coalitions when asked — but to keep hands off when not asked. The teacher may be vaguely aware, but not fully realize, that the principal also has to juggle, that he is often more vulnerable than she to initial pressure from powerful citizens, parents, or the school board. Restrictions on the principal are not readily apparent to a teacher, but even when she senses them she often needs to believe that the principal is powerful in order to fix blame for her frustrations. (p. 235)

Thus, the principal has a problem that few teachers see. He or she is expected to coordinate and control but often lacks the formal authority that goes along with these responsibilities. Think back to a familiar issue discussed in Chapter 7: power, authority, and control. Principals, like teachers, vary considerably in how they carry out their roles. Many teachers can tell lots of "principal stories" about the good ones and the bad ones under whom they have served. A principal's predicament is similar to that of a teacher. Formal authority is too narrow a base; for real effectiveness one needs to develop informal and functional authority.

Teachers resent principals who use formal authority alone. Because it is so limited, principals operating from this base tend to be authoritarian, are prone to use close supervision, and ultimately invoke coercive power. Larry talks of teacher resentment of these kinds of principal orientations:

> I think problems come about with a principal in a classroom when the principal has a dogmatic idea of what teaching and learning is and the teacher has a different idea of what teaching and learning is. The principal trying to impose his idea about teaching and learning upon that teacher is a real problem, especially when it can be demonstrated that students are learning with the teacher's methods.

Teachers also resent principals who abdicate authority, who do little or nothing to exert leadership. Larry again comments: "So often I see principals interested in simply making things run smoothly. To me a bad principal is somebody who just wants things to run smoothly."

The respected principals have earned important informal and functional authority to supplement that which comes with their formal position. They lead in ways that get the tasks done but also show personal concern for their faculties. These principals often have even and predictable dispositions. They are authentic people and leaders. They listen; they are accessible; they are often knowledgeable about pedagogy and curriculum. These principals have a vision of what their schools should be and of how to get there. When principals behave in these ways, teachers grant them functional authority to buttress their formal authority. They are respected, and they are able to lead despite restrictive union contracts, conflicting sets of role expectations, and other constraints.

Several of the case study teachers indicated a strong desire to receive feedback, especially positive feedback, from principals. Positive feedback shows concern for a teacher and it helps to earn functional authority for the principal. As Larry said about his first principal: "[He] had an ability to motivate and to pat people on the back. He liked positive reinforcement. That's stuck with me." Elsewhere he continued:

> The principal is so important for the teacher psychologically because you don't have kids coming by every day patting you on the back saying what a great job you are doing. Other teachers usually don't come around to tell you what a great job you are doing either. You've got to have someone with some kind of authority come by periodically and tell you, "Hey, you're okay. You're doing pretty well." I think a principal can be very important in this respect, especially in a teacher's formative years.

Clearly, Larry has higher respect for principals who show him respect and consideration. Ruth values a principal who listens because she likes to use her principal as a sounding board for new ideas.

> Once I had enough self-confidence that I didn't feel that by going to a principal I was admitting I wasn't top quality, I have found my principals very helpful. They can help in discussing children that I worry about, or curriculum decisions if I'm planning something new, or by just reacting to my pros and cons by questioning. Another thing I have learned is that every question they ask you is not a put-down. Many teachers will say, "I tried to do this, but he just kept asking me this, this, and this." You have to realize that you're going to the principal to brainstorm, and if you look at it like that, you can come out with ideas that are helpful.

When teachers propose a new idea, principals must ask about the proposal because ultimately they are responsible for the outcome. How principals listen and do the asking, however, makes a big difference in how teachers perceive them and in the amount of authority teachers grant them.

Principals may lose as well as gain functional authority. One of the quickest ways to lose authority is by failing to support teachers. Teachers see providing adequate disciplinary support and buffering them from unreasonable parents as two important aspects of a principal's job. Luberta feels strong disciplinary support from her principal. He is always close at hand. Jacquie notes: "I see the main job of the principal as supporting teachers with discipline. That's just the Number 1 problem altogether—discipline and backing the teachers." Sandy has experienced inconsistency in disciplinary support, in part because there are multiple principals in her school, one for each grade level.

If I have a junior and senior in the same class, and they are accused of the same crime, one might get a three-day suspension and the other might get a slap on the wrist. And the kids come into my class wanting to know, "Is that fair?" No, it's not fair.

Principals perceived to be inconsistent by teachers and students have less authority. At one point in his career Larry resigned both the departmental chairmanship and the sponsorship of the student council because of the lack of support and inconsistency he felt from his principal at that time.

His was administration by memo. He was real wishy-washy. You never knew where you stood. You thought you had some input into decisions, but you found later it was just a big sham. I wouldn't put up with that kind of thing. I simply resigned.

And there are times when Sandy does not perceive herself as being buffered from parents with complaints. From time to time she feels that she is "expected to defend" herself. In some cases she would prefer to deal directly with parents rather than have the principal act as an intermediary. But for a principal to act as Sandy suggests would be to abdicate part of the role for which he or she is held accountable by superiors.

Instructional Leadership

Having considered the activities principals must perform, the discussion returns to the more ideal conception of principals as educational and instructional leaders. There are principals who are instructional leaders, but not every principal can be so described. The experience of having an educational leader is noteworthy in the career of a teacher, as indicated by Ruth and Larry.

Recall from Chapter 1 that Ruth's second teaching position was in the city of St. Louis and that she took over a rambunctious class of second graders who by midyear had experienced 13 different substitutes. Edna Murphy, Ruth's principal, was a teaching principal; she taught first grade full time and also performed the duties of principal. Of her Ruth says:

She was one person whom I respected very much. I feel she really taught me to be a teacher. I was very impressed by how she could leave her first-grade room to do her principaling duties, and the children would continue to work very, very hard. She was also very willing to share, to critique, and to answer my questions. And if I came back to tell her that this particular thing didn't work, she could tell me why it didn't work.

Recall also from Chapter 1 that Larry's first principal left a lasting mark on him. At the secondary level where teachers are subject matter specialists, the kind of direct instructional assistance Ruth received from Edna Murphy is less likely to occur. Nonetheless, Larry's first principal was an educational leader in different ways. He stressed the importance of positive reinforcement for students, in part by modeling such behavior with his teachers. He also encouraged his faculty to experiment, to innovate, and to risk, knowing full well that they would sometimes fail. But he backed them up when they took the risks. Larry feels that having this principal at the beginning of his career helped him to be a better, more confident teacher.

In some respects excellent principals are much like excellent teachers: they rise above the minimal requirements of their jobs; they put themselves into the role in a way that transcends its stereotypic dimensions; they define a personal vision of the school and act to move it in that direction.

In their book, *The Effective Principal,* Blumberg and Greenfield (1980) present case studies of eight effective principals much like this book has presented five excellent teachers. They conclude that each principal is different and that the specific orientation and style used by one principal in a particular school would not necessarily be effective if transferred to any of the other seven schools they studied. As with good teachers, there is no set of behaviors that can be followed mechanistically to produce effective educational leadership. Blumberg and Greenfield (1980) did conclude, however, that all eight principals shared three dispositions: (1) Each established a personal vision of where the school should be moving and how, realistically, to get it there. (2) Each was proactive or seized initiative rather than waiting for directions from others. (3) Each was resourceful in getting what he or she needed to fulfill the vision.

Others who have observed and interviewed principals find that effective principals influence two dimensions of the school, school climate and instructional organization (Dwyer et al., 1983). School climate is analogous to the school's personality. It communicates expectations for all members of the school, and it sets the tone. A positive climate might include a high sense of morale among teachers; high expectations for teacher and student achievement; respect for all persons regardless of official status; and a tradition of teacher-principal communication in matters of curriculum and pedagogy. Less positive climates are, of course, imaginable.

Research studies indicate that a principal is the most important person in setting the climate of the school. The climate in turn has important positive or negative effects on teachers, students, and classroom learning. When asked how important the principal is in setting the tone or climate for the school, Jacquie replied, "Extremely important, extremely. The principal can make or break the school." And Larry noted, "The principal has got to set an intellectual climate that makes you want to be a good teacher."

A more recently developed concept closely related to establishing climate is cultural leadership (Kottkamp, 1984). In acting as a cultural leader a principal uses symbolic means to establish, maintain, and indicate shared norms and values in a school. Symbolic means may include creating and telling stories, sagas, or myths about exemplary teachers or students who embody desired values and behaviors; creating rituals that convey essential purposes such as student academic and service awards ceremonies (this is always done in athletics); and recognition dinners to honor outstanding teachers. Cultural leadership conveys purpose, goals, values, and expectations to teachers, parents, and students. Symbolic leadership can provide teachers with much support.

The other dimension of schooling that principals can affect is instructional organization. Specifically principals can affect such instructional issues as: time-on-task, or student engaged time, in academics; class size and composition; student grouping practices; curriculum practices including pace, sequence, and content coverage; evaluation and feedback about instruction; and instructional task characteristics such as clarity, joint problem solving, and active student participation (Bossert et al., 1982).

Although all principals may affect these dimensions of institutional organization, how they go about it matters. There are a number of popular approaches that can be adapted and sensitively integrated to bring about change among individual teachers in a particular school circumstance. On the other hand, they can be applied in an externally imposed, mechanistic, or technocratic fashion with little sensitivity to the positive or negative effects they may have on a teacher's instructional and learning environment. How aspects of instructional organization for individual teachers are affected by the increasing number of external mandates is largely dependent upon the actions taken by principals. Principals who are experts in pedagogy, learning theory, and curriculum are in a better position to influence aspects of instructional organization in useful, sensitive, and positive ways than principals who lack such a knowledge base. Some principals even take the risk of buffering their teachers from district mandated programs or approaches that in their professional judgments are likely to have deleterious effects on instruction and learning.

The instructional time-on-task monitoring system in Luberta's school can once again serve as an example. The intention of this program is to reduce the amount of noninstructional, nonproductive time in the school day. Luberta believes strongly in the rationale behind the program; however, it is understandable that the program creates some tension for her. Her principal, Mr. Benning, knows that good teaching cannot be created mechanistically. He demonstrates to his teachers that he is in full agreement with the *intention* of the district program and wants teachers to follow it, but he also understands that teachers will have to apply professional judgment and discretion if the spirit and purpose of the program are to be achieved. Knowing full well that he does not function optimally under externally imposed frameworks, Mr. Benning consciously strives to provide his teachers with the freedom to accomplish program goals through creative use of their own expertise. Therefore, Mr. Benning does not impose the program on her in a way that would create negative effects on her personalized, effective teaching style.

CONCLUSION

This chapter has presented a selected number of external influences that directly affect the work of teachers in classrooms. With the growing complexity of the social, political, and economic order has come a growing complexity of the educational systems and the needs to control and coordinate them. Three types of governance have had legal, formal influence upon the fashioning and refashioning of public education. The relative importance of the different types has changed over time and continues to change. Extralegal sources have also affected educational policy and operation; these too change with time.

At the local level, where as a new teacher you are most likely to experience the direct effects of influences from outside your classroom, are the school board and superintendent as well as the building principal.

As you think about becoming a teacher and spend time in schools, try to be aware of the external forces that permeate the boundaries of the classroom. Recall also the conclusion of Chapter 1 in which C. Wright Mills was cited. He argued that society affects the individual but the individual also affects society. Although the case study teachers have been influenced by their own teachers and are influenced in their classrooms daily by various levels of the larger society, they, as teachers, in turn now influence the society of today and tomorrow.

There are many more forces in the social order influencing schools and teachers than those mentioned in this book including: technology, especially TV and computers; demographic changes; economic cycles; racism; news media; changing parental and student attitudes and life styles; liberation of women; changes in teacher unions and associations; child abuse; drugs and alcohol; violence; vandalism; and teen pregnancy. You and your instructor may wish to discuss these and other influences. You might also ask teachers about how external forces affect their daily lives in classrooms. What you will find is that to be a teacher is to deal with a universe that goes far beyond the confines of the classroom walls. The decision to become a teacher should involve serious consideration of this reality.

ACTIVITIES

1. Observe, interview, and look for documentary evidence of types and sources of external control that affect the teacher. Sources of control might include federal, state, local, and extralegal. Within the district look for influences from the superintendent; other central office personnel, principals and supervisors; and students and parents.
2. Look at curricular guides, student and teacher handbooks, union contracts, attendance recording systems, and various paperwork requirements as means of coordinating and controlling efforts for the purpose of reaching mutually held goals.

3. You or your instructor may want to research in depth one or more external influences or governmental regulations that affect the conduct of school and the classroom processes carried out by teachers. Examples of topics are found in the chapter conclusion.

4. Interview several teachers concerning their perceptions of their principal. Ask what they want from a principal and whether they get it. If they have experienced several principals over time, ask about similarities and differences. Ask whether their principals have been real instructional and educational leaders or more oriented toward management and control of building, paper, and people.

5. Interview a principal. Ask what he or she wants from teachers. Ask what central office, parents and teachers want of him or her. Discuss your findings with peers and your instructor in an attempt to gain a better understanding of the role of the principal and the forces that act upon that office.

6. Ask teachers about the influence of the superintendent upon them.

7. Investigate and discuss current legislative proposals or executive actions at the federal, state, or local levels that are likely to influence teachers in the school where you are doing your observations. Also investigate recent judicial decisions or cases in progress that may have important educational impact.

8. Observe a board of education meeting, or better yet, several in one or more than one community. Examine the kinds of issues discussed at board meetings. How will these decisions affect classroom teachers? You might want to share your observations with other students who observed different boards. What themes were similar in the deliberations of those boards? What issues were unique? Was the style of the various boards (e.g., the emotional tone and the member-member and member-superintendent interaction) similar or different? Look for the relationship between the kind of community and the kinds of expectations and control exercised within the schools of that community.

REFERENCES AND SOURCES

Allen, H. P. (1950). *The federal government and education.* New York: McGraw-Hill.

Aufderheide, J. A. (1976). Educational interest groups and the state legislature. In R. F. Campbell & T. L. Mazzoni, Jr. (Eds.). *State policy making for the public schools* (pp. 176–216). Berkeley, CA: McCutchan.

Bestor, A. E. (1953). *Educational wastelands: The retreat from learning in our public schools.* Urbana, IL: University of Illinois Press.

Blumberg, A., & Greenfield, W. (1980). *The effective principal: Perspectives in school leadership.* Boston: Allyn & Bacon.

Bossert, S. T. et al. (1982). The instructional management role of the principal. *Educational Administration Quarterly, 18*(3), 34–64.

Boyer, E. L. (1983). *High school: A report on secondary education in America*. New York: Harper & Row.

Campbell, R. F. et al. (1985) *The organization and control of American schools* (5th ed.). Columbus, OH: Charles E. Merrill.

Deal, T. E., & Kennedy, A. A. (1981). *Corporate cultures: The rites and rituals of corporate life*. Reading, MA: Addison-Wesley.

Dywer, D. C. et al. (1983). *Five principals in action: Perspectives on instructional management*. San Francisco: Far West Regional Educational Laboratory.

Gross, N. (1958). *Who runs our schools?* New York: Wiley.

Howsam, R. B. et al. (1976). *Educating a profession*. Washington, DC: American Association of Colleges for Teacher Education.

Kimbrough, R. B. (1969). An informal arrangement for influence over basic policy. In A. Rosenthal (Ed.), *Governing education: A reader on politics, power, and public school policy*. New York: Doubleday.

Kottkamp, R. B. (1984). The principal as cultural leader. *Planning and Changing. 15(3)*, 152–160.

Lieberman, M. (1956). *Education as a profession*. Englewood Cliffs, NJ: Prentice-Hall.

Lieberman, M. (1960). *The future of public education*. Chicago: University of Chicago Press.

Lortie, D. C. (1975). *Schoolteacher: A sociological study*. Chicago: University of Chicago Press.

McPherson, G. (1979). What principals should know about teachers. In D. A. Erickson & T. L. Reller (Eds.), *The principal in metropolitan schools*. Berkeley, CA: McCutchan.

Plisko, V. W. (Ed.). (1984). The condition of education 1984. Washington, DC: U.S. Government Printing Office.

Quattlebaum, C. A. (1951). *Federal educational activities and educational issues before congress*. Washington, DC: U.S. Government Printing Office.

13

CAREER, WORK REWARDS, AND LIFE STYLE

INTRODUCTION

Work is a central element in adult lives. Excitement and satisfaction from work make life richer and more meaningful. Negative feelings about work or a sense of being trapped in something that has lost its excitement can color life with drab hues and undercut emotional health. All occupations put limits on life style whether they be limits of money, prestige and respect, or time to spend with family and in other pursuits.

This chapter considers teaching as an occupation and as a career.* It is important to take a close look at how becoming a teacher can affect your life, both immediately and during the course of a career. The issues examined are: the career structure of teaching, proposed changes in the current structure, work rewards and frustrations, and stages of development within a teaching career.

This chapter relies heavily on Lortie's *Schoolteacher* (1975), and upon the authors' recent research that updates Lortie's twenty-year-old data. In addition, it

*Throughout this text the terms *occupation* and *profession* have been used interchangeably. There is, in fact, an argument within the field as to whether or not teaching has a sufficiently developed knowledge base and sufficient autonomy to be considered a profession in the same sense as medicine or law. This book's position is that teaching is a profession. This is in contrast to Dan Lortie who uses the term *occupation* to describe teaching in *Schoolteacher* (1975). Since this chapter draws heavily upon Lortie's work, his terminology will predominate.

relies heavily upon interviews with the five case study teachers to make abstractions concrete. As you read, think about (1) how the structure of teaching is different from other occupations, (2) what rewards, frustrations, and changes others have experienced in teaching, and (3) how the career experiences of others resonate with your own career interests and definition of self.

THE STRUCTURE OF TEACHING CAREERS

The chapter begins with a focus on the absence of a career line in teaching and turns to Lortie's (1975) analysis of teaching for the basic argument.

Unstaged and Front-loaded Careers

When occupational rewards are discussed they often center on earnings. One approach is to look at the *income profile* of an occupation, or the typical pattern of earnings over the work life of an individual. Such profiles are structural and are related to the kind of organization in which the work is done. Some organizations, such as major corporations, are *tall*, that is they contain many levels through which it is possible for an employee to move. A beginning manager in such a corporation, for example, may start with a relatively low income, but he or she also has the possibility of moving up through a number of levels. Each upward movement may bring a major status shift and be accompanied by a sharp increase in income. Yet the kind of work he or she does remains management; it is simply pursued at a higher level and entails more responsibility. Thus, a manager in a corporation may have a career with a set of upward movements that bring significantly higher status and income. Further, the income profile of a successful manager will be in stages, that is, it will resemble a set of stairs or alternating plateaus and steep inclines. Not all managers will be successful; not all will have careers or staged income profiles over the course of their work lives; but the structure of management in the corporate world at least makes staged careers and income profiles possible.

The situation in teaching is very different. As Lortie (1975) explains: "Classroom teaching is notably unstaged" (p. 82). Rather than resembling a stair, the income profile of most teachers resembles an inclined plane with a gentle upward slope. It typically evolves from a uniform salary schedule with relatively small increments based on longevity and earning additional graduate or in-service credits. In addition the income profile is *front-loaded*. This means that a beginnner knows what he or she will be able to earn over the years and can see that with seniority the often fixed increments actually represent increasingly lower percentage gains. In essence, "one begins at a high level relative to one's ultimate earning potential" (Lortie, 1975, p. 84). Further, once the threshold of tenure is reached, "The status of the young tenured teacher is not appreciably different from that of the highly experienced old-timer" (Lortie, 1975, p. 85). More years of experience do not normally move one into a revered group of senior practitioners whose advice is eagerly sought by the less experienced. Lortie concludes that compared to other kinds of middle-class work, teaching is front-loaded, unstaged, and relatively careerless.

That the occupation of teaching is structured the way it is in comparison to so many other forms of middle-class work is not the result of individual teacher actions. Nor is it likely that individual teachers can change the situation very much. Rather, the explanation for the existing pattern in teaching is structural and historical.

Lortie traces the unstaged career path of teachers to the nineteenth century when school bureaucracies were developed in cities. A major problem faced by school boards was the constant need to recruit new teachers to staff schools that kept growing because of the immigrant influx. Thus the system of remuneration was focused on attracting new teachers rather than retaining those who were already in the work force. Turnover rates were relatively high. Even today, roughly half the teachers who enter teaching in a given year leave by the end of their fifth or sixth year of work. With the high turnover rates, teacher associations and unions have been comprised of high proportions of relatively young teachers. The bargaining strategies of these organizations often reflects the imbalance toward younger members. Consequently, even the organizations representing teachers have traditionally pressed for higher beginning salaries rather than for comparatively greater remuneration for experienced colleagues.

Only within the last ten years with the advent of declining enrollments that reduced the number of younger members have teacher organizations begun to trade off emphasis on beginning salaries for raising the salaries at the experienced end of the salary schedule. Further, the attempts to raise the high end of the schedules have met with resistance from school boards. From the perspective of many board members, faculties composed of increasingly experienced teachers are viewed more as "expensive" than "better" when compared to the period when there were many more novices who tended to keep overall expenditures lower. After all, board members are the ones who keep asking their fellow citizens to pay higher taxes. A new teacher costs about half as much as an experienced teacher costs. With an impending teacher shortage in the 1990s it is possible that there will be a shift back toward emphasis on higher beginning salaries in order to attract persons who might choose occupations other than teaching.

The relatively unstaged and front-loaded income profile of teaching has caused problems but has kept the cost of public education at a level that taxpayers would support. From the perspective of the accepted goals of schooling the largest problems have been in maintaining the motivation and effort of midcareer and older teachers. Two important motivating factors related to staged career structures are missing in teaching. First, staging creates institutionalized delayed gratification. Younger people are led to expend higher levels of effort in the hopes that they will eventually reach the same heights as the role models they see around them in the organization. Second, staging helps to "balance the relationships among effort, capacity, and reward" (Lortie, 1975, p. 85). Not everyone climbs the ladder to the top, nor is all the climbing "fair." But to the degree that those who are rewarded are perceived to be those who have talent and have expended effort, the reward system is viewed as legitimate and serves as motivation to invest oneself in work at a high rate.

The motivational and legitimizing aspects of a staged career path are absent in teaching. Because tenured teachers are extremely difficult to remove (barring some gross moral breach) and pay raises are automatic, teachers are fairly free to choose anywhere from a low to a high level of engagement in their work without changing the prospects for a known level of income. Lortie (1975) writes:

> The system of career rewards, in sum, works most satisfactorily for those who give teaching less than full commitment; "gainers" are teachers who plan on short-term or less than full-time engagement. We are witnessing consequences of a historical pattern; the career system in teaching continues to favor recruitment over retention and low rather than high involvement. (p. 99)

Thus, teachers who receive rewards do not always do so legitimately in the view of teachers who may actually work harder. Witness Jacquie discussing some of her peers: "I see so many teachers who aren't doing their jobs. I hate to say it, but I can understand the public saying, 'Well, we want to get some quality for our money if we're going to raise their salaries.' "

Getting Ahead by Getting Out

Not only does the present structure of teaching cause problems in keeping up the motivational levels of some who have job security, but it may actually encourage some very good teachers who seek financial and status improvement to leave the classroom. Lortie (1975) states: "The main opportunity for making major status gains rests in leaving classroom work for full-time administrative work" (p. 99). Staging in an educational career occurs at the point where one leaves teaching; a teaching career itself is unstaged.

By no means do all teachers seek to leave the classroom, nor are those who do seek to leave necessarily good teachers. Nevertheless, it is not possible to make a large status and financial step while remaining in the classroom. Therefore, numbers of teachers seek to get ahead by getting out of the classroom. Some step immediately into full-time administrative work. Others move into part-time quasi-administrative work or positions outside of the classroom in hope of eventually moving into full-time administrative work. Some teachers seek to become assistant principals, principals, central office or districtwide coordinators. Others move into department chairships or into guidance counseling, some with the goal of moving from there to full-time administration. Coaching has also traditionally been an activity that provides visibility and a certain degree of status and public recognition that is not available from the work teachers do within the classroom.

None of our case study teachers intends to enter full-time administrative work. Larry had been social studies department head, but he resigned five years ago because of a principal, now gone, under whom he found it difficult to work. At present, at least, he remains content as a classroom teacher.

The situation for Jacquie is more complex and illustrates another problem with the structure of teaching for many individuals. Jacquie is the activities coordinator in Robert E. Lee Junior High, but she did not seek the post. It started three years ago when her principal asked her to take over the sponsorship of the student council. Recall her description of the position:

> I assist the principal, direct the activities program. I coordinate and schedule club activities. My student council is responsible for most of the major activities—fund raising for schoolwide events; social activities, like dances and the prom for ninth graders; charitable ones, like the United Way; helping initiate new clubs; promoting school spirit and pride. . . . This year I'm in charge of the newspaper, which I use as a means of unifying the school and boosting morale of students and teachers. . . . In my school you have the administrative staff, and the guidance staff, and then you have me. I'm kind of in between a classroom teacher and an administrator.

For this extraclassroom work, Jacquie receives $500 a year. She commments: "It's nothing to speak of. It's supplementary just like the coaches get." The money is not important but, to Jacquie, the position is.

> I now think that this [position] is why I have survived so happily at this school—the support from the principal along with the respect I receive from the students. . . . They often treat me differently from a regular teacher. . . . I'm the one who organizes the major activities. . . . Of course, they don't want to get me angry or upset because I might say no. I like the extra duties and the respect I get from the students because of that particular position, and I don't know that I would want to give it up. . . . I do it because it's a challenge to do something that's successful in getting students to participate.

Being the activities coordinator also puts Jacquie in a unique position as a communication link between the administration and teachers. Because of the nature of her position she must work closely with the principal. Other teachers know this and seek her out to gain information about issues that involve his decisions. At the same time she is in a special and trusted position to convey information to the principal about how the faculty is feeling. In a way she serves as a barometer of how relationships in the school are going.

However, the important issue to understand about the activity coordinatorship for Jacquie is that it has varied her duties. She remains a classroom teacher and likes it, but she also does other things both during the school day and after school that break the sense of isolation that some teachers feel, give her a change of pace, a differential status, new responsibilities, and a challenge. She explains:

> If I had stayed with teaching only French and Spanish, I don't know if I would have liked it as much. I might have gotten bored. I've been teaching the same subject for 12 years at the same level, and it can get boring after a while. If I didn't have the activities, I probably would be less satisfied.

When asked whether she aspired to become an administrator, Jacquie said probably not because she would not like the paperwork and because "I wouldn't have any contact with the students, and it's the students that I enjoy. They're the ones who are really fun." This position is an interesting compromise that both gets her out of the classroom to have new and varied experiences and keeps her teaching because her energy and satisfaction levels are up. The additional money she receives does not make her career staged financially. However, she experiences more staging in the status she receives within the school and in the responsibilities and variation in work she experiences. So Jacquie has found a unique resolution to some of the dilemmas of the nondifferentiated position and unstaged career of classroom teacher. This resolution, however, like leaving to become an administrator, is not open to the majority of teachers, since only one such position exists at Lee Junior High and comparable positions do not exist in many schools.

Recent Reform Proposals: Merit Pay and Career Ladders

Recently, national commission reports and the tenor of public opinion have supported two plans that address some of the problems of motivation and work quality created by the unstaged and front-loaded income profile in teaching. The two plans are merit pay proposals of differing types and career ladders to which differential salary increments are tied.

In general, merit pay systems provide added salary for teachers whose performance is judged to be exemplary for a given year. Issues constituting merit pay proposals differ considerably. They include whether the payment is a lump sum or is added to the base for figuring future salary; whether merit is restricted to a certain percentage of teachers; whether the criteria for merit include only classroom performance, nonclassroom performance as well, or test scores; whether the evaluators are administrators, peers, students, or some combination of the three. The possibilities for combinations of these issues make for great complexity. Some school districts are implementing school-level merit systems whereby all teachers in a school judged meritorious receive merit increments.

Career ladder proposals differ in that they are not just concerned with distribution of monetary rewards. Rather, a career ladder sets up differentiated levels through which a teacher might pass in a career. As teachers move up the ladder by proven performance, they gain additional status, financial reward, and added or varied responsibilities. These responsibilities often include mentoring and supervising novices, demonstration teaching, curriculum development, and administration. At the same time, most of these proposals keep the teacher in the classroom as a teacher for a good portion of his or her time. Such proposals reward teachers with money, recognition, and responsibility for being master teachers. Career ladders, then, appear closer to the kind of staging found in corporate management or in the sort of differentiated activities Jacquie was able to pursue as activity coordinator. As with managers who remain managers while moving to higher levels of status and responsibility, career ladders allow teachers to remain teachers while moving to higher levels of status and responsibility.

There is disagreement, however, between the general public and teachers over the proposals to institute merit pay and career ladders. As part of the sixteenth annual Gallup Poll of the Public's Attitudes toward the Public Schools (G. H. Gallup, 1984) a representative sample of citizens responded to questions on career ladders and merit pay. On the career ladder question, with possible responses of *approve,* *disapprove,* and *no opinion,* 75 percent of the 1,515 adults interviewed in their homes approved of the idea of career ladders in which salary increases would be "based primarily upon demonstrated effectiveness in the classroom." On the merit pay question with the same three response categories, 65 percent of all respondents and 75 percent of those who had "heard or read anything about these programs" approved of the notion of merit pay. The general public clearly favors such proposals.

Teachers, on the other hand, do not view merit pay as a positive solution to educational problems. As part of the first Gallup Poll of Teachers' Attitudes toward the Public Schools (G. H. Gallup, 1984) 813 teachers responded to a mailed survey posing many of the same questions that had been asked of the general public several months earlier. On essentially the same question about merit pay, 32 percent favored whereas 62 percent opposed the general idea. Much of the teacher negativism toward merit pay proposals stems from the belief that subjectivity or favoritism rather than objective exemplary performance is likely to be the real basis for merit pay increments. Survey research conducted among 2,719 randomly selected teachers in Dade County, Florida, shows the degree of acceptability or unacceptability to teachers of various evaluation methods for merit rating. These data may be seen in Table 13.1. All of the proposed methods of evaluation received

Table 13.1   Responses of 2,719 randomly selected Dade County, Florida, teachers to
merit pay questions on 1984 survey (in percentages)

Many segments of society advocate merit or differentiated pay for teachers. Various pay systems are proposed. Please evaluate each of the following potential elements of a merit-differentiated pay system. Indicate whether (1) the element is unacceptable to you, (2) you are neutral toward the element, or (3) the element is necessary for your acceptance.

	Unacceptable to Me	Neutral	Necessary for Me
Merit raises assigned to a specified percentage of teachers in the system	80	14	6
Merit raises available to all teachers who meet the established criteria	22	17	61
Merit raises for exemplary classroom performance only	44	29	27
Merit raises for additional nonclassroom responsibilities only	69	20	11
Merit raises for both classroom performance and additional nonclassroom responsibilities	38	27	35
Additional pay tied to advancement through a career ladder of differentiated levels of duties, responsibilities, and months under contract (e.g., apprentice, senior, and master teacher levels)	24	26	50

Various evaluation criteria for merit-differentiated raises are also proposed. As in the question above, please evaluate the following criteria as potential components of a merit pay decision process.

	Unacceptable to Me	Neutral	Necessary for Me
Scores on teacher tests (e.g., National Teachers Exam)	61	25	14
Master's degree in a subject field or similar formal degree achievement	30	21	49
Classroom performance evaluated by administrators only	53	25	22
Classroom performance evaluated by fellow teachers only	62	26	12
Classroom performance evaluated by a team including an administrator, a fellow teacher, and a specialist in a subject field or in teaching methods	24	23	53
Student test scores	67	20	13

SOURCE: Unpublished results from Provenzo E. F., Jr., Cohn, M. M., & Kottkamp, R.B. *Teacher Work Incentives and Rewards: A Twenty Year Perspective.* National Institute of Education Research Project, 1985.

higher percentages of *unacceptable* than *acceptable* responses. Performance evaluations based on peer ratings and student test scores were the most unacceptable means of evaluation for this sample of teachers. The Metropolitan Life Survey of the American Teacher (Louis Harris & Associates, 1984), an interview study of 1,981 teachers, yielded a more positive response to the general question of merit pay (see Table 13.2). However, the wording of the question contained the phrase "if a teacher's merit can be judged on an objective standard." Research data indicate that teachers do not really believe that such decisions would be reached objectively. The Metropolitan survey also indicated that slightly less than half the teachers believed that merit pay would help to make teacher salaries comparable with other professions, and fewer yet believed that it would help to attract and retain good teachers.

Whether or not teachers like merit pay or career ladder proposals may have little to do with whether or not the reward systems are implemented. Some state legislatures have already or are in the process of mandating such programs. For the basic issues of occupational structure raised in this chapter, the real question is: Even if these proposals are implemented, will they change the basic career path available to teachers by making teaching more staged and less front-loaded? To make real changes in the potential career paths of teachers—major increments rather than a few hundred dollars—will cost taxpayers significant amounts. Thus merit pay may come, with attendant loud protests from teachers, without seriously modifying the career structure of teaching compared to other occupations. These are empirical questions that will be answered in the coming years.

Table 13.2   Teachers' attitudes toward merit pay (responses in percentages)

For each of the following statements about merit pay, please tell me whether you agree strongly, agree somewhat, disagree somewhat, or disagree strongly.

Number of Respondents—1,981	Agree Strongly	Agree Somewhat	Disagree Somewhat	Disagree Strongly	Not Sure
Merit pay could work if a teacher's merit can be judged on an objective standard.	34	37	16	1	
Merit pay would help make teachers' salaries more comparable with salaries in other professions.	18	31	20	30	2
Merit pay is an effective way of attracting and retaining good teachers in the profession.	14	25	21	38	1

SOURCE: Louis Harris and Associates, Inc., *The Metropolitan Life Survey of the American Teacher,* The Metropolitan Life Insurance Company, 1984.

The Carnegie Forum's Task Force
on Teaching as a Profession

In addition to the specific proposals for merit pay and career ladders that emanated from several reports on educational reform in the 1980s, the report of the Carnegie Forum's Task Force on Teaching as a Profession in the spring of 1986 called for a restructuring of the entire teaching profession. Chaired by Lewis M. Branscomb, Chief Scientist and Vice-President of International Business Machines Corporation, the task force declared that America's future is dependent upon a more enlightened and thinking citizenry and that the classroom teacher is the key to achieving that end.

> Textbooks cannot do it. Principals cannot do it. Directives from state authorities cannot do it. Only the people with whom the students come in contact every day can do it. (Carnegie Forum on Education, 1986, p. 46)

The report then suggested a plan for the "transformation of the environment for teaching" that would attract and empower the kinds of teachers needed to meet the challenge. Among the sweeping changes recommended were:

- Creation of a National Board for Teaching Standards that would set high standards and certify those who have reached them
- Restructuring of schools so that teachers would have more authority but, at the same time, be responsible for student progress
- Restructuring of the teaching force with a new category of Lead Teachers who would take a leadership role in redesigning schools and in teacher training
- Raising of requirements in teacher education so that a bachelor's degree in the arts and sciences would be a prerequisite for the professional study of teaching
- Development of new graduate programs leading to a Master of Teaching degree
- Recruitment of minority youngsters for teaching
- Making of teachers' salaries and opportunities competitive with those in other professions (Carnegie Forum on Education, pp. 45–47)

These ideas and ideals are now under debate, and their eventual implementation could dramatically alter the nature of the profession. As in the case of proposals for merit pay and career ladders, however, only time will tell.

WORK REWARDS

Having considered the current structure of the occupation and recent proposals to change that structure, the discussion now turns to what is known about the major rewards available to teachers. This discussion again draws heavily on the research Dan Lortie conducted 20 years ago as well as on a recent replication of his research in Dade County, Florida, and the five case study teachers.

Lortie (1975) describes three major types of rewards available to teachers: extrinsic, ancillary, and psychic or intrinsic.

Extrinsic Rewards

Lortie (1975) defines *extrinsic rewards* as:

> what we usually think of as the "earnings" attached to a role and involves money, income, a level of prestige, and power over others. These earnings are "extrinsic" in the sense that they exist independently of the individual who occupies the role; since they are experienced by all incumbents, they have an "objective" quality. (p. 101)

The extrinsic rewards available to teachers are not great. Teachers are typically neither wealthy nor famous. Beginning teacher salaries are often below the levels of other occupations whose beginning members have invested an equal amount in education and preparation. Because of the unstaged nature of teaching, mid- and later career salary differences between teaching and other occupations are even greater than at the beginning. Neither does teaching provide much of a base of prestige or power. Teaching is performed among children in isolation from most adults in the community. Some excellent teachers enjoy community-wide reputations for their fine work as parents sing their praises over the years, but this is not the typical lot of teachers.

Only the material benefits theme of the five major attractions to teaching is related to extrinsic rewards, and Lortie argues that there is a whole cultural explanation as to why extrinsic rewards have not been emphasized in teaching.

> The traditions of teaching make people who seek money, prestige, or power somewhat suspect; the characteristic style in public education is to mute personal ambition. The service ideal has extolled the virtue of giving more than one receives; the model teacher has been "dedicated." (p. 102)

Since not seeking high extrinsic rewards has been tied to the moral status that teachers have traditionally been accorded in the culture, it can be hypothesized that the increased militancy of teachers in pushing for extrinsic rewards through their unions and associations may have tarnished some of the special nonmaterial-based status teachers have possessed. Strikes are especially injurious to the public's view of a service occupation.

Ancillary Rewards

Lortie (1975) defines ancillary rewards as:

> simultaneously objective and subjective; they refer to objective characteristics of the work which may be perceived as rewards by some (e.g. married women might consider the work schedules of teaching to be rewarding while men might not). Ancillary rewards tend to be stable through time, and to be "taken for granted" rather than specified in contrasts; for example, people expect teaching to be cleaner than factory work. (p. 101)

The time compatibility theme as an attraction to teaching is most related to ancillary rewards. Further, ancillary rewards are more likely to be associated with reasons why people begin a particular occupation than their effort levels once in it. Lortie argues that such things as frequent holidays are often taken for granted and that they are received by all teachers equally. The employing organization has less ability to manipulate ancillary rewards than it does extrinsic ones in attempting to increase worker performance.

Psychic or Intrinsic Rewards

The third type of reward is primary among teachers.

> Psychic rewards consist entirely of subjective valuations made in the course of work engagement; their subjectivity means that they can vary from person to person. But they are also constrained by the nature of the occupation and its tasks; we would not expect lighthouse keepers to list sociability as a work reward or street cleaners to rejoice in opportunities for creative expression. (Lortie, 1975, p. 101)

The important difference between intrinsic rewards and the other two types is that they can fluctuate. The personally defined rewards that teachers can take from their work can be very high or very low. Effort makes considerable difference in gaining these kinds of rewards. For example, assuming that most teachers are rewarded by seeing their students learn and that the rate of student learning is in some way related to the amount of effort the teacher puts into classroom preparation and instruction, teachers should be able to increase their intrinsic rewards to some degree by working harder. The largest number of psychic rewards are related to classroom-based, task-related student outcomes. The organization and administration of a school can also either facilitate or hinder teachers in receiving desired intrinsic rewards. To the extent that the principal refrains from using the intercom as a convenient means to communicate with a teacher, he or she is able to help the teacher attain the personally defined rewards gained from seeing students learn in the process of working through a well-prepared, well-taught lesson free from interruption. Psychic rewards, then, are of primary importance to teachers because they are integrally tied to the motivation teachers possess to do a good job in the classroom.

One example of intrinsic rewards related to extraclassroom activity is Jacquie's role as activities coordinator. There is some extrinsic reward associated with that work, but most is psychic or intrinsic. She recounted how past coordinators had received the extra pay but done minimal work. Why, then, does Jacquie work so diligently in this job? Because in working hard she accomplishes things that are rewarding to her; she describes the position as providing all kinds of rewards that apparently the previous coordinators did not see. She works hard and feels rewarded.

Research Evidence on Rewards

In 1964 Lortie surveyed over 6,000 classroom teachers in Dade County, Florida. In the survey were four questions concerning the three types of rewards discussed above. In 1984 the authors repeated these four questions with a randomly selected group of 2,719 Dade County teachers. Both sets of responses are tabulated in Table 13.3 (Kottkamp, Provenzo, & Cohn, 1986).

Table 13.3   Dade County teacher responses in 1964 and 1984 to choices about extrinsic, ancillary, and intrinsic rewards (in percentages)

Extrinsic Rewards: Although few would call school teachers a "privileged class," they do earn money, receive a certain level of respect from others, and wield some influence. Of these three, from which do you receive the *most* satisfaction?

	1964	1984
The salary I earn in my profession.	14.3	14.2
The respect I receive from others.	36.6	26.3
The opportunity to wield some influence.	36.0	31.7
I receive no satisfaction at all from these things.	13.0	27.8

Ancillary Rewards: Which of the following things do you like best about teaching?

The relative security of income and position.	22.6	16.1

Table 13.3   (continued)

The time (especially summer) that permits travel, family activities, etc.	23.2	35.4
The opportunity it offers to earn a living without much rivalry and competition with other people.	4.8	2.8
Its special appropriateness for persons like myself.	34.1	28.6
None of these afford me satisfaction.	15.3	17.1

Intrinsic or Psychic Rewards: Which of the following is the *most* important source of satisfaction for you?

The opportunity teaching gives me to study, read, and plan for classes.	3.4	1.9
The chance it offers to develop mastery of discipline and classroom management.	1.1	1.4
The times I know I have reached a student or group of students and they have learned.	86.2	86.7
The chance to associate with children or young people and to develop relationships with them.	7.9	7.6
The chance it gives me to associate with other teachers and educators.	1.0	0.7
I receive no satisfaction from these.	0.3	1.6

Extrinsic, Ancillary, and Intrinsic Rewards: Of the features grouped below, the following is most important to me:

The salary and respect received and the position of influence.	11.9	11.3
The opportunities to study, plan, master classroom management, reach students, and associate with colleagues and children.	76.3	70.2
The economic security, time, freedom from competition, and appropriateness for persons like me.	11.8	18.4

The first question concerns satisfaction from extrinsic rewards. Teachers chose the most important from among *salary, respect, wielding influence,* and *no satisfaction* from any of these. Over the 20-year period, respect declined by 10 percent, wielding influence declined by 5 percent, and these 15 points shifted to no satisfaction from any of these. As one might expect, teachers have not found salary a major satisfaction. It is disturbing, however, to see both respect and influence decline while no satisfaction grows.

The second question concerns satisfaction from ancillary rewards. The choices were among *security, time schedules, lack of competition, special appropriateness,* and *no satisfaction*. In 1964 *special appropriateness* or the fit between the position, personality, and values received the highest response, 34 percent. *Security* and *time* each received about 23 percent. In the 20-year span *security* has dropped 7 percent, *time compatibility* has increased by 8 percent, *special appropriateness* has declined by 5 percent, and *no satisfaction* has grown by 2 percent. Apparently *time compatibility*, now the largest response, is of growing importance among teachers. One possible explanation for this is that 20 years ago women teachers were more likely to drop out of teaching for several years following childbirth; today the trend is to take a maternity leave and to return to the classroom within a short time. This has become increasingly a pattern in part because of the difficulty of reentering teaching due to the poor market conditions and because teacher unions have negotiated maternity leave policies that were nonexistent 20 years ago. Both Luberta and Sandy were able to make use of maternity leaves and to retain their full-time positions.

The third question concerns satisfaction from intrinsic or psychic rewards. Recall that these are the kinds of subjective rewards that teachers define personally. The choices were: *to study and prepare for classes*; *mastery of discipline and management*; *knowing a child was reached*; *developing relationships with children*; *associating with other teachers*; and *no satisfaction* from these. Unlike the other two questions, the responses to this one have remained constant across the 20-year span.

The final question asked teachers to choose from among the three categories of rewards, extrinsic, intrinsic, and ancillary, in that order. As can be seen, intrinsic or psychic rewards are the most important, but there has been a slight decline from 76 percent in 1964 to 69 percent in 1984. Extrinsic rewards have remained most important to a constant 11 percent or 12 percent of teachers across time while the growth across the 20 years has been in the ancillary category, which grew from 12 percent to 19 percent. Thus, slightly over two-thirds of teachers in 1984 viewed intrinsic rewards from the occupation as most important. These findings are in line with what we know about the structure of teaching as an occupation. Teachers do not as a rule become rich or famous, but many of them receive a deep inner sense of reward from service, working with children and adolescents — exactly the reasons that attracted many of them in the first place. Thus, there appears general consistency between what people entering teaching hope to find and what they actually receive as rewards. In order to make this more concrete, the next section looks at the satisfactions experienced by the case study teachers.

Work Rewards and Satisfaction: The Case Study Teachers

There are a number of ways of gathering evidence on what teachers find rewarding or satisfying. Some ways are direct, like simply asking, "What are the major sources of satisfaction for you in teaching?" Other ways are more indirect, like asking a teacher to describe a good day. Following are some of the responses of the case study teachers responding to the question about a good day. Ruth said that a good day occurs:

> when I've seen enthusiasm on the part of the kids; when their attention is focused on the task because they're really involved in the task. I think the days when I really feel the best are the days when I've got them to the point where I just stand there and I have nothing to do but respond to their production.

For Ruth, a really good day and the rewards and satisfactions that come from it are centered on seeing her carefully orchestrated teaching reach the point where the kids take over and become responsible for guiding their own learning. Earlier Ruth said that her most important goal was "motivating a child to function on [his or her] own." A good day for Ruth, then, is when her primary goal comes to fruition. All of the good feelings that surround such events are psychic or intrinsic rewards because they are subjective valuations; Ruth determines for herself the primary goal of teaching. When she sees evidence that it has been reached, she feels rewarded. No external agent can create these feelings in her. They flow from her self-definition of purpose as a teacher.

Recall that Larry commented on a good day in these terms:

> I get the feeling that something has clicked, that what I want to get across, gets across. I can see it in the eyes of the students, that they really are interested in what they heard or what they did or what they've seen. That's a good day!

Sandy, you may remember, described a good day with slow students in this way:

> A good day is when you have been going on and on about the presidency for days, and a kid who is very slow comes in with an article he has cut out of the newspaper, and you think that he probably never looks at the newspaper. He comes in saying, "Look, we talked about this in class yesterday," and you are surprised that he remembered. It's little things like that. Or a kid running in and saying, "Last night on the news they said exactly what you said." Like you didn't make it up after all. Something that you said in class, and they follow up on it. You mention something, and they go home and talk to their parents about it, and then they will come back and comment about it. . . . Or they will come in and say, "Thank you; I got the scholarship that you wrote the recommendation for." Or a kid will come in to tell you that he talked with his parents about something like you suggested and now everything is fine. Those are the things that really make my day. Or just a kid in the hall saying, "Oh, Hi! I haven't seen you in a while."

On good days for both Larry and Sandy rewards and satisfactions are psychic and closely tied to events in the classroom. Larry prides himself in getting across subject matter and "opening up the window, letting the light come in." His good days occur when he sees these things happen. For Sandy, especially with the slower students, her goals are broader than subject matter, though that too is important. Her good days are tied to evidence of learning but also to evidence that she is affecting their broader lives. For all three teachers a good day also relates to some of the basic attractions to teaching: the interpersonal theme, the service theme, and the continuation theme. Thus, regarding sources of satisfaction, Lortie's conceptual framework again ties together the experiences of the case study teachers.

The direct responses echo the indirect ones. As noted earlier, Larry says his satisfaction stems from "the intellectual satisfaction of communicating things that they should really know to be a good citizen, an aware citizen in this democracy." For Sandy, the satisfaction comes from "the daily rewards that you get, the kid who comes in and says, 'I really enjoy your class. What are we doing today? Is it exciting?' " It is obvious that the case study teachers receive personally defined or psychic rewards from working with students and seeing them grow, from being of service, and from seeing the results of their efforts to teach subject content.

In addition these teachers' work rewards come from a sense of their own growth. Chapter 10 discussed how Jacquie, Larry, and Sandy believe teaching has made them different and better individuals. Sandy's development will get more attention later in this chapter.

WHEN REWARDS DO NOT COME AND OTHER FRUSTRATIONS

Teaching can be very rewarding work; it can also be very frustrating. As Sandy has said, the highs are great and the lows make you think about quitting altogether. This discussion would not be complete without mentioning some of the unpleasant realities of teaching. Questions about lack of rewards and frustrations may also be asked directly or indirectly.

The Gallup Poll of Teachers' Attitudes toward the Public Schools in 1984 asked a question about the reasons why teachers leave the occupation. The question had nine possible responses, and teachers were allowed to choose more than one response. The Gallup organization had asked the identical question of a random sample of the American public in 1982. The 1984 Dade County research questionnaire also asked teachers why they thought teachers leave the profession. Ten response possibilities were included, seven of which were identical to those asked in the two Gallup polls. In all three surveys the respondents were asked to list three reasons why they thought teachers were leaving. The responses from the three different samples, two from teachers and one from the general public, are found in Table 13.4. Only the responses to the Gallup surveys are directly comparable because of identical response categories and because they report random national samples. However, it is meaningful to compare the general pattern of the responses across the two samples of teachers. In doing so it is important to know that Dade County encompasses the entire county containing Miami; that its schools range from inner city, through suburban, to rural; that there are large minority populations in the schools; but that some experts project that the general United States population will begin to resemble that of the Miami area in the decades following the year 2000.

Certain patterns in Table 13.4 are fairly consistent. *Low salaries* and *discipline problems* are seen by all three groups as the two most important reasons why teachers leave. However, both groups of teachers place *low salary* first and *discipline* second, whereas the general public reverses the order. Although these questions were asked indirectly about why others leave teaching, the teacher responses are probably projections of their own sense of why they might leave teaching. In this respect another finding in the Dade County study is important. Responses to the *discipline* answer were specific to individual schools. In some of

Table 13.4   **Perceptions of why teachers leave the classroom (in percentages)**

Many public school teachers are leaving the classroom. Here are some reasons that are sometimes given. Which three of these do you think are the main reasons why teachers are leaving their jobs?

	1982 Gallup Poll of the Public	*1984 Gallup Poll of Teachers*	*1984 Dade County Teachers*
Low teacher salaries	52	87	72
Discipline problems in schools	63	46	65
Low standing of teaching as a profession	15	38	21
Students are unmotivated, uninterested in school	37	37	24
Lack of public financial support for education	24	26	NA
Parents don't support the teachers	37	21	19
Outstanding teacher performance goes unrewarded	13	20	14
Difficulty of advancement	14	19	7
Parents are not interested in children's progress	25	11	NA
Frustration at being unable to achieve one's ideals as a teacher	NA	NA	24
A feeling of exhaustion or burnout	NA	NA	38
Greater job opportunities for women and minorities	NA	NA	10

NOTE: Figures add to more than 100 percent because of multiple answers. NA = question not asked on the survey.

the 247 schools in our sample all of the teachers mentioned *discipline* as one of their three responses; in other schools none of the teachers answered the *discipline* choice. Although *discipline* is the second response of teachers in both surveys, our data indicate that there is great variation in the amount of frustration teachers feel with disciplinary problems and that the level of frustration is related to the specific school and perhaps also the principal for whom they work.

The third-ranked teacher response on the Gallup poll was the *low standing of the profession*; in our survey that response ranked sixth. Dade County teachers ranked *exhaustion* or *burnout* third, a response not included in the Gallup survey. The other responses may be seen in Table 13.4.

If the focus is shifted from the individual responses to a broad view of the total cluster of responses from which teachers had to choose, it can be seen that most responses are about areas over which teachers as individuals have limited or no control. A number of the responses—*salary, low standing of the profession,* and *greater opportunities for women and minorities elsewhere*—are constrained by the structure of the occupation and the relationships of occupations within the national occupational structure. Other issues like *lack of financial support* and *lack of parent support* are beyond direct individual influence. Two responses on the Dade County survey deal with the direct frustration of the basic activity of teaching—*unmotivated students* and the *inability to reach one's ideals as a teacher*. As would be expected, reasons teachers impute to their colleagues who leave are closely related to the frustration of the major themes of attraction described initially in Chapter 1.

Not all teachers leave. Of those who stay some rarely receive the rewards and satisfactions they desire, whereas others receive great rewards. Both groups, however, are frustrated by similar events and circumstances. The other side of the good day is the bad day. On bad days teachers receive few or no psychic rewards; their desire to see students learn and grow is thwarted. On bad days the flow of lessons and psychic rewards is destroyed by student misbehavior or recalcitrance, interruptions from the intercom or assemblies, weather changes and impending holidays, or the teacher's being out of sorts.

Lortie (1975) concluded that "teacher complaint is almost ritualized" (p. 175). He identified two major categories of complaint: task and time use and interpersonal relationships. The Dade County interviews echo his findings. Time in school can be divided into instructional time during which teaching and learning occur—and the teacher is receiving psychic rewards—and noninstructional time during which psychic rewards are not likely to surface. Teachers complain about things that are noninstructional or that interrupt or eat away at instructional time or preparation for instruction. The list includes clerical duties, lesson interruptions and time pressures, duties outside the classroom, large classes, grading papers, and other forms of bureaucratic paperwork.

The interpersonal relationship complaints are targeted at four groups: troublesome students, administrators, parents and fellow teachers. Complaints about interpersonal relationships are really concerned with instructional time and tasks too because they focus on conditions that make effective instruction difficult. Teachers are disturbed by students who interrupt instruction or make a lesson almost impossible to pursue. They are disturbed by administrators who do not support them, who do not buffer them from interruptions and outrageous parental demands, who themselves create interruptions (the PA system is a favorite!) or who make demands that destroy the flow of instruction. Parents are a source of irritation when they demand special treatment for their child that takes away instructional time from other students, or when they make excessive demands. Colleagues bother teachers when they take up time that teachers wish to devote to lesson preparation or when they do not do their share of the necessary extra classroom work, such as maintaining discipline in the halls.

A few statements from the case study teachers will indicate they are not different from teachers in general in terms of frustrations and conditions that limit the receipt of psychic rewards. Ruth is frustrated when "the boys are more interested in the girls and the girls in the boys" than they are in the lesson. She continues:

> Another thing that frustrates me is when I go home not feeling good about teaching, the days when I ask myself what I could have done to help this child do better in this situation — or not being able to find the time to devote as much individual attention to that one, to get him over the humps that he's run into so he feels good about his work.

Knowing something of the setting in which Jacquie teaches, her response to what she likes least about teaching is almost predictable:

> discipline, constantly having discipline uppermost in your mind before you can teach. If I didn't have to worry about discipline——There's always going to be some kids in the class who are troublemakers, and if I didn't have to worry about that I could go ahead and be teaching all the time.

Jacquie works in a school where discipline can be a problem, but a look at her statement indicates that it troubles her not so much directly but because it keeps her from teaching. Larry also dislikes discipline.

> My worst experience is being a policeman in the hallway. You've got to break up fights. You've got to make sure if people are here or there. You've got to patrol the bathroom in some cases. That's the worst part about it.

He continues on another issue: "I don't get real turned on with doing a lot of book work. I don't like to record grades. I don't even like to write down lesson plans. I don't like a lot of paperwork."

Sandy also speaks of discipline problems because they keep her from teaching:

There are kids who I really think shouldn't be in school—a 19-year old freshman who only comes to sell his drugs and won't do a thing in your class. There's really nothing you can do with him. The school doesn't feel that they can do anything with him. They think that their hands are tied legally, or they are not willing to pursue it. Kids who are continually in trouble—we're talking about a tiny percentage—kids who are continually in trouble and the school won't do anything to them ... the perpetual troublemakers who are there not to get anything out of school, but who knows what— dope dealing or just to get into trouble. I don't understand their motivations. I can do without them, and I tend to get all those kids because they get kicked out of the other classes, and they put them into my room because they don't know where else to put them.

Thus, the case study teachers support Lortie's analysis of discontent. What bothers teachers are events that hamper the flow of teaching and learning and in doing so prevent them from receiving the major rewards available to them, the self-defined sense of accomplishment that centers on having reached a student or a class in a way that makes a visible difference.

BURNOUT AND LOSS OF MEANING

Teaching like any other occupation has its bad days and down times. The case study teachers have shown that they have bad days and that certain aspects of their work bother them. But on the whole they are still optimistic, energetic, and derive a deep sense of personal reward and meaning from their work with children and adolescents. However, for some, teaching eventually loses its meaning altogether.

Since the case study teachers do not experience work in this negative way, examples of other teachers who express nothing positive about their work are given. DeFabiis (1985) did an intensive interview study of New Jersey teachers with between 7 and 35 years of experience who were experiencing great amounts of job-related stress. Teachers reported the following kinds of feelings:

A very bad day or sometimes a failure or lack of success with a particular student can make you feel drained, make you feel like your efforts are wasted. It makes me feel like I am not making any kind of a contribution to what I do. And, of course, as soon as you feel like you are not successful you start to look at things outside the immediate work area, and then you start to look at how teaching has affected other parts of your life, such as planning for your future, security at home or in your private life, and that adds to the failure in the classroom. The feeling that even if I'm not satisfied with the results that are being turned out, whether it is my fault or not, I can't be satisfied particularly with all the things I am doing in my private life—where is this all taking me to?

It is an overall depression and fatiguing feeling, one that just drains the emotions out of you, and really kind of kills your optimism. What is the purpose of doing something or anything if you think that it's a foregone conclusion that it will either not be successful or that it will certainly not be meaningful, and it definitely will not be appreciated? (p. 81)

It is not as pleasant a job as I thought it would be. I don't think teachers are very happy people. Many teachers are frustrated—low salary, boredom in the classroom, and this rubs off on other teachers. I think you can see this in the teachers' room and things like that. I wasn't ready for that. You come into teaching with high expectations that you were going to change the world. You get shot down real fast. (p. 87)

I just realized that I can only relate a negative side to teaching. I'm having a hard time coming up with examples which would typify some of the joys of teaching. You know, I don't find too many other teachers expounding on the positive aspects of teaching. This reinforces my feelings. You know we're almost wallowing in it. (p. 91)

Obviously these teachers are at a stage beyond an occasional bad day. The last teacher also does not appear to interact with anyone like the case study teachers, who certainly have a more positive outlook. In popular terms, the three teachers speaking here are experiencing job burnout. Burnout has been variously defined (Cedoline, 1982) but typically is considered to include elements of emotional and physical exhaustion, psychological distancing from one's clients, and a sense of lack of accomplishment or of the impossibility of achieving what the job demands or one demands of oneself. Symptoms of burnout may include: fatigue and exhaustion, high blood pressure, poor mental health, impairment of decision-making skills, obsessive thoughts about work, marital problems, social withdrawal, cynicism, increased use of alcohol and drugs, depression, anger and self-deprecation (Cedoline, 1982, pp. 17–35).

This chapter will not go into all the predicted causes and prescribed cures for burnout and stress in teaching. Cedoline is a good source to begin with for those who are interested in pursuing this topic. It is also a popular issue in magazines and journals. Teachers do suffer stress and burnout, as do workers in all sorts of people-centered occupations. Such occupations include social work, nursing, child care, police work, and counseling. Not all teachers experience burnout. Certainly the case study teachers are not experiencing it. It is, however, a point to be considered by those who choose to teach.

PERSONAL DEVELOPMENT AND LIFE CYCLES IN TEACHING

This discussion has bounced back and forth between positive and negative aspects of teaching in an attempt to present a balanced view of the life of a teacher. In making any career decision, people need as detailed and realistic a picture as possible. Another way of gaining insights into the lifestyle of a teacher is to consider some of the changes and cycles that occur within the career. There are the obvious stages that many people pass through in adulthood: jobs, marriage, parenthood, retirement. However, within the last 10 years developmental psychologists have done a great deal of writing about less visible changes, stages, transformations, or cycles that adults pass through. Works by Gould (1978), Levinson (1978), and Sheehy (1976, 1982) have demonstrated that there is no such thing as growing up for good. Adulthood is not static but rather a continual process of growth and development. The task of growing up never stops! Because this is true the meaning one draws from an occupation and the investment one makes in it are likely to vary over the years of adult life.

To illustrate the issue of change within a teaching career, this section focuses on Sandy Snodgrass and the changes she has gone through during her 17 years as a teacher. These changes come from the intersection of her personal life, her evolving role as a teacher, and the social forces that bear upon both her work and her personal life. Sandy's career is not as long as that of Luberta or Ruth, but in some respects more changes have been condensed into it than into the careers of the other two teachers. Table 13.5 presents a graphic representation of the interacting changes in Sandy's life and career. Glancing at the table as you read may help you fit the various pieces of the discussion into a pattern.

Recall that Sandy began teaching directly out of college. During college she had begun to bloom, to have greater confidence in her abilities and to discover her great capacity for compassion and service to others. It was also the Vietnam War era in which Sandy, opposed to the United States involvement in Southeast Asia, worked as a volunteer with disabled veterans.

Her first year was typical in the sense that she really had to learn to be a teacher in her own right — to develop curriculum, to instruct, to give tests, to set up a different social system for each of her five classes, to earn authority with each group, to interact with parents, and to cope with the myriad of problems that first-year teachers experience. Her first year was atypical in other respects. She was one of the first women hired into a department that had been a largely male domain. Beyond that, her stance on the Vietnam War made her a radical in the eyes of some of her male colleagues (who since have gained respect for her). During her first few years most of her professional relationships were with other young, more liberal teachers.

Although she recalls being exhausted most of the time, Sandy made it through the trials of the first year pretty well until the very end. Then tragedy struck.

I had several students commit suicide all at the same time. And I just thought, "I can't keep up with this. I'm too involved." It happened right at the end of the school year, and I thought, "This is it! I quit. It's too much." But I went back, and I'm glad I did. But

Table 13.5 Sandy's teaching career

Year	68	70	72	74	76	78	80	82	84
Years of teaching	*1*	*3*	*5*	*7*	*9*	*11*	*13*	*15*	*17*
School-related issues	1st year; survival issues; exhaustion; extracurricular involvement; self-contained classroom; social studies: average students; student suicides; subject orientation	boredom	new issues of survival; excitement of new challenge; enter Cluster, team teaching: low and disaffected students; person orientation		tired; earn master's degree in special education	reduce extracurricular involvement because of family	leave Cluster—renewed energy; mix of regular, slow, and special education students; teach various social studies courses		
Personal issues	single; school consumes most of personal life space; opposition to Vietnam War				marriage; purchase house	family consumes more time	divorce; 1st son born; single parent	marriage	2nd son born
Societal, political, economic issues	Vietnam War era					special education legislation	growing conservatism, accountability, and back to basics; enrollment decline; increased technical support		

I was seriously considering quitting then and there. Probably the only reason I went back was that I wasn't sure what else to do. At the time the whole experience was very confusing.

When Sandy started teaching she was very much caught up in political science as a subject and very subject oriented in her teaching. The suicide of several students — not a typical beginning experience for most teachers — was one of the events that contributed to a change in her overall view of her role as a teacher. Through the first few years of her career she moved from a strict academic orientation to one that encompasses the whole student. Now when students come in excited about suicide or other issues that are not strictly part of the lesson plan, Sandy takes the time to deal with their real-life excitements and anxieties. During her first year she would have ignored the excitement and gone right ahead with her lesson.

At the beginning of her fifth year of teaching Sandy made a change that had lasting effects. She moved from teaching mostly regular students and a few slow classes in self-contained classrooms to the Cluster, a school-within-a-school alternative program for freshmen who were having difficulty in school for various reasons. The Cluster was housed in one large room, a former library. Three other teachers team taught in this large, open space with Sandy. She recalls the experience as a turning point in her career. Sandy entered the Cluster because she was experiencing boredom from teaching the same classes for four years.

In the Cluster I was never bored. It was neat. There were a lot of headaches in there, but I was never bored, and I learned a lot from working with the other three teachers. Some things I didn't like. We were real open, and we would tell each other, "You really messed up today when you did this," or "We should have tried this." It was constant self-criticism, which was good for me. It helped me to grow as a person and as a teacher. There has been a lot of carry-over. Things we did in Cluster I now do with regular kids. One example is that every student in my class gets called on at least once every hour. That's hard to do with a class of 35, but I learned to do it in the Cluster. It's just second nature now.

The Cluster was an important learning experience about self and teaching. But it also demanded so much that it might have led to burnout.

After four years with remedial kids I was just spent, exhausted emotionally and physically. I was ready for a change. I had forgotten that there were kids who care about school. I needed to get out of there. I needed to go off on my own for a while. I enjoyed the team teaching, but it was like when you live in a big family and you want to be alone for a while. When I was alone, I incorporated many of the ideas and things we had done in the Cluster into my regular classes. It was like a new beginning. Now I wouldn't mind team teaching like that again, but I needed to get away from it for a little while.

Sandy credits her administrators with being sensitive enough to understand her plight and her request to have a more normal teaching load. In a sense they helped to rescue her from physical, emotional, and intellectual overload. Her admonition to administrators is that if they can only see when a teacher really needs a change and allow the change to occur, "they'll see a new teacher emerge."

The Cluster experience was instrumental in Sandy's attitude change toward low-ability students and students with learning disabilities. Recall Sandy's statement:

> When I first started teaching I would just look down on them. And I looked at the people who taught them and thought, "Well you just can't do anything else. That's why you're working with them." And I thought to myself, "I would never have a room that was so loud and where kids were squirming around." And now when I think of teaching some of the slow kids—some of the things they did to me or I let them do—years ago I would never have believed that I would have changed that much in regard to them. And now I really enjoy teaching them. . . . I used to think, "Why don't you just quit school? You do not belong here." My attitude toward them has changed.

In addition to the Cluster experience, two other factors were instrumental in learning what and how to teach special students. Sandy enrolled in a masters degree program in special education while she was teaching in the Cluster. The knowledge gained in that program coupled with the results of new special education legislation that led to increased technical support from experts available through the countywide Special Education District provided Sandy with the knowledge, technology, and direct support she had lacked earlier in her career. This is a case in which larger forces in the environment resulted in significantly enhancing Sandy's ability to help her students learn. Today she individualizes her teaching and makes good use of each special student's individual educational plan (IEP). Learning disabilities are real, she believes, and the information now available to her helps her to plan alternative routes for reaching students with particular problems.

Toward the end of her Cluster teaching experience, Sandy also began a series of changes in her personal life that affected her teaching in numerous ways. Single for the first eight years of her career, she was married and bought a home. Sandy decided to take a maternity leave when her son was born and to return to teaching shortly after his birth. When her son was only a couple of years old, she found herself going through a divorce and becoming a working, single parent. Sandy has since remarried and enjoys life in a close and rewarding family, which now includes a second son.

Some of these personal transitions affected Sandy's teaching. One factor involved her investment of time and energy in her work.

> When I started teaching and was single I invested almost all of myself in my work. Teaching was my life. I didn't have anything else. All of my friends were teachers. I didn't mind staying after school every day to sponsor extracurricular activities, to go to

plays, and to watch basketball games. Everything in my life was really job oriented, and in the evening I would be completely drained and exhausted. Once I was married and had a child, I didn't want to spend as much time with the extra curriculum. Now, when I am in school I give them myself, but I still save a little energy for myself, whereas before I was being eaten up with school. Now I've got a home and a family. They are first in my life, and they get most of my emotional being.

At first look it may appear that Sandy does not put the effort into her work that she used to, but this is not really so. Family responsibilities have perhaps helped her to work more efficiently and to waste less emotional energy on things that she cannot change. One change has been her use of her one-hour planning period. When she was single she used this time to socialize with other teachers because there was time in the evening to complete her work at home. Now she uses time at school for work and as much as possible reserves her time at home for her family. This is not to say that she does not take work home. She comments, "I seem always to have a book in my hand, sometimes a child on my lap and a book in my hand."

The other important lesson that Sandy has taught herself is to worry less.

Over the years I've taught myself an important lesson. Years ago I'd come home and I'd be a nervous wreck over something that had happened at school or some kid who had a problem. I'd think, "How is he going to live with it?" Now it's not that I care less — I probably care more — but it doesn't eat away at me as much. Now I'm more able to come home and to leave my problems at school. It also doesn't take as much to make me happy as it used to, but it takes more to make me unhappy. Things don't bother me like they used to. I'm convinced that most of these kids are going to make it through adolescence, and they're going to come out fine no matter how horrible things seem now. Most of them are very adaptable. I've been at teaching long enough to see so many jerks turn out so fine that I just figure that kids I have today will too. I work hard and give the kids a lot of myself, but I'm just more relaxed about work than I was at first.

The experience of being a parent, and for a while a single parent, has also changed Sandy's orientation to teaching.

My perspective changed with becoming a mother. Now I think, "Would I want my kid in her class?" when I think about another teacher. I'll even ask myself at times whether I would want my child in my own class when I'm tempted to get lazy and throw in a unit that is just sort of filler until I get myself charged up to go into something in more depth. Then I think, "No, that's not right. I wouldn't want Matt to sit through a class and do this garbage." Being a parent has kept me on my toes. I'm more critical of teachers now because I have children. Mediocrity in other teachers bothers me a lot more now. It scares me to send my kid to public school or any school for that matter.

Single parenthood left Sandy with a permanent attitude change. Recall Sandy's statement regarding children from homes where there has been a divorce:

I can tell which kids are going through unhappy times at home. I have become more sensitive. At one time I would have thought, "You're from a divorced home. That's too bad, isn't it? It's a shame your parents are failures." Whereas now I'm not as condescending in my attitude toward children of divorce. At one time I would see on a kid's record a different name from the parents and say, "Oh my, a child from a broken home." But now that I am in that situation and have a son, I don't want him to be categorized or all of his problems blamed on the fact that he comes from a broken home.

The final thing that has come with parenthood for Sandy is a growing understanding that she really does like children. Years ago she did not know whether she could tolerate young children. Her interest was in adolescence. Now her house is filled with young children. The neighborhood kids seem to live at her house. She is interested in children of all ages and recently has been playing with the idea of teaching younger children some day.

These, then, are the major themes of change in Sandy's career. There have been other changes, too. Over the 17 years of her career the student population of her school has declined from 4,000 to 2,500. Smaller is better as she sees it. The students feel less anonymity and are easier to control. Students' attitudes have also become much more conservative since the radical Vietnam era when Sandy began to teach. When Sandy started teaching high school seniors, she was only four years older than her students. Today she comments that the age differential is great enough that they could almost be her children. In the beginning she had to work on maintaining a social distance between herself and the students so they would not think of her as a crony. Age has solved that problem by creating a natural distance.

When asked what she has gained and what she has lost by being a teacher rather than working in some other occupation, Sandy said the loss was simply money. But she commented that she was not very materialistic, and with a husband who made a good salary she really had no complaints about the kind of life style she was able to maintain.

What has she gained by being a teacher? Patience, open-mindedness, flexibility. Working with adolescents has helped her to stay younger in outlook and to remain more open-minded. Today she has close friends that range in age from their twenties through their fifties. Through teaching she has learned to relate to many age groups. Finally, Sandy has gained a sense of her genuine usefulness, as she puts it, a sense that only came after more than a decade of teaching because it took that long for her to be able to really see the impact that she had had on her students over those years.

Sandy's career has encompassed many changes both within her and within her work setting. Her career has also given her a deep sense of satisfaction and a growing sense of pride. There have been many frustrations too. But on balance the good clearly outweighs the bad. She is a teacher deep in her bones now, a natural. She seems to have learned when she needs a change and what will keep her energized to continue to reach students in both academic and personal ways.

CONCLUSION

This chapter has attempted to present some of the realities of teaching over the longer run that beginning teachers and those thinking about teaching often overlook. Beginning teachers are consumed with learning how to instruct students, how to manage a classroom, how to cope in order to make it through the first year. But after surviving the first year, issues of career, work rewards, and life style begin to surface. Individuals and the conditions in which they work also change over the course of their careers. It is better that these issues are raised before energy and talent are invested in preparation for a teaching career rather than after the first year of teaching.

The fit between an occupation and role and a person is important no matter what line of work one decides to pursue. Teaching has been a fairly stable occupation in terms of its career and reward structure. As we have seen, Sandy is satisfied with her life and work, but she is also aware that she is in a district and school that make it possible for her to reach her goals and to feel satisfied. She has friends who teach in both the inner city and suburban districts who discuss with her the problems encountered in their daily lives in school. Such circumstances may stem from a myriad of causes including difficult students and principals who make life unbearable. Luberta for one has found teaching in the inner city to be a joy. The point is that teaching always occurs in a particular context, and the context makes a difference depending on its fit with a particular individual at a particular point in his or her life and development. The Cluster experience was both positive and negative for Sandy. She believes she needed to get into it at one point to grow, and she needed to get out of it at another point to continue growing.

With the projected teacher shortage, the job market should be in your favor. Look carefully for a setting that will support the particular person you are and the particular goals you have as you begin to teach. A good way to begin that quest is to visit a wide variety of schools and interview a wide variety of teachers while you are still a student. To be a teacher is to have good days and bad days, but the better the match between the individual teacher and the school setting the better one's chances are that the good days will predominate.

ACTIVITIES

1. List the attractions that teaching holds for you. Are these realistic bases for making an important occupational decision?
2. What are the most and least attractive aspects of being a teacher? Use the material in Chapters 5 through 10 and Chapter 13 to guide your response. Ask yourself: "Do I wish to engage in these kinds of activities as my life's work?"

3. Interview several teachers who have been working for 10 years or more to gain additional perspectives on careers, satisfaction, life style, money, changes through the years, and so forth. You might want to interview one or more of your own elementary or secondary teachers whom you really respected. It is likely they will take such an invitation as a compliment. Ask them to be very open with you. Explain that now you are trying to understand the perspective from the other side of the desk. Themes for investigation can be:

- Satisfactions and dissatisfactions, including changes over time.
- Changes in perspective over time concerning general orientation toward teaching; importance of subject matter; classroom control and management; most important goals of teaching; views of student motivation; methods of instruction and student learning.
- The importance of work rewards over time.
- The relationship between personal and family events and teaching over time.
- Changes in the setting regarding attitudes, work satisfaction, energy flow, and so forth (if the teacher has experienced a number of different work settings, academic levels, and schools in different kinds of communities).
- The teacher's comments about being trapped in the work.
- A desire to become an administrator and why.
- Opinions about the issues involved in merit pay and career ladder proposals.
- Personal advice they might give you concerning teaching as a career.

4. Share answers and perceptions from your interviews with various classmates and your instructor. What patterns do you see?
5. What kinds of changes might be made in teaching as an occupation to make it more attractive to bright and capable young people in search of a fulfilling career choice?
6. Do more listening in the faculty lounge in the school where you observe. Concentrate on the relationships between teachers' teaching and their lives away from work.

REFERENCES AND SOURCES

Carnegie Forum on Education (1986). A nation prepared: Teachers from the 21st century [excerpts]. *Chronicle of Higher Education* (May 21), 43–54.

Cedoline, A. J. (1982). *Job burnout in public education: Symptoms, causes, and survival skills.* New York: Teachers College Press.

DeFabiis, W. G. (1985), *An interpretive study of the sources of teacher stress within an existentialistic framework.* Ed.D. Diss. Rutgers University, New Brunswick, NJ.

Gallup, A. (1984). The Gallup Poll of teachers' attitudes toward the public schools. *Phi Delta Kappan, 66*(2), 97–107.

Gallup, G. H. (1984). The sixteenth annual Gallup Poll of the public's attitudes toward the public schools. *Phi Delta Kappan, 66*(1), 23–38.

Gould, R. (1978). *Transformations.* New York: Simon & Schuster.

Kottkamp, R. B., Provenzo, E. F., Jr., & Cohn, M. M. (1986). Stability and change in the teaching profession: Attitudes over twenty years: 1964–1984. *Phi Delta Kappan, 67*(8), 559–567.

Levinson, D. et al. (1978). *The seasons of a man's life.* New York: Knopf.

Lortie, D. C. (1975). *Schoolteacher: A sociological study.* Chicago: University of Chicago Press.

Louis Harris & Associates (1984). *The Metropolitan Life survey of the American teacher.* New York: Metropolitan Life Insurance Company.

Sheehy, G. (1976). *Passages: Predictable crises of adult life.* New York: Dutton.

Sheehy, G. (1982). *Pathfinders.* New York: Bantam.

——14——

THE PROCESS OF BECOMING A TEACHER

INTRODUCTION

This book began with the brief life histories of five teachers and the reasons behind their career choices as well as a more general discussion of who teaches in America and why. This final chapter circles back to the decision to teach, but its approach is designed to help your own career decision making. Whether you are just exploring the possibility of becoming a teacher or are already involved in a teacher education program, it is important to understand at both an analytical and personal level the process of induction and socialization into the profession.

This discussion begins with the assumption that the process of becoming a teacher can be conceptualized in the following three stages: (1) making the decision, (2) participating in a teacher education program, and (3) getting through the first year of teaching. The first part of this chapter examines each of these three stages, citing, wherever appropriate, examples from the five case study teachers. The latter part of this chapter attempts to make these stages as immediate and close to your experience as possible by introducing five individuals who are currently in the process of becoming teachers. They speak frankly and openly about their decisions to teach and their experiences as student teachers and first-year teachers. As you read this chapter think about your own career interests and choices and whether becoming a teacher is a commitment you might be ready to make.

MAKING THE DECISION

Some Questions

Herbert Kohl, elementary school teacher and education critic, in an article entitled "Why Teach?" suggests a number of different motivations for entering the profession. The motivations he cites incorporate some of the categories of attractions that Lortie (1975) found in his research, but he mentions others as well. Kohl writes at a more personal level than Lortie, and his purpose is to help individuals who think they are interested in becoming teachers to examine honestly their motivations.

> Some young people choose teaching because they enjoy being with young people and watching them grow. Others need to be around young people and let their students grow for them. Teaching for some is a family tradition, a craft that one naturally masters and a world that surrounds one from childhood. For others teaching is magical because they have had magical teachers whose roles they want to assume. Teaching can be a way of sharing power, of convincing people to value what you value or to explore the world with you or through you. (p. 73)

If these reasons sound familiar it may be that they are essentially those that the five case study teachers gave about their own decisions to teach. For Ruth the decision revolved around the enjoyment she received from working with the children and watching them learn. For Jacquie and Luberta it was natural because they were surrounded by family members in education. Jacquie looked to her aunts and her uncle for role models and Luberta followed right in the footsteps of her two older sisters. For all three of our secondary people—Jacquie, Larry,and Sandy—the opportunity to convince others of the value of their subject areas was an initial driving force.

In addition to publicly acknowledged reasons, Kohl (1976) cites some cynical reasons as well:

> For some people teaching becomes a matter of temporary convenience, of taking a job that seems respectable and not too demanding while going to law school, scouting around for a good business connection or merely marking time while figuring out what one really wants to do as an adult. For others teaching is a jumping-off point into administration, research or supervision. (p. 73)

He also includes the motivations of many of the college students he knew in the late 1960s and early 1970s. Speaking of his own case he mentions two factors in his decision to become an elementary teacher: (1) teaching in an elementary school allowed him to do and to share the things he liked most, exploring the world and moving from subject to subject and project to project; (2) young children were more open, less inhibited (Kohl, 1976, p. 74). Life in elementary classrooms was, however, not exactly as Kohl had imagined it. In his early years he found young children could be open and creative, but they could also be "closed, destructive, nasty, manipulating"—all the things that he sought to avoid in the adult world. Eventually, Kohl (1976) had to "sort out the romance of teaching from the realities" (p. 74), and he recommends that those thinking of becoming a teacher start that process earlier than he did. In his view a good place to begin is with an honest examination of one's motivations. Arguing that the reasons one has for becoming a teacher will significantly affect one's work satisfactions, he suggests that prospective teachers begin questioning themselves about what they expect to gain from and give to teaching.

To guide the self-inquiry process, Kohl (1976) offers nine types of questions:

1. What reasons do you give yourself for wanting to teach? Are they all negative (e.g., because the schools are oppressive, or because I was damaged or because I need a job and working as a teacher is more respectable than working as a cab driver or salesperson)? What are the positive reasons for wanting to teach? Is there any pleasure to be gained from teaching? Knowledge? Power?

2. Why do you want to spend so much time with young people? Are you afraid of adults? Intimidated by adult company? Fed up with the competition and coldness of business and the university? Do you feel more comfortable with children? Have you spent much time with children recently, or are you mostly fantasizing how they would behave?

3. What do you want from the children? Do you want them to do well on tests? Learn particular subject matter? Like each other? Like you? How much do you need to have students like you? Are you afraid to criticize them or set limits on their behavior because they might be angry with you? Do you consider yourself one of the kids? Is there any difference in your mind between your role and that of your prospective students?

4. What do you know that you can teach to or share with your students?

5. Getting more specific, a prospective teacher ought to consider what age youngster he or she feels greatest affinity toward or most comfortable with. There are some adults who are afraid of high school or junior high school aged people (13- to 17-year-olds), while others are terrified at the idea of being left alone in a room with 24 six-year-olds.

6. Before becoming a teacher it is important to examine one's attitudes toward racial and class differences. Racism is part of the heritage of white Americans, and though it can be mostly unlearned, it manifests itself in many subtle ways.

7. Another, perhaps uncomfortable, question a prospective teacher ought to ask him- or herself is what sex-based motives he or she has for wanting to work with young people. Do you want to enable young boys or girls to become the boys or girls you could never be? To, for example, free the girls of the image of prettiness and quietness and encourage them to run and fight, and on an academic level, mess about with science and get lost in the abstractions of math? Or to encourage boys to write poetry, play with dolls, let their fan-

tasies come out and not feel abnormal if they enjoy reading or acting or listening to music?

8. What kind of young people do you want to work with? There are a number of children with special needs that can be assisted by adults with particular qualities. For example, there are some severely disturbed children — children whose behavior is bizarre, who are not verbal, who might not yet be toilet-trained at age nine or ten, who might be engaged in dialogue for hours at a time with creatures you cannot perceive.

9. Some people get along well in crowds, and others function best with small groups or single individuals. Before becoming a classroom teacher, it is important to ask oneself what the effect is on one's personality of spending a lot of time with over 20 people in the same room. (p. 74)

Some of Kohl's questions are important because they force one to confront some underlying motivations for going into teaching that frequently go unexamined. In Kohl's view, there are definitely some wrong reasons for deciding to teach — not knowing what else to do, wanting to right personal injustices, and being uncomfortable with adults are just a few of them. Individuals who start with these motivations are at best likely to be unsuccessful and at worst likely to be harmful to young people and perhaps even themselves.

Other questions on Kohl's list are important because they serve to differentiate the global career called teaching. As you have seen in the five case studies, elementary teaching is quite different from secondary teaching. Experienced teachers also tell you that there are tremendous differences within the two levels. Some first-grade teachers maintain that they do not enjoy working with fifth and sixth graders and some high school teachers contend teaching freshmen is much different from teaching seniors. When you add to this diversity the differences between regular and special or exceptional students (those who are retarded, emotionally disturbed, behaviorally disordered, blind, deaf, gifted, specially talented) the differences among students in general, college prep, vocational, and honors tracks; the differences between large and small schools, public and private schools, rich and poor schools, urban, suburban, and rural schools, the possibilities seem almost endless.

All of Kohl's questions are worthwhile in one way or another because they help individuals determine whether they are likely to receive the intrinsic rewards described in Chapter 13 that are at the heart of the profession. You should take the time to answer each of these questions for yourself.

Today, however, self-inquiry related to motivation and interests is not enough. In the 1980s as never before the decision to become a teacher often involves a confrontation of disapproval from peers, parents, and the general public. Throughout American history there have been mixed feelings about teaching as a legitimate career. To some, like Sandy Snodgrass's father, teachers have always been and always will be special, exalted individuals who affect young minds in important ways. To others, the often quoted statement of George Bernard Shaw, "Those who can, do. Those who can't, teach" has always been and will always be a truism. But for most people a teaching career falls somewhere in the vast middle ground; it is usually seen as a respectable occupation, particularly for bright women and idealistic young people.

Lortie (1975) captured some of the ambivalence around the profession when he wrote:

> Teaching . . . is honored and disdained, praised as "dedicated service," lampooned as "easy work." . . . teaching from its inception in America has occupied a special but shadowed social standing . . . real regard shown for those who taught has never matched professed regard. (p. 10)

The situation in the 1980s seems to be more problematic. There are many who no longer even profess regard for teachers. For example, the cover of a recent edition of *Newsweek* magazine featured a picture of a teacher with a dunce cap. Today, individuals who are considering teaching as a career run the risk of being thought of as foolish or not too bright. There are multiple, overlapping reasons for the decline in status of this career. Statistics and findings reported in July 1984 by Linda Darling-Hammond of the Rand Corporation explain some of the reasons for the more recent loss in status.

Some Concerns

Declining Salaries Despite years of collective bargaining by teacher organizations, the fact is that teachers' salaries have failed to keep pace with other occupational salaries. Between 1971 and 1981 average salaries for teachers actually declined by nearly 15 percent in real-dollar terms. The situation is equally gloomy for beginners as can be seen in Figure 14.1. Even when adjusted to reflect a 12-month salary equivalent, beginning salaries for teachers are lower than those in almost every other field that requires a bachelor's degree.

Increasing Dissatisfactions Although the salary news is depressing, the preceding chapter shows that individuals are attracted to teaching because of the intrinsic rewards related to helping young people develop and learn. Unfortunately, there are data to suggest that these rewards are less and less frequent. Teachers today express increasing dissatisfaction with the working conditions of schools. One way to see this increasing dissatisfaction is to look at the National Education Association's yearly poll of several thousand teachers. Each year the question is asked: If you could go back and start all over again, would you still become a teacher? Between 1971 and 1981 the proportion of respondents saying they would not teach again increased from 10 percent to almost 40 percent. Moreover, less than half of the current teaching force said that they planned to stay in teaching until retirement.

The factors that contribute to teacher dissatisfaction in the workplace are multi-

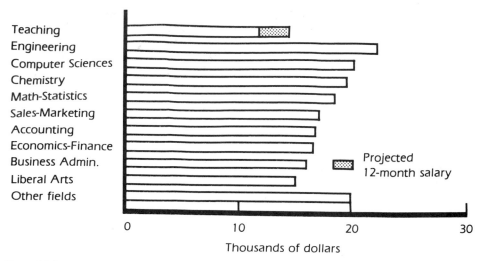

Figure 14.1   Beginning salaries of bachelor's degree graduates (from L. Darling-Hammond, *Beyond the Commission Reports: The Coming Crisis in Teaching*, no. R–3177–RC, 1984, The Rand Corporation)

ple. Teachers talk of a lack of physical support in terms of adequate materials and facilities, a lack of clerical support for the burgeoning paperwork, a lack of administrative support to protect them from interruptions and nonteaching responsibilities, and also a lack of support from parents in terms of general interest and the monitoring of homework. Many teachers today feel that they are not treated as professionals. Decisions that critically affect their classroom and school environments are frequently made by others and few opportunities for professional growth exist. Ironically this growing feeling of powerlessness stems, in part, from efforts over the last decade to improve education. In an attempt to raise standards and increase quality, many states have legislated accountability policies and minimum competency tests that have sought to and succeeded in standardizing and regulating teacher behavior. The reality is that many of these policies have become, from the perspective of teachers, dysfunctional. Teachers are not against accountability, but they are against policies that restrict their ability to make important classroom decisions that affect their ability to teach effectively. Darling-Hammond (1984) summarizes the problem in simple but clear terms:

> Highly prescriptive teaching policies often limit the curriculum to those subjects and types of thinking that are most easily tested; such policies also prevent the use of alternative teaching strategies that are more appropriate to students' learning needs and create paperwork burdens that distract from teaching time. The results are two-fold: emphasis on procedural conformity to narrowly configured objectives at the expense of more creative forms of teaching and learning; and dissatisfaction on the part of teachers who find their ability to respond to students' needs reduced. (p. 15)

Increased Options for Women and Minorities Another contributing factor to the declining public regard for teachers is the fact that there are now alternative career possibilities for women and minorities. Bright women have always been the mainstay of the teaching force, but figures show that academically talented women increasingly are pursuing other kinds of work. Between 1970 and 1980 the proportion of women receiving bachelor's degrees in education dropped from 36 percent to 18 percent. During that same decade women's occupational choices increased and shifted from the traditional fields of education, English, and the social sciences to business, commerce, and the health professions. The percentage of degrees granted to women in the biological sciences, computer sciences, engineering, and law increased tenfold.

Decline in Academic Ability of Teaching Force With declines in salary and satisfaction and increases in career options for women, the next finding is fairly easy to predict: the teaching profession is attracting and retaining fewer academically able individuals than in the past.

For example, the Scholastic Aptitude Test scores of students planning to major in education have traditionally been lower than those of others, but in the last 10 years the scores of potential education majors have declined even more (see Figure 14.2). The majority of those entering teaching come from the bottom group of SAT scores; at the same time, most of the few top scorers who become teachers leave the profession. For example, 28 percent of the lowest quintile of SAT scholars who graduated from high school in 1973 entered teaching and more than half said they planned to remain. Only 8 percent of the highest quintile went into teaching and only 25 percent of them said they planned to remain.

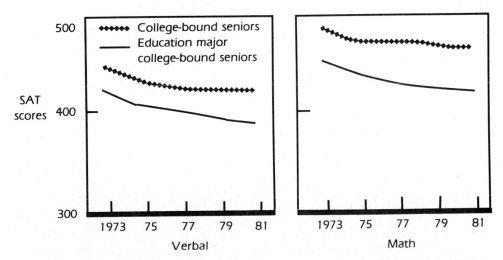

Figure 14.2 Declining academic ability of incoming teachers (from L. Darling-Hammond, *Beyond the Commission Reports: The Coming Crisis in Teaching*, no. R–3177–RC, 1984, The Rand Corporation)

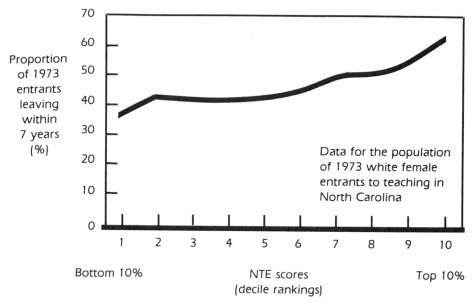

Figure 14.3   Attrition rates of teachers (from L. Darling-Hammond, *Beyond the Commission Reports: The Coming Crisis in Teaching*, no. R–3177–RC, 1984, The Rand Corporation)

Moreover, using the National Teacher Examination (NTE) as a measure, the teachers tested in 1973 in North Carolina who left the profession seven years later tended to be high scorers rather than low scorers (see Figure 14.3). By 1980 almost two-thirds of the top decile had left; in contrast, only about one-third of the bottom decile had left. The two measures of academic ability that the Rand study used, the SAT and the NTE, are open to serious question, particularly the NTE. Nonetheless, these statistics are included because experience on college campuses and in schools suggests that the basic conclusion of these charts is reasonable.

Given these factors, it is not surprising to find that the general public now as perhaps never before wonders why anyone of academic talent would choose teaching.

Some Hopeful Signs

Although the statistics cited by Darling-Hammond provide reasons for making the decision not to enter teaching, there are also a number of hopeful signs today that should encourage those who are now thinking about a career in teaching.

Recognition of Existing Problems   To begin with, the Rand Corporation published these statistics in order to bring about awareness of the need for change. As noted in Chapter 8 there have been many other reports that have documented the current problems of American education and almost all of these have focused on the need to improve the conditions of teaching. A *Nation at Risk* (National Commission on Excellence in Education, 1983), for example, argued in strong terms

> that not enough of the academically able students are being attracted to teaching; that teacher preparation programs need substantial improvement; that the professional work life of teachers is on the whole unacceptable; and that a serious shortage of teachers exists in key fields. (p. 22)

Similarly, Ernest L. Boyer (1983) described at length some of the difficult conditions under which teachers work. He called attention, for example, to the hectic daily schedule; the nightly lesson planning and reading of homework; the ever-growing pile of procedural work; the time given to important tasks such as student counseling; as well as the time given to menial tasks such as monitoring the halls, the cafeteria, and the bathrooms.

These reports have succeeded in capturing the attention of policy makers and the public at large, and there is now widespread recognition of the need to make the profession more attractive in order to recruit bright young people and to retain effective, experienced teachers in the classroom.

Proposals for Reform For almost every critique that has been published in the last several years there have been accompanying proposals for reform. These proposals hold the promise for significant improvement within the profession, and there are indications that some of these proposals will turn into policy. For example, the Commission on Excellence in Education (1983) recommended in A *Nation at Risk* that (1) teachers' salaries "should be increased and should be professionally competitive, market sensitive, and performance-based" (p. 30); (2) teachers be given an eleven-month contract so that they could have more time to develop curriculum and instructional strategies; (3) incentives such as grants and loans should be used to recruit able people into the profession.

To renew the profession Boyer (1983) recommended a number of changes, some major and some minor. To improve the working conditions he proposed that high school teachers be given

1. A reduced teaching load (no more than four formal classes).
2. A minimum of an hour for class preparation within the school day.
3. Freedom from noninstructional tasks.
4. Opportunities to develop their own curriculum and research projects.
5. More adequate rewards and recognition.
6. More support in terms of discipline.

To improve the salaries Boyer recommended "as a national goal, the salary for teachers should be increased by at least 25 percent beyond the rate of inflation over the next three years, with immediate entry level increases" (Boyer, 1983, p. 308).

To recruit more outstanding students into teaching, he recommended

1. Cadet programs in high school that encourage the most able students to become teachers.
2. Full tuition college and university scholarships for the top 5 percent of their gifted students who plan to teach in public schools.
3. A national teacher service, especially for those who plan to teach in science and mathematics. This would be a tuition scholarship program that would be for students in the top third of their high school graduating class and would require the recipient to teach at least three years in public school.

Boyer has many other recommendations related to the education of teachers and the development of a career pattern within the profession, but the point here is not the nature and number of proposals. Rather it is the fact that prestigious people and commissions are advocating that the profession must be altered to be more attractive. Hopefully advocacy will turn into action and those who decide to become teachers in the coming years will experience far better incentives, working conditions, salaries, recognition, and overall satisfaction.

An Increasing Demand for Teachers A third hopeful sign related to job opportunities is the increasing shortage of trained teachers. Although this is a serious problem for local school systems and society in general, it means that there will be many more employment opportunities for those entering the profession during the next decade. In addition, as qualified people became more and more difficult to hire, market conditions will make it possible for teachers to make greater demands supporting improved working conditions and higher salaries.

Population growth, particularly in the Sunbelt states, is responsible for much of this growth in the demand for teachers. In Texas, for example, which had 3.42 million public school students in 1970, it is expected that there will be a total of 5.25 million students by the year 2000. Florida's public school population, which was 1.56 million in 1984, is expected to grow to 2.1 million for the year 2000. California is expected to increase its 4.1 million students in 1985 to just under 5 million students in 1991 (Bowen, 1985, p. 63).

This growth in the need for teachers comes at a time when an unusually large number of people are coming up for retirement or seeking alternative careers. Enrollments in teacher training programs have been down over the past decade. As a result, it is clear that there will not be enough people to fill the needs of an expanding student population and replace those individuals leaving the profession. The next decade will be difficult for the public school system in the United States, but it will also be a period of opportunity and growth for those entering the teaching profession. It will, in a sense, be the best of times and the worst of times for making the decision to be a teacher.

PARTICIPATING IN A TEACHER
EDUCATION PROGRAM

For those who make the decision to become teachers the next step is usually to enroll in a teacher education program. In order to teach in any public school and in some private schools one needs a teaching certificate. Standards for certification are set by state boards of education, and certification is predicated on successful completion of a teacher education program at an accredited higher education institution.

Teacher education programs differ because state requirements vary and because the quality of higher education institutions differ. Also there are often program variations related to whether a higher education institution is public or private. Although public colleges and universities must conform completely to state standards, private ones ordinarily have some flexibility.

A national accreditation agency entitled the National Council of Accreditation for Teacher Education or NCATE sets standards and to some degree monitors teacher education programs throughout the country. NCATE evaluates programs, and those that meet its standards are said to be NCATE approved. Of particular importance is the fact that NCATE provides reciprocity. This means that when a person graduates from an NCATE program in one state he or she will be able to obtain certification in a number of other states.

Despite the existence of NCATE, teacher education programs have traditionally been viewed as less rigorous than other courses of study. Today, with so much attention focused upon the need for school reform, teacher education is under even more serious attack.

One of the most severe critics is Emily Feistritzer (1984) who argues that the absence of uniform standards in teacher education is a major stumbling block to excellence. Although Feistritzer is correct in asserting that there is considerable diversity in terms of standards and quality, there are, in fact, some common elements to be found within most programs. Almost every teacher education program, for example, begins with some kind of *foundations* course that gives the theoretical underpinnings of education. A variety of courses are considered to provide foundations, and these may include offerings such as history of education, philosophy of education, sociology of education, and educational psychology. The idea behind the foundations courses is that if a teacher understands how the disciplines of history, philosophy, sociology or psychology bear on education, the teacher will have a theoretical framework for practical decision making.

Methods courses form a second component of most teacher education programs. These are the courses on pedagogy, which focus on, for example, how to teach reading in elementary school, or how to teach math in secondary school. *Field experiences* are a third component of most programs. These are the courses that get students into the schools and may involve opportunities for observation, some participation, and student teaching. All three of these components build upon a general liberal arts background and, for secondary teachers, a major in the field to be taught.

Much of the criticism of teacher education revolves around the foundation and methods courses. Some argue that too much time is devoted to these courses and too little to courses in one's discipline; others maintain that these courses are too theoretical, poorly taught, or largely irrelevant. Teachers themselves frequently talk disparagingly about their training. Sandy's reflections on her education courses are fairly typical.

> Irrelevant and boring. And it's a shame, because they needn't be that way. . . . Having teachers come in to talk might have been helpful, rather than my teacher, who hadn't taught high school since — I'm not even sure if he ever had. I thought there were things that we could have done; my techniques of teaching social studies class were good. I remember he would tell us all kinds of things we could try with kids, and he was pretty current. But my other teachers were — it was just unbelievable. It was the joke of the school. The foundations course was just terrible . . . and the ed. psych. course was ridiculous. Adolescent psych. could have been fantastic, but it was a waste of time. I think they could have been good, but they weren't. And that was because they had some poor teachers in there. I definitely think we need these courses, but they should be better.

Larry has similar sentiments: "I think my preservice training was not very good. The classes I took in teacher education were simply not helpful."

Most teachers, however, feel very positively about student teaching in particular and about field experiences in general. They argue that more exposure to the real world of classrooms in preservice education better prepares teachers to deal with the realities of the job. Jacquie, Sandy, and Larry, for example, all maintain that they should have had more field experience prior to student teaching. In Jacquie's words:

> I was really unprepared for student teaching, and I didn't know what to expect at all in the classroom. There must have been a lot of complaints because the education department where I was trained a few years later started giving students more on-site experience before they got to be seniors.

Sandy concurs:

> People going into education need to start observing when they're freshmen and sophomores in college. I think a lot of people would soon realize that they don't want to be

teachers. Instead, you wait until you're in your senior year, and you have invested all of this, and you feel I can't get out now! I think that may have changed, but it was a crime. I had never seen a classroom until I went out to teach. No observations in anything!

Larry simply exclaims: "I did my student teaching my last quarter in college—of all the times to do student teaching!"

Although they would have liked a more extensive field experience both Larry and Sandy talk positively of their student teaching experiences, particularly the opportunity it provided them to get practical knowledge. According to Sandy:

I observed the first two weeks and then Mr. Shaefer turned it over to me totally. I feel that I had good preparation for teaching, not from my college classes, but from working in his room. I did all the tests and just everything. I've heard people say, "Student teaching did not prepare me. It was a waste of time." I found mine very valuable. I guess it was because I worked so hard too. I was so paranoid. I was such an overachiever and wanted to do my best and I learned how to make lessons and get things started. . . .

Larry also speaks of student teaching as a "really good experience." Like Sandy, he taught a great deal, and he even had opportunities to get involved in extracurricular activities.

Jacquie praises student teaching as well but talks primarily in terms of her cooperating teacher who has served as a role model for her entire teaching career.

I was very lucky to have a wonderful teacher. She saved me. I'm sure I never would have been successful at all if she had not shown me everything she knew. . . . She taught me everything I know, and she was just so helpful in the way she taught it to me—she taught me to make teaching fun and to enjoy teaching.

Although Jacquie acknowledges the enjoyable nature of the student teaching experience, all of the teachers could talk of the pressures and strain. Sandy put it this way:

I was exhausted when I was student teaching, and I felt the pressure of not disappointing my cooperating teacher. Plus I was working for a grade. Even back then social studies jobs weren't easy to find, so I was very concerned that I get a good grade in there. I remember being tired my first year of teaching, but no more so than in student teaching.

Although there is a long tradition of criticism that maintains student teaching is the only realistic and worthwhile component of teacher education, it is important to note that many exemplary teacher education programs and courses make meaningful links between theory and practice. The course you are enrolled in now is probably one of these. Moreover, a variety of recent initiatives seek to establish more rigorous standards for higher education institutions offering preparation for teaching. For example, the Holmes Group Consortium, a group of education school deans from large research universities, has proposed that teachers who desire to be career professionals should participate in a full year of post-baccalaureate professional study followed by an induction year in the schools that combines a paid internship with continued education (Atkin, 1985). Thus, teacher education, like teaching as a profession, is getting serious examination, and those who enroll in certification programs in the years ahead will probably be as well prepared as preservice teachers can be to face the inevitable challenges of their first year.

GETTING STARTED: THE FIRST YEAR

Student teaching is usually both stressful and exhausting, but the literature suggests that the first year of teaching can be really traumatic. Kevin Ryan et al. (1980) who studied the experience of the first year maintain that "it is particularly important for people considering careers in teaching to address some common beliefs about the first year and, also, to examine their own beliefs" (p. 4).

Ryan begins with the recognition that for some, whom he calls "the blessed few," the first year of teaching is both exciting and successful. Most, however, find the first year complex and difficult. The difficulties, according to Ryan et al. (1980), are numerous. Many arise from the fact that teaching every moment, every single day is different from what the novice expects. In his words:

> Having been in school those many years and having seen so many different teachers in so many different situations, many beginners think they know what it is like to *do* teaching. But alas, it fools them. The teacher's side of the desk is different. Behind it are hidden demands and subtleties which are quite unexpected. (p. 5)

Here, Ryan is echoing Lortie's concept of the misleading nature of the apprenticeship of observation mentioned in Chapter 1.

Ryan also argues that although one might think that student teaching gives novices a realistic picture of what lies ahead this, in fact, is not the case. He maintains that teaching under the guidance of a cooperating teacher in a carefully selected site rarely captures the experience of being in charge. The educational philosopher John Dewey articulated this position in 1904 and, based on his conviction that student teaching was inherently idealistic, proposed that student teaching should be a laboratory for learning theories. The practical survival skills and techniques, he argued, could be better learned on the job.

Related to this point is the reality that first-year teachers often take positions in schools that are very different from those they have previously known and are given assignments for which they have not been specifically trained. Luberta was trained as a secondary English teacher but her first job was in an elementary classroom. Similarly, Jacquie, whose primary training was in French, was hired to teach Spanish.

Finally, Ryan et al. (1980) maintain that novices are unprepared for the mental, physical, and emotional drain of teaching.

> There is always a strain to teaching, but it is particularly pronounced for beginners. They're like athletes who have trained for the season by reading, writing and discussing. They may know what to do, but their bodies cannot take the punishment of the game. . . . After a while, however, the beginning teachers' bodies and minds become toughened to their routine of school so that they can be on their feet for six hours, responding to the many different messages and events of classroom life. They get conditioned, but it can be hell until then. (p. 8)

THE FIRST YEAR: RECOLLECTIONS OF THE CASE STUDY TEACHERS

In a fundamental sense all five teachers belong to the category that Ryan labels the blessed few. Their first years were successful. Sandy and Jacquie, for example, were hired to take over their cooperating teachers' jobs, so they were both familiar and relatively comfortable with their assignments. Luberta took over a position that her sister had held and was familiar with the school in particular and small schools in general. Obviously, knowing something about the setting and the kinds of lessons one will be teaching is an advantage for a first-year teacher. Larry credits the fact that he had a strong background in his subject matter for his success as a beginner.

> The thing that helped me more than anything else in my teaching career is my academic background. As far as competence in the classroom, I could walk into the classroom and know what I was talking about. If I had had to worry about the kids and what was going on and about how to make new tests and about this whole new situation and then had to worry about the background—the knowledge content—then it would have been even worse. Of course the first year, I had to read a lot and really study a lot, but my background was a key for me. You've got to have that confidence; and when I spoke, the kids knew I knew what I was talking about, generally. Not that I always do or always did then, but in general I thought I had from the very beginning a pretty good connection with the subject I was teaching. Not that I'm ever going to stop learning or that I ever will know all I need to know.

Ruth credits the nature of the community and students of her first position with her initial success. As she describes the situation: "The children were in a com-

munity where the teacher was highly respected and there were no discipline problems. I did the things that the education courses say a teacher should do."

They were all successful, but they all experienced difficulties and exhaustion.
Both Larry and Luberta describe the experience as challenging. In Larry's words:

> I had big classes—there were 42 kids in each of my two freshman classes and 36 and 38
> in world history. Talk about challenging! And we also had a different kind of student
> coming here. It was the hippie era then, and we had a drug problem and a lot of all-
> around laxness. That was a real challenge. I was also challenged by the competition
> here. Some of my colleagues were very good teachers with a lot of background, and I
> was challenged to keep up with them. I had a principal who gave me a lot of good reac-
> tions and a lot of freedom. . . . I was scared; I worked hard, I came in early, and I stayed
> late. I remember I couldn't wait for Thanksgiving and Christmas vacation and when
> school was out for the summer, I was like a little kid excited about my
> vacation. . . . Teaching is a mental and physical drain—your mind works and it makes
> your whole body tense. I distinctly remember the first day of teaching. I was more
> physically exhausted than anything I could remember. It was incredible!

Luberta also found having students in Grades 1 through 4 in a single classroom a
challenging situation. Her reflections on the first year also validate that being in
charge for the first time can be quite different from part-time field experiences:

> I had spent some Friday afternoons working with my sister, so I had a little idea what a
> small school would be like. But, on the other hand, it's a completely different situation
> when you're in charge of it. I think this is the way you begin to devise methods of getting
> the job done. If you have any creativity in teaching, you start right there because you
> have to. It all worked out. I'm afraid I did a lot of practicing with those first classes, but I
> found some methods that really worked.

Other First Years: Beginning Again and Again

The previous discussion has focused on the challenges of the first year of a
teaching career. It seems important to mention, however, that the case study
teachers talk of other challenges in "other first years." Ruth and Sandy actually
found their second years more difficult because they were beginning again in new
situations, and in their cases, these new situations were more challenging than the
first year.

In Ruth's case the second year of her career was the "first year" because of its
challenging setting, the St. Louis Public Schools. It was with that move that she
really "learned to be a teacher." You may recall that Ruth encountered students who
bit, kicked, ate the crayons and paste, and used foul language. After three days she
lost her voice; nonetheless, after two days at home she returned to "conquer them."

For Sandy the first year of her career seemed relatively similar to student
teaching. She was hired at Lindbergh High School to take over Mr. Shaefer's

classroom while he went on sabbatical. With the next year, however, came the adjustment. She was transferred from seniors to ninth graders and from sociology to government. She describes her adjustment in this way:

> I used to be one of those who would look down on the ninth-grade teachers, thinking "can't you keep those beasts in their chairs." Then when I got the ninth graders, I saw a new animal. After the initial shock of finding kids who in some ways didn't seem wholly human, I really began to enjoy their enthusiasm. You could get them really interested very quickly—you just had to approach it from a different perspective.

Thus it was in Sandy's first year with ninth graders that her challenge came.

For Luberta and Jacquie there were challenging other first years that occurred long after the first year of their careers. Jacquie talks of her first year in her school in Miami, which was totally different from those she had known. Recall some of Jacquie's comments from Chapter 4 about her first day:

> I'll never forget the first day that I taught at my school. We were on the same pathway as the Miami International Airport, and the planes flew right overhead, and I thought they were going to crash into the school. You just had to stop class, what you were saying, and let the planes go over. Oh, there were so many things that were different. . . . The black and Hispanic cultures were virtually unknown to me. . . . The school was very old. . . . There was one set of books to be used for all classes. Students were not allowed to take them home . . . before it was just understood that the student would have a book to take home for homework.

Similarly, Luberta encountered new challenges when she moved from the two-room schoolhouse in the tiny town of Palmyra to the large St. Louis Public School system. One difference she recalls was the attitude of the students toward the teacher:

> When you were in Palmyra, just by virtue of having the job, you were somebody to be followed and paid attention to, but in St. Louis I found that you needed more than a presence to get any kind of following from the children. They were just a little tough in their resistance, sometimes, to you. But some of the approaches from Palmyra still worked.

In our view the experiences of the case study teachers indicate that there may be a number of first-year experiences in teaching. The fact that each of our teachers handled the first years of their careers successfully and subsequently were able to handle the succeeding challenges may say something about the importance of a successful first year. Their experiences may support the conclusion of Joseph Vaughn of the National Institute of Education who, along with his staff members, summarized the available literature on first-year teachers.

The conditions under which a person carries out the first year of teaching have a strong influence on the level of effectiveness which that teacher is able to achieve and to sustain over the years; on the attitudes which govern teacher behavior over even a forty-year career; and, indeed, on the decision whether or not to continue in the profession. (Ryan, 1980, p. 13)

ON BECOMING A TEACHER: REFLECTIONS OF SOME IN PROCESS

To add a contemporary flavor to this discussion about the process of becoming a teacher, the following section introduces the views of five young people who are currently at varying stages within that process. They're part of the new generation of teachers who will be replacing the Ruths, Sandys, Larrys, Jacquies, and Lubertas of this book. The School-based Teacher Education Programs (STEP) at Washington University are the constants in this section. One of these individuals is about to enter the secondary program, one has just completed the elementary program, and three have completed programs and are in their first year of teaching. A very brief description of the STEP programs follows.

The STEP Programs at Washington University

As noted earlier in this chapter there have been recent efforts to improve teacher education by adding more field experience. Zeichner (1981–1982) and others present a counterview that field experience is not necessarily beneficial. The issue in Zeichner's view is not the amount of fieldwork but "the quality of the experience that results" (p. 1).

The STEP programs at Washington University are the result of faculty efforts to improve the quality of the fieldwork experience and teacher education in general by combining methods courses and student teaching into something called a *professional semester*. After the completion of a sequence of courses in the social and psychological foundations of education, students then enroll in an integrated set of methods courses and fieldwork. The elementary professional semester is an 18-credit program that involves: reading methods (3 credits), math methods (3 credits), children's literature (3 credits), teaching-learning (3 credits), and student teaching (6 credits). Students work in the classrooms Monday through Thursday and attend methods classes all day Friday. The team of faculty members who teach on Fridays also supervises in the schools during the week and are therefore in a position to link course concepts to the field experience. The secondary professional semester is a 15-credit program that includes: teaching-learning (3 credits); reading in the content fields (3 credits); a course in the field to be taught (science methods, math methods, and so forth) (3 credits); and student teaching (6 credits). Students in the secondary semester teach in the morning and take their methods courses three afternoons a week. During the middle of the experience the secondary students are in the schools all day for six weeks. As in the elementary program, the team of methods instructors supervises in the schools. The chapter now turns to five individuals who have either just finished or are about to participate in the STEP programs.

Five Novices: An Introduction

Audrey Oka is a senior at Washington University and a long way from her home in Hawaii. Audrey is Japanese-American and the fourth generation of her family in Hawaii. Her mother studied in Japan before her family returned to the United States. She teaches preschool and is, in Audrey's eyes, really good at what she does. Her father, a salesman, graduated from the University of Hawaii. Audrey has a math major and a minor in business; she is about to enter the STEP secondary professional semester.

Meg Richardson from Miami, Florida, is also a senior at Washington University. She is an elementary education major and has just completed the elementary STEP program. She is starting the process of looking for a teaching job either in Miami or in St. Louis; eventually she would like to be a missionary in Latin America.

Audrey Oka

Karen Fairbank, Jim Ladwig, and Amy Speigel are all first-year teachers. Because the public school job market was tight in the year they graduated, each of them took positions in private schools.

Karen is older than the other two and practiced law for six years before she decided to become a secondary history teacher. She recently finished the secondary STEP program and is now in her first year at Thomas Jefferson High School, a small, independent college preparatory school that has mostly boarding students.

Jim is 22 years old and is in his first year of teaching at Oak Hill School, a suburban Catholic Elementary School that is part of the Villa Duschesne School in Ladue, Missouri. Jim recently completed the elementary STEP program and is teaching science to sixth graders at Oak Hill. He is not Catholic and is one of two males on the faculty (the other male is the gym teacher).

Amy Speigel is 22 years old and in her first year at Childgrove School, an elementary independent school in University City, Missouri, noted for its progressive educational philosophy.

Listen to what these five novices have to say about their decisions to become a teacher. Then consider how Audrey thinks about starting, how Meg feels after completing STEP, and how Karen, Jim, and Amy talk about their first year after STEP.

Meg Richardson

Karen Fairbank, Jim Ladwig, and Amy Speigel talking about their experinces as
beginning teachers

MAKING THE DECISION

All five of these young people encountered pressure against becoming teachers. As
an undergraduate math major, Audrey herself was ambivalent in terms of career.
She thought about teaching but also about business. Not surprisingly Audrey's
mother encouraged her to pursue a career in business. She was worried that
Audrey would not be financially secure on a teacher's salary. Audrey's friends were
initially surprised when she told them of her decision because they did not see
teaching as a high-status career; still they approved of her decision because they
thought that she would be a good teacher, that she had a lot to offer the kids. More
generally she admits that at first she was hesitant to tell people and always wanted
to add "I'm not doing it because there is nothing else that I could do."

> It *did* bother me at first. It was just a matter of sitting down and saying, "Do you really
> want to do this? The money isn't going to be great . . . ." then you realize, "well, that's
> not so bad." I think I could get internal satisfaction out of it—some gratification that
> can't be figured into a paycheck.

Audrey persists in the face of disapproval because of what she believes will be the internal satisfaction that comes from doing important work. She talks, for example, of how her experience in a church-sponsored summer program for middle-class youngsters of elementary school age in Hawaii helped her to recognize the important contribution a teacher can make.

> The more I got to know the kids, the more I saw how much these kids needed attention and to be accepted. I was surprised at the number of children who were coming from divorced homes or families where both parents work. They didn't have a lot of time with their parents. I saw how much these kids were hurting and suffering because they lacked attention. I'm very idealistic, but I think it is an essential quality for anyone choosing a career in education. On the other hand, I'm sure I will learn to be more realistic, as I don't think I will accomplish everything that I want to do. Ultimately, my decision to teach reflects my desire to influence kids, in the hope that our interaction will help give them a better sense of themselves.

She cites the following case in point:

> We had one child, Michael, who had a learning disability. He was bright in math and had highly developed verbal skills, but he struggled with writing and printing. The first year he attended the program, he was a first grader, an aggressive first grader at that. He was constantly frustrated and as a result often got into fights. Over three or four years, however, I've seen his whole attitude change. Not only is he doing better in school, but socially. He can deal with the other children and interact with them. He still gets frustrated with himself, but he doesn't try to hurt or bother others anymore. He's starting to ask questions such as, "*Why* am I this way?" His new attitude is evident when he says, "I *want* to be able to write," instead of tearing up his papers. It's really exciting to see him come this far, and you think that perhaps there are other kids out there who could also benefit from having someone help them and provide encouragement.

Observing the growth of young people like Michael over four summers ultimately led Audrey to select teaching instead of business.

> I knew I had to work with kids. I can't see myself becoming a member of the corporate world. I still get mad when I think about my classes in the business school because they always told us, "Your main objective is the maximization of profit." That's what they constantly said. And I think that all of the business students, or most of them, truly believe that. People, individuals, become commodities, and are used as a means to an end—that end being to make money. I just could not buy into that.

Although Audrey really enjoys working with elementary school children, she has decided to teach math at the secondary level. Her focus on math goes back to her own schooling.

I want to teach at the secondary level because I see it as a challenge. I recall my own high school friends being turned off to math at some point. Sometimes it could have been blamed on an inept teacher, but there were people in my classes who suddenly would simply hate mathematics. I could never understand it. They despised math while I was still loving it. I want to teach mathematics because I believe that the teacher can make the difference, if she is highly motivated and interested in what she has to offer students. If she can see different ways to present the material so as to stimulate the kids to think—creativity and insight are crucial here—then maybe they'll want to learn, maybe they'll be interested. I've had teachers who could not explain or perhaps did not care to explain; ones who didn't try to make the class interesting. The result was that some kids lost interest in the subject. I had a business professor who on the first day of class said, "I want you to sit back and relax. It's my job to stimulate you, motivate you, and get you to think. If I can't do that, then the guilt is on me, not you." I admired that bold philosophy; I keep it in the back of my mind, as an ideal for myself. I want to be able to say that.

Meg's decision to become a teacher was made in a similar way to Audrey's. In her early years in high school she wanted to be a teacher, but by the time she entered college she was focused on medicine as a career mainly because of status. After one semester in premed, Meg realized that medicine would be a mistake for her, and she began looking for other options. In her sophomore year she enrolled in a course in which she worked six hours a week in a third-grade class. She found the experience tremendous.

The teacher I worked with was a great example of what a real teacher should be. She was concerned with the kids, and she was making a difference in their lives. I loved it, I enjoyed teaching. I worked with one little boy who was Vietnamese. He was learning his second year of English. And just to see how excited he was to learn was something that I thought was more gratifying than any amount of money I could make.

Clearly Meg knows of the internal satisfaction Audrey talks about. Meg, however, has notions of helping and influencing others that go beyond the classroom. Her life goal is to be a missionary overseas, and teaching is obviously compatible with such work. Like Audrey, Meg encountered disapproval with her decision:

When I first told my friends from high school, they said, "Wow, we thought you were smart. Why are you going to be a teacher?" I immediately learned that it wasn't going to be easy. . . . I realized from looking at how our society views education now, and teachers—especially elementary teachers—that as a teacher I would only get gratification from the inside. And that I would have to have my own motivation.

Meg believes that people look down on teaching because of salary. "It's important to everybody to make a good living, to be able to support your family and support yourself." The major reason teaching is disparaged, she believes, is that the public does not understand what is involved in being a good teacher.

> I don't think people honestly believe that it takes an intelligent person to be a good teacher. . . . I think they realize that it takes a clever person, who is creative, but I don't think they perceive teachers as highly intelligent individuals. I obviously disagree. Teachers have to be thinkers. We are professionals and should be thought of as such.

Meg found misconceptions even within her own family. When talking to her mother after her first week of student teaching, Meg recounted how her cooperating teacher "comes early, leaves late, and carries piles of work home." Mrs. Richardson said to Meg, "Oh, she must be a new teacher." Meg then said to her mother, "No, she's been teaching for 37 years." According to Meg, her mother was genuinely surprised, and Meg now feels that she converted her mother by giving her an inside picture of what is involved.

As a first-year teacher Karen Fairbank still finds people, particularly her students, surprised that she left law practice to go into teaching. They ask, "How could you give up all that money?" or "Why would you rather be with us?" She, however, has no regrets, even with the heavy load of the first-year teacher:

> What I found happening to me when I was practicing law was that I was under a lot of pressure to produce all the time. You never really got any feedback if you did well. You just got feedback if you screwed up in some way. And it was a constant flow of work — 8:00 A.M. I show up, go home 7 or 8 P.M. at night. Even in the corporate field which I thought would be a little less stressful, it was still like that. And I had to fight for a day off and vacation time. I enjoyed the challenges of being a lawyer. I enjoyed the material that I was discovering and finding out about, as tough as it was and as tough as law school was. But after I had been doing it for about six and a half years I just realized I never really was enjoying the work I was doing. And I decided I had to just take a break and figure out whether it was law, or the job, or my life, or what it was that was making me unhappy. So I got away from law for three years to do entirely different things, and finally after doing some substitute teaching just to earn extra money . . . people began to suggest going back to school for certification and a masters. And when I did that I found I enjoyed it, and found that when I started student teaching I just loved what I was doing. My response after that . . . is that the quality of life is so greatly improved despite working harder than I did as a lawyer. Now I get up at 6 A.M. and watch the news and read the newspaper so I have some choice tidbits to share with my 9 o'clock United States history class. And then, I rarely leave school before 6 P.M. and then I get home, have dinner, and work until about 1 A.M. I know that these long hours come with being a first-year teacher, but even so I feel it is worth it because I am enjoying work so much more. I am really involved in what I'm doing. I love the kids, and I love being able to talk. I like the intellectual stimulation I am getting all the time — I am learning new things all the time — I like the fact that my views are respected, that I'm successful, and that I hear I'm successful all the time. I get feedback every day, whether it's from kids, parents, or teachers. And the money just can't

compensate for that kind of personal feeling as well as the time away where you just can do anything else that's not connected with your work life. And I just love that. I have so many things that interest me. . . .

Jim Ladwig also claims that he gets raised eyebrows from everybody about his decision to teach. Students ask, "Why do you teach?" Other teachers ask, "Why are you doing this?" According to Jim, "They just can't figure out what I'm up to. But for me, it's a commitment I made a long time ago." Jim's commitment is an ambitious one.

For me, teaching is a way to participate in the development of a society — from within. My decision to become an educator is directly related to my dedication to the ideal of building a world attentive to its own development. My concern is for the role of the teacher as an individual within a global society.

Jim admits that his reason for becoming a teacher sounds "arrogant and idealistic"; nonetheless, he believes it is this kind of idealism and vision that educators in today's world must have if they are to meet the tough challenges in front of them. This global perspective has, in fact, greatly helped him face the difficult decisions of a first-year teacher.

As a first-year teacher I often find myself making decisions that control how the time in my classroom will be spent. The set of ideals I have developed with this global perspective in mind often influences decisions in my classroom. I feel the decisions I've made have been more judicious and wise than they would have been without this concern. I can't help but feel that education in America has suffered greatly because of the nearsightedness of those within the profession. One of the only ways to combat this problem is to attract people who actively address these issues within the context of their daily lives. Progress is hindered when people in the schools do not see that there are much greater concerns than those affecting their small, individual realities.

Amy Speigel talks about becoming a teacher "because it was so natural." As a little girl she always played teacher, but by junior high she wanted to be a "doctor or something that real people do." As she got older she also recognized that teaching was a feminine occupation, and she felt that if she became a teacher it would perpetuate the feminization. During college she explored other options. At first when anyone suggested she would be great with children, she resented it and felt pushed in that direction. Eventually, however, she took some education courses, which "felt right," and decided that teaching was, in fact, for her.

Amy also encountered some disapproval regarding the decision, particularly from her parents' friends. What shocked her the most, however, was that her professors and advisors seemed surprised to learn that she did indeed intend to teach, rather than go on to graduate or law school.

Here then are five young, academically talented people who have chosen to become teachers despite all of the obvious problems with the profession today. Clearly they all have options and they all have thought seriously about the choice.

ANTICIPATING THE STEP PROGRAM: AUDREY OKA

Of the five, Audrey naturally has the most anxiety. She has made the decision but has not tested it out in the classroom. She talks about that anxiety in this way:

> I have high anxiety because I always get anxious when I'm in unfamiliar situations. . . . I worked with elementary school kids. I would feel comfortable student teaching there. But I haven't really worked with adolescents, and that provokes some questioning and fear inside of me. I don't know if I can relate to them as well as I would like to. I'm also a perfectionist. I guess I'm looking at student teaching as a time when it's going to be okay to explore and okay to fail, and I want to get a wide variety of experiences. I'd like to work with maybe three or four different grade levels, like 9, 10, and 11 if I can, and see where I would fit in best, where I feel most comfortable, teaching different levels of kids. I want to test my ability to teach kids who are having difficulty with math. I want to just experience all of this and hopefully get a flavor for what I'd feel most comfortable teaching.

Although the anxiety is there so is the realization that she made a thoughtful decision that is right for her. She advises others to consider the decision with equal care.

> I don't think you should just go into it as a final option—"I have nothing else I want to do and so I'll give this a try." I think that in order to be a successful teacher, in order to be an effective teacher, you need to have thought it out, thought about your values, your goals—for yourself as well as for your students—why you're going into it and whether you are serious about it or not. To me, when you deal with kids, impressionable kids at that, you have so much to mold in your own hands and you can't take it lightly. At this time, there is a lot of discouragement about going into teaching, and we all need to deal with the decision and be aware of its consequences. Is it important enough to me that I can withstand what others think and the low salary? I don't see it as something that you can just plunge into and then quit halfway through.

PARTICIPATING IN THE STEP PROGRAM: MEG RICHARDSON

For Meg the experience of her STEP professional semester was all-consuming in terms of time and overwhelming in terms of scope and effort; yet it was also more fun than she ever imagined. Meg captures some of the time-consuming quality in this statement:

First of all you spend your entire day there. You no longer have an hour or so between classes to take a break. That's the joke. When the kids go to gym, you have maybe 20 minutes and then something unexpected always comes up, and you have to deal with it. So that when you come home at night, probably not 'til 4:30 or 5:00, you're dead tired. Then, when you finally feel like you've got a break, you're faced with piles of planning and assignments. It's especially difficult in student teaching, coming into a situation where you don't know, and you can't plan beforehand in the summer. It takes all your time to be ready . . . that's what you feel like as a teacher; you've got to be ready for anything all the time.

Occasionally Meg felt resentment over the time commitment and rebelled under the work load. She missed her friends and she missed the good times she had come to associate with her college life:

The first party I went to was probably in October sometime. I had about four people come up to me and say, "Oh, are you in for the weekend?" and "Oh, where are you working?" Some thought I had graduated, some people thought I was back in Florida. I went to that party because I said, "I'm not staying home another Friday and Saturday and Sunday. I'm going to go out." And it was a mistake. You just don't have time to do anything else.

Meg gave up a great deal in the way of social activities, but she maintains that she also received a great deal of satisfaction and insight from the experience. She learned a lot about the need to be prepared, but the hardest lesson that she recalls involved an incident related to discipline.

The hardest day I had was when someone stepped on my ego, and I responded in what I think was an improper way. I think it stemmed from the fact that I was tired. One kid said something that upset me, and my mistake was in not having some kind of response. . . . I remember when we talked in our educational psychology class about the ripple effect and how what you do with one student affects the others. Well, right after that I was reading a story. A girl that is always out of the room came in late after lunch while I was reading. The kids started laughing, and I thought it was this one boy behind me, making faces. I turned around and immediately without asking questions first said, "Why are you doing. . . . " He said, "I didn't do anything, it was Alicia." And so I said, "Okay, well, what happened? Did she come in doing something funny?" . . . then I said, "Alicia, you go outside and try to come back in again—better yet, just stay in the hall and think about how you're supposed to walk into the room." She went outside. The door was open, and she said some things very angrily. I never heard exactly what she said, but I sort of did. I'm not insecure, but I was just like struck down dead. I could not come back from it. I just walked outside, and I couldn't even say anything to her. I just looked at her and I walked back into the room. I couldn't go on. I said to the kids, "Just take out a book and read, quietly." And the worst thing was they all yelled. "Yea!" So I felt worse. But I just said, this is ridiculous. I cried a little. But I just sat at my desk and read a book. It was so quiet in the class you could have heard a pin drop.

What really upset Meg was that she had worked consciously to build a sense of shared understanding with her students, but she felt that she, at least for a moment, had lost it!

> I felt like up until then the class and I were working together, but that week I felt like it was a battle. And I let that happen. That's a pitfall you have to avoid. If you get outside of being a part of the class, you have problems. You have to be the teacher *with* the class, but here I found myself battling them instead of working with them.

But for Meg the vast majority of the days were exciting and fun. She talks, for example, about a literary project she did with her students.

> When I first announced that we were going to do it, the kids responded with a nice "ugh." But after a while they started getting into it. We did some brainstorming and they began to get excited. Seeing them do that made everything come alive for me. That's what keeps the teacher going, when you see the kids turn on to something.

The major understanding that Meg seems to have taken from her clinical experience, however, is the overwhelming nature of the teaching job. How, she wonders, will she be able to reach each and every student in the classroom? This question first hit her immediately after she had participated in some parent-teacher conferences.

> After the parent-teacher conferences, I was really overwhelmed because I found myself sitting there with every parent saying, "This is the strategy for your child" . . . all these great plans. The next Monday I was like, oh wow, there's 20 of these plans that we have going. What are we going to do here? How are we going to meet the needs of everyone?

Fortunately Meg has not become immobilized by the complexity of the teaching task. Rather it has challenged and inspired her.

> If you lose your vision, then you have lost the game. You do get a little disillusioned. Your dreams come down to earth a little bit more. But if you can keep the vision, you have goals to shoot for.

She even has a plan for realizing some of those goals:

> You need to look at everything and take what's good from it and take what's good from the theories. You have to know your dreams, but also know your limitations. And you have to remember that each kid is an individual. It's going to take a little bit of each of those theories to reach each kid.

With that blend of idealism and realism Meg probably will have the kind of successful first year that belongs to the blessed few.

GETTING STARTED: KAREN, JIM, AND AMY

Karen, Jim, and Amy are about halfway through their first year of teaching. When they were asked about their initial reactions, the conversation began with the all-consuming nature of the job. Karen put it this way:

> Even with student teaching, you never really get the idea of the amount of time and preparation involved. I know the first year is the hardest, but nothing prepares you for how overwhelming it can be.

Amy was surprised by how much parents expected her to know and how much she was viewed as an authority or expert regarding children.

> Not only am I asked to diagnose and deal with learning disabilities, but parents expect and need me to provide much more than math and science. We have a lot of single parents in our school and they seem to need and want support . . . I don't know if it's appropriate for me to give advice and sometimes I don't feel like I have the knowledge or experience.

She worries about being able to live up to their expectations but she also admits "it's nice, in one sense, that no one seems to think of me as a 22-year-old, fresh out of school."

Jim was surprised and frustrated by some of the pedagogical practices he has observed.

> To walk into a classroom, a science class, where they claim to teach the methods of science, and the teacher is testing students totally on a memorization of word-for-word definitions of vocabulary words, is surprising.

Karen was particularly surprised at the nonteaching tasks she was expected to perform.

One of the major frustrations for all of them is to figure out how to do their best and still retain their physical stamina and their perspective. Jim expressed the tension well, when he said, "I always feel like I'm not doing as much as I can, but at times I can't help thinking I'm being too serious." Karen concurred:

> You get all these ideas in your head of what makes a good teacher and you try to be all of those things all of the time and you can't. And that's your mistake — you have to kick

yourself once in a while to realize that you can't be this perfect person all the time, and yet at least with me I keep feeling that I have to be and that if I do anything less, the kids are missing something.

Karen also finds that she becomes so immersed in her work that sometimes she finds it difficult to shut down and keep from boring dates who say, "Can't you talk about anything other than your students?"

Although their comments about the challenges of classroom practice were not surprising, their comments about the need for educational theory were quite unexpected. Each in one way or another talked of the importance of pedagogical theory and their disappointment with its absence in the school environment. Karen has found, for example, there is too much rote memory expected of the history students. She recalls from her education courses the importance of giving meaning to facts and of having clear, overarching objectives.

> I still give them dates, but only those relevant to them. They have to remember when certain things happened, but I have a lot fewer, and it is not as memorization oriented. That's the kind of thing that really bothered me because it didn't seem like there was any real purpose other than just memory. I really do think about lesson planning and objectives. I ask myself if I am trying to get them to remember a date or if I am trying to give them a feel for what it is to study history. And there's a real difference. I have to keep reminding myself what it is I'm trying to do. Sometimes you tend to forget but I think that is one of the most important things we learn as teachers . . . to figure out what the objective is and how to implement it.

Amy agrees both with Karen and with the educational philosopher John Dewey:

> Now that I'm away from it, I feel like I didn't have enough theory . . . that's the kind of thing that it's hard for me to get on my own. A lot of the survival skills that I was given I would have been able to get on my own because once you're in the classroom, either you do or you don't.

Moreover, Amy finds that when she tries to discuss with colleagues issues that are somewhat academic, she gets little response:

> I find that teachers resent talking about content and methods. When I try to pull something in, it's like I'm being really arrogant, real cerebral. I don't know how to approach that, but when I say something I get this kind of reaction: "Oh, you're just out of school . . . you're so academic." I don't really think that I'll change in that way.

Jim also believes that there is far too little educational theory guiding school practice. Jim thinks that such theory should be within the consciousness of all teachers as they encounter and influence the lives they intend to educate.

Theory offers the only hope for confronting the serious problems in schools. The commonly found practices of the real world of teaching are results of feeble attempts to find symptomatic cures for problems that will persist until skillful analysis finds the true sources of the overly abundant problems found in our schools. Only once the source is found can we execute the application of methods to prevent the problems of schools from ever arising. Today, teachers are faced with the challenging endeavor of locating the roots of our schools' problems, developing preventative practices, and applying these theoretical practices within a realistic world. . . . The idealistic nature of teacher education course work should not be left in the college classroom. It is meant to be applied in the classrooms we are to control.

It is four months into the first year, and Karen, Jim, and Amy are clearly struggling. They are struggling with theory and practice issues and with personal issues; yet, they also sound as if they could join the growing ranks of Ryan's blessed few. At the very least for each of them the first year has been a great personal growth experience. Jim talked of the importance of graduating from college and finding a way into the society that allows one to express one's individuality. Karen, like Herbert Kohl, has found in teaching "a chance to use all your talents . . . and explore all your interests." Finally, Amy describes her growing sense of self in these terms:

I joked with my friends when I took the job. I said it was a great place to make mistakes and in my school I am really being encouraged to make mistakes. I've taken a lot of risks, and I think that's really what's kept me going. I never felt competent or secure enough to take those kinds of risks in a university setting. My greatest fear was not just failing, but not doing my best. But this year I have taken risks with these kids and I have seen that they're okay and I'm still okay.

A major focus of this chapter has been on the risk as well as the excitement that is part of becoming a teacher in contemporary America. The risk, however, is not for everyone. Is it for you?

CONCLUSION

To answer the question, Is it for me? one needs to have a clear understanding of what "it" is. The purpose of this chapter and of the book as a whole has been to contribute to your understanding of the teaching profession. In the language of our legal colleagues, we have presented our case. Our clients have been teachers in contemporary America. Our cause has been the development of the individual—teacher as well as student—and the development of society to its fullest potential. A society can only be as clear and forward thinking, knowledgeable, productive, and just as its individual citizens. In turn, the knowledge, skills, and values that individuals bring to their society are inextricably bound to the education they have received. As John W. Gardner (1968) has said: "We know in our bones that over the long haul what we do in education has the greatest relevance to building the kind of society we want."

At the core of the educational process stand excellent classroom teachers. Our argument has been, however, that to achieve excellence in teaching is no simple task. Rather, it is a complex and serious undertaking that demands the highest levels of knowledge, thought, and action and requires continual decision making. To build our argument we have presented the works of significant educational theorists and researchers. To make our case vivid and concrete we have called upon five expert witnesses who have been recognized not only by us but by students, peers, and administrators alike. By examining the specific ways in which they think about and create physical, social, intellectual, and personal environments for learning in their particular settings we have been able to convey a more general and theoretical understanding of what it means to be a teacher in contemporary society. Their classroom stories reveal, in sharp relief, the complexities of the profession, its promise and possibilities as well as its problems. Their differing school and community contexts demonstrate some of the external forces that deeply affect what teachers can and cannot do on a daily basis within the confines of their classrooms. As a result of their eloquent testimony and skilled practice, we have gained valuable insights into the multiple and shared meaning of excellence in teaching.

Finally, we have maintained that the decision to become a teacher must be based upon an understanding of the organizational, professional, and educational contexts of teaching as well as a genuine understanding of oneself. To give a contemporary flavor to our case, the concluding chapter introduced a new generation of novice teachers who shared something of the pleasure and pain, sacrifice and significance associated with their decisions to become teachers in America today.

We believe that now you are in possession of the necessary evidence to make a decision yourself. You have facts and figures, theories, concrete cases, and conceptual lenses to see in the fullest sense of the word what it means to be a teacher and to decide whether a teaching career is for you. Our final instructions are to weigh the evidence carefully, for America needs teachers, but only those with intellect, knowledge, social responsibility, personal integrity, and professional commitment will do.

If you feel that you have what it takes, and it clearly takes a lot, we invite you to join the three of us, Ruth, Luberta, Sandy, Larry, and Jacquie, as well as the new generation, Audrey, Meg, Karen, Jim, and Amy, in our commitment to the profession of teaching and to the achievement of excellence for ourselves, for our students, and for our future as a society.

DISCUSSION QUESTIONS

1. What kinds of changes might be required in order to improve the status of teaching in America? Will teaching ever become a high-status profession such as law or medicine?
2. How do you feel about the current pressures for "bright" people to do something other than teach?
3. What similarities do you see between the new generation's motivation to teach and the motivations of the five case study teachers? What differences do you see?
4. What differences and similarities do you see among Audrey, Meg, Karen, Jim, and Amy?
5. From what the case study teachers and the new-generation teachers say, what do you think will be the most difficult part of teacher education? What will be the greatest reward of teacher education?

ACTIVITIES

1. List the reasons why you might consider teaching as a career. Compare your reasons with the themes that Lortie describes (Chapter 1) and with the motivations and questions that Kohl suggests (Chapter 14). How do you reconcile the motivations you feel and the current data (Rand Report) on the conditions of teaching?
2. Compare your motivations with those of Audrey, Meg, Karen, Jim, and Amy.
3. List your concerns about participating in a teacher education program. Then talk to those who are either recently graduated from a teacher education program or in the process of student teaching. Determine whether or not your concerns are justified.
4. Interview several first- or second-year teachers and find out what they see as the major problems of getting started. Solicit their advice on how to begin so that you might be one of Ryan's blessed few. Compare these perspectives with the ones you gathered from the teachers with 10 or more years of experience.

REFERENCES AND SOURCES

Atkin, J. M. (1985). Preparing to go to the head of the class. *The Wingspread Journal* (Summer, special section on teacher education), 1–3.

Bowen, C. (1985). And now, a teacher shortage. *Time*, July 22, p. 63.

Boyer, E. L. (1983). *High school: A report on secondary education in America.* New York: Harper & Row.

Darling-Hammond, L. (1984). *Beyond the commission reports: The coming crisis in teaching.* Santa Monica, CA: The Rand Corporation.

Dewey, J. (1904). *The relation of theory to practice in education.* Third yearbook of the National Society of Scientific Study of Education. Chicago: University of Chicago Press. Reprinted in *The relation of theory to practice in education.* Cedar Falls, IA: The Association of Student Teaching, 1962.

Feistritzer, C. E. (1984). *The making of a teacher: A report on teacher education and certification.* Washington, DC: National Center for Education Information.

Gardner, J. (1968). *No easy victories.* New York: Harper & Row.

Kohl, H. (1976). Why Teach? *Teacher, 94*(3), 73–78.

Lortie, D. C. (1975). *Schoolteacher: A sociological study.* Chicago: University of Chicago Press.

National Commission on Excellence in Education. (1983). *A nation at risk: The imperative for educational reform.* Washington, DC: U.S. Government Printing Office.

Ryan, K. (1970). *Don't smile until Christmas: Accounts of the first year of teaching.* Chicago: University of Chicago Press.

Ryan, K. et al. (1980). *Biting the apple: Accounts of first year teachers.* New York: Longman.

Zeichner, K. (1981–1982). Reflective teaching and field based experiences in teacher education. *Interchange, 12*(4).

APPENDIX A

The following is an example of an ethnographic report written after five weeks of observation in a secondary classroom. The focus of the report was on the social climate of the classroom. We include the paper as an example of a carefully done undergraduate student's observation paper. We wish to emphasize that this is simply one example of how an ethnographic report may be written.

FIELDWORK ANALYSIS

EDUCATIONAL PSYCHOLOGY 4052

MIDTERM PAPER

Audrey Oka

Preparing to be a "classroom microethnographer" is similar to learning to drive a car. One can try to get a feel for it by reading and doing simulations but the skill is learned and developed only through experience. One must take powers of observation and perception into the classroom and attempt to record interactions as quickly and accurately as possible. Over the course of five weeks, this (aspiring) microethnographer has progressed in her ability to collect data in the classroom to the point where she feels some sense of control over the situation. I present first a description of the classroom setting I observe-participate in, and secondly, a comparative analysis of that microcosm. In addition to the concepts found in the Education 4052 readings, I will refer to a second classroom that I observed at the school.

DESCRIPTION:

My observations are done at Shaw Junior High School, located in a white, upper-class district in the suburbs of Dallas. The setting is a seventh grade math class taught by Mrs. Jenning. I sit in on her fifth and sixth hour classes--a standard math class and an advanced group that studies pre-algebra respectively. The sessions are large; each having approximately thirty pupils. The kids are predominantly Jewish. There are two or three blacks and orientals in each section.

Mrs. Jenning is in her first year at Shaw. She was described to me by Ms. Andrew, school counselor, as "vivacious, energetic, and relating well to the kids." Although she has done some substitute teaching with this age, this is her first attempt as a secondary educaiton teacher. Her teaching background lies in the younger elementary age (Kindergarten-third grade). Displayed on her desk is a 9x11 photograph of her five-year old daughter. Mrs. Jenning is an attractive woman, about thirty years of age. Through observations and a conversation we had regarding the chaperoning of an upcoming school event, I realized that she is single. I am not sure about the surrounding

circumstances, but found this fact quite interesting. What kinds of
perceptions develop based on marital status and how does marital status affect
classroom behavior?

diagram of Mrs. Jenning's classroom:

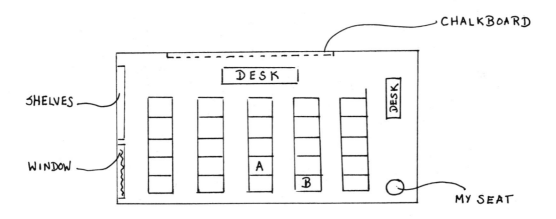

     The seating arrangement does not allow room to walk across rows because
there is no room between the chairs in a column. In addition, the last row of
chairs is flush up against the back wall and in order to get to someone in
another row, the teacher has to do a lot of traversing. For example, if Mrs.
Jenning was helping student A and then needed to get to student B, she has to
go up the column of students and down the next column instead of crossing
directly from A to B. This also worked against Mrs. Jenning by aiding pupils
in the back row who know that she could not come up on them from behind. In
order to check their behavior, Mrs. Jenning would have to approach them from
the front, always in full view of the students, and allowing them adequate time
to terminate their antics.

2

The room temperature usually runs at 78-80°F, which made it difficult for me to concentrate. The pupils never complained in my presence, but I don't doubt that they were quite uncomfortable. The excessive warmth could have made it hard to think and pay attention.

The room is constructed so that oustide noises do not filter in, except for the bells that periodically ring during the period. (The eighth graders are on another schedule). Thus, once the class settles down, there is little, if any, audible or visual distraction for the students.

I was introduced to both classes as "Miss Oka, a student at Washington University who is interested in teaching. She will be here to observe and help us." I take my place at the back corner of the room, near the "backrow action." The class period is spent in a variety of activities. Part of the hour is devoted to correcting homework papers together, reviewing for exams, or receiving new lesson material. During these times, I observe the ongoing interactions from my seat or correct papers at Mrs. Jenning's desk. Each day, time is given for the pupils to begin work on their assignment. Mrs. Jenning then circulates around the room, and she allows me to do the same. We spend the time clarifying the material and checking procedures to make sure the students are on the right track.

Shaw Junior High has a computer room that is used to orient the pupils with the data systems world. Interestingly, the computer room has become a form of incentive for many pupils, especially the boys. They know that by finishing an assignment early, the will probably be granted use of a terminal. On several occasions, Mrs. Jenning would take half of the class to work on the computers and would leave the other half of the class with me. She provided me with worksheets and a guide to follow, and then allowed me to present the concept to the students and to control the class. This exposed me to being in front of a class without the pressure of a full classroom.

In addition to Mrs. Jenning's class, I spent a few days observing Mrs. Williams' eighth grade classes. These two classes were much smaller—fourteen students who were of a different temperament than the seventh graders. These kids were more subdued and seemed docile in comparison to their younger, eager-to-please counterparts. Observing her classes has given me more insight into Mrs. Jenning's classroom style. I would like to begin my analysis by drawing upon both sets of observations in discussing the influences on teacher roles.

THE ANALYSIS:

Teacher Roles

Both teachers are well-liked by the students and have attained a "friend" relationship with the pupils characterized by good rapport, humor in the class, and a sense of comfortable openness on both sides. I discern primary and secondary roles for both teachers. The primary role is how the students perceive and respond to this perception from sizing up the teacher. I define the secondary role as being a result from the primary role in some way. It is more subtle than the primary role; often a reaction to it. It is interesting to note however, that Mrs. Jenning and Mrs. William have attained their roles in different ways. The "friend" role is Mrs. Jenning's primary role but is the secondary role for Mrs. William.

Mrs. Jenning frequently jokes with the students. One incident occurred the day before a student body dance.

> Mrs. Jenning: "How many of you are gonna dance? How many
>
> of you are going to ask someone to dance? Raise your hand
>
> if you want to dance?"

She continued to inquire about current dancing styles. On another day, Mrs. Jenning has six pupils seated in a circle with her to grade their worksheets. As she is reading off answers she asks, "Am I going too fast?" To the replies of "no," she reads off an answer really quickly. It is warmly received with laughter.

Mrs. Jenning's style of dress helps to further the friend image. She
wears bright colors and fashionable, preppy outfits. Stylish pinks, purples,
and reds convey a sense of youth and beauty that helps the kids identify with
her.

Mrs. Jenning's secondary role is that of the authoritarian. Although a
seeming contradiction to her primary role, the authoritarian role is necessary
to keep that open, fun communication intact. For, while the teacher is their
friend, she must maintain control and their respect. Thus, comments like
"Heather, don't say 'what' to me" or "I will work the problem. Raise your hand
if you have anything to say." (10/20) remind the students that Mrs. Jenning is
in reality, not their equal, but someone who commands their respect.

Mrs. William, in her early forties, has had more experience with the
junior high age group. Additionally, she has five children of her own, most of
whom are past this age. Her experience is clearly reflected in her teaching
style and her rapport with the class. I classify her primary role as maternal.
She does not interact with the students as one of them, but rather, she treats
them as her peers—adults. She rarely raises her voice in Mrs. Jenning's
regimented manner. Instead, such comments as "Let's go" or "I have confidence
in you" project unity and encourgement to the pupils.

Mrs. William dresses in a matronly fashion, again reflecting her primary
role. Her wool sweater and blue gathered skirt are more conservative and
subdued than Mrs. Jenning's attire and convey an older, maternal image to the
students.

Out of this develops the secondary role as a friend. Because the eighth
graders are respected as mature, responsible adults, a friendship and ease
develops as a natural consequence.

5

Their teaching styles also vary because of different goals. Mrs. Jenning, according to Bloom's Taxonomy, places emphasis on knowledge and application of methodology. She feels that many students can't understand the theory behind the procedures. From observation: "If you can't understand the mathematical logic behind it, just learn the rules -- how to do it." There is a danger to her leniency however, best exemplified by a student's comment of, "I thought we just do it because you said so."

Mrs. William has a different response to the kids' inability to think. She stresses the analysis objectives that Bloom outlines. When working on a concept, she questions the class, "What gives us the right to do that step?" or "I am looking for something to tie the whole (process) together." Thus, by encouraging the students to talk, analyze, and discover why, she is teaching them to think.

Pupil Perceptions

The concept of the self-fulfilling prophecy is taken up by both Delamont and Smith & Geoffrey. The school employs an interesting system of core-teacher teams whereby a team of four teachers--in English, Science, Math, and American Studies--teach their subject to the same students. The core team has free periods at the same time and meets regularly to discuss students and teaching strategies. From the teachers' point of view, this concept allows the team to compare notes about a child and to develop a better conception of him/her based on additinoal information from one's colleagues. Yet, as the opportunities to obtain "guilty knowledge" (Delamont, p. 57) expand, so does the potential for a vicious cycle of self-fulfilling prophecy. A great deal of Mrs. Jenning's free periods is spent in conferences with parents. Information gained here is almost certainly shared with other team members in the interest of better understanding the child's background. Thus, guilty knowledge comes not only from other teachers, but from interactions other teachers may have with the

child's parents. Delamont (p. 57) notes that whether favorably or unfavorably,
"the teacher's classroom behavior may be considerably altered by the possession
of this private information."

Chris is one of the three black pupils in Mrs. Jenning's sixth period
advanced class. My initial observations of him read like this:

"Sitting upright, alert, paying attention. Involved in his
work. Uninhibited boy; talkative and outgoing.

1:40 -- 'I have a couple of questions. I think I did
something wrong.'"

His eagerness to learn as indicated by his posture and class involvement struck
me and when I approached Mrs. Jenning about him, she admitted that she too was
once impressed with Chris' seeming enthusiasm. However, it was revealed to her
through team meetings, that Chris is near failing in every class and his
reading level was put at the 25% percentile, way below the norm. Chris comes
from a divorced home and while his parents are supportive, Mrs. Jenning
questions his abiilty to succeed. She went on further to say that he is
irresponsible and difficult to trust because he constantly exaggerates about
his skills and abilities. The guilty knowledge obtained may help Mrs. Jenning
to get a clearer picture of Chris, but she has also come to expect less from
him than other class members. Certainly, her expectations may be justified
conclusions based on Chris' class performance, but how much of it does Chris
pick up and incorporate into his own personal expectations for success? When
these low expectations or even disappointments in a student's performance are
communicated to a child, a vicious cycle begins that may end up with self-
fulfilling prophecy--student failure. Certainly, the same could hold true at
the other end of the scale. Take Diane, another pre-algebra student who sits
in the front row of class. Each day, Diane has the privilege of erasing the
chalkboards before class. She was selected because "she is a reasonable,

dependable student." It has become an attraction of sorts for the girls, who cluster around Diane and watch. Attempts to clean the board by others are discouraged by Mrs. Jenning, because it is Diane's job. The self-fulfilling prophecy may come into effect again if Diane senses the teacher approval and incorporates that into her self-image.

Authority Establishment

In chapter three, Geoffrey and Smith describe the process of "grooving the children" whereby Geoffrey establishes control early in the term. Not having been present during the initial encounter (Delamont), I don't know if Mrs. Jenning laid the disciplinary foundations in the same fashion or not. It seems very important for her to have control over the kids before she begins the class. She assumes what I call the "attention stance and call" at the front of the room. Standing tall, with hands clasped in front of her or with her arms crossed, Mrs. Jenning will call for attention. "Fifth hour, look up here!" (9/29) is not uncommon and if necessary, a second admonition of "I'm waiting for you to settle down," conveys her sense of urgency and propriety to the students. She makes a lot of eye contact at this time, making certain that everyone is with her and ready to go. My observations show that this became standard procedure as the weeks went by.

In contrast to this method was the way Mrs. William handled her classes of eighth graders. In a much more relaxed fashion, she approaches her podium, opens her book, and begins speaking. Soon the murmurings cease, as the students realize that she is starting the lesson. Thus, Mrs. William manages to focus their attention on her without directly calling or demanding it. This gives her more authority because the class knows that she will not wait for them. They have less manipulative power here.

8

Control in Mrs. Jenning's classroom is enforced throughout the period.
For example, amidst shouts from the group, she said, "I only call on those who
are sitting nicely and have their hand up" (10/6). As an example of Smith and
Geoffrey's "I mean it/Follow Through" stages of Belief Establishment, consider
the following: The portion of class time allotted for doing homework is
considered a privilege not to be abused. One period, as the students'
chattering and hand-raising for help increased, Mrs. Jenning's comment took on
an "I mean it" quality: She threatened to double the homework and refuse to
help them if the noise continued. Two minutes later: "Okay! Miss Oka and I
will no longer help you today. There is too much loud talking and you are
relying on us too much. For the rest of class, if you have a question, just
refer to your notes or your text. Is that understood?" To complete this
"follow through" stage, she promptly assigned more homework as promised. This
type of disciplinary measure is not needed often and when it was used, proved
to be quite effective in re-establishing control and authority.

Cooperation vs Competition

I was surprised to find the level of competition in the classroom to be so
low. There is a much greater sense of cooperation both among the students and
with the teacher. This is perhaps a result of the friendship relationship and
good rapport discussed earlier. Jules Henry would have found favor with the
school system as the de-emphasis of competition begins with the grading
process. They refrain from using the A-F scale and instead, report progress on
a 1-4 point scale which doesn't connote as much pressure as letter grades do.

Among students, there appears to be a protective obligation and mutual
respect for each other. On my first day of observation, fifth period was
grading homework sheets. The boy sitting closest to me was correcting Aaron's
paper which was totally wrong. Each time he had a question regarding a
homework problem, he was careful to say "this person" in reference to Aaron.

9

At the end of the task, he muttered under his breath, "poor Aaron."

The "egg-beater kid" offers another interesing glimpse into pupil relations. Mrs. William related the details about one student in her advanced class who, although is very intelligent, is an eccentric. He commonly loses texbooks and/or notes daily. She described him as having "hair that was combed with an egg beater." I was surprised to learn that he is not subjected to ridicule by his peers, but is treated with respect, humor, and patience.

Jules Henry, in "Golden Rule Days," talks about carping criticism which can cultivate feelings of competition. Mrs. Jenning, like the "unique Miss Smith" Henry refers to (p. 302), on many occasions makes remarks that help steer away from carping criticism.

One day, as the homeworks were being corrected, Aaron disagreed with one of the answers. As Mrs. Jenning tried to understand his questions, other pupils in the class declared that he was wrong. Instead of agreeing with the class (they were right) she discouraged their remarks with, "Aaron just wanted to voice his opinion. He's entitled, isn't he?" By deterring the carping criticism, Mrs. Jenning helps to change the negative attitudes toward others and to create a healthier, cooperative spirit.

Further evidence of the cooperative bond that exists between teacher and children took place when Jenning left the room. Although the room became more active, the students took responsibility for their behavior:

> Kim: Shhh!
>
> (Steve goes to sharpen a pencil)
>
> Student: You're not supposed to...
>
> Steve: She'll never know.
>
> Sam: Let's put on our best behavior.
>
> (whispering)
>
> Kim: Sam, please be quiet. Sam, shut up!

10

(Mrs. Jenning walks back in)

Another observation demonstrates the fun and love for Mrs. Jenning the students have: She had gone outside to break up a scuffle in the hall. The class could hear the "battle" outside. The following discussion ensued:

A: Let's stand up when Mrs. Jenning comes in.

B: Should we, really? Let's applaud.

(General agreement from group)

Mrs. Jenning returns and some students cheer and applaud her. She faces the class, bows, and flexes her muscles for them. Class breaks up with laughter.

Mrs. Jenning's classroom does not have the high levels of noise, freedom, and creativity as Mr. Jeffries did (Henry, p. 317). However, I think she allows "limited liberation," if there is such a thing, for her students. It is important for her to be able to control the noise and to be in a position of authority but she managed to encourage cooperation and freedom within the group.

In this paper, I've tried to evaluate several social aspects of a classroom that I have been observing. By discussing teacher and pupil perceptions, the establishment of authority, and the degree to which cooperation is central in the classroom, I hope to have presented a clearer understanding of some of the factors that are in play in the classroom today.

INDEX

Y

Z